# Nonprofits and Advocacy

# NONPROFITS AND ADVOCACY

Engaging Community and Government in an Era
of Retrenchment

EDITED BY

Robert J. Pekkanen, Steven Rathgeb Smith,
AND Yutaka Tsujinaka

JOHNS HOPKINS UNIVERSITY PRESS    BALTIMORE

© 2014 Johns Hopkins University Press
All rights reserved. Published 2014
Printed in the United States of America on acid-free paper
2 4 6 8 9 7 5 3 1

Johns Hopkins University Press
2715 North Charles Street
Baltimore, Maryland 21218-4363
www.press.jhu.edu

Library of Congress Cataloging-in-Publication Data

Nonprofits and advocacy / engaging community and government in an era of retrenchment /
edited by Robert J. Pekkanen, Steven Rathgeb Smith, and Yutaka Tsujinaka.
pages    cm
Includes bibliographical references and index.
ISBN 978-1-4214-1349-5 (pbk. : alk. paper) — ISBN 1-4214-1349-3 (pbk. : alk. paper) —
ISBN 978-1-4214-1350-1 (electronic) — ISBN 1-4214-1350-7 (electronic)
1. Nonprofit organizations—United States. 2. Advocacy advertising—United States.
3. Policy sciences—United States. I. Pekkanen, Robert. II. Smith, Steven Rathgeb, 1951–
III. Tsujinaka, Yutaka, 1954–
HD62.6.N693 2014
361.7′630973—dc23          2013032248

A catalog record for this book is available from the British Library.

*Special discounts are available for bulk purchases of this book. For more information,
please contact Special Sales at 410-516-6936 or specialsales@press.jhu.edu.*

Johns Hopkins University Press uses environmentally friendly book materials,
including recycled text paper that is composed of at least 30 percent post-consumer
waste, whenever possible.

CONTENTS

## Part Two: Organizational Politics, Strategy, and Tactics

Nonprofit advocacy across a wide range of issues has received unprecedented attention in recent years. The decision of the US Supreme Court in the 2010 *Citizens United v. Federal Election Commission* case, allowing unlimited campaign contributions of corporations and wealthy individuals, unleashed a torrent of spending on general elections. In particular, political action committees (PACs and even Super-PACs) such as Crossroads GPS, Restore Our Future, and Priorities USA Action spent huge sums on the 2012 US presidential campaign. These PACs are typically organized as 501(c)(4) tax-exempt organizations. Further, the presidential campaign and a host of high-profile Senate and House races called attention to the mobilization of citizens at the local level by nonprofit organizations including charitable 501(c)(3) organizations, churches, political parties, unions, and trade associations such as chambers of commerce.

President Barack Obama's reelection led to a lot of speculation about the actual impact of the flood of Super-PAC cash on the election (Freeland, 2012). Since a disproportionate amount of Super-PAC money was spent to defeat President Obama and Senate Democrats, the natural reaction to Obama's victory and the victories of many targeted Senate Democrats such as Elizabeth Warren of Massachusetts was to question the impact of this spending. Indeed, it would appear likely that the Super-PACs changed the national political conversation and even the candidate's positions. Super-PACs have thus had an important influence even if the election's outcome was not what many of the Super-PACs desired (Bouie, 2012).

In addition to Super-PACs, the advocacy of a wide assortment of nonprofits has received media attention. The intense political controversy surrounding the Susan G. Komen Foundation's decision to end its funding of Planned Parenthood (and the subsequent reversal of this decision) highlighted the complex dilemmas for nonprofits in a highly polarized political environment. PAC activity is also evident in religious groups, such as church leaders who have been active in opposing gay marriage referenda and President Obama's health-care reform law. Many ballot initiatives across the country—from the legalization of marijuana in Colorado and Washington State to charter schools and gay marriage—have attracted the involvement of countless nonprofit organizations and their supporters.

While the focus has been on US electoral politics during 2012, nonprofits have also been increasingly active in advocacy efforts that target corporations, especially national and international nonprofits active in environmental causes and fair labor practices (Yaziji and Doh, 2009). For instance, Greenpeace has pressured corporations through aggressive advocacy to adopt certain environmental practices and to reduce the use of genetically modified foods (Yaziji, 2004). A coalition of nonprofit advocacy organizations has tried to preserve old-growth forests by targeting large companies such as Staples that sell paper goods (O'Rourke, 2004).

The growth of nonprofits has also meant more nonprofit engagement in local politics. As detailed by Jeffrey M. Berry and Kent E. Portney in chapter 1, nonprofits are now active in a host of municipal issues, from zoning to economic development to social welfare. Despite this activity, however, many nonprofits are less engaged in policy advocacy than would be expected or predicted, given the history of nonprofits advocacy dating back to the nineteenth century (Skocpol, 1999). Political scientists have long studied interest groups (Berry, 1977; Moe, 1980; Walker, 1991), but they have rarely directly investigated nonprofits as a distinct example of interest group advocacy. Further, scholars of nonprofits and philanthropy have tended to approach advocacy by nonprofits without a direct engagement in the rich political science literature on interest groups and political participation, with some exceptions (see Bass et al., 2007; Berry and Arons, 2003; Jenkins, 2006). This volume unites political science and nonprofit scholarly perspectives to further our understanding of nonprofit advocacy, an increasingly vital topic to the future of American democracy.

Following the introductory chapter, part one contains research on local nonprofit organizations and their engagement in advocacy. In chapter 1, Jeffrey M. Berry and Kent E. Portney present detailed findings on the role of nonprofits in urban politics, especially small community groups such as neighborhood associations. In chapter 2, we evaluate research on nonprofit advocacy in Seattle and Washington, DC. Elizabeth Boris and Matthew Maronick focus in chapter 3 on nonprofit agencies that contract with government agencies for various social and health services. These agencies have a deep stake in the policy process but often face constraints on their ability to undertake advocacy; the authors provide insight into this complex relationship between nonprofits and government. The fourth chapter, by Carol J. DeVita, Milena Nikolova, and Katie L. Roeger, evaluates nonprofit advocacy in the Washington, DC, metropolitan region. Part one's concluding chapter by Jennifer E. Mosley presents her detailed research on the advocacy of homeless service providers in Chicago; her findings have broad relevance to our understanding of nonprofit advocacy and strategy overall.

Part two reflects a more national focus to our research agenda. In chapter six, Dara Z. Strolovitch examines the advocacy of national nonprofits following the tragedies of Hurricane Katrina and the September 11 attacks. Kristin Goss follows with a comprehensive analysis of the evolution of advocacy by national women's groups between 1920 and 2000. Doug Imig in chapter 8 presents his findings on advocacy by national children's organizations over the course of the twentieth century. Jodi Sandfort's chapter addresses advocacy by coalitions and associations representing nonprofit human service agencies, which have increasingly attracted interest. The book's final chapter, by Gary D. Bass, Alan J. Abramson, and Emily Dewey, connects the academic research on nonprofit advocacy with the world of nonprofit practice, and provides specific observations and suggestions for nonprofit organizations to improve the extent and effectiveness of their advocacy.

ROBERT J. PEKKANEN AND STEVEN RATHGEB SMITH

### REFERENCES

Bass, Gary D., David F. Arons, Kay Guinane, and Matthew F. Carter. 2007. *Seen but Not Heard: Strengthening Nonprofit Advocacy.* Washington, DC: Aspen Institute.

Berry, Jeffrey M. 1977. *Lobbying for the People: The Political Behavior of Public Interest Groups.* Princeton, NJ: Princeton University Press.

Berry, Jeffrey M., with David F. Arons. 2003. *A Voice for Nonprofits.* Washington, DC: Brookings Institution Press.

Bouie, Jamelle. 2012. "Did Republican Mega-Donors Waste Their Money? Maybe Not." *The Plum Line* (blog), *Washington Post*, November 9, http://www.washingtonpost.com/blogs/plum-line/post/did-republican-mega-donors-waste-their-money-maybe-not/2012/11/09/87f8e0ec-2a8a-11e2-bab2-eda299503684_blog.html.

Jenkins, J. Craig. 2006. "Nonprofit Organizations and Policy Advocacy." In *The Non-profit Sector: A Research Handbook*. 2nd ed., edited by Walter W. Powell and Richard Steinberg, 307–32. New Haven, CT: Yale University Press.

Moe, Terry M. 1980. *Incentives and the Internal Dynamics of Interest Groups*. Chicago: University of Chicago Press.

O'Rourke, Dara. 2005. "Market Movements: Nongovernmental Organization Strategies to Influence Global Consumption and Production." *Journal of Industrial Ecology* 9, no. 1–2: 115–28.

Skocpol, Theda. 1999. "Advocates without Members: The Recent Transformation of American Civic Life." In *Civic Engagement in American Democracy*, edited by Theda Skocpol and Morris Fiorina, 461–510. Washington, DC: Brookings Institution.

Walker, Jack L. 1991. *Mobilizing Interest Groups in America: Patrons, Professions, and Social Movements*. Ann Arbor: University of Michigan Press.

Yaziji, Michael. 2004. "Turning Gadflies into Allies." *Harvard Business Review* February: 110–15.

Yaziji, Michael, and Jonathan Doh. 2009. *NGOs and Corporations: Conflict and Collaboration*. Cambridge: Cambridge University Press.

This book represents the product of two collaborative research projects, and, as one might guess, there are many people to thank.

The two surveys of nonprofits in Seattle and Washington, DC, led by Robert J. Pekkanen and Steven Rathgeb Smith, were conducted by the Survey Research Division (SRD) of the University of Washington and the Urban Institute, respectively. We thank Diane Christiansen, Kimberly Cooperrider, Charlotte Eidlin, Kate Fernandez, Amy Haslund, Andrea Valdez, and Danielle Woodward at SRD, and Elizabeth Boris and Carol J. DeVita at the Urban Institute. Support for these surveys came from two projects funded at the University of Tsukuba by the Ministry of Education of Japan and the Japan Society for the Promotion of Science and headed by Yutaka Tsujinaka: "A Comparative and Empirical Study of the Structural Changes in Politics and Transformations in Pressure Groups, Policy Networks, and Civil Society in Japan since 2009," grant-in-aid for scientific research (S) led by Yutaka Tsujinaka (2010–15), and "A Comparative Empirical Study on the Three-Level Civil Society Structure and Governance in Japan, South Korea, the United States, Germany and China in Comparative Perspective," specially promoted research, MEXT, led by Yutaka Tsujinaka (2005–10). As described in this book, Yutaka's pioneering surveys of nonprofits in over a dozen countries were the initial spark for this project on American nonprofit advocacy. We also thank Jae Young Choe and Takafumi Ohtomo at the University of Tsukuba for their assistance.

We would like to thank at the University of Washington Hironori Sasada (now at the University of Hokkaido) and Anne Buffardi (now at Oxfam International) for excellent research support early in the project, and Saadia Pekkanen for her advice. We are grateful for the support of the Nancy Bell Evans Center for Nonprofits and Philanthropy at the Evans School of Public Affairs at the University of Washington, and Filemon Gonzales, Dvorah Oppenheimer, Toni Read, and Diane Scillo at the Jackson School of International Studies. Julita Liauw Eleveld, program manager of the Nancy Bell Evans Center, was especially helpful in the early stages of the project. The Georgetown Public Policy Institute supported this project, and the Graduate School at Georgetown University as well as the University of Tsukaba provided financial support for an authors' conference in 2011. Deborah Auger, Joseph Galaskiewicz, Kirsten Grønbjerg, and Karla Simon provided incisive comments as discussants at this conference. Kate Anderson Simons, during her time as a graduate student at Georgetown, provided excellent research assistance to the project. Natalie C. Alm also provided invaluable and timely assistance with the editing process for the manuscript.

A terrific advisory committee composed of nonprofit community leaders in Seattle assisted us with the design and implementation of the survey. In Seattle, we would like to thank Putnam Barber, Mary Kay Gugerty, David Harrison, and Cory Sbarbaro for their advice and feedback on the Seattle survey.

We also thank Keiko Sato. David Reingold and Kirsten Grønbjerg (again) provided insightful comments as discussants on an International Studies Association meeting panel in San Francisco.

This project would have been impossible without the fantastic group of authors represented on the following pages.

At Johns Hopkins University Press, Henry Tom provided early encouragement for us to bring our manuscript to the Press for review and publication. Our current editor, Suzanne Flinchbaugh, provided sage and thoughtful advice throughout the process and contributed to the shaping of the manuscript. We greatly appreciate her enthusiastic support for our book.

Robert wishes to thank his family for their perpetual support. Steven would like to express his enduring gratitude to his wife, Penny, for her support.

# Nonprofits and Advocacy

# Nonprofit Advocacy

## Definitions and Concepts

ROBERT J. PEKKANEN AND STEVEN RATHGEB SMITH

Although nonprofit advocacy has received plenty of attention in recent years, we have relatively little understanding of how nonprofits advocate for themselves and their strategic considerations. These central research questions animate this volume, and each chapter illuminates part of the answer. This introduction outlines the key theoretical issues involved in the analysis of advocacy and provides a more detailed definition of advocacy. We explore three main themes that allow for deeper understanding of advocacy in theory and practice: (1) limitations on advocacy, (2) the significance of venue, and (3) the conditions under which advocacy can be successful. We also introduce a remarkable set of international surveys—the Japan Interest Group Surveys, or JIGS.[1]

## Advocacy Behavior's Stubborn Resistance to Definition

Advocacy behavior generally resists scholarly analysis for three critical reasons. First, advocacy is difficult to measure, partly because advocacy covers a broad range of actions—from organizing a massive demonstration to encouraging board members to write letters to the editor of the local paper. As we explain, these activities constitute advocacy despite their diversity. Moreover, even if we consider a single action, intensity of effort could matter. Dashing off a quick letter is one thing, but spending hours or days crafting a thoughtful and substantive epistle is a substantially different endeavor; intensity of effort can be difficult to quantify and assay for observers. How hard is the actor trying? Quantifying results is one thing, but as volumes of management studies reveal, measuring effort is not quite as straightforward. Adding to the complexity, not all advocacy efforts occur in the same venue;

besides a range of actions, we must also investigate a range of venues to fully understand advocacy. It is not just about lobbying politicians. For example, nonprofits may also channel their advocacy through the courts, as advocates for environmental causes or deinstitutionalization of the mentally ill have demonstrated. Thinking more generally, we see that advocacy actions can be directed at politicians, bureaucrats, the courts, or the general public, and might be undertaken on the federal, state, local, or even international level. We regard the analysis of "advocacy venue" as a major contribution of this book, and return to it below.[2]

Second, causality is difficult to determine when assessing success. Even if we had a complete record of all advocacy behavior by nonprofits, we would still face some challenges in knowing how and when it met with success. One especially nettlesome problem in particular is measuring policy change in a consistent metric across issue areas. Did environmental policy change more in the 1990s than employment policy, or the reverse? Even if we can reliably mark change, though, causality can be murky; we often have trouble assessing exactly why policies were adopted, modified, or abandoned. Advocates and their targets may both have incentives to distort the effectiveness of lobbying. Advocates might exaggerate their success, either to heighten their own importance or because they mistakenly believe they were actually instrumental in changing minds or policies. Politicians may tell voters they were persuaded after hearing from a nonprofit, but do so only out of a desire to conceal motives less likely to gain accolades. Persuasion is notoriously difficult to measure accurately in politics, although advances have been made in the field of international relations (Kawato, 2010).

Third, advocacy is fungible. As wide as is the range of actions available to a nonprofit that decides to advocate, the nonprofit is similarly presented with a set of choices about whether to advocate directly or to find a surrogate. The nonprofit might establish a parallel organization, perhaps a 501(c)(4) dedicated to lobbying. Or the nonprofit might be a local chapter of a larger organization, in which case it might delegate lobbying to another chapter in the state, or perhaps the national headquarters. Then again, the nonprofit might enlist the aid of a dedicated group (see Boris and Maronick, chap. 3, this volume). These options are similar to the choices faced by corporations that choose to lobby directly or to delegate the work to a trade association or chamber of commerce. And even these dimensions leave out choices such as whether to lobby alone or in coalition with like-minded organizations.

Despite these challenges, attention to nonprofits advocacy is growing, including a number of recent valuable contributions that have come from surveys similar to our own. Berry and Arons (2003) led a national survey of nonprofits (excluding universities, hospitals, religious groups, and private foundations). Gary Bass and colleagues investigated advocacy by nonprofits through multiyear surveys and research (see Bass et al., 2007; OMB Watch, Tufts University, and Center for Lobbying in the Public Interest, 2002). Child and Grønbjerg (2007) studied Indiana nonprofits. Salamon and Geller (2008) analyzed a nationwide survey of nonprofits in four major social service fields. To answer similar questions, Nicholson-Crotty (2011) examined National Center for Charitable Statistics (NCCS) data on nonprofit activities and organizational characteristics. Jennifer E. Mosley (2010) investigated advocacy by nonprofit human service agencies in the Los Angeles area. Dara Strolovitch (2007) conducted an in-depth survey of women's, racial minority, and economic justice organizations and the engagement of these organizations in policy advocacy. More recently, Independent Sector (2012), a national organization representing nonprofits, released a major study of nonprofit advocacy, particularly at the national level. This volume aims to contribute to this developing literature and to a broader understanding of nonprofit advocacy in a period of political turbulence, fiscal crisis, and intense interest in citizen participation, as well as the potential contributions of nonprofits to community representation. As a first step toward this goal, though, we need to carefully define "nonprofit advocacy," an admittedly elusive term.

## Advocacy and Nonprofits: The Double Definitional Dilemma

We face some definitional difficulties in studying advocacy that have complicated advancing our understanding of the actual behavior. These challenges come on top of the conceptual and measurement problems discussed above. Moreover, when coupled with "advocacy," even the term "nonprofit" is not as straightforward as it appears at first blush, although definitions of advocacy, lobbying, and political activity overlap. Simply put, *advocacy is the attempt to influence public policy, either directly or indirectly.* We stick with advocacy, but we mean to use the term in a neutral way that is, in practice, close to the broad "political activity" employed by Chaves et al. (2004), Salamon and Geller's (2008) "advocacy," and Leech's (2010) "lobbying."[3] Although our focus in this book is on advocacy to government, our definition also covers advocacy behavior on other actors. For example, nonprofits could advocate to corporations (or other nonprofits) to change their behavior (O'Rourke,

2005). To the extent that these efforts are directed at changing behavior that encroaches upon public policy areas, we consider this targeting of corporations also to be advocacy. So it is advocacy when nonprofits try to change corporations' environmental practices or gender discrimination rules. It is not advocacy when nonprofits try to get corporations to make changes disconnected from larger public policy concerns. A campaign to revive a beloved flavor of ice cream at Baskin-Robbins is not advocacy, regardless of how delicious that flavor might be. In this broader usage, our definition is consistent with Jenkins (2006), who argued that advocacy was "any attempt to influence the decisions of any institutional elite on behalf of a collective interest" (267). Moreover, our definition includes efforts by nonprofits that span coalitions, such as transnational ones, or that seek to engage actors charged with multinational governance (e.g., the United Nations, the World Trade Organization, etc.) or domestic coalitions that include other nonprofits or types of actors (Keck and Sikkink, 1998).

Tactics by nonprofits to influence the policy-making process span a dizzying range. Getting up close and personal, the nonprofit's staff might spend their time lobbying legislators directly. They might also devote their attention to the bureaucrats implementing policy (we discuss below the importance of "venue choice," a major theme of this volume). The organization could send delegates to testify at public hearings (see Goss, chap. 7, this volume), or it could organize a rally, demonstration, march, or boycott. The group might commission research on the topic and then publicize the results in press releases to frame an important issue on favorable terms. In addition, the nonprofit might decide to organize a letter-writing campaign on a particular issue, to pen an op-ed for the local paper, or to post information or views on its website. Nonprofits can pursue an "insider" strategy such as cultivating long-term relationships with government administrators as well as develop classic "outsider" strategies such as demonstrations or email alerts (see Mosley, chap. 5, this volume). Or the organization could seek like-minded allies to press its arguments collectively (see Boris and Maronick, chap. 3, this volume). The nonprofit might delegate its advocacy function to an affiliated 501(c)(4) or hire a lobbyist. It might join an advocacy coalition composed of other types of nonprofits such as a statewide child welfare association that represents their specific interests as well as those of other member organizations. To complicate matters further, a nonprofit might engage in an activity considered by some scholars as advocacy (e.g., letter writing), but the organization itself might only consider advocacy to be active, overt strategies such as public demonstrations or lobby days at the state capital. This tremendous diversity in advocacy strategies (and we have only scratched the surface) complicates the definitive definition and measurement of advocacy.

Figure I.1 represents the relationship among various types of activities under our definition of "advocacy." Within this overall term, we designate several activities as special subsets, or types, of advocacy. The horizontal axis of figure I.1 spans "insider" to "outsider" strategies. Calling for demonstrations or getting people into the street to protest are classic outsider strategies. Insider strategies, on the other hand, might entail speaking directly with politicians and bureaucrats in private meetings. On the vertical axis appears the continuum of "indirect" and "direct." We contend that some activities are more directly related to advocacy, while others fit within the broad definition of advocacy but might be only indirectly contributing to the attempt to influence policy. So buttonholing a politician to lobby in a face-to-face meeting, for example, would count as direct advocacy. Yet engaging in public education or outreach activities might indirectly influence the policy-making process by shaping the "frames" of understanding of the general public, or specific populations within it. For instance, an environmental organization might engage in public education about climate change, with the view that the more people know about it the more likely they are to pressure politicians to alter policy. Still, we consider this to be indirect influence. Such indirect activity causes the most difficulty and ambiguity of understanding, probably because it has a "dual use" function. We thus regard public education as a form of advocacy, but at the same time differentiate it from overt political activity such as lobbying.

Turning to the shapes occupying figure I.1, the largest oval is "political activity." Here we include overt or self-consciously political efforts. "Lobbying" nestles in snugly as a subset of this class of activity, closer to the insider pole than, say, the more general "policy advocacy" and much closer than "protest." "Public education" remains outside of the overt political activity sphere but within advocacy as an indirect means to influence policy.

For our purposes, the term "advocacy" covers a broad range of activity. This wide array of strategies leads Chaves et al. (2004) to prefer the term "political activity." Also, as Berry and Arons (2003) observe, terms such as "advocacy" and "lobbying" carry legal implications that could make some nonprofits squeamish about the labels (see also OMB Watch, Tufts University, and Center for Lobbying in the Public Interest, 2002). Berry and Arons (2003) found that responses to their survey varied greatly when they asked

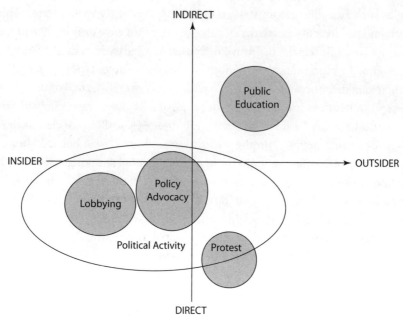

*Figure I.1.*

groups if they "advocate," "lobby," or "educate." Lobbying appeared to have
the most negative connotations, and 29% of groups responded that they
"never lobby"—nearly twice as many (15%) as those who said that they "never
advocate." The Internal Revenue Service (IRS) also has legal definitions on
what constitutes lobbying, which undoubtedly influences a nonprofit's understanding of the term. "Advocacy" sounds nearly as positive as "educate,"
which only 12% of Berry and Arons's respondents say they never do. The
terms and definitions we employ are significant not only to create an analytical language for scholars to dissect nonprofit behavior, but also because these
terms can powerfully affect the responses received in surveys.

Beth Leech (2010) argues for a broad definition of lobbying. Salamon and
Geller (2008) introduce an analytical distinction between policy advocacy
and lobbying. "Policy advocacy" is the more general term and "aims to influence government policy at the federal, state, or local level and can encompass
a range of activities, including conducting research on public problems, writing Op-Ed pieces on issues of public policy, building coalitions, or participating in a group working to formulate a position on a matter of policy" (4).
Lobbying is a specific subset of policy advocacy and involves communicating
the organization's positions to policymakers either directly (direct lobbying)

or by mobilizing the general public (grassroots lobbying). We find this distinction useful because it provides greater precision to our analytical vocabulary, and we hope it will become accepted in the literature. Currently, many authors use the terms interchangeably.

Our approach is to define advocacy broadly, but also to identify specific types of behavior within advocacy. These types of advocacy could be analyzed separately and still advance our overall understanding; for example, as Kristin Goss (chap. 7, this volume) focuses on hearings. Because of the problems of studying advocacy discussed above, this targeted research on different types of advocacy may be a particularly promising approach. For example, nonprofits, as noted above, can target corporations as a way to achieve important policy goals such as fair trade, improved working conditions in developing countries, and a reduction in greenhouse gases. A case in point is the Rainforest Action Network, which has been pressuring leading banks to avoid investments in "dirty coal" as a strategy to tackle climate change and greenhouse gases. The National Resources Defense Council is currently trying to mobilize citizens to protest the plans of large, multinational oil companies to develop a large tar sands mine in northern Canada.

Although we say that the phrase "nonprofit advocacy" brings up a double definitional dilemma, the "nonprofit" half is more straightforward. First, nonprofits in the United States are a diverse set of tax-exempt organizations. One might expect 501(c)(4)s to engage in advocacy, but the term "nonprofit" can include all nonprofits or only 501(c)(3)s, even though our expectations of nonprofit behavior would be different for groups with varying legal status. Second, is nonprofit advocacy a distinctive type of organizational or group advocacy? In other words, what types of the behaviors described above do we mean by the term "nonprofit"? Aseem Prakash and Mary Kay Gugerty (2010) have persuasively argued the merits of analyzing advocacy nongovernmental organizations as "special types of firms which function in policy markets" (3). Studying the advocacy behavior of nonprofits is beset with all the above difficulties, as well as a few challenges indigenous to the field. Perhaps the first to come to mind is the skittishness many nonprofits have about engaging in, much less admitting to, advocacy. This hesitancy is at least in part due to uncertainty about the legal permissibility or consequence of advocacy (Berry and Arons, 2003; Salamon and Geller, 2008). Reluctance to identify advocacy presents an empirical research hurdle, but a conceptual puzzle remains: should nonprofits be isolated from other interest groups for study?[4] Is nonprofit advocacy distinct in any way except for legal categories from the advocacy engaged in by corporations, for example? In studying nonprofit advocacy by itself, do we put on blinders that limit our understanding of advocacy as a general phenomenon? After all, the number of corporations in the *Washington Representatives Directory* dwarfs those of public interest, social welfare, or identity groups put together (Schlozman, 2010, 433). We could also turn the question around by conceptualizing goal-oriented political actors as having a variety of means to pursue their political ambitions. They could contribute to a political party sharing their vision (or, if we are talking about an individual, she could run for political office herself). Creating a nonprofit is but one option available to achieve political goals. When is it more likely to be undertaken?

## Themes of the Volume

The authors of this volume all examine advocacy. Although each scrutinizes the topic through a different lens, we can nevertheless identify three recurrent themes: (1) the limitations on advocacy, (2) the significance of venue, and (3) the conditions under which advocacy can be successful.

### Limitations on Advocacy: Whose Interests?

A central issue for our understanding of advocacy and nonprofits is determining who advocates, which has two essential components. First, whose interests do the organizations represent? Elected and unelected public officials alike respond to various constituencies, and interests need not be well organized (or even organized at all) in order to receive some attention. Nevertheless, it has been a truism of the field that organized interests will be advantaged over unorganized interests in the policy arena. E. E. Schattschneider (1960) famously remarked a half-century ago, "the flaw in the pluralist heaven is that the heavenly chorus sings with a strong upper-class accent" (35), and Mancur Olson's (1965) seminal work on collective action and the role of selective incentives in prompting organizational participation has been widely accepted as at least a partial basis for understanding why some interests are more likely to succeed in organizing than others. The challenges of collective action have direct consequences for our conceptions of equity, democracy, and representation. Kay Schlozman (2010) argues that "political scientists should pay attention not only to explaining where groups come from but also to understanding the kinds of interest and concerns that have vigorous representation—and those that do not" (426). Further, she usefully raises the provocative question of what an "unbiased" organizational population would look like—how many economic interest groups and how many based on race or on hobbies (428)? The first-order consideration, therefore, is about which interests have organizations to represent them.

A second-level question is, among organizations, which groups engage in more (and more successful) advocacy? We could further engage in sophisticated questions about representation by distinguishing whether groups seek to represent the interests of their actual members (if they have members) or of some larger group of possible members. After all, group members may have different preferences and characteristics than individuals who do not choose to join the organization, even if both would fit under the same category of possible members (Schlozman, 2010, 427). Does a bowling league represent only those who have joined, or does it seek to represent the interests of all bowlers, or all people who might become bowlers under the right conditions? Dedicated league bowlers are likely to have different preferences from those of casual bowlers. Many groups have no members at all, instead being dominated by paid professionals (Skocpol, 1999) or having at least no human members, representing instead firms, hospitals, or universities (Schlozman, 2010; see also Lang, 2013 on how this connects to legitimacy). Dara Strolovitch (2007) calls our attention to how marginality and identity intersect in a way that affects representation even in organizations whose mission is to represent the marginalized. But it is this second-level question that the JIGS (discussed below) position us to address.

Which nonprofits advocate? This is one of the most frequently asked questions about nonprofits and advocacy, and the answer provides essential context for further investigations of advocacy behavior. After all, if only a tiny minority of nonprofits engaged in advocacy, even scholars with an interest in nonprofits might generally be less interested in the topic. Indeed, scholars might have to reconsider our research methodology to analyze the phenomenon. Several chapters in this volume investigate our approach to determining who advocates from different perspectives. Robert J. Pekkanen and Steven Rathgeb Smith (chap. 2) and Carol J. DeVita, Milena Nikolova, and Katie L. Roeger (chap. 4) examine in detail the factors associated with a greater likelihood to advocate. Jennifer E. Mosley (chap. 5) investigates similar questions, with a focus on the advocacy role of the executive directors in nonprofit human service agencies.

We have some evidence on the limitations of advocacy from the JIGS as

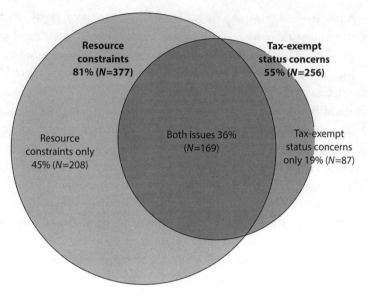

Resource
constraints
81% (*N*=377)

Tax-exempt
status concerns
55% (*N*=256)

Resource
constraints only
45% (*N*=208)

Both issues 36%
(*N*=169)

Tax-exempt
status concerns
only 19% (*N*=87)

*Figure I.2.* Limitations on advocacy according to data from Japan Interest Group Surveys. Total, *N* = 1137; yes, *N* = 464; no, *N* = 673. Note that these figures are for the organizations that say they have to limit their advocacy only; 673 respondents said they did not limit their efforts. Source: US JIGS 2 data set

well. We asked groups that did not advocate if they limited their advocacy because of resource problems or concerns about tax-exempt status. Figure I.2, which draws on the JIGS data described below, presents the answers to this question.

### *Venue: Where Do Nonprofits Advocate?*

Where do nonprofits advocate? Do nonprofits prefer to make their case to politicians or to the bureaucracy? Do nonprofits act at the local, state, or national level? A number of factors could shape nonprofit strategies on venue choice. Some of these factors could be internal to the nonprofit itself. A nonprofit active across a state but not outside it, for example, might be more likely to approach the state government than local or national governments. Nonprofits with limited resources might find local government more approachable than the federal government. The field in which the nonprofit operates could also be a factor. Our survey provides good information on these kinds of factors.

Other factors may be at work in shaping decisions about venue, such as longitudinal variation in the political opportunity structure (Scheiner et al., 2013). Changes in the relationship between state and federal government, or between politicians and bureaucrats, could also affect nonprofits' decisions on where to advocate. Then again, nonprofits might adopt a complex strategy of choosing a venue depending on the characteristics of the particular issue. The issue of venue choice remains a rich area to explore for advocacy research, and we hope to return to it in more detail in future research projects.

Several chapters in this volume call attention to the importance of venue. Jeffrey Berry and Kent Portney (chap. 1) argue that venue matters because city politics are a qualitatively different arena from national politics. So we can expect to see patterns of nonprofit advocacy at the city level that are different from what we observe at the national level. In chapter 4, Carol J. DeVita, Milena Nikolova, and Katie L. Roeger also suggest that differences exist in advocacy depending upon the level of government.

## *How Can Nonprofits Advocate Successfully?*

Chapter ten focuses directly on the lessons of contemporary academic research on nonprofit advocacy for policymakers and nonprofit staff, volunteers, and supporters. Gary D. Bass, Alan J. Abramson, and Emily Dewey offer a theoretically informed primer on how to advocate successfully, with direct relevance to the work of nonprofit executive directors. Many other chapters in this volume inform our understanding of successful advocacy.

We realize that nonprofits have many options when it comes to how to advocate, including the examples outlined above that range from authoring an op-ed to visiting a legislator to organizing a mass demonstration. Another set of choices exists as well. Nonprofits can choose to advocate by themselves, in coalitions, or through delegations. Chapters three and nine show how these choices can make a difference to the success of advocacy.

This is not to say that success comes easily. Although we would like to know how much effort nonprofits devote to advocacy in order to succeed, we cannot completely determine this in terms of the amount of time and money nonprofits spent on advocacy. Results from other scholars engender caution. Salamon and Geller (2008) found that although many nonprofits engaged in some kind of advocacy or lobbying activity, few devoted many resources to the objective. Only 14% of those organizations that engaged in policy advocacy spent as much as 2% of their overall budget on these political activities, and "they are far from the center of organizational focus and tend to attract relatively limited commitments of time, resources, and attention" (7). Salamon and Geller (2008) also note that the great majority of nonprofits (90%) concede, "Nonprofits like mine should be more active and involved in policy advocacy" (7).

Resource constraints significantly limit the ability of nonprofits to undertake advocacy. In our study of nonprofits in Seattle and Washington, DC, we find conclusive evidence of this capacity problem in the responses of nonprofits in our study sample to our question on this issue (Pekkanen and Smith, chap. 2, this volume). Further, implicit evidence derives from the support for the resource mobilization arguments we and others have found in analyzing nonprofit advocacy (see Pekkanen and Smith, chap. 2, this volume; De Vita et al., chap. 4, this volume). Constraints include money and staff, of course, but also time and expertise. The information costs involved in fully understanding the IRS regulations on political activity, for instance, are not negligible. Scholars have found that uncertainty over the legal environment may act as a substantial restraint on organizations that might otherwise engage in advocacy (Bass et al., 2007; Boris and Maronick, chap. 3, this volume).

## The JIGS: Seattle and Washington, DC

The JIGS provide important empirical evidence for two chapters in this volume. Because the survey data are used throughout this book, we provide background information on the surveys here, rather than replicating it in the chapters where it appears.

The data sets featured in this volume are based on surveys of nonprofits in Washington, DC, and Seattle. But the surveys themselves are part of a much larger international project, the JIGS project. The JIGS project has surveyed interest groups in over a dozen countries since the turn of the twenty-first century. Tens of thousands of groups have completed the JIGS, which represent one of the most important sustained international efforts at surveying interest groups. One of the editors of this volume, Yutaka Tsujinaka of the University of Tsukuba, initiated the JIGS project and has continued to lead it as it enters its second decade. Because many key questions on the surveys are replicated in each country, it provides an extremely comprehensive comparative database with which to explore international nonprofit activity. The contributions to this volume exploit only the US data, but we hope to engage in meaningful international comparisons in the near future. Other scholars associated with the JIGS project have already utilized the data to investigate the nonprofit sector in other countries (Tsujinaka, 2002; Tsujinaka and Mori, 2010; Tsujinaka and Yeom, 2004; Tsujinaka et al., 2009).

In the United States, the Survey Research Division of the University of Washington implemented our King County, Washington, survey through the Nancy Bell Evans Center on Nonprofits and Philanthropy at the Evans School of Public Affairs. The Center on Nonprofits and Philanthropy at the Urban Institute in Washington, DC, implemented the DC survey. Carol J. De-Vita directed the survey team.[5] Working with the JIGS team to maximize international comparability, Robert J. Pekkanen and Steven Rathgeb Smith designed surveys for nonprofit organizations in King County, which includes Seattle. DeVita joined the team and advised on survey design for the Washington, DC, metropolitan area survey. We sampled nonprofit organizations in these two areas, receiving 1,501 responses in Seattle and 571 in Washington, DC.[6] We oversampled 501(c)(4) organizations in Washington, DC, in order to obtain sufficient observations. Our respondents were mostly 501(c)(3) organizations (92%, $n$ = 528 in Washington, DC; 77%, $n$ = 1,064 in King County) but also included 501(c)(4)s (8% in Washington, DC; 4% in King County). In King County, we were also able to include many (19%) nonprofits with different legal statuses (14.25%, $n$ = 195) or without legal status (4.24%). These "other" legal statuses include both those who replied only "nonprofit" ($n$ = 46) and those who identified as 501(c)(6) organizations ($n$ = 45).

We surveyed nonprofits in the Seattle area in 2009. To identify the target population, we used the Washington secretary of state's list of registered nonprofit organizations in the state, restricting ourselves to those located in King County. King County is large, encompassing not only all of the city of Seattle but also adjoining suburban regions incorporated as cities themselves, such as Lynnwood, Bellevue, and Edmonds. Registration involves having an agent file registration papers, but the registration process is not particularly onerous. From these 8,000 organizations, we located and verified activity and contact information for 4,297 (53.7%). Because they were outside of our research target, we dropped homeowner associations, condominium owner associations, and individual churches (2,851, or 35.6%), as well as organizations no longer functioning or active, or no longer active in King County (786, or 9.8%). We were unable to locate 66 (0.8%) organizations and were forced to drop them from the sample frame. We found addresses (95%), phone numbers (54%), and email addresses (48%) for the groups we had identified as active in King County and otherwise fitting our criteria ($n$ = 4,297). We contacted groups via email if we had an email address, and by post if not. We tracked this postal response, as well as whether groups responded through the Internet (75.1%), on paper (21.5%), or by phone (3.4%), but found no significant differences in these group characteristics). We sent in advance a contact letter that introduced the survey and identified a board of advisors of local nonprofit leaders who had endorsed the survey. We subsequently followed up with emails and postcards, and if still no response, we then made telephone calls. In the course of our surveying, we found an additional 314 (7.9%) groups to be outside of our survey parameters (mostly homeowner associations) and excluded them from the results, leaving 3,983 eligible organizations. We received 1,227 (30.8%) completed responses to the survey, as well as 274 (6.9%) partial responses. A relative handful of nonprofits (113, or 2.8%) refused to respond, but most uncollected data came from the majority of groups that simply never responded (2,369, or 59.5%).

The Urban Institute conducted the Washington, DC, survey from January to July 2010. The survey drew a stratified random sample from the Urban Institute's NCCS 2007 and 2008 "core" files of all 501(c)(3) and 501(c)(4) public charities filing annual financial returns (Form 990) with the IRS. Hospitals, foundations, homeowner associations, grant-making foundations, and higher education organizations were excluded, leaving 10,581 organizations satisfying the criteria in the sampling frame. A total of 3,300 groups were randomly selected. The NCCS was stratified by region, size of organization, and type of nonprofit prior to sampling, and 501(c)(4) organizations were oversampled. Organizations were contacted by mail, email, and phone. A contact letter was printed on the Urban Institute's letterhead and signed by Carol J. DeVita, who led the DC survey. The survey questionnaire was mailed in batches from February 18 through April 21, 2010. Two postcard reminders were sent to nonrespondents, as were three emails (to those whose email addresses were available). Telephone calls were made to nonrespondents, too, ending on May 15, 2010. The survey was also available throughout this period through the Internet. Ultimately 565 completed responses and six partial responses were received, yielding a response rate of 17.8%.

Because of differences in the survey procedure, we analyze Seattle and DC data in parallel in most cases in this volume. The Seattle survey results cover organizations not captured in our DC survey, including a limited number of 501(c)(6) organizations and other tax-exempt organizations. Also, the Seattle organizations appear to be smaller than those in DC. Indeed, nearly four out of ten of our Seattle respondents (39%, $n = 1,111$) had budgets of less than $25,000. Moreover, the survey instruments were different. The Seattle survey was slightly longer (36 questions to the DC survey's 31) and included a skip pattern that allowed groups to avoid all policy advocacy questions if they answered "no" to a gateway question (this means that the overall Seattle advocacy responses could be lower than if the survey had been identical to the DC survey). In most cases identical wording was preserved for the overlapping questions, but even minor perturbations of question sequence and overall length could affect responses. We believe the surveys are comparable.

With this in mind, our book is distinguished from earlier works on nonprofit advocacy by its detailed empirical research on local and national organizations; its investigation of specific, understudied questions related to nonprofits such as strategy, venue, and effectiveness; and its integration of scholarship on political science and nonprofits to inform the research on advocacy. Given this approach, the book also has direct relevance to our conceptual understanding of nonprofit advocacy. But the book also contains rich information on advocacy strategy and effectiveness, so our research can be especially useful to policymakers and the staff and volunteers of nonprofits who are interested in enhancing the engagement of nonprofits in the policy process and improving their advocacy effectiveness.

### NOTES

1. We describe JIGS (Japan Interest Group Surveys) below. The JIGS include recent surveys in Washington, DC, and Seattle that form the empirical basis for chapters 2 and 4.

2. For now, we note that these measurement problems beset only the advocacy behavior we can observe; however, a bigger problem is that a lot of nonprofit advocacy occurs in private settings such as meetings rather than in public forums such as marches and demonstrations.

3. Our discussions with Gary Bass helped clarify these dimensions of the definition. See also Prakash and Gugerty (2010), who call advocacy "systematic efforts (as opposed to sporadic outbursts) by actors that seek to further specific policy goals" (1).

4. This is similar to the existential question faced by nonprofit scholars of "why nonprofits?" (Hansmann, 1980; Salamon, 1987; Smith and Lipsky, 1993; Weisbrod, 1988).

5. The authors are deeply grateful to their colleagues who made these surveys possible.

6. For convenience and familiarity, we will refer to the King County survey as the "Seattle survey" and reference results as "Seattle" on occasion in this chapter. However, only 25% ($n = 341$) of our organizations in the King County survey reported serving only the citizens of Seattle. We similarly refer to the Washington, DC, metropolitan area survey as the "DC survey" even though only 42% ($n = 237$) of the

organizations were located in the District of Columbia, with 35% in Virginia and 23% in Maryland.

## REFERENCES

Bass, Gary D., David F. Arons, Kay Guinane, and Matthew F. Carter. 2007. *Seen but Not Heard: Strengthening Nonprofit Advocacy*. Washington, DC: Aspen Institute.

Berry, Jeffrey M., with David F. Arons. 2003. *A Voice for Nonprofits*. Washington, DC: Brookings Institution Press.

Chaves, Mark, Laura Stephens, and Joseph Galaskiewicz. 2004. "Does Government Funding Suppress Nonprofits' Political Activity?" *American Sociological Review* 69: 292–316.

Child, Curtis D., and Kirsten A. Grønbjerg. 2007. "Nonprofit Advocacy Organizations: Their Characteristics and Activities." *Social Science Quarterly* 88, no. 1: 259–81.

Hansmann, Henry. 1980. "The Role of Non-Profit Enterprise." *Yale Law Journal* 89: 835–901.

Independent Sector. 2012. *Beyond the Cause: The Art and Science of Advocacy*. Washington, DC: Independent Sector. http://www.independentsector.org/uploads/advocacystudy/IS-BeyondtheCause-Full.pdf.

Jenkins, J. Craig. 2006. "Nonprofit Organizations and Policy Advocacy." In *The Nonprofit Sector: A Research Handbook*. 2nd ed., edited by Walter W. Powell and Richard Steinberg, 307–32. New Haven, CT: Yale University Press.

Lang, Sabine. 2013. *NGOs, Civil Society, and the Public Sphere*. New York: Cambridge University Press.

Leech, Beth L. 2010. "Lobbying and Influence." In the *Oxford Handbook of American Political Parties and Interest Groups*, edited by L. Sandy Maisel and Jeffrey M. Berry, 531–51. New York: Oxford University Press.

Kawato, Yuko. 2010. "Imagining Security: The U.S. Military Bases and Protests in Asia." PhD diss., Department of Political Science, University of Washington.

Keck, Margaret E., and Kathryn Sikkink. 1998. *Activists beyond Borders*. Ithaca, NY: Cornell University Press.

Mosley, Jennifer E. 2010. "Organizational Resources and Environmental Incentives: Understanding the Policy Advocacy Involvement of Human Service Nonprofits." *Social Service Review* 84, no. 1: 57–76.

Nicholson-Crotty, Jill. 2011. "Nonprofit Organizations, Bureaucratic Agencies, and Policy: Exploring the Determinants of Administrative Advocacy." *American Review of Public Administration* 41, no. 1: 61–74.

Olson, Mancur. 1965. *The Logic of Collective Action*. Cambridge, MA: Harvard University Press.

OMB Watch, Tufts University, and Center for Lobbying in the Public Interest. 2002. "Strengthening Nonprofit Advocacy Project (SNAP): Overview." October 29, http://www.ombwatch.org/files/npadv/FinalSNAP_Overview.ppt.

O'Rourke, Dara. 2005. "Market Movements: Nongovernmental Organization Strategies to Influence Global Consumption and Production." *Journal of Industrial Ecology* 9, no. 1–2: 115–28.

Prakash, Aseem, and Mary Kay Gugerty. 2010. "Advocacy Organizations and Collective Action: An Introduction." In *Advocacy Organizations and Collective Action*, edited by Aseem Prakash and Mary Kay Gugerty, 1–24. New York: Cambridge University Press.

Salamon, Lester, M. 1987. "Partners in Public Service: The Scope and Theory of Government Nonprofit Relations." In *The Nonprofit Sector: A Research Handbook*, edited by Walter W. Powell, 99–117. New Haven, CT.: Yale University Press.

Salamon, Lester M., and Stephanie Lessans Geller with Susan C. Lorentz. 2008. "Nonprofit America: A Force for Democracy?" Listening Post Project Communique No. 9, Center for Civil Society Studies, Johns Hopkins University, Baltimore. http://ccss.jhu.edu/wp-content/uploads/downloads/2011/09/LP_Communique9_2008.pdf.

Schattschneider, E. E. 1960. *The Semi-Sovereign People: A Realist's View of Democracy in America.* New York: Holt, Rinehart, and Winston.

Scheiner, Ethan, Robert Pekkanen, Michio Muramatsu, and Ellis Krauss. 2013. "Why Do Interest Groups Contact Bureaucrats Rather Than Politicans? Evidence on Fire Alarms and Smoke Detectors from Japan." *Japanese Journal of Political Science* 14, no. 3: 283–304.

Schlozman, Kay. 2010. "Who Sings the Heavenly Chorus? The Shape of the Organized Interest System." In *Oxford Handbook of American Political Parties and Interest Groups*, edited by L. Sandy Maisel and Jeffrey M. Berry, 425–50. New York: Oxford University Press.

Skocpol, Theda. 1999. "Advocates without Members: The Recent Transformation of American Civic Life." In *Civic Engagement in American Democracy*, edited by Theda Skocpol and Morris Fiorina, 461–510. Washington, DC: Brookings Institution.

Smith, Steven Rathgeb, and Michael Lipsky. 1993. *Nonprofits for Hire: The Welfare State in the Age of Contracting.* Cambridge, MA: Harvard University Press.

Strolovitch, Dara Z. 2007. *Affirmative Advocacy: Race, Class, and Gender in Interest Group Politics.* Chicago: University of Chicago Press.

Tsujinaka, Yutaka, ed. 2002. *Gendai nihon no shiminshakai rieki dantai* [Civil Society and Interest Groups in Contemporary Japan]. Tokyo: Bokutakusha.

Tsujinaka, Yutaka, and Hiroki Mori, eds. 2010. *Gendai shakai shūdan no seiji kinō—Riekidantai to shiminshakai* [Political Functions of Contemporary Social Groups—Interest Groups and Civil Society]. Tokyo: Bokutakusha.

Tsujinaka, Yutaka, Robert Pekkanen, and Hidehiro Yamamoto. 2009. *Gendai nihon no jichikai chounaikai* [Neighborhood Associations and Governance in Contemporary Japan]. Bokutakusha: Tokyo.

Tsujinaka, Yutaka, and Jaeoho Yeom, eds. 2004. *Gendai Kankoku no shimin shakai rieki dantai* [Civil Society and Interest Groups in Contemporary Korea]. Tokyo: Bokutakusha.

Weisbrod, Burton. 1988. *The Nonprofit Economy.* Cambridge, MA: Harvard University Press.

# PART ONE

# THE LOCAL AND NATIONAL DIMENSIONS OF NONPROFIT ADVOCACY

# CHAPTER ONE

# The Group Basis of City Politics

JEFFREY M. BERRY AND KENT E. PORTNEY

Most nonprofits are local in nature. A high percentage is neighborhood based, serving the interests of a compact and relatively small area of a city or town. Although we do not know what percentage of the nation's more than 1.1 million 501(c)(3) nonprofits operate at the city or neighborhood level, we do know that nonprofits are playing an increasingly greater role in urban political systems.[1] In this chapter we analyze nonprofit advocacy in city politics, emphasizing their interaction with local policymakers. First, we discuss what we call the "politics of place" in cities, examining the participation of three types of citywide and neighborhood nonprofits. Second, we develop two lines of inquiry and articulate a set of hypotheses that grow out of a theoretical construct relating to low barriers to entry. Next, after describing the empirical methodology, we test those hypotheses with data derived from large-scale surveys in 50 of the nation's largest cities.

Cutting across these specific lines of inquiry is a more normative concern: how might nonprofits empower themselves in city politics? To the degree they're engaged in advocacy, nonprofits often speak for those who are chronically underrepresented in the political process. (See Robert J. Pekkanen and Steven Rathgeb Smith's introduction to this volume for an elaboration of what constitutes nonprofit advocacy.) Are there ways in which nonprofits can design their organizational structures and allocate their resources to maximize their influence in city government? This may seem like a relatively straightforward question, but for nonprofits there are many complicating factors. Resources can be scant, sometimes to the point of amounting to little more than a few volunteers' time. Their expertise and experience may be no match for that possessed by city councilors and agency bureaucrats. Nevertheless, nonprofits can and do influence public policy, and here we look for patterns that may help us to understand advocacy in the context of city government.

## The Politics of Place

Not long ago, American cities were seen as dying, destined to be repositories of the poorest and most marginal among us. For a variety of reasons the pendulum has swung back, and the future of cities seems brighter (Glaeser, 2011). Most striking, perhaps, is that many major cities are gaining populations after a long period of decline. Rising energy prices and lengthening commutes are among the reasons that make cities more attractive to some who might otherwise choose a suburb. Cities themselves have demonstrated imagination in nurturing neighborhoods with attractive amenities, building light rail systems, adding new parks, and enhancing village-like commercial centers (Florida, 2012; Glaeser et al., 2001). The great variety of neighborhoods and different types of housing and levels of housing price points add to the marketability of city life. Although a sense of community, of belonging and identifying with one's neighbors, can develop in suburbs and cities alike, it is certainly the case for some that city neighborhoods stand out as more inviting, more communal by nature.

The changing face of cities in the postwar era is reflected in the growth of three types of nonprofits that we focus on here: social service providers, environmental groups, and neighborhood associations. The federal government's response to both central city poverty and the civil rights movement was to move strongly toward an expansion of social services as providing income maintenance came to be seen as insufficient. Beginning in 1962, social policy began to emphasize rehabilitation, giving clients the skills and support they needed to enter the work world and to provide for themselves. Such services are labor intensive and require either an increased number of bureaucrats or outsourcing. Outsourcing was the choice, and nonprofits were the vehicle. Steven Rathgeb Smith (2002) has noted that this shift to delivery of services through nonprofit providers is nothing short of a "transformation" of our welfare system. He writes, "nonprofit social service agencies have a more central role in society's response to social problems than ever before" (150). But social service nonprofits do more than implement programs. State and local bureaucracies involve nonprofits in planning and depend on them for program evaluation. State and local governments have been forced to lay off more and more employees during the recent economic downturn, and as social welfare agencies shrink, the remaining bureaucrats may become even more dependent upon assistance from nonprofits.

The environmental movement's emergence in the late 1960s and 70s was most visible in national politics. A number of venerable, older organizations like the Sierra Club and Audubon Society experienced skyrocketing membership and many new activist organizations formed as well. More recently, cities have become centers of environmental activism. A strong environmental profile has become part of some cities' attraction, and individuals who are concerned about the environment will find a lot to like about many of the nation's central cities. In the area of sustainability, cities have taken the lead in this country, and impressive, creative policies and programs have been implemented across the nation (Portney, 2013). Smart-growth initiatives have coupled housing, transportation, and renewable energy endeavors in urban neighborhoods; such efforts build on collaborations with existing environmental groups, but they spawn them, too. Another source of new activism is partnerships between nonprofits and government or nonprofits and for-profits in the production and promotion of energy-efficient goods and "greener" utilities (Fitzgerald, 2010). Spurred by the pursuit of climate protection, many national and international organizations have now turned their attention to ensuring that the environment and sustainability are represented in the local nonprofit sectors of cities.

Our third nonprofit sector, comprising neighborhood organizations, has become ubiquitous in cities. Few cities operate effective and comprehensive citywide systems with officially recognized neighborhood associations possessing real authority (Berry et al., 1993). Even when cities do develop a citywide system, neighborhood empowerment can fall far short of what was envisioned. In Los Angeles, with its recently constructed ambitious citywide system, the results have been mixed at best (Musso et al., 2004). The city has not given sufficient powers to its many neighborhoods. But in many American cities independent neighborhood associations are common, and while they are not the most stable organizations in urban society, we have found in our research across different projects that they are regarded as authentic and credible representatives of their neighborhoods.

Over time, the political ecology of cities has changed. Every city has lost many of its longtime corporate citizens as major companies have merged, migrated to the suburbs, or moved their headquarters to reflect a new global focus. There are new, large companies that have established themselves in metropolitan areas, but those corporations in the emergent growth sectors of the American economy—such as high tech, telecommunications, and biotechnology—have tended to locate outside the central city. Today there are fewer large-scale companies in central cities, and those that remain often have less interest in local politics than was true a generation ago. Research on corporate leadership in cities conducted by Royce Hanson and his colleagues (2010) concluded, "Our results suggest that the institutional autonomy, time, and personal connections to the central cities of many CEOs have diminished and that the civic organizations through which CEOs work appear to have experienced lowered capacity for sustained action" (1).

The largest and most prestigious nonprofits—universities, medical centers, local foundations—have moved into this partial vacuum and become increasingly important as both employers and as civic leaders. Smaller nonprofits, too, have benefitted, because without strong business leadership of political coalitions there is opportunity for a new set of activists. Even though they are forbidden from participation in electoral politics, 501(c)(3)s can be links between city hall and neighborhoods. The leadership of nonprofits, including citywide civic organizations, social service agencies, environmental groups, and neighborhood associations, are prized members of any candidate's campaign or governing coalition. They are skilled professionals who spend a good deal of their time building alliances with other organizations in their neighborhoods. Even though nonprofits do not endorse candidates, it is easy for leaders to communicate to followers who the organization's friends are. Sociologist Nicole Marwell (2004) documents the case of the Lindale Center for Service (LCS), which serves a Latino community in New York. It is part of a "triadic exchange operation" where the state assemblyperson (a former director of the LCS) provides crucial help to the nonprofit. Reciprocally, the state assemblyperson benefits as a shadow political institution, the Lindale Democratic Club, draws on the LCS's staff and constituency in the community (280).

The role of nonprofits is greatly enhanced by the "politics of place." In cities, most day-to-day decision making by government involves a specific neighborhood or area of the city. Whether a school matter, law enforcement problem, transportation issue, siting a new facility, or constructing a new office building, the decision typically involves a specific neighborhood. Observe any neighborhood in any city and the organizations the city government must consult with, appease, or simply inform are primarily nonprofits. By way of comparison, a small or midsize nonprofit is much more likely to be in contact with government than a small or midsize business. Nonprofits in health care, social services, and community development are also recipients of government grants, contracts, and, in some cases, dedicated income streams, like that for the nation's 4,600 community development corporations (CDCs). City hall finances are thus intertwined with an array of non-profit organizations. Yet despite the strong rationale for ongoing interaction between city government and nonprofits, it may be the case that either non-profit passivity or opposition by city policymakers stands in the way of ex-panding nonprofit advocacy.

## Access and Barriers

Interest group influence is built upon access to policymakers, and the con-cept of access is at the core of any analysis of advocacy groups operating at any level of government. If access of all interest group sectors to government is not equal (and it never is), then there is bias in the system. A considerable portion of all interest group research has been built around the measure-ments of such bias, determining those sectors and groups that are favored by policymakers along with those that are not. Such inequity has profound im-plications for democratic theory, and the most influential scholars of interest group politics—Dahl (1961), Lowi (1969), Mills (1956), Olson (1968), Schatt-schneider (1960), and others—have been preoccupied with the question of equality and inequality in access.[2]

We define interest group access as the opportunity to meet with policy-makers on issues of central concern to the organization. Assigning a degree of interaction that demarcates access from lack thereof is arbitrary, as there are too many contingencies for each and every issue. An advocacy group may just want to check with a staffer to make sure that the committee is not going to hold hearings on a proposal that the organization opposes. If so, a single phone call may satisfy the group that nothing more needs to be done at the present time. On another issue, that group may feel it needs to be in constant contact with the committee as it goes through the painstaking process of marking up a complex piece of legislation. Conceptually it is helpful to think of a continuum, stretching from no access at one end to incorporation and even collaboration toward the other pole. We use "incorporation" to mean that an interest group has an ongoing relationship with policymakers, and this regular interaction promotes an exchange of views at all stages of the policy-making process.[3] The optimum relationship for an interest group is a collaborative partnership with policymakers. In such a relationship govern-ment officials and staffers will sometimes initiate contact with the advocacy group as they seek out solutions, information, or political support.

In national politics relatively few groups are incorporated into a collaborative relationship. There are simply too many organizations within each policy community. Policymakers are consequently in a position of having to be selective about with whom they meet and how much time they spend with client groups and other advocacy organizations. We have no way of knowing how many groups operate in Washington, as there is no comprehensive census of organizations that lobby in one form or another. Kay Schlozman's (2010) research has served as a baseline of sorts, as she has utilized the *Washington Representatives Directory* at four points in time to delineate the evolution of the Washington, DC, interest group community. Her latest calculations (for 2006) put the aggregate number of Washington-based organizations at close to 14,000, which compares to close to 7,000 in 1981 (443). But this figure does not include organizations that utilize contract lobbyists or are headquartered in another city. Nevertheless, it is clear that the Washington interest group community is enormous and continues to grow.

## Comparisons

Even though this chapter deals with city-level interest group politics, the theorizing that guides interest group scholarship is largely derived from research on national-level groups. The empirical findings that shape our understanding of interest group behavior also follow from studies of Congress and Washington agencies.[4] In the work we have read on city politics there seems to be an implicit assumption that interest group politics at the local level is generally just a smaller version of what takes place on the national level. Yet there is no theory of interest group politics that persuades us that city-level interest group politics is largely similar to the lobbying world in Washington. Rather, the assumption about cities encompassing a smaller version of national interest group politics appears to be more a reflection of the lack of impact of the research conducted at the local level.

Our views are also shaped by an earlier study of Massachusetts cities, where we found three critical differences between interest group politics at the local and national levels (Berry et al., 2006). The first difference is that the mix of groups on the local level is sharply at odds with what is found in Washington. There are clear measures of the makeup of both the population of interest groups at the national level, as well as the mix of groups that are actually involved in lobbying work. Returning to Schlozman's (2010) work, her 2006 calculations reveal that just over half of all Washington lobbies are corporations, business trade groups, and professional associations. State and local governments are another 12%. Combining some of her categories, the total of all citizen advocacy groups and nonprofits comes to around just 9% (433). A study by Baumgartner et al. (2009) of Washington lobbying, which categorized groups actually working on a random sample of 98 issues, found that corporations, business trade groups, and professional associations were 46% of all groups that lobbied, close to Schlozman's population figure. But citizen groups were fully 26% of all groups that lobbied, quite a bit higher than Schlozman's population aggregate. Baumgartner et al.'s (2009) analysis had no separate category for nonprofits (9).

In our earlier study the proportion of business and professional groups that were active in eight eastern Massachusetts cities was just 20%. The remainder comprised citywide citizen groups (31%), neighborhood associations (24%), and other types of nonprofits (26%). These figures were not the result of a random sample but rather were derived from interviews with city councilors, administrators, and representatives of advocacy organizations (Berry et al., 2006, 15). We subsequently coded all outside organizations that subjects mentioned in the course of each interview, and most references came from a question that inquired about what issue they were spending the most time on that week. Even allowing for the imprecision associated with this method, there is no question that the mix of local advocacy organizations is strikingly different from what can be found at the national level.

The second difference that was highly evident is in the density of the interest group populations. As noted above, the numbers of groups in each policy area at the national level is enormous. In the health-care field alone there were 3,600 lobbyists working in Washington in 2009, up from 2,300 a decade earlier.[5] Unfortunately there are no comparable statistics for local politics. In contrast, however, Paul Peterson (1981) has gone so far as to describe local politics as "groupless politics" (116). There is hyperbole in his assessment, but there is also a convincing explanation as to why the overall numbers of groups in a city appear to be modest. As the figures cited above indicate, most groups in Washington represent business interests. Unlike Washington, though, cities do relatively little in the way of regulation and therefore there is less reason for local businesses to organize (Portney, 2007). An important exception to the low level of regulation in cities is in the area of land use and business mobilization. Developers, construction firms, and business trade councils as well as labor unions mobilize on behalf of project proposals.

The third difference is largely a consequence of the lower density of groups. At the national level there is a high barrier to entry for lobbying.

There are so many groups competing for attention from policymakers that officials have little choice but to construct high barriers for individual groups to breach. If legislators, agency administrators, and their staffs did not set such limitations, they would be overwhelmed by meetings with interest group representatives. Instead they carefully pick and choose among all who want to see them and ration their direct interaction with client organizations. Although we used different methodologies for the 2006 study and this more recent research, we observed the same low barriers to entry for groups wanting access to city councilors or agency administrators. City policymakers do not need to wall themselves off from organized interests because they are not inundated with demands to meet with groups. Rather, there appears to be a manageable equilibrium between interaction with lobbying groups and carrying out the other parts of their job.

### Low Barriers, Different Politics

The theoretical foundation of this chapter is the idea of low barriers to entry for city-level interest groups (Berry, 2010). If we relax the assumption that we would make for Washington politics—that high barriers make it difficult for all but the most influential and important groups to have regular access to policymakers—we anticipate finding a considerably different pattern of political behavior by local advocacy organizations. In Washington, for example, research shows that at any one time a relatively large proportion of interest groups is working hard to find someone in government to simply listen to their concerns. As such, many organizations expend a significant amount of their resources working on issues on the periphery of the agenda because they cannot find policymakers to take up their cause. A substantial amount of lobbying goes nowhere because policymakers refuse to engage: calls are not returned, memos receive no response (Baumgartner et al., 2009). With the low barrier to entry that we expect to find in city governance, the initial response from local government should look far more welcoming than what is found in Washington.

We have organized our inquiry around two central hypotheses that can be tested with our survey data (described below). First, if barriers to entry are low, then *all* interest group sectors should have generally high access to city councilors and administrators. Why would we expect this to be true? Without high barriers to entry, it certainly becomes more difficult to exclude groups. In Washington, with the barbarians always at the gate, interest groups understand that access is privileged and may be infrequent. In cities, norms and expectations are created out of the high access that exists. Another feature of city politics is that there are formal requirements under federal, state, and even local law for citizen participation opportunities. At the very least, such programs create entry points for participation on some issues and raise expectations for meaningful, ongoing dialog.

A second, related hypothesis relates to the opportunity for real collaboration. Organized interests want to be partners in policy making, not a beseeching entity that is knocking at the door asking for a meeting. But why might some groups be incorporated as collaborators while others are not asked to the bargaining table as plans are being designed or compromises negotiated? Aside from the ideology of the councilors or administrators, it could be the case that some groups are more valuable to policymakers because of what they can bring to the table. We look here at whether groups that have the capacity to produce research stand a better chance of being incorporated into the policy-making process. Berry and Arons (2003) found the research capacity of nonprofits to be directly related to their access to government (132–36).

The null hypothesis is that research capacity makes no difference. The underlying supposition as to why this hypothesis will be borne out is that, for policymakers, an efficient path to getting things done is to bring in all stakeholders and to create processes that lead participants to buy into an ultimate resolution (Altshuler and Luberoff, 2003). The Berry and Arons study included only medium- and large-sized nonprofits (more than $25,000 in annual income), and some operated at the state level, where barriers to entry are likely higher. Unlike the Berry and Arons study, which was restricted to the judgments of only the advocates, we have data from the policymakers themselves.

## Survey Methods

The data on which this analysis is based come from a 2009 survey of local officials and advocates in 50 of the largest 54 cities in the United States. The four largest cities—New York, Los Angeles, Chicago, and Houston—were excluded from the survey because of the challenges presented by their scale. The 50 surveyed cities have 2007 population sizes ranging from 1.5 million in Phoenix to 336,000 in Tampa. In other words, these cities represent the entire universe of US cities in this population range. Between June and August

2009, questionnaires were mailed to all city councilors or commissioners, a specific subset of city administrators, and to a selected set of representatives of advocacy organizations in each of these cities.[6] We used a multimodal approach, offering subjects the choice of filling out a paper questionnaire they received in the mail or going to a website and answering the same questions online. Follow-up prompts to initial nonrespondents took the form of personalized emails and a link to the website.[7] City councilors' and administrators' mailing and email addresses were collected from each city's respective websites.

Overall, questionnaires were mailed to the entire population of 541 councilors,[8] and 190 responded. Of the 541 councilors identified, we were unable to reach ten, yielding an adjusted response rate of 35.8%.[9] The project also involved identifying and surveying an average of about 18 city administrators in each city. The administrators we targeted were all leading officials at the heads of departments or bureaus with some relevance to environmental affairs or economic development. Titles of such offices and the organization of responsibilities differed from city to city. Generally, though, we identified organizations in areas such as environmental protection, sustainability, public works, parks and recreation, public utilities, water and wastewater management, office of the city manager, economic development, and planning. Questionnaires were mailed to this entire population of 885 city administrators, and 413 responded. Thirty-seven of these questionnaires were returned as "undeliverable," and we were not able to locate appropriate replacement administrators. The adjusted response rate was 48.7%.

Identifying interest group advocates was more challenging. There are no city-level directories of advocacy organizations, and there was no easy way for us to ascertain which groups exist in each of 50 large cities. Each member of a small staff of research assistants was assigned a set of cities and set out to determine which groups were active in the political arena. The primary sources of information came from monitoring each city's newspapers, conducting web-based research, and talking to informants. In the end we assembled a list of approximately 25 leading advocacy organizations in each city.[10] Since we identified the groups, this cohort does not represent a random sample. Although we could not reach all of the groups, we are confident that we identified organizations that had been active in the immediate period prior to our survey. We mailed 1,250 questionnaires to local group leaders, and 557 responded. Perhaps owing to the transient nature of many local nonprofit groups, some 119 of these questionnaires were returned as undeliverable without identifiable alternative address or contact information. Thus the adjusted response rate is 49.2%.

The larger project from which this chapter is drawn focuses on sustainability and environmental protection, as well as on economic development. Our researchers paid particular attention to the environmental sector and searched broadly for organizations working on related issues before the city. Since we do not know the population of groups within each city, we cannot assess the degree to which environmental groups were oversampled. We also looked aggressively for business groups, as we wanted to contrast environmental policy making and advocacy with economic development policy and business-related lobbying. In the process of simply identifying groups, we found that business advocacy is highly concentrated in local peak associations, principally a chamber of commerce and often a real estate developers group.[11] Likewise, the number of labor unions is not great, as local AFL-CIO councils can dominate a city's labor landscape. Other unions identified included municipal workers locals and Service Employees International Union (SEIU) locals.

Neighborhood associations were included, but locating their addresses was a problem, and they are surely underrepresented overall. In the context of city governments, neighborhood associations are no one thing. In cities without rules about neighborhood associations, anyone can organize a group and declare it the neighborhood association for a particular area. In other cities there is at least formal recognition of neighborhood associations with official, city-sanctioned boundaries for each neighborhood. This is the case in Tucson, Arizona, but the neighborhood associations have no authority beyond a state law that gives associations and their residents certain rights relating to standing in criminal cases. The Barrio Anita Neighborhood Association is one of the many in the Tucson, but it has no newsletter and does not seem particularly active. In contrast, the city of Portland, Oregon, has a well-developed citywide system of 95 neighborhood associations. They are grouped into seven regional coalitions and under city law have authority in critical areas, affecting the quality of life in a neighborhood, including zoning.[12] For those cities that do have officially recognized neighborhood associations, our identification process made no distinction between an association affiliated with the city and any other neighborhood advocacy organization. Any one neighborhood may be populated by a number of different groups, and all were eligible to be included in our surveys.

## Data Analysis

As discussed above, our expectation is that access to city officials should be universally high. But what reasoning may lead us to think that the hypothesis might not be correct? The urban politics literature is replete with studies documenting the special role of business in policy making, including Charles Lindblom's (1977) argument that government's door is always open to business, regardless of who is in power, because everyone is dependent on business for income growth and wealth creation. Likewise, Molotch (1976) argues that the "growth imperative" in cities requires business collaboration. But whether the urban political landscape has changed significantly in recent times is an open question.

### *Public Officials' Perspectives*

In order to assess the degree of access to city policymakers, we asked city councilors and city administrators similar questions regarding the levels of contact—telephone calls and face-to-face meetings—they had with different groups. Councilors were asked whether they had contact with each of seven different types of groups "over the last month or so," and table 1.1 summarizes these results. City administrators were asked to report the frequency of contacts (weekly, monthly, annually, never) with each type of group "over the past year or so," and these results are summarized below.

City councilors report substantial contact with all four types of groups examined here. Business groups, by which we mean both business associations and specific corporations, show a high level of contact. Over 42% of city councilors reported having contact with business groups over the previous month. Yet contact with neighborhood associations is actually higher, at 56.8%. Nonprofit organizations do not fare as well, with councilors reporting contact about half as often as with neighborhood associations. And environmental groups fare considerably worse, with only 11.9% of councilors reporting contacts in the previous month.

Table 1.2 shows a similar pattern for city administrators. Keeping in mind that table 1.2 shows contact "over the past year or so," business contact seems high. Nearly 90% of the city administrators we questioned reported contact with business. Neighborhood associations came in second, with a little over three quarters of the administrators reporting contacts. Nonprofits came in

TABLE 1.1.
City Councilors' Contact with Groups over One Month

|  | Business Groups | Nonprofit Organizations | Neighborhood Associations | Environmental Groups |
|---|---|---|---|---|
| Contact over the last month | 42.1% | 28.6% | 56.8% | 11.9% |
| No contact | 57.9% | 71.4% | 43.2% | 88.1% |
| Total | 100% | 100% | 100% | 100% |
| N | 190 | 185 | 185 | 185 |

TABLE 1.2.
City Administrators' Monthly Contact with Groups over the Past Year

|  | Business Groups | Nonprofit Organizations | Neighborhood Associations | Environmental Groups |
|---|---|---|---|---|
| Contact at least once a month | 89.1% | 67.8% | 76.0% | 52.4% |
| Contact less than once a month | 10.9% | 32.2% | 24.0% | 47.6% |
| Total | 100% | 100% | 100% | 100% |
| N | 368 | 404 | 404 | 401 |

third, with just over two thirds, and environmental groups had the least contact, with administrators at just over half.

From their own perspective, local public officials believe that they offer high levels of access. Business enjoys a privileged position, but that access is not entirely closed off for other kinds of organizations. Neighborhood associations in particular seem to enjoy nearly equal access, even if nonprofits—and especially environmental groups—do not. Barriers to entry appear low, though we need also to examine group advocates' perceptions, as policymakers could exaggerate their openness as a means of promoting a positive self-image.

## Advocacy Groups' Perspectives

Our effort to measure access from the perspective of local nonprofit and advocacy groups relied on a different question. We asked our sample of advocates in the 50 cities, "When you pick up the phone and call a city official,

TABLE 1.3.
Likelihood of the Group Leader Receiving a Return Phone Call

| | All Groups | Business Groups | Nonprofit Organizations | Neighborhood Associations | Environmental Groups | All Other Groups |
|---|---|---|---|---|---|---|
| Almost always | 40.9% | 50.8% | 43.4% | 40.9% | 36.0% | 28.1% |
| Usually | 51.2% | 43.4% | 51.2% | 40.9% | 53.9% | 63.2% |
| Usually not | 6.6% | 5.7% | 5.4% | 13.6% | 7.9% | 5.3% |
| Almost never | 1.3% | 0.0% | 0.0% | 4.5% | 2.2% | 3.5% |
| Total* | 100% | 100% | 100% | 100% | 100% | 100% |
| N | 557 | 122 | 166 | 22 | 178 | 57 |

The significance of chi-square equals 0.038. "All other groups" includes faith-based and church groups, labor unions, and "others."

*Some columns do not sum to 100% due to rounding errors.

how likely is it that you'll either get through to that person or that your call will be returned?" The results are revealing, as summarized in table 1.3.

Fully 92% of all respondents said that it is "almost always the case I'll get through or my call will be returned" or that "usually I'll get through or my call will be returned." Under 7% said they "usually don't get through," and only 1% said they "almost never get through." When we divide the respondents according to the type of group they represent, the three different types of nonprofits show only modestly lower levels of access than that possessed by business. Compared to access in Washington, this represents an impressive level of group access.

The issue of having a phone call returned does not tell the whole story, and may not represent a high or demanding level of access, because it presumes that the group initiates contact. Might the story look different if the dynamic changes direction, whereby city officials initiate contact? To answer this question, we asked leaders to report how often on average over the past year city officials approached the executive director, staff, or members of the organization's board to discuss policy decisions of mutual interest. These results are reported in table 1.4.

When the measure of access is perhaps a little more demanding, the frequency of contact is not nearly as high. Across all groups, only a little over 30% of the group leaders report contact with the group being initiated by city officials twice a month or more, and just over 11% report contact four or more times a month or more. When broken down by the type of group, the role of business groups becomes somewhat clearer. According to the groups themselves, city officials initiate contact with business groups more fre-

TABLE 1.4.
Frequency of the Group Leader Being Approached by City Government

|  | All Groups | Business Groups | Nonprofit Organizations | Neighborhood Associations | Environmental Groups | All Other Groups |
|---|---|---|---|---|---|---|
| Never | 22.5% | 22.1% | 20.1% | 31.8% | 26.4% | 14.3% |
| Once a month | 47.2% | 33.6% | 48.2% | 31.8% | 57.9% | 46.4% |
| Two to three times a month | 19.0% | 27.9% | 18.9% | 36.4% | 9.6% | 23.2% |
| Four or more times a month | 11.3% | 16.4% | 12.8% | 0.0% | 6.2% | 16.1% |
| Total | 100% | 100% | 100% | 100% | 100% | 100% |
| *N* | 542 | 122 | 164 | 22 | 178 | 56 |

The significance of chi-square equals 0.00. "All other groups" includes faith-based and church groups, labor unions, and "others."

quently than with other kinds of groups, and these differences appear to be statistically significant. Yet a relatively small proportion of all types of groups report that they are "never" contacted by city officials, again suggesting that the overall level of access of groups is fairly high.

The bottom line on access, whether seen from the perspective of city officials or group leaders, whether involving contacts initiated by groups or by city officials, is that groups appear to have a significant opportunity to affect local policy. Is that access equal across all types of groups? The answer would appear to be no, as business organizations occupy a preferred position. Still, other types of groups also enjoy some level of access to local officials. Even environmental groups, which demonstrate the lowest scores in these tests, have a significant degree of access. Barriers to entry in the policy-making process are truly low in city politics.

## Inclusion and Incorporation

The second broad hypothesis involves a more challenging test for advocacy groups: collaboration and incorporation into the policy-making process. To what degree are local groups part of collaborative policy making, and are some types of advocacy organizations more likely than others to be included in policy and program decision processes?

## Public Officials' Perspectives

We asked city councilors and city administrators how likely different kinds of groups were to be "included in informal bargaining and negotiation with city officials" on issues of economic development and environment. Presumably this question moves beyond simple contacting and interaction to tap a more active and influential role of groups in actual policy decisions. The responses from city councilors are summarized in table 1.5. Once again, we observe a highly privileged position for business, with a much lesser role for other types of groups.

When administrators were asked which groups were likely to be involved in policy decisions, the pattern of responses was almost identical to those of city councilors. The preeminent position of business in terms of incorporation into city policy making could not be more clear. A more surprising finding is that neighborhood associations also score highly on incorporation. Exclusion is minimal across the board.

## Advocacy Groups' Perspectives

The question posed to group leaders asked how open and inclusive (or closed) the decision process in the city is. Specifically, group leaders were asked, "When your city's government is formulating new policies, how would you describe this process?" Respondents were offered response categories that said "Policymaking is usually inclusive with all the stakeholders brought into the process. Sometimes the process is inclusive; other times participation by stakeholders is limited or nonexistent. In most cases the process is closed to some stakeholders while open to other stakeholders who are favored by city officials. Or the process is generally closed off to all stakeholders." The picture reflected by table 1.6 looks contrasts starkly from that painted by city officials.

The vast majority of leaders from all types of groups consider the policy-making process in their respective city to be "sometimes inclusive," and sometimes "participation by stakeholders is limited or nonexistent." Business leaders and nonprofit leaders see the process as a bit more inclusive, with neighborhood association and environmental group respondents seeing the process as more limited. But the differences are not great, and the chi-square test fails to reach statistical significance.

Are some kinds of groups more likely than others to be incorporated into the policy-making process? The answer depends on whom you ask. Accord-

TABLE 1.5.
City Councilors' Reports of the Likelihood of Groups Being Included in Informal
Bargaining and Negotiation

|  | Business Groups | Nonprofit Organizations | Neighborhood Associations | Environmental Groups |
|---|---|---|---|---|
| Very likely to be included | 92.6% | 35.2% | 57.1% | 45.0% |
| Maybe included, maybe not | 4.7% | 50.8% | 32.8% | 38.3% |
| Not very likely to be included | 2.7% | 14.0% | 10.2% | 16.7% |
| Total* | 100% | 100% | 100% | 100% |
| N | 150 | 179 | 177 | 180 |

*Some columns do not sum to 100% due to rounding errors.

TABLE 1.6.
Group Leaders' Description of the Policy-Making Process

|  | All Groups | Business Groups | Nonprofit Organizations | Neighborhood Associations | Environmental Groups | All Other Groups |
|---|---|---|---|---|---|---|
| Always inclusive | 16.6% | 19.8% | 18.2% | 13.6% | 11.2% | 23.2% |
| Sometimes inclusive, sometimes limited | 58.1% | 57.9% | 55.2% | 59.1% | 61.8% | 55.4% |
| Mostly closed | 24.2% | 20.7% | 25.5% | 22.7% | 27.0% | 19.6% |
| Very closed | 1.1% | 1.7% | 1.2% | 4.5% | 0.0% | 1.8% |
| Total* | 100% | 100% | 100% | 100% | 100% | 100% |
| N | 542 | 121 | 165 | 22 | 178 | 56 |

The significance of chi-square equals 0.360. "All other groups" includes faith-based and church groups, labor unions, and "others."

*Some columns do not sum to 100% due to rounding errors.

ing to local public officials, business groups enjoy a privileged position. Yet when you ask business leaders whether the policy-making process is open and inclusive, they are no more likely than leaders of other kinds of groups to say yes. Clearly, none of the types of group leaders we surveyed seems to have a majority willing to report that the policy-making process is "always inclusive" or "mostly closed." In a survey of national and local business leaders, Sidney Verba and Gary Orren (1985) found that these executives rated their own influence with government as modest, part of a pattern they called "influence denial" (189).

## Explaining Group Access

The cross-tabulations provide a basic description of differences in access by various types of groups, but by themselves provide little or no information about what actually accounts for this variation in access. The data at hand permit us to build a more detailed picture. In order to do so, we construct some simple multivariate regression models, which allow us to determine whether there are specific variables that explain a significant amount of the variance in access. It also enables us to see whether any observed business advantage is produced by other variables.

Earlier analysis (table 1.1) showed that business groups and neighborhood associations shared unusually high access to city councilors, at least in terms of councilors reporting frequent contact with them. How do we begin to explain differences across councilors? Why do some councilors report more frequent contact with business or with neighborhood associations? Our focus here is on a small number of potential explanatory variables. First and foremost, does the ideology of the councilor and of the city play a role in determining access? We might expect conservative councilors to be more receptive to business contacts than moderate or liberal councilors. If the need to cultivate business transcends ideology, then it should not just be conservative councilors who report greater contact. We also look at the quality of information that business groups provide when contact is made, as reported by the councilors.

Table 1.7 shows that the explanatory power of different variables for contacts with business and contacts with neighborhood associations is not strong. Contacts with business groups seem to be driven more by the perception that business groups provide high-quality information than by either the ideology of the individual councilor or the perceived ideology of the city as a whole. Controlling for the ideology of the councilor, the quality of information provided by business groups seems to be a primary reason why councilors are in contact with business groups. The results for contacts with neighborhood associations show a different pattern. Here perceptions of the quality of information provided by neighborhood groups do not explain contacts one way or another. But it does seem to be true that conservative councilors are more likely to report such contacts than liberal ones. Recent contact with neighborhood associations seems to be influenced more by political ideology of the individual councilor than by the other factors.

Patterns for city administrators' business contacts are also not strong, as

TABLE 1.7.
Explaining City Councilors' Contacts with Business and Neighborhood Associations

| | Contact with Business | | Contact with Neighborhoods | |
| --- | --- | --- | --- | --- |
| | Beta | Significance | Beta | Significance |
| Quality of information provided by group (business or neighborhood) | **+.182** | **.021** | +.133 | .088 |
| Conservative political ideology of councilor | −.099 | .222 | **+.144** | **.069** |
| Conservative political ideology of city as a whole | +.076 | .342 | −.064 | .421 |
| $R^2$ | | .039 | | .034 |
| Significance | | .090 | | .122 |

Boldface indicates statistically significant results.

shown in table 1.8. None of the variables is correlated with business community contacts. Such contacts are not related to the quality of information provided, or to either the ideology of the administrator or of the city as a whole. The results for contacts with neighborhood associations are considerably stronger. Both the quality of information and the liberal ideology of the administrator seem to help explain administrators' contacts with neighborhood associations.

## Explaining Incorporation

Earlier analysis documented the advantage that business organizations have in terms of being included and incorporated in policy decision-making processes. Inclusion of neighborhood associations also exceeded that of other kinds of groups except business groups. Can incorporating business and neighborhood associations be explained in terms of political ideology? Or are other factors at work?

Turning first to city councilors, table 1.9 looks at inclusiveness of the business community and of neighborhood associations. Inclusiveness of the business community is not related to the quality of information provided by business groups, or by political ideology, per se. Councilors in cities that are highly committed to the private sector report greater inclusion of the business community. The strongest relationship that we have found is with the length of service of the councilor. Councilors who have served for a longer

TABLE 1.8.
Explaining City Administrators' Contacts with Business and Neighborhood Associations

|  | Contact with Business | | Contact with Neighborhoods | |
|---|---|---|---|---|
|  | Beta | Significance | Beta | Significance |
| Quality of information provided by group (business or neighborhood) | +.064 | .235 | **+.232** | **.000** |
| Conservative political ideology of administrator | −.074 | .170 | **−.127** | **.015** |
| Conservative political ideology of city as a whole | −.008 | .877 | −.072 | .167 |
| $R^2$ | | .008 | | .076 |
| Significance | | .387 | | .000 |

Boldface indicates statistically significant results.

period of time are much less likely to report that business is included, and more recently elected councilors report greater inclusiveness for business. Analysis of inclusiveness of neighborhood associations shows an absence of statistically significant findings. None of the variables in the model helps to explain inclusiveness of neighborhood associations in policy decisions.

Results for city administrators look different from those for city councilors, as presented in table 1.10. First, neither of the models is terribly robust. In other words, it seems much more difficult to explain the variance in administrators' reports of inclusiveness. Second, none of the explanatory variables is correlated with inclusiveness of business. Variation in the inclusiveness of the policy process to the business community cannot be explained by political ideology, by the quality of information offered by business groups, by administrators' views on how committed the city is to the private sector, or by the length of service of the administrator. Third, in a slightly stronger model, inclusiveness of neighborhood associations seems to be related to the quality of information these kinds of groups provide to administrators. When administrators report that neighborhood associations provide high-quality information, they also report that neighborhood associations are likely to be involved in policy decisions.

## Conclusions

The future for America's cities is bright. In increasing numbers, Americans are deciding that urban living is the best option at the price they can afford,

TABLE 1.9.
Explaining City Councilors' Reports of the Inclusiveness of Policy Process to the
Business Community and Neighborhood Associations

| | Inclusiveness of Business | | Inclusiveness of Neighborhoods | |
|---|---|---|---|---|
| | Beta | Significance | Beta | Significance |
| Quality of information from group | +.085 | .321 | +.065 | .432 |
| Conservative ideology of councilor | −.097 | .280 | +.052 | .527 |
| Conservative ideology of city as a whole | −.042 | .642 | −.068 | .409 |
| City commitment to the private sector | **+.160** | **.062** | +.079 | .344 |
| Years served on city council | **−.259** | **.003** | −.002 | .981 |
| $R^2$ | .112 | | .020 | |
| Significance | .009 | | .684 | |

Boldface indicates statistically significant results.


TABLE 1.10.
Explaining City Administrators' Reports of the Inclusiveness of Policy Process to the
Business Community and Neighborhood Associations

| | Inclusiveness of Business | | Inclusiveness of Neighborhoods | |
|---|---|---|---|---|
| | Beta | Significance | Beta | Significance |
| Quality of information from group | +.095 | .116 | **+.185** | **.001** |
| Conservative ideology of administrator | +.024 | .692 | −.065 | .235 |
| Conservative ideology of city as a whole | +.094 | .112 | −.038 | .490 |
| City commitment to the private sector | +.036 | .543 | +.074 | .172 |
| Years served on city council | −.059 | .313 | +.013 | .807 |
| $R^2$ | .025 | | .046 | |
| Significance | .196 | | .008 | |

Boldface indicates statistically significant results.

and most cities have grown in recent years, many by double-digit increases (Glaeser and Shapiro, 2003). The variety of neighborhoods, housing options, cultural amenities, and availability of mass transit are appealing qualities for many. Suburban living remains attractive to be sure, and larger employers often find office parks off the interstate to be their best choice. Still, young people starting out in their careers, entrepreneurs, and others who find networking a necessary component of their work lives may find cities to be attractive for their professional pursuits. Any enduring rise in energy prices will surely accelerate urban population growth.

Population growth, even from a skilled and professional workforce, does not in and of itself create a greater role for nonprofits in the governance of cities. But the changing ecology of cities has created greater opportunities for nonprofits to become instrumental parts of the policy-making process. We see this as a positive development, but not because of the partial vacuum created by a lower density of large corporate entities headquartered in cities and active in their politics. Rather, as students of both nonprofits and city politics, we believe that a pluralistic city is desirable, as all sectors of the city should be vigorously represented. Not all nonprofits work with low-income and disadvantaged populations, but those that do are of critical importance in the vitality of our democracy. The reality of the collective action problem means that among all advocacy sectors, only nonprofits supported by contracts, fees for service, or philanthropy have a strong interest in speaking on behalf of the disadvantaged.

The evidence in this chapter is based on three separate surveys, and the resulting data point toward an important story about advocacy. Four findings stand out:

First, unlike national politics, the barriers to entry into the urban policy-making system appear to be low. Access to policymakers is easily available. Not all types of groups enjoy the same level of access, but no particular type of group among those examined here are totally shut out. Incorporation is more selective, but there are large numbers of nonprofits from various advocacy sectors that have ongoing, collaborative relationships with city officials.

Second, neighborhood associations, which tend to possess little in the way of resources other than the time of their volunteers, are highly valued by city policymakers. The surveys do not tell us exactly why, but we believe that the "politics of place" that characterizes city politics is a large part of the reason. So many important decisions facing policymakers involve a specific neighborhood, whether it be a matter involving resource allocations, project siting, zoning, economic development, or schools. Councilors and administrators know that gaining approval (or at least acquiescence) from residents is highly desirable, if not effectively required. Neighborhood associations are a means to that end. For neighborhood associations there is great opportunity to become involved, but considerable challenges as well. Volunteers must be mobilized on a continuing basis, and effective advocacy requires more than simply stating a neighborhood preference.

Third, business retains a privileged position in city politics. This is hardly surprising, and big business's reduced footprint in city politics may make the cooperation of remaining business entities all the more valuable. There are times when business and nonprofit interests are at odds, such as a firm wanting to develop a particular parcel of land and environmental groups trying to stop the company. Often, though, business and nonprofits are aligned. Peak civic associations are composed of leaders from both the for-profit and nonprofit sectors. Individual firms and nonprofits might work together, for example, on neighborhood economic redevelopment. It is common for private developers and a local CDC to collaborate in planning a project. Business leaders populate the boards of nonprofits (DeSocio, 2007), and these relationships offer 501(c)(3)s more entrée into government.

Fourth, the specific attributes of nonprofits that city policymakers find valuable are not clear. In particular, we explored whether the quality of information transmitted from nonprofits to policymakers, as reported by policymakers, made a difference in terms of access and incorporation. There are some signs suggesting that a real research capacity could be beneficial, but the findings differ depending on whether the policymakers are city councilors or city administrators. Among councilors, the quality of information from business organizations affects contacts with business, but the quality of information generated by neighborhood associations does not seem to affect contacts with such organizations.

The opposite pattern seems to be true for city administrators. When administrators report that business has high-quality information, they do not necessarily have greater contact with businesses. Yet when they report that neighborhood associations have high-quality information, they have significantly greater contact with these groups. Taken together, this suggests that neighborhood associations (and perhaps other nonprofit organizations) with the ability to generate high-quality information might be better advised to seek interactions with city administrators than with city councilors. The quality of information also seems to have some relationship to how inclusive city administrators are with respect to neighborhood associations.

For nonprofits, the greatest challenge to becoming involved in city policy is making the decision to become involved. Nonprofits tend to regard themselves as nonpolitical and are acculturated by the limits on lobbying in section 501(c)(3) to believe they should be nonpolitical (Berry and Arons, 2003). Yet at the city level, section 501(c)(3) should not present any problem for advocacy, as lobbying before city councils appears to fly under the radar of the IRS. Lobbying by nonprofits is perfectly legal, and the legal limits on lobbying do not even apply to advocacy before administrative bodies. Rather, the constraint is a self-imposed one, as nonprofits are often poorly prepared for advocacy. In a small organization overwhelmed by the demands of clients, government relations may simply be a job that belongs to no one. The door to government is wide open. Nonprofits may want to walk through it.

## NOTES

1. This figure is for 2009. There are close to 1.6 million nonprofits of all types. Data are available from the Urban Institute's National Center for Charitable Statistics at http://nccsdataweb.urban.org/PubApps/profile1.php?state=US.

2. Not all forms of interest group influence are directly exerted through access to policymakers. Most fundamentally, dominant societal values are transmitted through political socialization.

3. The concept of "incorporation" in urban politics is most closely associated with Browning et al.'s (1984) study of city councils. They were focused on minority representation on councils, and they defined incorporation as "the extent to which group interests are effectively represented in policy making" (25). We focus on frequency of interaction as a meaningful indicator of effective representation, as this operationalization lends itself better to the limitations of survey research.

4. This has not always been the case. The central work in the debate over pluralism, Robert Dahl's *Who Governs?* (1961), was based on his study of local politics in New Haven, Connecticut.

5. These numbers were calculated by the authors from OpenSecrets.org and aggregate the following categories: pharmaceuticals/health products, hospitals/nursing homes, and health professionals.

6. The three questionnaires can be found at http://ase.tufts.edu/polsci/faculty /berry/ under "Cities Face the Future." The administrator questionnaire is available at http://ase.tufts.edu/polsci/faculty/berry/question-admin.pdf.

The councilor questionnaire is found at http://ase.tufts.edu/polsci/faculty/berry

/question-city.pdf, and the group leader questionnaire is found at http://ase.tufts
.edu/polsci/faculty/berry/question-group.pdf.

7. To incentivize respondents to fill out the questionnaire, we offered them the
opportunity to win one of three $100 gift cards from Amazon.com. The mailings
included a prepaid (stamped) postcard allowing the respondent to provide a name
and to be entered into the gift card raffle. This mailing also included a $1 bill, which
Dillman et al. (2009, 238–42) suggest exerts significant influence on the response rate.

8. We use the generic term "councilor" here, although some cities may refer to
their representatives as aldermen (as in Milwaukee), supervisors (as in San Francisco), or commissioners (as in Portland).

9. Most city councilors in Columbus, Ohio, declined to participate citing a local ordinance that prohibits administration of such surveys. Even so, one councilor
responded.

10. The instructions to our research assistants are recorded in a detailed memo
that we prepared, "Strategy for Developing List of Advocacy Organizations," which
is available by request.

11. Individual corporations also fell outside of the set of organizations targeted for
the survey of advocates. But the surveys sent to city councilors and administrators
included questions that asked respondents to evaluate corporate activities along with
those of other advocacy sectors.

12. See http://cms3.tucsonaz.gov/hcd/neighborhood-associations and http://www
.portlandonline.com/oni/index.cfm?c=28385.

### REFERENCES

Altshuler, Alan, and David Luberoff. 2003. *Mega-Projects*. Washington, DC: Brookings Institution Press.

Baumgartner, Frank R., Jeffrey M. Berry, Marie Hojnacki, David C. Kimball, and
Beth L. Leech. 2009. *Lobbying and Policy Change*. Chicago: University of Chicago
Press.

Berry, Jeffrey M. 2010. "Urban Interest Groups." In *The Oxford Handbook of American Political Parties and Interest Groups,* edited by L. Sandy Maisel and Jeffrey M.
Berry, 502–15. Oxford: Oxford University Press.

Berry, Jeffrey M., with David F. Arons. 2003. *A Voice for Nonprofits*. Washington, DC:
Brookings Institution Press.

Berry, Jeffrey M., Kent E. Portney, Robin Liss, Jessica Simoncelli, and Lisa Berger.
2006. *Power and Interest Groups in City Politics*. Cambridge, MA: Rappaport Institute for Greater Boston, Kennedy School of Government.

Berry, Jeffrey M., Kent E. Portney, and Ken Thomson. 1993. *The Rebirth of Urban
Democracy*. Washington, DC: Brookings Institution Press.

Browning, Rufus P., Dale Rogers Marshall, and David H. Tabb. 1984. *Protest Is Not
Enough*. Berkeley: University of California Press.

Dahl, Robert A. 1961. *Who Governs?* New Haven, CT: Yale University Press.

DeSocio, Mark. 2007. "Business Community Structures and Urban Regimes." *Journal of Urban Affairs* 29, no. 4: 339–66.

Dillman, Don, Jolene Smyth, and Leah Melani Christian. 2009. *Internet, Mail, and Mixed Mode Surveys: The Tailored Design Method.* 3rd ed. New York: Wiley.

Fitzgerald, Joan. 2010. *Emerald Cities.* New York: Oxford University Press.

Florida, Richard. 2012. *The Rise of the Creative Class, Revisited.* New York: Basic Books.

Glaeser, Edward. 2011. *The Triumph of the City.* New York: Penguin.

Glaeser, Edward, Jed Kolko, and Albert Saiz, 2001. "Consumer City." *Journal of Economic Geography* 1: 27–50.

Glaeser, Edward, and Jesse Shaprio. 2003. "City Growth: Which Places Grew and Why." In *Redefining Urban and Suburban America*, edited by Bruce Katz and Robert E. Lang, 13–32. Washington, DC: Brookings Institution Press.

Hanson, Royce, Harold Wolman, David Connolly, Katherine Pearson, and Robert McMannon. 2010. "Corporate Citizenship and Urban Problem Solving: The Changing Civic Role of Business Leaders in American Cities." *Journal of Urban Affairs* 32, no. 1: 1–23.

Lindblom, Charles E. 1977. *Politics and Markets.* New York: Basic Books.

Lowi, Theodore J. 1969. *The End of Liberalism.* New York: Norton.

Marwell, Nicole P. 2004. "Privatizing the Welfare State: Nonprofit Community-Based Organizations as Political Actors." *American Sociological Review* 69: 265–91.

Mills, C. Wright. 1956. *The Power Elite.* New York: Oxford University Press.

Molotch, Harvey. 1976. "The City As Growth Machine: Toward a Political Economy of Place." *American Journal of Sociology* 82, no. 2: 309–22.

Musso, Juliet, Christopher Weare, and Terry L. Cooper. 2004. *Neighborhood Councils in Los Angeles: A Midterm Status Report.* Los Angeles: USC Urban Initiative.

Olson, Mancur. 1968. *The Logic of Collective Action.* New York: Schocken.

Peterson, Paul E. 1981. *City Limits.* Chicago: University of Chicago Press.

Portney, Kent E. 2007. "Local Business and Environmental Policies in Cities." In *Business and Environmental Policy: Corporate Interests in the American Political System*, edited by Michael E. Kraft and Sheldon Kamieniecki, 299–326. Cambridge, MA: MIT Press.

———. 2013. *Taking Sustainable Cities Seriously.* 2nd ed. Cambridge, MA: MIT Press.

Schattschneider, E. E. 1960. *The Semi-Sovereign People.* Hindsdale, IL: Dryden Press.

Schlozman, Kay. 2010. "Who Sings in the Heavenly Chorus? The Shape of the Organized Interest System." In *The Oxford Handbook of American Political Parties and Interest Groups,* edited by L. Sandy Maisel and Jeffrey M. Berry, 425–47. Oxford: Oxford University Press.

Smith, Steven Rathgeb. 2002. "Social Services." In *The State of Nonprofit America,* edited by Lester M. Salamon, 149–86. Washington, DC: Brookings Institution Press.

Verba, Sidney, and Gary Orren. 1985. *Equality in America.* Cambridge, MA: Harvard University Press.

# CHAPTER TWO

# Nonprofit Advocacy in Seattle and Washington, DC

ROBERT J. PEKKANEN AND STEVEN RATHGEB SMITH

How do nonprofits advocate? This central research question animates this volume. We adopt an empirical approach to investigating this question, relying here on data gleaned from surveys of nonprofits in King County, Washington (hereafter Seattle), and Washington, DC. We provide details of these surveys in the introduction to this volume; they were designed to illuminate a number of issues in nonprofit advocacy. Our analyses focus on answering the question of which nonprofits advocate.

## Defining Advocacy

We follow the definition of advocacy advanced in the introduction to this volume: "advocacy is the attempt to influence public policy, either directly or indirectly." In this chapter, we operationalize advocacy as specific responses by organizations to certain survey questions. More specifically, we define a group that engages in advocacy for our analysis below as a group that answered one of five questions on our survey in a specified way. We counted as an advocacy group any nonprofit that identified itself as such in the field question. But we also used measures of reported behavior, in part because of the sensitivities groups display toward identifying themselves as engaged in lobbying or advocacy. Also, we believe survey results are more reliable when they report responses to questions about specific actions. We thus analyze advocacy below in the context of specific responses to questions on our surveys. In other words, when groups tell us that they do something that we consider advocacy, we call it advocacy. We counted as an advocacy group any organization that reported becoming involved in public policy or advocacy, employing a lobbyist, or affiliating with a political action committee or 501(c)(4) that had advocacy as part of its mission. Finally, we counted as an advocacy group any organization that reported trying to influence government policy at the local, state, or national level.

Using such responses to these questions as our measure of advocacy, we found that 31.9% of Seattle organizations were "advocating organizations" (figs. 2.1 and 2.2). This is comparable to the percentage (27%) found by Child and Grønbjerg (2007) in their study of Indiana nonprofits (266), although far less than that (73%) identified by Salamon and Geller (2008, 1) and lower also than Chaves et al. (2004) found for congregations (over 41%). By implication, Berry and his colleagues find an even higher proportion, 85% if one counts all groups declining to report that they never engage in advocacy (OMB Watch, Tufts University, and Center for Lobbying in the Public Interest, 2002, 17). Differences in the scope of organizations surveyed, survey methods, definition of advocacy, and the geographic region targeted probably account for the divergent results. Only further empirical investigation can be conclusive, but we suspect that what is counted as advocacy and the wording of questions could be enough to create such a wide variation.

Figures 2.3 and 2.4 provide an overview of the different types of nonprofit organizations in the DC and Seattle. Figure 2.5 provides information on the budget size of the Seattle organizations in the study. One notable aspect of figure 2.5 is the large number of small nonprofits, mirroring the national composition of the nonprofit sector.

## Why Do Nonprofits Advocate?

One of the most frequently asked questions about nonprofits and advocacy is which nonprofits advocate. This sensible, basic question provides some context for further investigations of advocacy behavior. After all, if only a tiny minority of nonprofits engaged in advocacy, even those with an interest in nonprofits might generally be less interested in the topic, or perhaps scholars would have to reconsider our research methodology to analyze the phenomenon. So a first step is to consider what proportion of nonprofits advocate, which we do below. Our analysis connects this chapter to one of the central themes of the volume, namely, the limitations on advocacy; we see specification of the conditions under which advocacy is (more) likely to occur to be intimately related to the obverse question of which nonprofits are (less) likely to engage in advocacy. And our data are only the latest to show that some nonprofits and not others engage in advocacy.

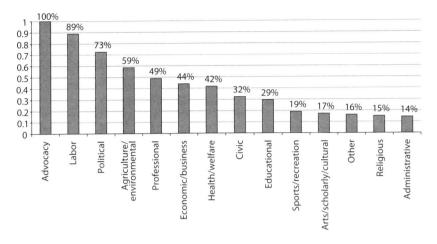

*Figure 2.1.* Percent of organizations engaging in advocacy by field (Seattle).

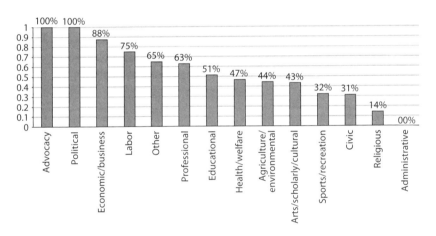

*Figure 2.2.* Percent of organizations engaging in advocacy by field (Washington, DC).

Noticing that some but not all nonprofits engage in advocacy naturally leads observers to ask why some nonprofits but not others advocate. This question has received a good deal of attention in the literature (see Prakash and Gugerty, 2010). The question is usually framed as some variation on *what characteristics of nonprofits are associated with behavior defined as advocacy?* Such framing permits testing of various hypotheses. It does not answer some fundamental questions about nonprofits per se, such as those raised in the

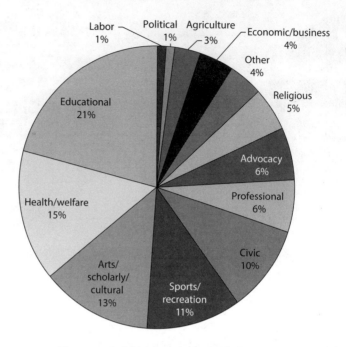

*Figure 2.3.* Field of organization (Seattle).

book's introduction about the difference (if any) between interest groups and nonprofits. Still, it is a valuable way to organize an investigation. Child and Grønbjerg (2007) provide an excellent example in establishing their hypotheses, and we follow it in this section. We set up more general propositions before we operationalize our hypotheses, however, in order to more clearly show both our analytical logic as well as the specifics of how we test.

Some of the most prominent arguments in the literature about what makes groups advocate have to do with resource availability, the field of the group, and reliance on government funding. We investigate these issues below. But arguments have also been made about a variety of other factors, such as legal status, age of the group, and organizational mission.

Our first proposition pertains to resource mobilization, which figures prominently in the literature on nonprofits but is borrowed from sociology and studies of social movements (see Grønbjerg, 1993; Pfeffer and Salancik, 1978; Smith and Grønbjerg, 2006; Thompson, 1967). The logic here is simple: the more resources a nonprofit has, the more likely it is to organize, either

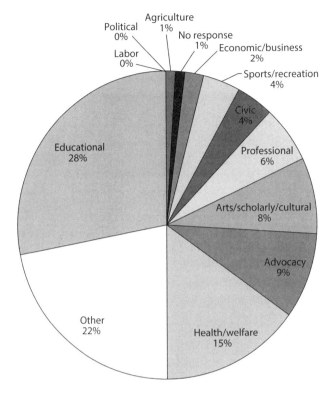

*Figure 2.4.* Field of organization (Washington, DC).

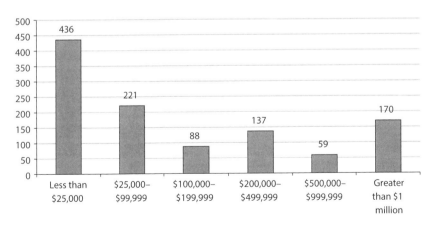

*Figure 2.5.* Budget size of Seattle organizations (*n* = 1111).

because it has sufficient resources to devote to advocacy or because it feels more keenly the need to defend its interests in the policy arena, or some combination of these factors.

Proposition 1: The greater an organization's resources, the more likely it is to engage in advocacy.

Given the few candidates for key resources—such as money, staff, expertise, or access to information technology—we recast proposition 1 for testing into a few related hypotheses. We lack good measures for expertise or access to information technology in our survey, so we focus on money and staff.

Our measure of budget stems directly from responses to our survey question about the size of the budget. We hypothesize rather straightforwardly that the larger an organization's budget, the more likely that it will be an advocating organization.

H1a [Resources-budget]: Higher reported budgets will be associated with a greater likelihood of being an advocating organization.

We then turn to an analysis of the relationship between staff size and advocacy. In line with the resource mobilization argument, our second proposition is also straightforward. The larger a group's staff, the more ability it will have to advocate, which in turn leads to more advocacy *ceteris paribus.*

The first hypothesis we operationalize from this proposition is a measure of total human resources. In the survey, we asked groups to specify the number of their full-time employees, part-time employees, regular volunteers, and episodic volunteers. Episodic volunteers could contribute to the organization's ability to advocate. But such volunteers might take staff time away from advocacy activity (there may be an issue of omitted variable bias here, too—groups that engage in activities that utilize many episodic volunteers may have a mission that is not compatible with advocating—but we do not investigate this directly). So we refine the total human resources measure into a measure that excludes episodic volunteers only and test for correlation between that measure and advocacy. We also considered that volunteers might actually detract from an organization's ability to advocate, because full-time staffers might have to spend their time and energy on training or coordinating the volunteers and thus have less time for advocacy. We also tested a measure of staff that captured the ratio of full-time staff to volunteers. We present these three hypotheses, H1b, H1c, and H1d, and their results below.

H1b [Resources-staff]: Greater total human resources (full-time staff, part-time staff, regular volunteers, and episodic volunteers) will be associated with a greater likelihood of being an advocating organization.

H1c [Resources-staff]: Greater numbers of regular human resources (full-time staff, part-time staff, and regular volunteers) will be associated with a greater likelihood of being an advocating organization.

H1d [Resources-staff]: A higher ratio of paid staff (full-time staff, part-time staff) to volunteers (regular volunteers, episodic volunteers) will be associated with a greater likelihood of being an advocating organization.

Not just the total amount of resources, but also where they come from, may be important. Another topic that has received a great deal of attention in the literature is the effect of government funding on nonprofit advocacy. Some scholars suggest that government funding might dampen the advocacy activity of nonprofits. For instance, funding might cause nonprofits to be hesitant to pursue advocacy for fear of jeopardizing their relationship with government funders (Bass et al., 2007; Chaves et al., 2004; Reid, 2006). Other scholars suggest that government funding might actually prompt more engagement in advocacy because nonprofits would have a more direct connection to public policy (Chaves et al., 2004; Kramer, 1987; Salamon, 1987) In addition, Smith and Lipsky (1993) argue that government funding prompts more advocacy activity by nonprofits, but it tends to be advocacy focused on issues and concerns related to the organization, such as funding and regulations, rather than more general issues related to service users and their community (see also Mosley, chap. 5, this volume). Bass et al. (2007), Berry and Arons (2003), and others suggest that nonprofits might be hesitant to advocate because they are uncertain about the legally permissible levels of advocacy with or without government funding.

Proposition 2: Government funding will be positively correlated with advocacy.

Question 34 asks about the percentage of the 2008 budget that comes from government funding, which "includes grants, fees, Medicaid, Medicare, contracts, etc., all funding that comes from federal, state, or local government."

H2 [Government funding]: A larger share of the 2008 budget coming from government will be positively correlated with advocacy.

Another staple of the empirical literature on nonprofit advocacy is that the field of the group affects advocacy. Different fields of activity present different public policy environments in which nonprofits must operate. Variation in this public policy environment could lead nonprofits to be more or less active in advocacy (Child and Grønbjerg, 2007, 261).

Proposition 3: Different fields present different public policy environments, and thus nonprofits in certain fields will be more likely than those in other fields to engage in advocacy.

Our proposition is unspecific about which fields will lead nonprofits to greater likelihoods of advocacy. Good arguments can be made for several fields. One approach would be to create deductive hypotheses based on the characteristics of a field that would be most likely to lead nonprofits to advocate. For example, government funding is more prevalent in health than for religion. So we might expect that groups (even if they do not receive funding themselves) in fields with heavy government funding might be more active than groups where funding is scarce. The same logic could apply to regulation. Where regulation is heavy, groups might feel a greater need to be involved in shaping policy. Where regulation is light, groups might shy away from advocacy. Similarly, groups might be involved in advocacy in policy arenas with greater policy contestation, where partisan bickering by political parties or the involvement of powerful corporate or other social actors is more prevalent. Some fields might just be considered more politically salient than others. Unfortunately, we lack good metrics for many of these possible independent variables, and instead rely on an inductive approach and our extant knowledge of the public policy environment (although guided by the logic above).

Specifically, we hypothesize that nonprofits in educational, health, and professional fields will be more likely to engage in advocacy. Health and educational nonprofits operate in both policy environments dominated by government spending and where many direct service providers exist (Smith and Lipsky, 1993). Professional groups are usually formed to advance the interests of professions, which frequently overlaps with attempts to shape the public policy environment. The environmental policy arena, for example, is one of fierce competition (Child and Grønbjerg, 2007).

H3a [Field-health]: Nonprofits in the health field are more likely than average to engage in advocacy.

H3b [Field-education]: Nonprofits in the education field are more likely than average to engage in advocacy.

H3c [Field-professional]: Nonprofits in the professional field are more likely than average to engage in advocacy.

We also consider that the age of a nonprofit could affect its likelihood of advocating. Older, more established nonprofits could be more likely to engage in advocacy because of their organizational history or experience, or perhaps they have come to fill a leadership position in the field.

Proposition 4: The age of nonprofits affects their likelihood of engaging in advocacy.

To investigate this possibility, we frame the following hypothesis.

H4 [Age]: The older the nonprofit, the more likely it is to engage in advocacy.

The mission of the nonprofit could also affect its decision to engage in advocacy behavior. It is easy to imagine that some nonprofits have missions that avoid any kind of political activity, either because of a particular aversion or because their niche in the field does not lead them to encounter as many policy issues as other groups within the same field.

Proposition 5: The central mission of nonprofits affects their likelihood of engaging in advocacy.

To investigate this possibility, we frame the following hypothesis.

H5 [Mission]: Nonprofits that identify education of the public as a goal are more likely to engage in advocacy.

Another possibility, arguably related to the previous two propositions, is that nonprofits established at different periods in history could have been shaped by the political and regulatory environment of the time. Child and Grønbjerg (2007) suggest that organizations formed in the 1960s could be more likely to engage in advocacy, while organizations that formed in the 1990s, when advocacy was more likely to be discouraged, would be less likely to engage in advocacy.

Proposition 6: The founding period of nonprofits affects their likelihood of engaging in advocacy.

To investigate this possibility, we frame the following two related hypotheses.

H6a [Period]: Nonprofits formed in the 1960s are more likely to engage in advocacy.

H6b [Period]: Nonprofits formed in the 1990s are less likely to engage in advocacy.

Some nonprofits are local chapters of a larger organization, while others are independent groups. Skocpol (1999), for instance, argued that the federal structure of the US political system shaped civic organizations into a parallel tripartite form.

Proposition 7: Independent nonprofits are more likely to engage in advocacy than nonprofits that are local chapters of larger organizations.

To investigate this possibility, we frame the following hypothesis.

H7 [Chapter]: Nonprofits that are local chapters of larger organizations are less likely to engage in advocacy than other nonprofits.

Skocpol (1999) examined the relationship of members to the professional staff of nonprofits, warning that "advocates without members" brought different political consequences than an engaged public. Foley and Edwards (2002) conducted an empirical investigation of organizations in the peace movement and found differences in political activity based on membership structure. For example, groups whose members are other organizations were more likely to adopt nonpartisan or "insider" strategies (27).

Proposition 8: Nonprofits with members are more likely to engage in advocacy.

We asked a question in our survey about members. If the organization responded that it had members, we asked a follow-up question about member involvement. Organizations could select from a frequency variable with five gradations ranging from "never" to "very often" to answer about a variety of modes of member involvement. Most of these modes involved governance issues, such as electing the board of directors or being involved in management. Some of the modes involved interaction among the members in person or through electronic means. Besides asking whether an organization had members, we also investigated whether greater member control of governance (higher frequency of electing board of directors, interacting with the board of directors, or being involved in decision making and management) was associated with more advocacy. As a third possibility, we checked whether greater member interaction (in person or electronically) correlated with higher levels of advocacy. To investigate these possibilities, we frame the below hypotheses.

H8a [Members]: Nonprofits with members are more likely to advocate.

H8b [Members]: Nonprofits with members involved in governance (performing decision making and management, electing the board of directors, or meeting and talking with the board of directors) are more likely to advocate.

H8c [Members]: Nonprofits with members who interact (in person or electronically) are more likely to advocate.

We also asked groups that did not advocate if they limited their advocacy because of resource problems or concerns about tax-exempt status. Figure 2.6 presents the results of that question.

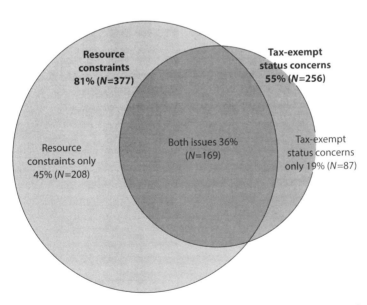

*Figure 2.6.* Limitations on advocacy according to data from Japan Interest Group Surveys. Total, $N = 1137$; yes, $N = 464$; no, $N = 673$. Note that these figures are for the organizations that say they have to limit their advocacy only; 673 respondents said they did not limit their efforts. Source: US JIGS 2 data set

TABLE 2.1.
Descriptive Statistics and Independent Variables

| | Seattle | | | | Washington, DC | | | |
|---|---|---|---|---|---|---|---|---|
| | Mean | SD[a] | Minimum | Maximum | Mean | SD | Minimum | Maximum |
| Budget ($ in thousands) | 3,217.24 | 52,852.57 | 0 | 1,500,000.00 | 1,957.25 | 6,509.70 | 0 | 73,000.00 |
| Annual budget of $1 million or more | 0.15 | 0.36 | 0 | 1 | 0.26 | 0.44 | 0 | 1 |
| Annual budget of $100,000–$999,999 | 0.29 | 0.45 | 0 | 1 | 0.41 | 0.49 | 0 | 1 |
| Paid staff and volunteers | 161.75 | 605.39 | 1 | 10,005 | 208.83 | 789.98 | 1 | 9,920 |
| Paid staff and volunteers (excluding episodic volunteers) | 39.90 | 173.03 | 0 | 3,508 | 61.26 | 298.99 | 0 | 4,920 |
| Ratio of paid staff to volunteers | 0.32 | 2.03 | 0 | 49 | 1.35 | 4.50 | 0 | 49 |
| Percentage of budget from government funding | 0.10 | 0.22 | 0 | 1 | 0.22 | 0.33 | 0 | 1 |
| Health and welfare (0,1)[b] | 0.16 | 0.37 | 0 | 1 | 0.24 | 0.43 | 0 | 1 |
| Education (0,1) | 0.22 | 0.41 | 0 | 1 | 0.29 | 0.46 | 0 | 1 |
| Professional (0.1) | 0.07 | 0.25 | 0 | 1 | 0.06 | 0.23 | 0 | 1 |
| Mission of educating the Public (0,1) | 0.34 | 0.47 | 0 | 1 | 0.37 | 0.48 | 0 | 1 |
| 501(c)(3) charity | 0.80 | 0.40 | 0 | 1 | 0.92 | 0.27 | 0 | 1 |
| Age in years | 28.18 | 24.77 | 3 | 151 | 20.74 | 15.09 | 2 | 73 |
| Local chapter of a national organization (0,1) | 0.18 | 0.38 | 0 | 1 | 0.13 | 0.34 | 0 | 1 |
| High level of member engagement | 0.46 | 0.50 | 0 | 1 | 0.42 | 0.49 | 0 | 1 |
| Moderate level of member engagement | 0.09 | 0.29 | 0 | 1 | 0.15 | 0.36 | 0 | 1 |
| Founded in the 1960s | 0.04 | 0.21 | 0 | 1 | 0.04 | 0.20 | 0 | 1 |
| Founded in 1990–2002 | 0.33 | 0.47 | 0 | 1 | 0.35 | 0.48 | 0 | 1 |

[a]SD, standard deviation.
[b]Responses were assigned a value of 0 if they responded no and a value of 1 if they responded yes.

Acting in coalition or delegating advocacy functions can mitigate resource constraints (see Boris and Maronick, chap. 3, and Sandfort, chap. 9, this volume). The various modes of advocating present another research opportunity. We have gathered some data on this topic in our surveys and hope to expand upon it in future. Table 2.1 shows the descriptive statistics for this analysis.

## Data Analysis

We created six separate models to test our hypotheses for both the Seattle and DC surveys. The six models vary slightly on how the resource variables are included. Models 1, 3, and 5 include a variable for all human resources (staff, regular volunteers, and episodic volunteers), while models 2, 4, and 6 contain a variable for regular human resources (staff and regular volunteers only). Models 1 and 2 contain a continuous variable for the age of the organization; models 3 and 4 contain a binary variable for whether the organization was founded in the 1960s; and models 5 and 6 contain a binary variable for whether the organization was founded in 1990 to 2002. Because the coefficients were similar across all six models, results are reported in this section from Model 1 unless otherwise noted. Tables 2.2 and 2.3 present the full results of our regressions.

In the Seattle survey group, a significant association between budget and engaging in advocacy exists. Compared to organizations reporting annual budgets of less than $100,000, organizations with budgets of $100,000 to $999,999 were more likely to engage in advocacy by a factor of 0.685. Organizations with an annual budget of $1 million or more were more likely to engage in advocacy by a factor of 1.327. These results suggest that the larger an organization's budget, the more likely it is to engage in advocacy, holding all other factors in the model constant.

A relationship between the percentage of government funding and engaging in advocacy is also apparent. For every one percentage point increase in government funding, the likelihood that an organization engages in advocacy increases by a factor of 0.014. Organizations that educate the public are also positively associated with engaging in advocacy. Further, the degree to which organizations involve members is associated with an organization engaging in advocacy, with organizations that involve members in governance being more likely to do so.

The results from the DC survey group show a greater number of significant associations between advocacy by nonprofits and the variables in our

TABLE 2.2.
Logistic Regression of Engagement in Advocacy on Independent Variables and Odds Ratios: Seattle Survey

| | Model 1 | Model 2 | Model 3 | Model 4 | Model 5 | Model 6 |
|---|---|---|---|---|---|---|
| Annual budget of $1 million or more | 1.327[a] (−4.95)[b] | 1.199[a] (−4.50) | 1.335[a] (−5.07) | 1.194[a] (−4.58) | 1.336[a] (−5.08) | 1.198[a] (−4.58) |
| Annual budget of $100,000 to $999,999 | 0.685[a] (−3.52) | 0.670[a] (−3.46) | 0.694[a] (−3.62) | 0.673[a] (−3.53) | 0.705[a] (−3.68) | 0.683[a] (−3.59) |
| Total human resources (square root) | 0.00259 (−.24) | | 0.00394 (−.38) | | 0.00348 (−.34) | |
| Total regular human resources (square root) | | 0.0327 (−1.66) | | 0.0342 (−1.77) | | 0.0329 (−1.70) |
| Ratio of paid staff to volunteers | −0.0214 (−0.76) | −0.0265 (−0.88) | −0.0215 (−0.76) | −0.0284 (−0.92) | −0.0218 (−0.78) | −0.0276 (−0.92) |
| Percentage of budget from government funding | 1.439[a] (−3.61) | 1.369[a] (−3.42) | 1.429[a] (−3.58) | 1.358[a] (−3.38) | 1.436[a] (−3.60) | 1.368[a] (−3.41) |
| Health and welfare (0,1)[c] | −0.179 (−0.70) | −0.218 (−0.85) | −0.183 (−0.71) | −0.221 (−0.86) | −0.196 (−0.77) | −0.232 (−0.91) |
| Education (0,1) | −0.323 (−1.54) | −0.34 (−1.62) | −0.33 (−1.56) | −0.348 (−1.65) | −0.33 (−1.56) | −0.345 (−1.64) |
| Professional (0,1) | 0.568 (−1.81) | 0.57 (−1.79) | 0.576 (−1.83) | 0.578 (−1.81) | 0.56 (−1.77) | 0.563 (−1.76) |
| Mission of educating the public (0,1) | 1.606[a] (−9.41) | 1.611[a] (−9.53) | 1.602[a] (−9.42) | 1.612[a] (−9.55) | 1.598[a] (−9.38) | 1.606[a] (−9.51) |
| 501(c)(3) charity (0,1) | −0.141 (−0.69) | −0.166 (−0.82) | −0.16 (−0.79) | −0.178 (−0.88) | −0.145 (−0.71) | −0.164 (−0.80) |
| Age in years | 0.00196 (−0.54) | 0.000896 (−0.25) | | | | |
| Local chapter of a national organization (0,1) | −0.192 (−0.88) | −0.191 (−0.87) | −0.164 (−0.77) | −0.177 (−0.83) | −0.178 (−0.84) | −0.189 (−0.88) |
| Members involved in governance (0,1) | 0.498[d] (−2.48) | 0.497[d] (−2.48) | 0.510[e] (−2.61) | 0.497[d] (−2.55) | 0.495[d] (−2.48) | 0.485[d] (−2.43) |
| Members interact but are not involved in governance (0,1) | −0.0495 (−0.15) | −0.114 (−0.35) | −0.0486 (−0.15) | −0.116 (−0.36) | −0.0484 (−0.15) | −0.114 (−0.35) |
| Founded in the 1960s | | | 0.444 (−1.29) | 0.453 (−1.32) | | |
| Founded in 1990–2002 | | | | | −0.14 (−0.76) | −0.124 (−0.67) |
| Constant | −1.700[a] (−6.51) | −1.716[a] (−6.57) | −1.674[a] (−6.49) | −1.708[a] (−6.63) | −1.605[a] (−5.92) | −1.646[a] (−6.07) |
| Observations | 833 | 833 | 833 | 833 | 833 | 833 |
| Pseudo r-squared | 0.1591 | 0.1614 | 0.1602 | 0.1627 | 0.1594 | 0.1618 |

[a]Statistically significant at 1%.
[b]Parentheses denote t statistics.
[c]Responses were assigned a value of 0 if they responded no and a value of 1 if they responded yes.
[d]Statistically significant at 10%.
[e]Statistically significant at 5%.

TABLE 2.3.

Logistic Regression of Engagement in Advocacy on Independent Variables and Odds Ratios: Washington, DC, Survey

| | Model 1 | Model 2 | Model 3 | Model 4 | Model 5 | Model 6 |
|---|---|---|---|---|---|---|
| Annual budget of $1 million or more | 1.786[a] (−14.97)[b] | 1.807[a] (−15.09) | 1.852[a] (−16.13) | 1.874[a] (−16.20) | 1.841[a] (−16.25) | 1.867[a] (−16.39) |
| Annual budget of $100,000–$999,999 | 0.311[a] (−3.82) | 0.320[a] (−3.94) | 0.323[a] (−3.99) | 0.332[a] (−4.10) | 0.314[a] (−3.88) | 0.325[a] (−4.02) |
| Total human resources (square root) | 0.0220[a] (−5.50) | | 0.0223[a] (−5.55) | | 0.0220[a] (−5.45) | |
| Total regular human resources (square root) | | 0.0276[a] (−4.14) | | 0.0277[a] (−4.15) | | 0.0271[a] (−4.01) |
| Ratio of paid staff to volunteers | −0.0259[a] (−3.46) | −0.0316[a] (−4.24) | −0.0268[a] (−3.57) | −0.0325[a] (−4.34) | −0.0271[a] (−3.60) | −0.0327[a] (−4.36) |
| Percentage of budget from government funding | 0.699[a] (−5.86) | 0.708[a] (−5.93) | 0.683[a] (−5.73) | 0.694[a] (−5.81) | 0.678[a] (−5.67) | 0.688[a] (−5.76) |
| Health and welfare (0,1)[c] | −0.469[a] (−4.81) | −0.411[a] (−4.28) | −0.469[a] (−4.81) | −0.410[a] (−4.26) | −0.439[a] (−4.38) | −0.385[a] (−3.89) |
| Education (0,1) | −0.00811 (−0.10) | 0.000922 (−.01) | −0.00731 (−0.09) | 0.00337 (−.04) | 0.00998 (−.12) | 0.0177 (−.21) |
| Professional (0,1) | −0.366[b] (−2.37) | −0.336[b] (−2.20) | −0.355[b] (−2.30) | −0.324[b] (−2.13) | −0.335[b] (−2.18) | −0.310[b] (−2.03) |
| Mission of educating the public (0,1) | 1.743[a] (−22.84) | 1.724[a] (−22.74) | 1.740[a] (−22.81) | 1.720[a] (−22.71) | 1.747[a] (−22.84) | 1.726[a] (−22.72) |
| 501(c)(3) charity (0,1) | −0.0417 (−0.31) | −0.0433 (−0.33) | −0.0839 (−0.64) | −0.0835 (−0.64) | −0.0811 (−0.62) | −0.0828 (−0.63) |
| Age in years | 0.00336 −1.32 | 0.00358 −1.41 | | | | |
| Local chapter of a national organization (0,1) | 0.194 (−1.90) | 0.195 (−1.91) | 0.202[b] (−1.98) | 0.204[d] (−2.00) | 0.203[d] (−1.99) | 0.204[d] (−2.01) |
| Members involved in governance (0,1) | 0.462[a] (−5.25) | 0.498[a] (−5.70) | 0.493[a] (−5.74) | 0.531[a] (−6.23) | 0.501[a] (−5.80) | 0.539[a] (−6.27) |
| Members interact but are not involved in governance (0,1) | −0.354[a] (−3.38) | −0.298[e] (−2.87) | −0.353[a] (−3.37) | −0.294[e] (−2.84) | −0.350[a] (−3.35) | −0.293[e] (−2.83) |
| Founded in the 1960s | | | −0.145 (−0.85) | −0.0998 (−0.59) | | |
| Founded in 1990–2002 | | | | | 0.0816 (−1.12) | 0.0706 (−.97) |
| Constant | −1.107[a] (−7.17) | −1.095[a] (−7.11) | −1.024[a] (−6.98) | −1.012[a] (−6.93) | −1.071[a] (−7.21) | −1.049[a] (−7.09) |
| Observations | 4,949 | 4,949 | 4,949 | 4,949 | 4,949 | 4,949 |
| Pseudo r-squared | 0.1902 | 0.1881 | 0.1901 | 0.1878 | 0.1902 | 0.1879 |

[a]Statistically significant at 1%.
[b]Parentheses denote $t$ statistics.
[c]Responses were assigned a value of 0 if they responded no and a value of 1 if they responded yes.
[d]Statistically significant at 10%.
[e]Statistically significant at 5%.

hypothesis. Resources, both human and financial, appear to be positively associated with advocacy. Compared to organizations reporting annual budgets of less than $100,000, organizations with budgets of $100,000 to $999,999 were more likely to engage in advocacy by a factor of 0.311. Organizations with an annual budget of $1 million or more were more likely to undertake advocacy strategies by a factor of 1.786. The more human resources an organization reported, measured by staff and staff plus volunteers, the greater the likelihood that the organization does advocacy. Against our hypothesis, the ratio of staff to volunteers shows a negative relationship in two of the models, with organizations with more volunteers per staff member being more likely to participate in advocacy. Interestingly, in DC, an average of 14 volunteers per paid staff of ten was evident, while in Seattle an average of only 3.5 volunteers for every paid staff of ten was reported.

Consistent with the Seattle results, the percentage of government funding shows an increase in the likelihood that an organization will undertake advocacy. Field of the organization is significant in the DC model, with organizations in the health/welfare and professional fields less likely to engage in advocacy.

Organizations that educate the public as part of their mission are more likely to participate in advocacy by a factor of 174. Level of member engagement also appears to be positively associated with advocacy for organizations in which members are involved in governance. Organizations in which members have a moderate level of engagement (i.e., they interact but are not involved in governance), however, are actually less likely to engage in advocacy than organizations with low levels of member participation. Moreover, Models 2–6 appear to suggest that organizations that are local chapters of national organizations are more likely to advocate than organizations that are themselves national organizations or independent local organizations.

Across both data sets, three variables emerge as consistent predictors of whether an organization does advocacy: budget, percentage of government funding, and a mission of educating the public. We also find support for the idea that member engagement promotes advocacy. In addition, we find at least partial support for the resource mobilization hypotheses.

## Conclusions

Advocacy is an important part of what nonprofits do. In this chapter, we have framed the question of the limitations on advocacy as one in which we see what organizational characteristics are associated with a greater propensity to advocate. We answer these questions through empirical analysis based on our new surveys conducted of nonprofits in Seattle and Washington, DC.

The first question in studying advocacy and nonprofits is how to define advocacy. We have argued in this chapter and the volume's introduction for a broad understanding of the term: "the attempt to influence public policy, either directly or indirectly." Underneath this broad rubric, we believe that specific and more limited terms can helpfully be used to delineate specific types of advocacy. Besides unpacking advocacy into component parts, we also argue for a more sophisticated understanding of advocacy as involving choices about venue (e.g., state versus federal), means, and coalition partners.

We find that groups are more likely to advocate when they have more financial resources and government support, confirming earlier research, but also discover new results in that the mission and governance of the group matters. Groups whose mission is educating the public are more likely to advocate. In addition, groups that involve members in governance were also more likely to engage in advocacy. This mix of factors provides additional support for earlier research findings, but also extends the scope to new areas.

Our findings are directly relevant to the understanding of the role of nonprofit organizations in a democratic society. As noted by Bass et al. (2007) and Berry and Arons (2003), nonprofits have often been reluctant to engage in advocacy. Our results suggest that nonprofits can increase their involvement with the policy process through deliberate efforts to make advocacy a central part of the mission of the organization (see also Independent Sector, 2012). Our results may suggest that greater efforts to incorporate the community as members of a nonprofit may promote more advocacy. More member engagement in organizational affairs offers nonprofits a larger potential pool of people for advocacy, and, in some circumstances, members may push the board and staff of a nonprofit to participate in the policy process. By engaging members in organizational governance and advocacy, nonprofits may also promote greater community building and social capital. Skocpol (1999) has lamented the decline of local nonprofits' citizen engagement and their historic role of mobilizing citizens for participation in the policy process. Our results indicate that, while this lack of engagement remains a challenge for nonprofits, it is also possible for nonprofits to reclaim or adopt advocacy and participation as a central goal of their mission and programmatic priorities.

### ACKNOWLEDGMENTS

The authors would like to acknowledge the excellent research assistance of Kate Anderson Simons in the preparation of this chapter and the financial support of the Georgetown Public Policy Institute at Georgetown University and the Nancy Bell Evans Center for Nonprofits and Philanthropy at the Evans School of Public Affairs at the University of Washington.

### REFERENCES

Bass, Gary, David F. Arons, Kay Guinane, and Matthew F. Carter. 2007. *Seen but Not Heard: Strengthening Nonprofit Advocacy*. Washington, DC: Aspen Institute.

Berry, Jeffrey M., with David F. Arons. 2003. *A Voice for Nonprofits*. Washington, DC: Brookings Institution Press.

Chaves, Mark, Laura Stephens, and Joseph Galaskiewicz. 2004. "Does Government Funding Suppress Nonprofits' Political Activity?" *American Sociological Review* 69: 292–316.

Child, Curtis D., and Kirsten A. Grønbjerg. 2007. "Nonprofit Advocacy Organizations: Their Characteristics and Activities." *Social Science Quarterly* 88, no. 1: 259–81.

Foley, Michael W., and Bob Edwards. 2002. "How Do Members Count? Membership, Governance, and Advocacy in the Nonprofit World." In *Exploring Organizations and Advocacy: Governance and Accountability*, edited by Elizabeth J. Reid and Maria D. Montella, 19–32. Washington DC: Urban Institute. http://www.urban.org/UploadedPDF/410532_advocacyII.pdf.

Grønbjerg, Kirsten. 1993. *Understanding Nonprofit Funding: Managing Revenues in Social Services and Community Development Organizations*. San Francisco: Jossey-Bass.

Independent Sector. 2012. *Beyond the Cause: The Art and Science of Advocacy*. Washington, DC: Independent Sector. http://www.independentsector.org/uploads/advocacystudy/IS-BeyondtheCause-Full.pdf.

Kramer, Ralph M. 1987. "Voluntary Agencies and the Personal Social Services." In *The Nonprofit Sector: A Research Handbook*, edited by Walter W. Powell, 240–57. New Haven, CT: Yale University Press.

OMB Watch, Tufts University, and Center for Lobbying in the Public Interest. 2002. "Strengthening Nonprofit Advocacy Project (SNAP): Overview." October 29, http://www.ombwatch.org/files/npadv/FinalSNAP_Overview.ppt.

Pfeffer, Jeffrey, and Gerald R. Salancik. 1978. *The External Control of Organizations: A Resource Dependence Perspective*. New York: Harper and Row.

Prakash, Aseem, and Mary Kay Gugerty, eds. 2010. *Advocacy Organizations and Collective Action*. Cambridge: Cambridge University Press.

Reid, Betsy J. 2006. "Advocacy and the Challenges It Presents for Nonprofits." In *Gov-*

*ernment and Nonprofits: Conflict and Collaboration*, edited by Elizabeth T. Boris and C. Eugene Steuerle, 343–72. Washington, DC: Urban Institute.

Salamon, Lester M. 1987. "Partners in Public Service: The Scope and Theory of Government-Nonprofit Relations." In *The Nonprofit Sector: A Research Handbook*, edited by Walter W. Powell, 99–117. New Haven, CT: Yale University Press.

Salamon, Lester M., and Stephanie Lessans Geller with Susan C. Lorentz. 2008. "Nonprofit America: A Force for Democracy?" Listening Post Project Communique No. 9, Center for Civil Society Studies, Johns Hopkins University, Baltimore. http://ccss.jhu.edu/wp-content/uploads/downloads/2011/09/LP_Communique9_2008.pdf.

Skocpol, Theda. 1999. "Advocates without Members: The Recent Transformation of American Civic Life." In *Civic Engagement in American Democracy*, edited by Theda Skocpol and Morris Fiorina, 461–510. Washington, DC: Brookings Institution.

Smith, Steven Rathgeb, and Kirsten Grønbjerg. 2006. "Scope and Theory of Government-Nonprofit Relations." In *The Non-Profit Sector: A Research Handbook*. 2nd ed., edited by Walter W. Powell and Richard Steinberg, 221–42. New Haven, CT: Yale University Press.

Smith, Steven Rathgeb, and Michael Lipsky. 1993. *Nonprofits for Hire: The Welfare State in the Age of Contracting*. Cambridge, MA: Harvard University Press.

Thompson, James. 1967. *Organizations in Action*. New York: McGraw-Hill.

# CHAPTER THREE

# Shaping the Government–Nonprofit Partnership

## Direct and Indirect Advocacy

ELIZABETH T. BORIS AND MATTHEW MARONICK
WITH MILENA NIKOLOVA

The Great Recession of 2007–10 affected families, communities, businesses, nonprofits, foundations, and governments at all levels. Unemployment increased and tax revenues declined. Philanthropic giving decreased as demands for supportive services increased. Despite the recent economic recovery, federal, state, and local governments today are still in severe fiscal distress, which is likely to continue for several years. State revenues are particularly hard hit, and since most states cannot run deficits, they are slashing spending to balance their budgets. The federal government is also tightening its belt, but it is trying to balance the need to rebuild the economy with the increasing pressure for deeper program cuts to stem the growing federal deficit.

The impact of this fiscal crisis raised the visibility of government contracting policies that impose costly inefficiencies on nonprofits through delayed payments and other policies (Denhardt and Auger, 2008; Michigan Nonprofit Association, 2009; National Council of Nonprofits, 2009). With the slow and uncertain economic recovery, weak philanthropic giving, and the proposed budget cuts in government programs that support many human service organizations, many nonprofits face a bleak future.

The National Survey of Nonprofit-Government Contracting and Grants (Boris et al., 2010) was designed to document the impact of the recession on nonprofits, their experiences with government contracting and grants processes, and the interaction of the two in calendar year 2009. The findings reveal how, in the face of shrinking resources and increasing needs, many human service providers cut back on staff, benefits, and programs. The results also detail problems that nonprofits encounter in their government funding relationships, including late payments, inadequate reimbursements, and complex paperwork requirements that have exacerbated the effects of the recession.

While studies suggest that human service nonprofits have traditionally been reluctant to advocate or lobby (Berry, 2003; Boris, 2012; Jenkins, 2006; Salamon and Geller, 2008), research also shows that they interact with government on a regular basis. Much of the scholarship on nonprofit advocacy focuses on individual organizational advocacy, often asking whether receipt of government money inhibits or promotes advocacy. Findings from this national survey document convincingly that human service nonprofits funded by government provide both direct feedback to government funding agencies and indirectly advocate through coalitions and associations. In this chapter, we explore the types of feedback, one-on-one meetings, formal feedback avenues, and advocacy through coalitions and associations and then focus on the determinants of advocacy through coalitions and associations.

The research questions we address are:

1. What characteristics differentiate human service nonprofits that advocate through coalitions and associations from those that do not?
2. Are some of the problems nonprofits experience with government contracts and grants processes more likely to lead organizations to advocate than others?

In the first part of this chapter, we describe research on coalition advocacy and the findings from the National Survey of Nonprofit-Government and Grants (Boris et al., 2010). We then model the characteristics that predict advocacy through coalitions and associations and discuss the findings.

## Advocacy through Coalitions

Advocacy is defined in overlapping ways and encompasses many types of activities, forms, venues, and goals, aptly described by Robert J. Pekkanen and Steven Rathgeb Smith in the introduction to this volume. Following them we favor a broad definition: "advocacy is the attempt to influence public policy, either directly or indirectly." This definition puts into sharp relief the necessity to look beyond advocacy activities undertaken by nonprofits themselves to the actions taken on their behalf (and usually with their membership dues) by organizations and associations linked to them.

While much of the research on nonprofit advocacy has focused on the individual organization's direct activities, there is growing attention to the role that coalitions and associations play in providing a voice for nonprofits in the policy process (Boris and Krehely, 2002; Boris, 2012; see also Pekkanen and Smith's introduction, and DeVita et al., chap. 4, this volume). Such advocacy is often cost-effective and enables individual organizations to maintain a low profile while permitting them to have their concerns promoted to policymakers by professionals with expertise in government relations and lobbying.

Alexander (2000) stresses that nonprofit coalitions and collaborations provide a number of resources to individual nonprofits, namely "grants, contracts, donated professional services, referred clients, and media attention" (Alexander, 2000, 298). Kramer (2000) and Reitan (1998) conclude that nonprofit coalitions increase the visibility of smaller nonprofits for core funding and may provide exposure and legitimacy to newer organizations as well as increase the efficiency of service provision through various collaborations (Oliver, 1990). Most importantly, nonprofit associations often join with other like-minded groups because large coalitions leverage scarce resources and shield smaller groups from economic vulnerability (Boris and Krehely, 2002). As Smith (2010) argues, the recession has fueled considerable efforts to pursue coalition building because "funding cutbacks often promote nonprofit organizations to join together to influence public policy, sometimes through formal coalitions and associations representing nonprofit interests" (623).

A study of immigrant-serving organizations in Washington, DC (De Leon et al., 2009) emphasizes the effectiveness of coalition building among area nonprofits. Several nonprofit directors mentioned that they gained credibility and saw legislators become more receptive to their minority constituencies through the effective mobilization of coalitions. One nonprofit officer commented, "We get a united voice (through coalitions) . . . become stronger and can more clearly articulate our issues and concerns to the powers that be." Immigrant-serving nonprofits also stress that coalitions provide opportunities to pool resources, forge partnerships, and share innovative programming ideas with other nonprofits. As one director noted, "we can't work in silos. We have to work on a more broad level . . . and you get creative minds working together around a table, and you come up with some really fantastic concepts and ideas."

Guo and Acar (2005) found that larger organizations engage in collaborations more frequently than smaller organizations, and other research suggests that funding patterns may factor into the decision to collaborate. In their study of 1,512 nonprofit organizations in 12 metropolitan regions, Jang and Feiock (2007) found that organizations with a larger share of private donations and membership dues were less likely to engage in collaborations because "private support allows nonprofits to operate autonomously in service delivery and avoid the individual costs of engaging in collaboration."

In earlier research (Boris, 2012), we found that successful coalition building is especially pervasive in the fields of poverty alleviation and civil rights. Poverty has become increasingly visible over the last decade as high-profile leaders like Bono, former President Bill Clinton, and Bill Gates have turned their attention toward the suffering and needs of people in less developed countries. Concerts and online fundraising to help the victims of floods, tsunami, earthquakes, and civil wars have sensitized many Americans to the devastation of poverty on an international scale.

Poverty alleviation gained even more traction with the economic downturn that began in 2007; the demand for basic necessities expanded as average Americans lost their jobs and their homes. Taking advantage of this focus on poverty, numerous coalitions associated with poverty alleviation have increased their visibility and made poverty a political agenda item. Well-known antipoverty coalitions such as the Coalition to End Homelessness, the Coalition on Human Needs, and the Half in Ten Campaign have rallied supporters to communicate with political leaders and have expanded awareness of poverty as a growing national problem.

Many of their efforts have borne fruit in legislative consciousness raising. In January 2008, a "Sense of the Congress" resolution passed that called for a reduction in poverty by half in the coming decade, stating that "policy initiatives addressing poverty have not kept pace with millions of Americans." The National Governors Association allotted funding to support poverty summits. In addition, many states and local governments are now adopting antipoverty goals. Both the Half in Ten Campaign and the Coalition on Human Needs have continued to push the agenda of poverty alleviation with concerted efforts to extend unemployment benefits, raise awareness about the plight of immigrant families, and organize rallies in every state in the union. With this research as a background, we decided to include a measure of coalition advocacy in our survey of human service nonprofits that receive contracts and grants from government agencies.

## National Survey of Nonprofit Contracting and Grants

The survey, described in *Human Service Nonprofits and Government Collaboration* (Boris et al., 2010), was undertaken as part of a project conducted in partnership with the National Council of Nonprofits with a grant from the Bill and Melinda Gates Foundation. We employed a stratified random sampling strategy including 501(c)(3) human service providers in the United States that reported $100,000 or more in expenses to the IRS on Form 990 in 2009 (the latest available data at the time). These organizations directly serve children, families, and seniors with programs such as child care, youth development, senior care, food, shelter, counseling, disaster relief, and more. Nine thousand organizations were surveyed and 3,500 responded, of which 2,153 had government contracts and grants. Responses were weighted to provide national-, state-, and sector-level analyses. The survey was conducted early in 2010, capturing experiences related to 2009, a year of deep recession, state budget crises, and high unemployment.

This is the first study to investigate systematically across the country the scope of local, state, and national government contracting and grants with human service nonprofits, the types of requirements and how they differ, and the experiences that nonprofits encounter when funded by government contracts or grants. It provides both national and state-by-state data on human services organizations that receive government funding through grants and contracts.[1]

## Scope of Government Contracts and Grants

Relationships between governments and human services nonprofits are multifaceted and extensive. Our findings indicate that federal, state, and local governments provided approximately $100 billion in grants and contracts to an estimated 33,000 human services organizations in 2009 (Boris et al., 2010). That translates to about 200,000 grants and contracts with nonprofit human service providers, an average of six per organization, although smaller nonprofits tended to have fewer grants and contracts than larger ones. The complexity of nonprofit relationships with government can be appreciated when we realize that half of these nonprofits had contracts with local, state, and national government agencies.

Government was the largest source of support for three of five of these organizations, while donations were the largest source for 19% of organizations, and fees were the largest source of support for 16%. While government dollars far outweigh other revenue sources and enable nonprofits to serve more people, government support also entails real costs in terms of payments that do not cover the full cost of programs, restrictions on administrative cost recovery, application and reporting burdens, and late payments. One surprising finding is that about half of human service nonprofits reported that at least one of their contracts or grants required them to provide matching funds, and 60% reported having to match 25% or more of government resources, no mean feat given the findings on reduced philanthropic resources reported below.

## Impact of the Recession

The recession had a deep impact on the finances of most human services nonprofits (table 3.1). We found widespread decreases in all revenue sources—government, individuals, foundations, corporations, earned interest, and fees. Nonprofits responded by making cuts to their budgets, including salaries, benefits, staffing, and programs.

In response to decreased revenues, 82% of human service nonprofits cut back in a variety of ways (fig. 3.1). The most common responses were to cut back on internal resources, staff-related expenses, and reserves. Many borrowed funds or sought lines of credit. Employees took the brunt of the cutbacks, with half of nonprofits freezing or cutting salaries and 38% cutting staff. Only about a fifth of organizations reduced programs, and somewhat fewer organizations (17%) reduced the number of people served.

Even after deep cutbacks, about 40% of nonprofits ended 2009 with a deficit, and 39% drew down reserves. While some of the reported deficits are likely because of late payments from government contracts, these nonprofits

TABLE 3.1.
Revenue Changes Reported by Human Service Nonprofits with Government Contracts and Grants in 2009

| Source of Revenue | Decrease (%) | Remain the Same (%) | Increase (%) |
|---|---|---|---|
| Investment income | 72 | 18 | 10 |
| Corporate donations | 59 | 28 | 13 |
| State government agencies | 56 | 30 | 14 |
| Federated giving (e.g., United Way) | 53 | 38 | 9 |
| Private foundations | 53 | 31 | 17 |
| Individual donations | 50 | 29 | 21 |
| Local government agencies | 49 | 40 | 11 |
| Fees from self-paying participants | 39 | 40 | 20 |
| Fees from government as third-party payer (e.g., Medicaid) | 34 | 47 | 19 |
| Federal government agencies | 31 | 39 | 30 |
| Other | 52 | 24 | 24 |

Source: Urban Institute, National Survey of Nonprofit-Government Contracting and Grants, 2010

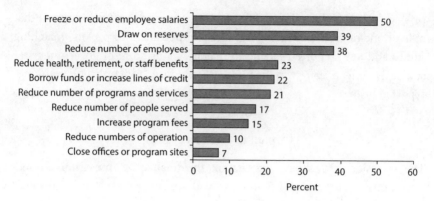

*Figure 3.1.* Cutbacks by human service nonprofits in 2009. Source: Urban Institute, National Survey of Nonprofit-Government Contracting and Grants, 2010

are operating close to the edge of fiscal sustainability, raising questions about whether nonprofits will be able to secure bridge loans to tide them over and, if they do, how they will pay the interest. Many are barely hanging on and will have a difficult time surviving if the economy does not gather steam.

## Problems with Government Contracts and Grants

Nonprofits that receive funding from government agencies must navigate many types of grants and contracts and a variety of requirements. Governments require different reporting formats, outcome measures, and financial accounting, which add up to costly and inefficient burdens for both partners. There is little standardization across government agencies. When asked about their experience with government contracts and grants, five major problems stand out (fig. 3.2). Two thirds of organizations reported that government payments do not cover the full cost of contracted services; three quarters mentioned the complexity of and time required for reporting on contracts and grants as well as for the application process; over half reported that government changes to contracts and grants created problems, and a similar number reported that late payments—beyond contract specifications—created difficulties for them.

We found that nonprofits reporting problems with government contracts or grants were significantly more likely than those who did not report such problems to make cutbacks in staff and programs described above (fig. 3.3). In other words, the contracting process itself added to and exacerbated the

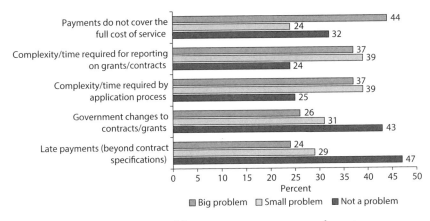

*Figure 3.2.* Key problems reported for government contracts and grants.
Source: Urban Institute, National Survey of Nonprofit-Government Contracting and Grants, 2010

impact of the recession for many nonprofits. For example, 58% of those reporting that government contracts did not cover the full cost of programs froze or reduced salaries, compared to 38% that did not report that problem. They were also more likely to reduce number of employees.

Other types of cutbacks were also significantly related to problems experienced by nonprofits. For example, 45% of those that reported government made changes to their contracts cut staff, compared to 31% that did not experience that problem, and 32% of nonprofits that had problems with late government payments borrowed money, compared to 12% that did not.

The survey results reveal a contracting and grants system that is fragmented, complex, and entails high costs to nonprofits. It is a system that has real and often negative consequences for the ability of nonprofits to serve those in need, especially in a time of severely constricted resources. The logical question is, how do nonprofits try to address these problems?

## Nonprofit Feedback and Advocacy on Contracting Issues

When asked if they provided feedback to government agencies on contracting and grants issues through meetings, formal mechanisms, or advocacy through coalitions or associations, 62% of nonprofits replied that they did. The largest organizations were more likely (68%) than the smallest ones (56%) to provide feedback and were much more likely to engage in indirect advocacy (table 3.2). Multipurpose human service organizations and those providing

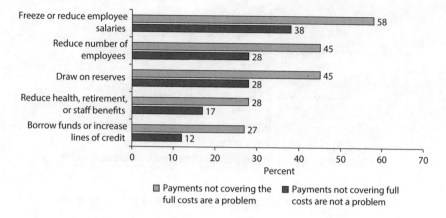

*Figure 3.3.* Cutbacks by human service nonprofits in 2009 by payments not covering full cost of contracted services. Source: Urban Institute, National Survey of Nonprofit-Government Contracting and Grants, 2010

employment services were more likely to provide feedback than other types of human service organizations. There were also variations among nonprofits that operated in different states; for example, organizations in Maine were much more likely to provide feedback (85%) than nonprofits in Connecticut (40%). These differences are likely related to the political economy and the formal and informal relationships forged between nonprofits and state and local governments. This is a fertile area for additional research.[2]

Of the nonprofits that provided feedback, three quarters provided it in direct meetings with funding agencies; 42% did so through official government feedback mechanisms and 55% relied on indirect advocacy through affiliated organizations or coalitions. Regardless of the problems encountered, nonprofits were more likely to discuss issues directly with the funding agency than through official channels or indirectly through advocacy. There is little difference by size among nonprofits that used official feedback mechanisms, suggesting that perhaps such mechanisms are not widely available, accessible, or perceived to be effective means for resolving problems. Size, however, is a clear determinant for indirect advocacy. Larger nonprofits (with more than $1 million in expenses) were much more likely than smaller organizations to engage in advocacy through an association or coalition.

Meeting with the funding agencies appears to be the most common way to articulate problems and seek solutions. One explanation might be that there are established relationships that must be nurtured, and that nonprofits pre-

TABLE 3.2.
Percentage of Human Service Nonprofits That Provide Feedback to Government and
Advocate in Coalitions or Associations, by Expenditure Size

|  | Total (%) | $100,000 to $249,999 (%) | $250,000 to $999,999 (%) | $1 Million or More (%) |
|---|---|---|---|---|
| Provide feedback to government (N = 31,302) | 62 | 56 | 59 | 68 |
| Method of providing feedback (N = 19,384) |  |  |  |  |
| During meetings with funding agencies | 76 | 70 | 74 | 79 |
| Through official government feedback mechanisms | 42 | 41 | 41 | 43 |
| Through indirect advocacy (affiliated organizations or coalitions) | 55 | 42 | 47 | 66 |

Source: Urban Institute, National Survey of Nonprofit-Government Contracting and Grants, 2010

fer to work within the system as the most direct way to solve problems, an indication of institutionalism that theorists often reference. This finding might be one explanation for the low level of advocacy that is typically reported in studies. Most observers note that nonprofits are often in contact with government officials, but they do not view those interactions as falling under the rubric of advocacy.

Our data suggest that much of the interaction of human service organizations and government agencies is likely to involve specific problem solving. Yet the finding that over half do engage in indirect advocacy—a full two thirds of the largest nonprofits—is also telling. The problems with government contracting are systemic, severe, and not amenable to one-off solutions. There is power and cover for individual organizations that belong to coalitions or associations that advocate for change when individual efforts do not achieve results; it is also cost effective. Although one could view the recession as a crisis that might encourage additional advocacy (see Strolovich, chap. 6, this volume), these problems are ongoing, complex, and not amenable to sound bites and slogans.

That 55% of nonprofits (10,562 of the 19,360) reported giving feedback to government in 2009 through coalitions and affiliated organizations advocating on their behalf could be explained by resource dependency theory, which predicts collaboration and alliances in the face of threatening external environment and funding uncertainty (Foster and Meinhard, 2002; Reisch and

Sommerfeld, 2003). A follow-up study after the current economic recession could be useful in exploring resource dependency implications over time.

Organizations with five or more government contracts or grants are much more likely to engage in direct advocacy (63%) than those with only one (42%). (See table 3.3.) While the number of contracts may be viewed as an indirect measure of organizational size, this finding suggests that even multiple formal interactions with government agencies do not curtail indirect advocacy activities.

Nonprofit human service organizations reporting that it was a small or big problem that government payments did not cover the full cost of contracted services were more likely to engage in indirect advocacy than those for whom it was not a problem (see table 3.4). While these results tended to support our hypotheses, we searched for firmer ground.

## Determinants of Indirect Advocacy

To analyze the determinants of indirect advocacy through coalitions and associations, we created a logistic regression model using explanatory variables that are both practically and theoretically important (Chaves et al., 2004; Child and Grønbjerg, 2007; Schmid et al., 2008; see also Pekkanen and Smith, chap. 2, and De Vita et al., chap. 4, this volume). Among the controls are *size*, measured by expenditures, which may be related to institutionalization (Schmid et al., 2008) and capacity. The *number of government contracts* may also be related to size, but we hypothesize that, controlling for size, the larger the number of contracts and grants, the more of a stake the organization has in promoting better government practices.

*Government funding* is identified in the literature as theoretically important in modeling advocacy (Chaves et al., 2004; Child and Grønbjerg, 2007; Schmid et al., 2008), although some researchers find a positive relationship

TABLE 3.3.
Percent of Human Service Organizations That Engage in Indirect Advocacy,
by the Number of Government Contracts and Grants

| Number of Contracts and Grants | Number | Percent |
| --- | --- | --- |
| One government contract/grant | 1,562 | 42 |
| Two to four government contracts and grants | 4,576 | 53 |
| Five or more government contracts and grants | 4,425 | 63 |

Source: Urban Institute, National Survey of Nonprofit-Government Contracting and Grants, 2010

TABLE 3.4.
Percent of Human Service Organizations That Engage in
Indirect Advocacy, by the Extent of Problems with Payments
Not Covering the Full Cost of Contracted Services

| Extent of Problem | Number | Percent |
|---|---|---|
| Not a problem | 1,999 | 46 |
| Small problem | 2,178 | 57 |
| Big problem | 4,821 | 64 |

Source: Urban Institute, National Survey of Nonprofit-Government
Contracting and Grants, 2010

and others no relationship. We hypothesize that a *higher proportion of government revenues* will increase the propensity of human service nonprofits to advocate.

*Indicators for field of activity* are included to reflect the hypothesis that there may be different cultural norms in different fields. While all nonprofits in this sample are human service organizations, we further distinguish them as follows: multipurpose human services, housing, and shelter; crime and legal related; community and economic development; and youth development. We created an "other" category that includes employment, food, agriculture, nutrition, public safety, and disaster relief.

We also include *regional indicator variables* (i.e., Northeast, Midwest, and West, with the South being the reference group) to account for regional variation in advocacy activities because state-by-state data indicate significant differences. We hypothesize that different political and economic considerations might be detectible regionally.

Finally, we introduce two indicator variables related to specific problems with government contracting and grants: *insufficient payments* and *complexity of and time required to report on contracts and grants*, expecting that both would be associated with advocacy activities because both were highly problematic for nonprofits in the survey.

## Findings

The logistic regression results are shown in table 3.5. We find that, controlling for other variables, organizational size is a key determinant of coalition advocacy activities, echoing the results of other studies. Large organizations (i.e., those with annual expenditures of more than $1 million) are significantly more likely than small organizations (i.e., those with annual expenditures between $100,000 and $249,000) to engage in indirect advocacy, possibly because the larger organizations have more resources and capacity. Both a larger number of government contracts and grants and higher proportions of government funding only marginally increase the propensity of organizations to engage in indirect advocacy, but in the hypothesized direction. Results by field were not robust, but crime- and legal-related groups were less likely to advocate than the groups in the "other" category. Regional variation was only a marginally significant determinant of indirect advocacy, with groups in the Northeast more likely to advocate than those in the South.

Turning to the indicator variables for problems with contracting, insufficient government payments were not associated with statistically significant differences in advocacy, but nonprofits that considered government reporting requirements to be a problem were significantly more likely to engage in indirect advocacy than those that did not consider such requirements to be a problem.

## Discussion

As expected, the size of organizations is a strong determinant of indirect advocacy. Organizations with greater resources have more capacity to engage in collective advocacy activities. The finding that organizations with greater numbers of government grants and contracts are marginally more likely to engage in indirect advocacy than others suggests that heavy involvement with government agencies does not generally squelch collaborative advocacy activities. This is also true for organizations that receive larger proportions of government funds than others. Receipt of government funding does not appear to generally silence or dampen collaborative advocacy activities, even among organizations that are largely dependent on government resources to deliver their services, but the marginal significance of the finding means that further analysis is required. While fields of activity and regional variation also have only modest indications of differential impact, the results suggest that we should look more closely at particular fields of activity and regional variation in future analyses, especially since Robert J. Pekkanen and Steven Rathgeb Smith (chap. 2, this volume) also find some interesting regional variations between Seattle and Washington, DC.

These results add weight to arguments that government funding does not stifle the voices of nonprofits (Pekkanen and Smith, chap. 2, and DeVita et al.,

TABLE 3.5.
Logistic Regression of the Determinants of Indirect Advocacy

| Variable | Indirect Advocacy |
|---|---|
| Organizational size categories (Reference group: expense size small, $100,000 to $249,999) | |
| Expense size: medium ($250,000 to $999,999) | 0.135 |
| | [0.221] |
| Expense size: large ($1 million or more) | 0.787[a] |
| | [0.226] |
| Number of contracts and grants (Reference group: one contract and grant) | |
| Nonprofit with two to four contracts and grants | 0.393[c] |
| | [0.219] |
| Nonprofit with five or more contracts and grants | 0.411[c] |
| | [0.234] |
| Government funding (percentage) | 0.004[c] |
| | [0.002] |
| Insufficient payments (1 = yes) | 0.285 |
| | [0.179] |
| Reporting complexity and time (1 = yes) | 0.635[a] |
| | [0.193] |
| Field of activity (Reference group: Other) | |
| Human service: multipurpose | −0.259 |
| | [0.279] |
| Housing and shelter | −0.107 |
| | [0.320] |
| Crime and legal related | −0.977[b] |
| | [0.394] |
| Community and economic development | −0.472 |
| | [0.374] |
| Youth development | −0.245 |
| | [0.408] |
| Region (Reference group: South) | |
| Northeast | 0.369[c] |
| | [0.218] |
| Midwest | 0.106 |
| | [0.204] |
| West | −0.040 |
| | [0.209] |
| Constant | −1.194[a] |
| | [0.399] |
| Number of observations | 990 |
| $F$ statistic | 4.79[a] |

Source: Urban Institute, National Survey of Nonprofit-Government Contracting and Grants, 2010
Brackets indicate standard errors.
[a]Where $p < 0.01$.
[b]Where $p < 0.05$.
[c]Where $p < 0.1$.

chap. 4, this volume) and suggest that analyses of nonprofit advocacy look more closely at indirect or collective advocacy through coalitions and associations, as well as at advocacy at the government funding agency level. Research that only considers individual lobbying and advocacy activities is likely to miss a major avenue of advocacy in the nonprofit sector.

That said, this research does not get to the effectiveness of any of the feedback mechanisms, one-on-one discussions, formal feedback mechanisms, or advocacy through coalitions. The findings of the national survey suggest that for almost a third of human service nonprofits the contracting relationship is worse than in prior years, and for almost two thirds it is the same. Conversations with nonprofit leaders and government professionals on the implications of this research suggest that the economic recession and slow recovery may provide a unique opportunity to find solutions to some of the systemic problems in the government–nonprofit contracting and grants processes.[3] Both are trying to do more with less. Both would like to streamline and simplify costly and redundant processes. Both are seeking ways to demonstrate their effectiveness and accountability. This seems like a recipe for mutual problem solving that could lead to better outcomes for communities. There is already a working group in Montgomery County, Maryland, and one in Washington, DC, to seek better ways of partnering, and similar efforts are underway in other states and localities.

Advocacy on behalf of better and more efficient government contracting and against budget cuts for human services does not have the visceral appeal of antipoverty, civil rights, and environmental campaigns. But those efforts do provide lessons for human service organizations about the importance of working together to effect change. Currently the National Council of Nonprofits, state associations, and others are mobilizing nonprofits to become advocates for better partnerships between government and nonprofits that conduct work on their behalf. Some of their recommendations are that governments should:

- adopt standard application and reporting formats in collaboration with nonprofits,
- implement on-time payment processes,
- create feedback mechanisms and procedures for resolving problems, and
- set up nonprofit liaisons at various levels of government.

Another avenue of action is to strengthen collaborative advocacy activities of human service organizations. As nonprofits take on more responsibilities for delivery of government-mandated services, it is clear that they are struggling to have a greater voice in the policies that affect their missions. Human service nonprofits must be able to use electronic media to project their voices in an increasingly crowded policy environment, where a multitude of causes are competing for attention.

Sanson (2008) argues that "the most powerful tools in this new era of politics are cell phones, online videos, blogs and social networking sites such as Facebook." More importantly, the use of Internet technology is beginning a process of leveling the playing field for nonprofits that would otherwise be incapable of reaching a mass audience to promote an advocacy agenda in local, state, or national politics. McNutt (2008) emphasizes this point, stating, "electronic advocacy provides a competitive advantage for advocacy groups that make use of it."

Research by Boris and Krehely (2002) demonstrates how nonprofits increase their access to funding, members, and referrals by tapping into the resources of other, like-minded organizations. The Internet is providing such opportunities. Nonprofits are even harnessing satellite mapping and state-of-the art data gathering to forge partnerships, strengthen collaborations, and avoid the redundancy of services within regions. Propelled by technology provided by groups like the National Center for Charitable Statistics through its Community Platform, nonprofits now have the capacity to examine what resources are present within their region and to create interconnected communities where nonprofits, social services, and community resources work in harmony to produce positive outcomes for various stakeholders.

## Conclusions

There are widespread and serious problems in the government–nonprofit contracting and grants relationship. In the context of an economy still feeling the effects of a deep recession and ongoing concerns about cutting the federal deficit and balancing state budgets, the pressure on nonprofits will only increase as government resources decline. Nonprofits must ramp up their engagement with government, and they must effectively use a wider variety of tools such as direct negotiations, coalitions, and Internet advocacy. They must communicate effectively and advance alternatives. They can:

- help governments to understand the problems,
- offer collaborative approaches to help craft solutions that lead to more efficient and effective services,

- seek a seat at the table for decisions that affect the services provided by nonprofits,
- provide a voice for constituents who will be affected by government decisions, especially budget and service cuts, and
- strengthen collective advocacy to provide a stronger presence and voice in policy debates.

Nonprofits and government agencies working together can eliminate many of the problems identified in our survey, but it will be slow going to develop agreement on workable solutions. There must be public will to change, and nonprofits will need to band together to build that will. Times are tough and resources will be scarce for the foreseeable future. With good will, nonprofits can contribute to a civil dialogue leading to solutions that benefit all.

### NOTES

1. The report, a brief summary, and state-by-state findings can be downloaded from the Urban Institute website (www.urban.org).
2. The National Council on Nonprofits, a collaborator on this project, is developing information on contracting policies in different states, and we plan to delve more deeply into these issues.
3. The Nonprofit Roundtable of Greater Washington, held on February 2, 2011, at the Urban Institute in Washington, DC.

### REFERENCES

Alexander, Jennifer. 2000. "Adaptive Strategies of Nonprofit Human Service Organizations in an Era of Devolution and New Public Management." *Nonprofit Management and Leadership* 10, no. 3: 287–303.

Berry, Jeffrey M., with David Arons. 2003. *A Voice for Nonprofits*. Washington, DC: Brookings Institution Press.

Boris, Elizabeth T., Erwin de Leon, Katie L. Roeger, and Milena Nikolova. 2010. *Human Service Nonprofits and Government Collaboration*. Washington, DC: Urban Institute Press.

Boris, Elizabeth T., and Jeff Krehely. 2002. "Civic Participation and Advocacy." In *The State of Nonprofit America*, edited by Lester M. Salamon, 299–330. Washington, DC: Brookings Institution Press.

Boris, Elizabeth T., with Matthew Maronick. 2012. "Civic Participation and Advocacy." In *The State of Nonprofit America*, edited by Lester M. Salamon, 394–422. Washington DC: Brookings Institution Press.

Chaves, Mark, Laura Stephens, and Joseph Galaskiewicz. 2004. "Does Government Funding Suppress Nonprofits' Political Activity?" *American Sociological Review* 69, no. 2: 292–316.

Child, Curtis D., and Kirsten A. Grønbjerg. 2007. "Nonprofit Advocacy Organizations: Their Characteristics and Activities." *Social Science Quarterly* 88, no. 1: 259–81.

De Leon, Erwin, Matthew Maronick, Carol J. DeVita, and Elizabeth T. Boris. 2009. *Immigrant Integration and Community-Based Organizations in the Washington, D.C. Metropolitan Area.* Washington, DC: Urban Institute Press.

Denhardt, Kathryn G., and Deborah Auger with Maria P. Aristigueta and Lauren Miltenberger. 2008. *Forward Together Project: Research Report.* Newark: University of Delaware.

Foster, Mary K., and Agnes G. Meinhard. 2002. "A Regression Model Explaining Predisposition to Collaborate." *Nonprofit and Voluntary Sector Quarterly* 31, no. 4: 549–64.

Guo, Chao, and Muhittin Acar. 2005. "Understanding Collaborations among Nonprofit Organizations: Combining Resource Dependency, Institutional and Network Perspectives." *Nonprofit and Voluntary Sector Quarterly* 34, no. 3: 340–61.

Jang, Hee Soun, and Richard C. Feiock. 2006. "Public versus Private Funding for Nonprofit Organizations: Implications for Collaboration." *Public Performance and Management Review* 31, no. 2: 174–90.

Jenkins, Craig. 2006. "Nonprofit Organizations and Political Advocacy." In *The Nonprofit Sector: A Research Handbook.* 2nd ed., edited by Walter W. Powell, 307–32. New Haven, CT: Yale University Press.

Kramer, Ralph M. 2000. "A Third Sector in the New Millennium?" *Voluntas: International Journal of Voluntary and Nonprofit Organizations* 11, no. 1: 1–23.

McNutt, John. 2008. "Advocacy Organizations and the Organizational Digital Divide." *Currents* 7, no. 2: 1–16.

Michigan Nonprofit Association. 2009. *Trends in Government Funding.* Lansing: Michigan Nonprofit Association.

National Council of Nonprofits. 2009. *Special Report Number 8.* Washington, DC: National Council of Nonprofits.

Oliver, Christine. 1990. "Determinants of Interorganizational Relationships: Integration and Future Directions." *Academy of Management Review* 15, no. 2: 241–65.

Reisch, Michael, and David Sommerfeld. 2003. "Interorganizational Relationships among Nonprofits in the Aftermath of Welfare Reform." *Social Work* 48, no. 3: 307–18.

Reitan, Therese C. 1998. "Theories of Interorganizational Relations in the Human Services." *Social Service Review* 72, no. 3: 285–309.

Salamon, Lester M., and Stephanie Lessans Geller with Susan C. Lorentz. 2008. "Nonprofit America: A Force for Democracy?" Listening Post Project Communique No. 9, Center for Civil Society Studies, Johns Hopkins University, Baltimore. http://ccss.jhu.edu/wp-content/uploads/downloads/2011/09/LP_Communique9_2008.pdf.

Sanson, Angela. 2008. "Facebook and Youth Mobilization in the 2008 Presidential Election." *Gnovis* 8, no. 8.3: 162–74, http://gnovisjournal.org/files/Facebook-Youth-Mobilization.pdf.

Schmid, Hillel, Michal Bar, and Ronit Nirel. 2008. "Advocacy Activities in Nonprofit Human Service Organizations: Implications for Policy." *Nonprofit and Voluntary Sector Quarterly* 37, no. 4: 581–602.

Smith, Steven Rathgeb. 2010. "Nonprofit Organizations and Government: Implications for Policy and Practice." *Journal of Policy Analysis and Management* 29, no. 3: 621–25.

# CHAPTER FOUR

# Nonprofit Advocacy in the Nation's Capital

CAROL J. DEVITA, MILENA NIKOLOVA, AND KATIE L. ROEGER

Civil society advocacy lies at the heart of democratic government. In the United States, the ability to assemble and petition the government is explicitly stated as a constitutional right, and although these rights are afforded to individuals, nonprofit organizations typically play a key role in giving "voice" to the views and concerns of their constituents in the public arena.

Nonprofits have historically played a major role in US social movements and political reforms. They have championed such causes as civil rights, women's rights, labor reforms, the environment, and children and family issues. Many organizations that play prominent roles in these national debates are household names: National Association for the Advancement of Colored People, National Organization for Women, American Federation of Labor and Congress of Industrial Organizations, Sierra Club, Children's Defense Fund, AARP, Christian Coalition, and National Rifle Association, to name a few.

While most research on nonprofit advocacy focuses on large, national organizations (Andrews and Edwards, 2004; Child and Grønbjerg, 2007; Foley and Edwards, 2002), this approach skews our understanding of how most nonprofits engage in advocacy and overlooks what locally oriented nonprofits do to foster civic engagement. Importantly, civic participation and nonprofit advocacy are not limited to large, national organizations; small and less well-known nonprofits, particularly at the local level, promote civic engagement and partake in public interest advocacy.

Despite their important role, many nonprofits are unaware that they engage in advocacy because they perceive it as only lobbying and electoral campaigns (Berry and Arons, 2003). Advocacy work actually runs along a vast continuum of activities, ranging from the identification of issues and agenda setting to educating the public about issues, lobbying, and even partisan electoral activities (Boris and Krehely, 2002; Reid, 2006). The misconception that advocacy entails only direct actions hampers our ability to measure and understand the breadth and depth of nonprofit advocacy activities (see Pekkanen and Smith, introduction, and Boris and Maronick, chap. 3, this volume).

Moreover, although most advocacy work is unregulated, the existing regulations, which are often embedded in tax codes, are complex and fragmented. This maze of regulatory requirements discourages some nonprofits from taking an active role in any form of civic discourse for fear of violating the regulations and perhaps losing their "charitable" 501(c)(3) status and thereby the ability to receive tax-deductible contributions. As a result, the regulatory framework is another factor affecting nonprofit involvement in advocacy.

To people living outside the Beltway, Washington, DC, is a mecca for policy advocates and lobbyists. Jeffrey M. Berry and Kent E. Portney point out in chapter 1 that nonprofit advocacy is essentially about the "politics of place," and the nonprofit sector in the Washington, DC, metropolitan area encompasses both city or local politics and national politics. But not all nonprofits in the nation's capital work on national issues, and there is scant research that compares the advocacy activities of national nonprofits with their locally oriented counterparts. Using 2010 survey data from a representative sample of nonprofit organizations in the DC region, this study begins to fill this gap. It investigates the number of nonprofits in the region that try to influence policy making and the levels of government that they try to influence. It also examines whether nonprofits conduct their advocacy work alone or in coalitions, and their self-perceptions of effectiveness. The analysis explores how advocacy varies by organizational type and size and compares national groups with those that are more locally and regionally focused.

In this chapter, we examine five research questions:

1. How many and what percentage of nonprofits in the DC region engage in advocacy?
2. What level of government (federal, state, or local) do nonprofits try to influence?
3. To what extent is nonprofit advocacy conducted by the organization's own efforts or through coalitions and hired lobbyists?
4. To what extent is advocacy work proactive (to enact new policies) or reactive (to stop or modify policies)?
5. How much influence do nonprofit leaders believe they have in shaping public policy?

## Survey Design and Methods

In collaboration with the University of Washington in Seattle, the Urban Institute's Center on Nonprofits and Philanthropy designed a survey to study the types of nonprofits that engage in advocacy in the DC metropolitan area, how they conduct their activities, and the venues or levels of government they target. The survey used a stratified random sample of 3,300 nonprofit organizations in the Washington, DC, metropolitan area so that organizations of different sizes, types, and geographic locations within the metropolitan area were represented.[1] Both 501(c)(3) and 501(c)(4) organizations were included in the sample, although 501(c)(4) organizations were oversampled to ensure adequate representation in the final results. Hospitals and higher education organizations were excluded because these organizations tend to be much larger and more complex structures than other types of nonprofits. Data from the Urban Institute's National Center for Charitable Statistics (NCCS) were the source of the sampling frame, which consisted of 10,581 organizations in the DC metropolitan area that filed a Form 990 with the Internal Revenue Service in years 2007 or 2008, the most current data available at the time of the study.[2]

To ensure that the survey results are generalizable to all nonprofits in the DC region and to correct for oversampling of 501(c)(4) organizations, we assigned statistical weights to the data. The weights match the responding organization's characteristics such as size, type, region, and subsection code—i.e., 501(c)(3) and 501(c)(4)—to the sampling frame. In addition to producing representative results, the weights also mitigate potential nonresponse bias. Further information about the survey is in this chapter's appendix.

## Analysis Strategy

Descriptive statistics show the characteristics of nonprofit organizations in the DC region that engage in advocacy and the types of activities they use to influence public policy. Three logistic regression models examine the determinants of nonprofit advocacy, namely:

- the levels of government that nonprofits try to influence (i.e., federal, state, or local),
- whether organizations use proactive or reactive strategies to influence policy, and
- the organization's perception of how much influence it has on the policy-making process.

Previous research and theoretical frameworks guided the selection of the variables used in these models. The organization's legal status, for example, is an important control variable because many 501(c)(3) organizations are reluctant to engage in advocacy for fear of losing their public charity status and the ability to receive tax-deductible contributions (Berry and Arons, 2003). Berry and Arons (2003) also show that location is important. Nonprofits in the nation's capital may be more likely than those in other locations to have a fuller understanding of the types of advocacy activities permitted under current tax codes and may have more access to national policymakers. Furthermore, an organization's age, size,[3] and field of nonprofit activity[4] are good predictors of engaging in advocacy because these factors influence the structure and capacity of a nonprofit organization (Berry and Arons, 2003; Chaves et al., 2004; Child and Grønbjerg, 2007; Schmid et al., 2008).

Because of the prevalence of national and international nonprofits in the DC region, it is important to distinguish them from locally and regionally oriented nonprofits. Survey respondents were asked to self-identify as a national, international, regional, or local group. It is expected that national and international organizations will be more active in the policy-making arena.

Finally, the regression models examine the importance of hiring a professional lobbyist for engaging in advocacy work. Enlisting the services of a lobbyist will not only increase the likelihood that a nonprofit will engage in advocacy, but also the organization's perception of influence and effectiveness.

## Findings
### The DC Region's Nonprofit Sector Is Both Similar to and Unique from Other Communities

In many ways, the nonprofit sector in the DC region is similar to that in other communities and generally reflects the national pattern of nonprofit activity.[5] The largest category of nonprofits in the region is human services, which accounts for one in four nonprofits (fig. 4.1). Education groups are the second-largest component of the sector (19%), while nonprofit health and arts organizations each account for one in ten organizations. These four major categories combined represent about two thirds of the region's nonprofit sector. The remaining third is a composite of organizations that engage in a range of nonprofit activities (such as environmental, animal-related, disaster prevention, community service clubs, and veterans' organizations) that are found in every community but cannot be classified into a single category for analytic purposes.

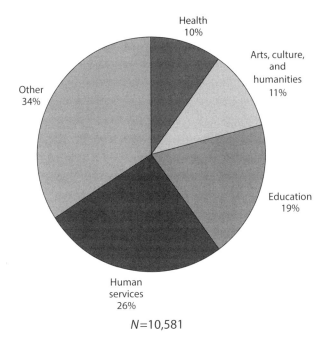

*Figure 4.1.* Responding organizations by field of activity. Source: Urban Institute, Survey of Nonprofit-Government Relations in the Greater Washington, DC, Metropolitan Area, 2010

As in other geographic areas, the vast majority of nonprofits in the DC area are classified as 501(c)(3) (or charitable) organizations. Specifically, 92% of the DC region's nonprofits are 501(c)(3) organizations; fewer than one in ten are 501(c)(4) groups. A chief distinction between these two categories is that 501(c)(3) organizations are subject to limits (and, in some instances, prohibitions) on engaging in political activities. In contrast, 501(c)(4) organizations may lobby and participate in political campaigns so long as these activities are not the organization's primary purpose. Moreover, unlike those made to 501(c)(3) organizations, donations made to 501(c)(4) organizations are not tax deductible.

There are a number of characteristics that make DC-area nonprofits unique, however. First, the region's nonprofit sector crosses several state lines, including Maryland, Virginia, and the District of Columbia.[6] While two in five nonprofits are located in the District of Columbia, one in three is located in Northern Virginia, and one in four is in the close-by Maryland suburbs (table 4.1).

TABLE 4.1.
Characteristics of Responding Organizations, by Region and
Self-Identified Geographic Scope

| Characteristic | Number | Percent |
|---|---|---|
| Region | | |
| District of Columbia | 4,291 | 41 |
| Maryland surrounding countires | 2,650 | 25 |
| Northern Virginia surrounding counties | 3,640 | 34 |
| Total | 10,581 | 100 |
| Self-identification | | |
| National or international nonprofit | 4,609 | 44 |
| Local, state, or regional nonprofit | 5,879 | 56 |
| Total | 10,488 | 100 |

Source: Urban Institute, Survey of Nonprofit-Government Relations in the Greater Washington, DC, Metropolitan Area, 2010
  Ninety-two respondents did not provide information on the geographic area they serve.

Also unique is the relatively high percentage (44%) of nonprofits that identify themselves as "national" or "international" organizations. Still, more than half (56%) of the region's nonprofits indicate that their geographic focus is local, state, or regional.

Perhaps because of the large number of nationally focused nonprofits in the DC area, the average size of organizations in the region is somewhat larger than the national average. As figure 4.2 shows, about one in four nonprofits in the DC region has a budget over $1 million, compared with one in six nationally. In contrast, most nonprofits nationwide (47%) have expenditures of less than $100,000, compared with 36% of nonprofits in the DC region.[7]

## How One Measures Advocacy Matters

As Robert J. Pekkanen and Steven Rathgeb Smith indicate in their introduction to this volume, it is difficult to define and measure the concept of advocacy because it covers such a broad range of activities. The simplest and most encompassing definition is that advocacy attempts to influence public policy either directly or indirectly. How one operationalizes the definition of advocacy, however, matters for understanding the extent to which nonprofits engage in this activity. When asked directly if their organization is "involved in public policy or advocacy," nearly half (48%) of DC-area nonprofits an-

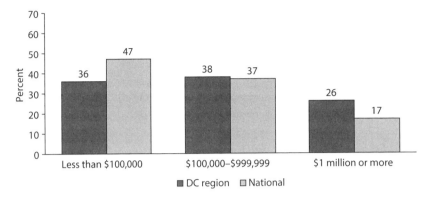

*Figure 4.2.* National and Washington, DC, region nonprofit organizations by expense size. Sources: Urban Institute, Survey of Nonprofit-Government Relations in the Greater Washington, DC, Metropolitan Area, 2010; Urban Institute, National Center for Charitable Statistics, Core Files (Public Charities and 501(c)(4) Organizations)

swered affirmatively. As we include other aspects of advocacy into the definition, such as if the organization is affiliated with a political action committee (PAC) or if it employs a lobbyist, the percentage of organizations that might be considered active in the policy arena increases.

In this study, we define advocacy as having engaged in *any* of the following actions:

- was "involved in public policy or advocacy,"
- was affiliated with a PAC or was a PAC,
- employed a lobbyist,
- worked alone or in a coalition to enact or stop a policy, or
- has engaged sometimes, often, or very often in one or more of 12 specific activities (e.g., assisted in drafting a bill, provided expertise, contributed public comment, solicited signatures, organized a demonstration, provided media with information, etc.).

By these criteria, 67% of DC-area nonprofits engage in advocacy.[8] Of these nonprofits, only 12% employed a lobbyist and 19% were a PAC or affiliated with a PAC.

Table 4.2 illustrates the extent to which organizations with particular characteristics are likely to engage in advocacy. Advocacy work is most prevalent among education and health nonprofits, for example. More than 70% of these groups meet our criteria for advocacy, whereas just under half (49%) of arts

TABLE 4.2.
Characteristics of Organizations That Engage in Advocacy

| Characteristic | Number | Percent |
|---|---|---|
| Overall | 6,930 | 67 |
| Field of activity | | |
| Arts | 553 | 49 |
| Education | 1,413 | 73 |
| Health | 782 | 71 |
| Human services | 1,764 | 67 |
| Other | 2,418 | 68 |
| Region | | |
| District of Columbia | 2,949 | 71 |
| Maryland surrounding counties | 1,514 | 57 |
| Northern Virginia surrounding countries | 2,467 | 69 |
| Self-identification | | |
| National or international nonprofit | 3,216 | 71 |
| Local, state, or regional nonprofit | 3,676 | 64 |
| IRS subsection code | | |
| 501(c)(3) | 6,336 | 66 |
| 501(c)(4) | 594 | 76 |
| Expenditure size | | |
| Less than $100,000 | 2,061 | 56 |
| $100,000 to $999,999 | 2,713 | 68 |
| $1 million or more | 2,156 | 81 |

Source: Urban Institute, Survey of Nonprofit-Government Relations in the Greater Washington, DC, Metropolitan Area, 2010
  The estimates are based on the number of organizations that provided answers to the questions.

organizations do. Location in the District of Columbia is a strong determinant of engagement in advocacy work. Within the region, just over 70% of all nonprofits in the District of Columbia report some type of advocacy activities, compared with 69% in Northern Virginia and 57% in Maryland. Not surprisingly, a relatively higher proportion (over 70%) of nationally focused nonprofits and 501(c)(4) organizations engage in advocacy, compared with 64% of their locally oriented counterparts.

Finally, consistent with previous research, an important determinant of advocacy is organizational size. Roughly 80% of nonprofits with expenditures of $1 million or more engage in some type of advocacy. In contrast, 56% of small nonprofits and 68% of midsized nonprofits participate in advocacy.

## *Nonprofits Typically Use "Public Education" and Not Direct Action to Advocate*

As previous research suggests, nonprofits generally do not engage in the most overt forms of advocacy such as demonstrations and drafting legislation. Among DC-area nonprofits, the most frequent form of advocacy is attending meetings (table 4.3). In particular, more than 80% indicated that they attend meetings at least sometimes; nearly half (48%) do it often or very often. Although the survey did not ascertain the types of meetings, it is likely that these meetings are with government administrators, as suggested by Elizabeth T. Boris and Matthew Maronick (chap. 3, this volume).

Roughly two thirds of the region's nonprofits contribute public comment on policy issues, form alliances with other groups, provide expertise on issues, and provide the media with information. As expected, these types of activities are more prevalent among large and midsized organizations rather than small organizations, among national rather than local groups, and among DC-based rather than Maryland or Northern Virginia nonprofits. On average, health nonprofits were especially likely to provide expertise, contribute public comment, and form alliances, while arts groups were most likely among all groups to provide media with information.

TABLE 4.3.
Advocacy Activities Nonprofits Undertake When Making Requests or Appeals to the Government

| Activity | Number | Percent |
|---|---|---|
| Attend meetings | 5,651 | 83 |
| Contribute public comment | 4,651 | 70 |
| Form an alliance with other groups | 4,651 | 70 |
| Provide expertise | 4,475 | 67 |
| Provide media with information | 4,132 | 62 |
| Ask members to call or send letters/emails to the government | 3,757 | 56 |
| Seek the involvement of influential local figures | 3,641 | 55 |
| Make statements at press conferences | 2,410 | 37 |
| Solicit signatures | 1,937 | 30 |
| Place opinion ads on television and in newspapers or magazines | 1,465 | 22 |
| Assist in drafting bills | 1,331 | 20 |
| Direct actions (demonstration, strike, etc.) | 737 | 11 |

Source: Urban Institute, Survey of Nonprofit-Government Relations in the Greater Washington, DC, Metropolitan Area, 2010
  The estimates are based on the number of organizations that advocate and provided answers to the questions.

About half of the region's nonprofits that advocate encourage their members to write or call government offices and even seek the assistance of influential people to appeal to government on their behalf. Organizations of all sizes are about as likely to partake in these activities, with larger organizations only slightly more likely to do so. Also, 501(c)(4) organizations are most likely to ask members to send communications to government, while arts, culture, and humanities groups are least likely to do so, 75% compared with 48%, respectively.

Activities such as soliciting signatures, placing opinion pieces in the media, helping to draft legislation, or taking direct actions such as holding demonstrations are far less prevalent. Large national organizations, 501(c)(4) nonprofits, health, and DC-based groups are more likely than their counterparts to assist in drafting bills, for example. But small and large groups and groups in all three jurisdictions report a roughly similar frequency of engaging in direct actions.

## Advocacy Work Is Conducted in Coalitions

Advocacy work in the nation's capital is conducted primarily through coalitions. Only 8% of nonprofits that engaged in advocacy did so exclusively on their own. Nearly half (48%) conducted their advocacy both in coalitions and sometimes alone, and about two in five nonprofits (44%) worked only in coalitions.

This pattern is fairly consistent across most dimensions of the sector, although there are a few exceptions (table 4.4). A relatively high percentage of arts organizations (20%) conduct their advocacy work exclusively on their own, while the majority of health organizations work only in coalitions. Similarly, small nonprofits have a propensity to advocate alone (14% do so exclusively), while the majority of large nonprofits conduct advocacy only in coalitions. This finding may suggest that small organizations have difficulty networking with their peers or other organizations in the sector, a topic that deserves further investigation. The majority of national nonprofits and 501(c)(4) organizations tend to work in coalitions and sometimes alone.

## Regression Models

Our regression models tested the determinants of three key aspects of nonprofit advocacy: (1) the level of government being influenced, (2) proactive

TABLE 4.4.
Characteristics of Organizations Advocating Alone and in Coalitions

| Characteristic | Both Alone and in a Coalition (%) | Alone Only (%) | In a Coalition Only (%) | Total (%) |
|---|---|---|---|---|
| Overall | 48 | 8 | 44 | 100 |
| Field of activity | | | | |
| Arts | 35 | 20 | 45 | 100 |
| Education | 47 | 12 | 41 | 100 |
| Health | 44 | 3 | 53 | 100 |
| Human services | 46 | 8 | 46 | 100 |
| Other | 54 | 5 | 41 | 100 |
| Region | | | | |
| District of Columbia | 45 | 9 | 46 | 100 |
| Maryland surrounding counties | 58 | 3 | 39 | 100 |
| Northern Virginia surrounding countries | 45 | 10 | 45 | 100 |
| Self-identification | | | | |
| National or international nonprofit | 58 | 4 | 38 | 100 |
| Local, state, or regional nonprofit | 38 | 12 | 50 | 100 |
| IRS subsection code | | | | |
| 501(c)(3) | 45 | 8 | 47 | 100 |
| 501(c)(4) | 69 | 13 | 18 | 100 |
| Expenditure size | | | | |
| Less than $100,000 | 54 | 14 | 32 | 100 |
| $100,000 to 4999,999 | 47 | 9 | 45 | 100 |
| $1 million or more | 44 | 3 | 52 | 100 |

Source: Urban Institute, Survey of Nonprofit-Government Relations in the Greater Washington, DC, Metropolitan Area, 2010
The estimates are based on the number of organizations that provided answers to the questions.

versus reactive strategies, and (3) perceptions of influence on the policy process. Each model included the following independent variables: geographic location, organizational age and size, field of activity, national or local orientation, and incorporation status. Models 2 and 3 included an additional variable for whether the organization employed a lobbyist. In all regressions, we used the sample weight to ensure that the results are generalizable to the universe of nonprofits in the DC region.

### Model 1: Predictors of Which Level of Government Is Influenced

Nonprofits have a choice of venues in which to conduct their advocacy work. They may try to influence one or multiple levels of government—federal, state, and local. Using a series of survey questions,[9] we constructed a variable to identify which level(s) of government an organization tries to influence. For example, the *influence federal government* variable is coded as one for organizations that indicated they enacted, stopped, or modified policies at the federal level, either alone or in coalitions. The variable is zero if the organizations indicated that they did not enact, stop, or modify policies at that level of government. The same procedures are applied for the creation of the variables *influence state government* and *influence local government*, respectively.

Table 4.5 shows the results of the logistic regression model for the determinants of the level of government being influenced. In this model, organizational size is a powerful predictor of nonprofit advocacy. The larger the nonprofit, the more likely it is to influence government at all levels. Likewise, other studies have found that size predicts nonprofit advocacy (Child and Grønbjerg, 2007; Schmid et al., 2008), which corroborates our findings and enhances the external validity of our study.

As expected, our results also indicate that location matters for advocacy. Compared with nonprofits located in the Maryland and Virginia suburbs, being in the nation's capital increases the likelihood that organizations will attempt to influence federal government policies, but not policies at the state or local levels of government.

Organizational age has a positive effect on the likelihood of influencing levels of government. While Child and Grønbjerg (2007) found that age is not a robust predictor of nonprofit advocacy, our results are plausible, as older organizations are likely to have greater knowledge of the rules and requirements of advocacy work. Older organizations are also more likely to have developed the capacity and the organizational skills to engage in such activities.

The organization's field of activity shows variability as a predictor of advocacy activities by level of government. Relative to organizations in the "other" category (such as environmental, animal, and veterans organizations), for example, education nonprofits are significantly more likely to attempt to influence policy at all three levels, though they are marginally more likely to influence federal government policy. Health organizations are more likely than organizations in the "other" category to influence policy at the federal level, while human services nonprofits are only marginally more likely to influence state governments.

As expected, organizations with a national or international focus are significantly more likely to influence federal government and significantly less likely to influence local governments. Both of these coefficient estimates are

TABLE 4.5.
Logistic Regression of the Determinants of the Level of Government Nonprofit Influence

| Variable | Influence Federal Government | Influence State Government | Influence Local Government |
|---|---|---|---|
| Located in DC | 0.579[b] | -0.264 | 0.171 |
| | [0.227] | [0.224] | [0.225] |
| Age | 0.016[b] | 0.013[c] | 0.014[c] |
| | [0.008] | [0.007] | [0.007] |
| Organizational size | | | |
| Expense size: medium | 0.651[b] | 0.661[b] | 0.578[b] |
| | [0.283] | [0.266] | [0.255] |
| Expense size: large | 1.323[a] | 1.504[a] | 0.880[a] |
| | [0.312] | [0.306] | [0.309] |
| Field of activity | | | |
| Arts, culture, and humanities | -0.219 | -0.309 | -0.022 |
| | [0.443] | [0.430] | [0.397] |
| Education | 0.667[c] | 0.863[a] | 0.682[b] |
| | [0.346] | [0.315] | [0.314] |
| Health | 1.089[a] | 0.449 | -0.040 |
| | [0.359] | [0.360] | [0.399] |
| Human services | 0.174 | 0.509[c] | 0.409 |
| | [0.297] | [0.279] | [0.283] |
| National/international organization | 1.631[a] | -0.152 | -1.146[a] |
| | [0.244] | [0.230] | [0.248] |
| Public charity | -1.1211[a] | 0.929[b] | -0.645 |
| | [0.432] | [0.387] | [0.394] |
| Constant | -2.261[a] | -1.310[a] | -1.115[a] |
| | [0.482] | [0.423] | [0.427] |
| N (using sample weight) | 544 | 540 | 536 |
| Chi-square | 129.793[a] | 53.390[a] | 49.985[a] |

Source: Urban Institute, Survey of Nonprofit-Government Relations in the Greater Washington, DC, Metropolitan Area, 2010
Brackets indicate standard errors.
[a]Where $p < 0.01$.
[b]Where $p < 0.05$.
[c]Where $p < 0.1$.

significant at the 1% significance level. Finally, public charities—i.e., 501(c)(3) organizations—are significantly less likely than their 501(c)(4) counterparts to attempt to influence federal and state governments.

## Model 2: Predictors of Proactive and Reactive Forms of Advocacy

The types of advocacy undertaken by DC-area nonprofits reflect both the strategies perceived to be effective and the potential access that advocates have to decision makers. These strategies are likely to be temporal in nature, changing over time to respond to shifts in policy and political conditions. But these cross-sectional survey data shed light on an important theme raised in chapter 1 of this volume, namely, the conditions by which nonprofits try to maximize their effectiveness in the policy arena.

In this analysis, proactive advocacy comprises attempts to enact a new policy at the federal, state, or local levels. Reactive advocacy is one that aims at stopping or modifying a policy. Since organizations can be both proactive and reactive in how they influence government, we explore the determinants of these two advocacy strategies separately.

As table 4.6 shows, being located in the nation's capital, compared with being in the Maryland or Virginia suburbs, does not affect the likelihood of being involved in enacting or stopping or modifying policies. Hiring a lobbyist, however, has a statistically significant impact on increasing the likelihood of organizations engaging in both proactive and reactive advocacy. Hiring a lobbyist likely increases the organization's advocacy effectiveness by bringing in expert advocacy skills. Furthermore, organizational age predicts the likelihood of proactive but not reactive advocacy actions. But organizational size is again a statistically significant predictor of engaging in both proactive and reactive advocacy, which dovetails with the findings of other studies (Child and Grønbjerg, 2007; Schmid et al., 2008).

As in the previous model, the field of nonprofit activity predicts the likelihood of proactive and reactive advocacy only in certain cases. Compared to organizations in the "other" category, for example, arts nonprofits are significantly less likely to use either type of advocacy strategy. Health organizations, however, are statistically more likely than "other" organizations to be proactive than reactive in their advocacy. Finally, compared with 501(c)(4) organizations, public charities, which are 501(c)(3) organizations, are significantly less likely to engage in proactive advocacy and marginally less likely to be involved with stopping or modifying policies.

## Model 3: Predictors of Perceived Influence

Self-perception of policy influence or effectiveness can encourage (or discourage) the leadership of a nonprofit organization from participating in the policy process. Executive directors and their governing boards may be more willing to allocate a greater share of resources to advocacy and political participation if they perceive or anticipate a favorable outcome for their

TABLE 4.6.
Logistic Regression of the Determinants of Whether Nonprofits
Engage in Proactive or Reactive Advocacy

| Variable | Proactive Advocacy | Reactive Advocacy |
|---|---|---|
| Located in DC | 0.254 | 0.200 |
| | [0.213] | [0.203] |
| Age | 0.014[b] | 0.010 |
| | [0.007] | [0.007] |
| Organizational size | | |
| Expense size: medium | 0.639[a] | 0.523[b] |
| | [0.246] | [0.226] |
| Expense size: large | 1.172[a] | 1.234[a] |
| | [0.291] | [0.278] |
| Field of activity | | |
| Arts, culture, and humanities | −1.077[b] | −0.631[c] |
| | [0.462] | [0.376] |
| Education | 0.628[b] | 0.728[b] |
| | [0.309] | [0.291] |
| Health | 0.732[b] | 0.411 |
| | [0.348] | [0.340] |
| Human services | 0.495[c] | 0.442[c] |
| | [0.264] | [0.252] |
| National/international organization | 0.217 | −0.134 |
| | [0.226] | [0.216] |
| Public charity | −0.903[b] | 0.714[c] |
| | [0.391] | [0.378] |
| Employed a lobbyist | 2.106[a] | 1.939[a] |
| | [0.480] | [0.490] |
| Constant | −1.201[a] | −0.711[c] |
| | [0.422] | [0.406] |
| *N* (using sample weight) | 541 | 542 |
| Chi-square | 107.572[a] | 85.915[a] |

Source: Urban Institute, Survey of Nonprofit-Government Relations in the
Greater Washington, DC, Metropolitan Area, 2010
Brackets indicate standard errors.
[a]Where $p < 0.01$.
[b]Where $p < 0.05$.
[c]Where $p < 0.1$.

organization or position. In Model 3, we looked at the determinants of the organization's perceived influence.[10] We asked organizations how politically influential they consider themselves in the geographic area they serve. The dichotomous dependent variable *perceived influence* has a value of one for organizations that reported strong or very strong political influence and a zero for organizations with no, very little, and some political influence.

The results in Model 3 show that being located in Washington, DC, does not affect nonprofits' perceived political influence in the geographic areas they serve (table 4.7). But hiring a lobbyist increases the probability of organizations reporting strong political influence. The results show that while factors such as self-identifying as a national or an international organization as well as the field of activity have no impact on how influential organizations perceive themselves to be, public charities were significantly less likely to report having strong or very strong political influence. In part, these findings support Jeffrey M. Berry and Kent E. Portney's conclusions (see chap. 1, this volume), that if nonprofits are able to lower barriers and gain access to decision makers, they have more positive attitudes about their effectiveness in the policy process.

## Conclusions

Nonprofit advocacy in the nation's capital exhibits both place-based and national characteristics. Most of the region's nonprofits are located in the Maryland and Virginia suburbs outside Washington, DC, and they indicate that they focus on local, state, and regional issues, not on national policies and politics. These organizations are more likely to advocate in their state capitals and at local council meetings than on Capitol Hill. In contrast, nonprofits located in the District of Columbia are significantly more likely to direct their advocacy activities at the federal government than at state or local government. This finding suggests that nonprofits in the DC region are likely to specialize in the venue they chose to influence (i.e., federal, state, or local government), not shop for an audience that is receptive to their issues and concerns. But the analysis did not explore whether nonprofits test their ideas among different types of decision makers (e.g., legislators, the governor or county executive, administrative officials, political parties, or others) within a particular level of government. Further research might shed light on the conditions and circumstances in which nonprofits engage in successful venue shopping.

Moreover, DC-area nonprofits tend to engage in indirect rather than direct advocacy. For example, the vast majority of nonprofits in the survey reported that they try to influence public policies by attending meetings. Although the survey did not ascertain the types of meetings, it is likely that many are with government agencies about contracting issues and policy-related topics (see Boris and Maronick, chap. 3, this volume). A significant number of nonprofits also indicated that they engage in activities that might fall under the designation "public education," such as contributing public comment or

TABLE 4.7.
Logistic Regression of the Determinants of
Organizations' Perceived Influence

| Variable | Perceived Influence |
|---|---|
| Located in DC | 0.317 |
| | [0.383] |
| Age | –0.019 |
| | [0.013] |
| Organizational size | |
| Expense size: medium | –0.133 |
| | [0.494] |
| Expense size: large | 0.964[c] |
| | [0.505] |
| Field of activity | |
| Arts, culture, and humanities | 0.188 |
| | [0.637] |
| Education | 0.219 |
| | [0.549] |
| Health | –0.381 |
| | [0.669] |
| Human services | –0.280 |
| | [0.506] |
| National/international organization | 0.529 |
| | [0.432] |
| Public charity | –1.310[b] |
| | [0.560] |
| Employed a lobbyist | 1.157[b] |
| | [0.494] |
| Constant | –1.983[a] |
| | [0.654] |
| N (using sample weight) | 550 |
| Chi-square | 28.321[a] |

Source: Urban Institute, Survey of Nonprofit-Government
Relations in the Greater Washington, DC, Metropolitan
Area, 2010
Brackets indicate standard errors.
[a]Where $p < 0.01$.
[b]Where $p < 0.05$.
[c]Where $p < 0.1$.

providing information to the media. Direct action activities, such as demonstrations or assisting in drafting bills, are the purview of only about one in four nonprofits.

As several other chapters in this volume show, organizational size is a strong predictor of engaging in advocacy. It is a key predictor of the types of actions taken and the perceptions of influence, regardless of whether the nonprofit is focused on national or local policies. Large nonprofits in the DC region are not only more likely than small and midsized groups to be active in the policy arena, they also are more likely to focus on national issues. Furthermore, they are more likely to engage in both proactive and reactive advocacy strategies, and they are more likely to hire a lobbyist to represent their interests. Given their greater resources (both human and monetary resources), large organizations are better positioned than smaller ones to invest in policy-related advocacy if they chose to do so.

Most nonprofits in the survey (64%) indicated that they had no or little political influence in the geographic area they serve. Larger nonprofits, 501(c)(4) organizations, and groups that employ a lobbyist, however, are significantly more likely than their counterparts to perceive their influence as strong or very strong. Field of activity and national or local orientation have little explanatory power in terms of predicting the organization's perception of affecting public policy.

Many aspects of nonprofit advocacy remain unexplored. We know little about why and how organizations decide to engage in advocacy, for example. Do board members and executive directors understand the value of political activity for their organization and their community? Are staff, community members, and other stakeholders included in the decision-making process? Practitioners could benefit from research that helps identify the types of political skills and strategies that lead to effective participation in the political process. Nonprofit scholars might also look to other social science disciplines such as economics, political science, or sociology for generating hypotheses and building explanatory models to explore the multidimensional nature of advocacy and the complexities of the advocacy process.

### APPENDIX: SURVEY DESIGN AND ADMINISTRATION

#### Background and Objectives

The Center on Nonprofits and Philanthropy at the Urban Institute conducted a survey in the Washington, DC, metropolitan area to examine the extent to which local nonprofits are represented in the public policy domains in the region. The study was developed in conjunction with the University of Washington, Seattle. The DC study began in January 2010 and ended in July 2010.

#### Population and Sample

The survey was based on a stratified random sample of nonprofit organizations in the Washington, DC, metropolitan area to ensure that organizations of different sizes, types, and geographic locations were represented in the study. The Urban Institute's National Center for Charitable Statistics (NCCS) compiled the list of names, addresses, and, when available, phone numbers and email addresses of organizations in the sample. The 2007 and 2008 NCCS "core" files were used to draw the sample. These core files contain all 501(c)(3) and 501(c)(4) public charities with gross receipts of $25,000 or more that file an annual Form 990 financial return with the U.S. Internal Revenue Service (IRS). Only organizations that are considered "active" by the IRS were included in the study.

To be compatible with the Seattle survey, we excluded hospitals and higher education organizations from the master list because these organizations tend to be much larger and more complex structures than other types of nonprofits. We also excluded foundations (i.e., organizations that file Form 990-PF), homeowner associations, and grant-making foundations (classified as T2, T3, T7, and T9 under the National Taxonomy of Exempt Entities). The NCCS database identified 10,581 nonprofit organizations in the Washington, DC, metropolitan area that file with the IRS and satisfy all of the selection criteria outlined above. The master list restrictions and exclusions were done to achieve comparability with a larger international study.

Although the NCCS database underrepresents small nonprofits, time and budget constraints did not allow us to supplement it with local lists that might contain smaller organizations. But any attempt to supplement the NCCS list is likely to be incomplete, and we would lose our ability to generalize to the broader population. Therefore we decided that the best sampling strategy was to use the NCCS data set as our sampling frame. This enabled us to generalize to the full population of nonprofits in the Washington, DC, metropolitan area with the caveat that some smaller groups may be missing.

For this study, a total of 3,300 organizations were randomly selected. To ensure a representative random sample, we stratified the NCCS list by region, size of organization, and type of nonprofit prior to selecting the sample. In addition, because of the smaller number of nonprofits classified as 501(c)(4) organizations, we oversampled the 501(c)(4) organizations to ensure that they could be analyzed separately.

To maximize the number of respondents, we contacted organizations through mail, email, and phone. This strategy was designed to stretch our resources and to ensure a good response rate. Participation in the survey by organizations was voluntary.

## Survey Instrument

The Urban Institute research team worked with the Seattle study's principal investigators, Robert J. Pekkanen and Steven Rathgeb Smith, to finalize and format the survey instrument. The questionnaire was divided into five sections: (1) basic information about the organization, (2) information about the organization's members, (3) how the nonprofit interacts with other organizations and groups, (4) information about the organization's involvement in affecting public policy, and (5) the organization's leadership and finances.

The questionnaire was designed to be administered by mail and Internet. Only one response was collected over the telephone. The paper version was 12 pages long, printed on letter-size paper. Depending on the questions answered and the skip patterns, the online version contained as many as 42 screens, which included an introduction page and a survey submission page.

## Data Collection and Contact Procedures

The first contact was an advance letter sent to all 3,300 organizations in the sample. The letter was printed on the Urban Institute's letterhead and signed by Carol J. De-Vita, the DC study's principal investigator. The letter announced the survey, highlighted its importance, and asked for respondents' voluntary participation. It also provided respondents with the opportunity to take the survey online by giving them a link, username, and password, as well as a telephone number and an email address to contact if they had any questions about the questionnaire or the study.

The next step was to mail questionnaires to potential respondents. The survey packet included a cover letter that provided more information about the study, the 12-page questionnaire, and an envelope with prepaid postage and the return address for respondents to send the completed surveys.

Eligible nonrespondents were sent several reminders about the survey. First, postcard reminders were sent in two batches to a sample of the respondents. Second, nonrespondents with email addresses were contacted and reminded about the study three times. Third, telephone contacts with nonrespondents were initiated.

## Response Rate

There were 571 completed questionnaires, yielding a response rate of 18%.

## Weights

To ensure that the survey results are generalizable to the population of nonprofits in the DC region and to correct for the fact that we oversampled 501(c)(4) organizations, we assigned each completed interview a survey weight. The weights were designed to match the respondents' characteristics such as size, type, region, and subsection code—i.e., 501(c)(3) and 501(c)(4)—to the sampling frame. Two weights were created: one *sample* weight and one *population* weight. Both weights will generate the same percentage estimates. The sample size for the sample weight equals the final survey sample size ($n = 571$). The population weight is the sample weight scaled up to match the universe sample size ($n = 10,581$). In addition to producing representative results, the weights also mitigate potential nonresponse bias.

### NOTES

1. The Washington, DC, metropolitan area is defined as the District of Columbia, two Maryland counties adjacent to the District of Columbia (Montgomery and Prince George's Counties), and nine jurisdictions in Northern Virginia, namely the City of Alexandria, Arlington County, the City of Fairfax, the City of Falls Church, Fairfax County, Loudoun County, City of Manassas, City of Manassas Park, and Prince William County.

2. Nonprofit organizations with an annual gross income of $25,000 or more are required to file the annual financial Form 990 with the IRS. Organizations below this filing threshold are underrepresented in the survey.

3. The literature shows that organizational size can be operationalized in various ways; that is, by using the number of employees (Child and Grønbjerg, 2007; Schmid et al., 2008) and budget or expenditures size (Berry and Arons, 2003; Chaves et al., 2004; Schmid et al., 2008), or number of volunteers (Schmid et al., 2008). We tested the models with two of these variables (number of employees and expenditures) and found that the expenditure variable provided more robust estimates than number of employees. We therefore used expenditures as a proxy for organizational size in the analysis.

4. Field of activity was identified using the National Taxonomy of Exempt Entities codes that are part of the NCCS database used to draw the sample.

5. Nationally, the distribution of nonprofits is as follows: human service, 34%; education, 18%; health, 12%; arts, 11%; all other types, 25%. See Wing et al. (2010).

6. Also note that there are a dozen city and county governments that may oversee and interact with these nonprofit organizations.

7. In the companion Seattle study (see chap. 2, this volume), about 15% of nonprofits have budgets greater than $1 million, while almost 60% have budgets below $100,000. One in four Seattle nonprofits is in the midsize range, with budgets between $100,000 and $1 million.

8. We tested various criteria for defining advocacy. Under a broader definition (i.e., organizations that seldom, sometimes, often, or very often engaged in the 12 specific activities), 73% of nonprofits might be considered engaged in advocacy. Under a more stringent definition (i.e., only organizations that often or very often engaged in the 12 specific activities), 56% of nonprofits engaged in advocacy. Because advocacy work can be episodic, we selected a definition that included "sometimes" but excluded "seldom" and "never."

9. Through a series of questions, the respondent was asked if the nonprofit worked alone to successfully enact, stop, or modify a specific policy at either the federal, state, or local level. The respondent was then asked if the organization worked in a coalition to successfully enact, stop, or modify a specific policy and at which level of government.

10. Schmid et al. (2008) find a positive significant correlation between advocacy and political activity and the organization's perceived influence on public policy agenda setting, as defined by these authors.

REFERENCES

Andrews, Kenneth T., and Bob Edwards. 2004. "Advocacy Organizations in the U.S. Political Process." *Annual Review of Sociology* 30: 479–506.

Berry, Jeffrey M., and David F. Arons. 2003. *A Voice for Nonprofits.* Washington, DC: Brookings Institution Press.

Boris, Elizabeth T., and Jeff Krehely. 2002. "Civic Participation and Advocacy." In *The State of Nonprofit America,* edited by Lester M. Salamon, 299–330. Washington, DC: Brookings Institution Press.

Chaves, Mark, Laura Stephens, and Joseph Galaskiewicz. 2004. "Does Government

Funding Suppress Nonprofits' Political Activity?" *American Sociological Review* 69, no. 2: 292–316.

Child, Curtis D., and Kirsten A. Grønbjerg. 2007. "Nonprofit Advocacy Organizations: Their Characteristics and Activities." *Social Science Quarterly* 88, no. 1: 259–81.

Foley, Michael W., and Bob Edwards. 2002. "How Do Members Count? Membership, Governance, and Advocacy in the Nonprofit World." In *Exploring Organizations and Advocacy, Governance and Accountability* 2, edited by Elizabeth J. Reid and Maria D. Montilla, 19–32. Washington, DC: Urban Institute. http://www.urban.org/url.cfm?ID=410532.

Reid, Elizabeth. 2006. "Advocacy and the Challenges It Presents for Nonprofits." In *Nonprofit and Government: Collaboration and Conflict,* edited by Elizabeth T. Boris and C. Eugene Steuerle, 343–71. Washington, DC: Urban Institute Press.

Schmid, Hillel, Michal Bar, and Ronit Nirel. 2008. "Advocacy Activities in Nonprofit Human Service Organizations: Implications for Policy." *Nonprofit and Voluntary Sector Quarterly* 37, no. 4: 581–602.

Wing, Kennard T., Katie L. Roeger, and Thomas H. Pollak. 2010. "The Nonprofit Sector in Brief: Public Charities, Giving, and Volunteering, 2010." Washington, DC: Urban Institute.

# CHAPTER FIVE

# From Skid Row to the Statehouse

## How Nonprofit Homeless Service Providers Overcome Barriers to Policy Advocacy Involvement

JENNIFER E. MOSLEY

The role of the nonprofit sector in advocating for the public good has been a topic of recent increased scholarly attention. Drawing on existing research on social movements and interest groups, this work has investigated the degree to which nonprofit organizations of all types are involved in policy advocacy, the barriers they face, and how this involvement varies among organizations (Andrews and Edwards, 2004; Bass et al., 2007; Berry and Arons, 2003; Chaves et al., 2004). As a result of this research, new questions have emerged. Research has shown that organizational characteristics such as professionalization and a higher degree of collaboration are associated with increased advocacy involvement, for example, but it has not confirmed the mechanisms by which this works (Mosley, 2010). Alternatively, several issues are thought to serve as barriers to advocacy involvement—e.g., fear of legal ramifications or lack of capacity—but more information is needed to address which barriers are most central in the minds of managers or how they may work together (Bass et al., 2007). Additionally, there is increased recognition that the answers to these questions may be different for nonprofits involved in different policy fields (Child and Grønbjerg, 2007; Stone and Sandfort, 2009). How these barriers may function to limit advocacy involvement is a major theme of this volume.

Nonprofits operating in human service fields provide a useful case to explore how barriers and incentives operate when it comes to policy advocacy. They are important because human service nonprofits are thought to be critical players in advocating on behalf of marginalized communities. Advocating human service nonprofits can help procure resources and improve policies by serving as vital information conduits regarding how policy is working on the ground. But because they are organized primarily to provide services, not to conduct advocacy, they also face substantial barriers to advocacy participation. These barriers include severe resource constraints, a lack of experience and knowledge about policy advocacy, and confusion about what they are legally able to do (see Bass et al., chap. 10, this volume, for more information on the barriers and incentives nonprofits face around advocacy). Unfortunately, how these barriers interact, or why some organizations are able to overcome them and others are not, is still unknown. Human service nonprofits also have higher-than-average levels of dependence on government funding, and both they and their clients frequently interface with public policy regulations. This institutional context complicates any claims regarding "outsider" status and may present unique barriers and incentives for advocacy participation.

If scholars are to understand how to help develop and strengthen advocacy among human service nonprofits, we must develop more specific knowledge of how advocacy is experienced inside organizations, including how managerial beliefs and priorities interact with organizational constraints and the institutional context. Central to this understanding must be what motivates human service nonprofits to become involved in advocacy, which barriers are most pervasive in limiting or silencing advocacy activity, and what organizational and institutional structures facilitate involvement.

Building on previous work in this area (Bass et al., 2007; Berry and Arons, 2003; Child and Grønbjerg, 2007; Mosley, 2010), this chapter addresses these three things by looking in depth at a single policy field: services for the homeless. I argue that in order to advance the research on nonprofit advocacy, we need to pay greater attention to the specific context in which it takes place and unpack the organizational and institutional processes that incentivize and constrain action. Only then can we more fully understand the conditions under which advocacy can be successful—a major goal of this volume. To do this, I first review previous research findings, pointing to the key questions that scholars have yet to fully address. I then present findings from a qualitative study of homeless service providers in Chicago that was designed to shed additional light on some of these questions.

This chapter addresses three major barriers to advocacy participation that have been proposed and received empirical support in the literature. These are concerns about Internal Revenue Service (IRS) regulations, limited capacity, and lack of supportive and knowledgeable leadership. After presenting data that help to adjudicate which are most central and why, I then explore three organizational characteristics or practices that have been associated with increased advocacy involvement and demonstrate the mechanisms by which they help organizations overcome the barriers mentioned above: use of collaborative networks, government funding, and issues of professional leadership. Three specific research questions are addressed. The first two—(1) what activities do organizational leaders consider advocacy? and (2) what are the most serious barriers to advocacy participation?—provide the necessary background to explore the central question of this chapter: (3) what organizational characteristics best position organizations to overcome those barriers?

## Literature on Human Service Nonprofits and Policy Advocacy

As noted above, while the recent scholarly attention placed on nonprofit advocacy has answered many important questions, like all complex topics, it has led to the development of more questions. In this section I review the major findings that have resulted from this increase in attention, pointing to where more information is needed. These findings fall into three broad categories: (1) definitions of advocacy, (2) barriers to involvement, and (3) actions and characteristics that facilitate involvement.

### *Definitions of Advocacy*

As Robert J. Pekkanen and Steven Rathgeb Smith point out in their introduction to this volume, defining advocacy is tricky business. The wide range of tactics that can be understood as advocacy complicate both the practice and measurement of advocacy. For this reason, understanding how managers define advocacy is important because it is impossible to fully understand what keeps organizations from participating in advocacy if researchers and managers do not have a shared understanding of the topic. Unfortunately, the nature of survey research might lead researchers to underestimate participation and thus overestimate barriers. In survey research, the meanings of specific terms are not open to negotiation. Researchers have a choice between leaving terms undefined (and thus privileging the definition of the respondent, which remains unknown and can be a devastating threat to reliability) or defining them a priori (which leads to greater reliability regarding the findings but may compromise construct validity).

The second approach, defining for respondents what is meant by specific terms like "advocacy," is generally preferred. As a result, surveys have asked respondents about advocacy using slightly different definitions, and it is unclear which definition produces the most valid answers. This also makes comparability across studies difficult. Alternatively, some researchers choose to ask about involvement in specific activities, and use those to estimate advocacy involvement (Allard, 2009; Donaldson and Shields, 2009; Schmid et al., 2008). This approach cleverly sidesteps the definitional problems and increases reliability, but it limits our understanding of advocacy to only a few specific agreed-upon activities. Another approach is to rely on information reported on the Form 990 (e.g., Nicholson-Crotty, 2007) but doing so is likely to severely underestimate actual advocacy participation, as organizations are not required to report any advocacy activity that is not lobbying.

Research from the Strengthening Nonprofit Advocacy Project (SNAP) highlights the importance of understanding more about how managers define advocacy (Bass et al., 2007; Berry and Arons, 2003). Anticipating that words like "lobbying" may be loaded for some managers, researchers systematically varied the words "lobbying," "advocacy," and "educate" in a single question to see if responses would vary accordingly. Not surprisingly, they found that many more managers responded positively to questions about "educating" than they did about the others (Bass et al., 2007).

To help shed light on how human service managers define advocacy and assess the degree to which their definitions are in alignment with those of researchers, managers in this study were explicitly asked how they defined advocacy and lobbying, and what activities they included in that definition. They were also asked about their participation in lobbying or other tactics researchers often consider advocacy, but without having those tactics labeled as such. This approach is in alignment with the broad definition of advocacy—"advocacy is the attempt to influence public policy, either directly or indirectly"—advocated by Robert J. Pekkanen and Steven Rathgeb Smith in this volume.

## Barriers to Advocacy Involvement

Researchers have hypothesized that several barriers may keep human service nonprofits from participating in advocacy. The barriers that are most often mentioned are concerns about IRS regulations, limited capacity, and lack of supportive and knowledgeable leadership, although there are certainly others. While previous research has informed us that each of these barriers exist, we do not know which barriers are most central for which types of organizations or how these barriers may work together. Understanding more about how these barriers limit advocacy involvement is a major goal of this volume.

First, the potential barriers that come with the IRS regulations that restrict lobbying for 501(c)(3) organizations and prohibit activities such as electioneering are a central concern of many scholars. These regulations are complex and can be confusing, but they are attached to severe sanctions, including the loss of 501(c)(3) status. Research has shown that many nonprofits are confused about the rules and that fear of sanctions leads some organizations to opt out of advocacy altogether (Bass et al., 2007; Berry and Arons, 2003). More research is needed, however, on how different types of nonprofits interpret these regulations, and how this barrier interacts with other important organizational characteristics and barriers, such as size and professionalization.

Another advocacy barrier for nonprofits is a lack of capacity (Bass et al., 2007; Child and Grønbjerg, 2007; Mosley, 2010), which may be a particular issue in the human services field. The field in general is faced with severe resource constraints, and organizations are compelled to spend the majority of their resources on service provision (Hasenfeld, 1992). The capacity barrier is not simple, however, as capacity stands in for many issues and is measured in different ways depending on the study (generally either by number of full-time employees or size of budget). The actual barrier may be a lack of staff, a lack of financial resources, or a combination of the two. Capacity may also serve as a proxy for political connections (e.g., smaller organizations may have a harder time getting their "foot in the door"). This research addresses what specific aspects of capacity hinder advocacy for human service nonprofits.

Finally, research has shown that executive directors have primary responsibility for advocacy, as staff members often lack the time, expertise, or authority to be involved (Bass et al., 2007; Salamon and Geller, 2008). In many cases the decision to be involved in advocacy comes down to one or two individual leaders in an organization, which can create a barrier if that individual lacks training in advocacy, believes that advocacy is outside of the organization's mission, or does not believe advocacy will have meaningful benefits. Some scholars have thus hypothesized that human service managers may hesitate to be involved in advocacy for reasons of knowledge or expertise (Schneider and Lester, 2001). Research has shown that organizations with highly educated managers are more likely to be involved in advocacy (Mosley, 2010), but much more information is needed on what aspects of leadership are important. Leadership barriers include managers' beliefs, access to professional networks, understanding of legal constraints, and personal passion. In this study the relationship between advocacy involvement and managerial practices and beliefs is explored in order to discover if one or more of these barriers is primary.

### What Characteristics or Actions May Help Overcome Barriers to Advocacy Involvement?

Given these barriers, and the importance of advocacy involvement for the well-being of both human service organizations and their vulnerable clients, it is important to know what can help organizations overcome them. For some organizations, overcoming barriers may mean becoming involved in advocacy in the first place, and for others it may mean expanding their advocacy involvement to a more meaningful level. There are several variables that may facilitate advocacy in this way, and all may operate via a variety of mechanisms that are not well understood. In this chapter I investigate three—collaborative networks, government funding, and issues of professional leadership—by looking at how they may counteract specific barriers and the mechanisms by which they do this. I also assess the effect of specific incentives and barriers found in distinct policy fields.

First, collaboration is one of the most common tactics chosen by human service organizations involved in advocacy (Mosley, 2009) for a number of reasons. Collaboration may increase legitimacy, access to knowledge about policies and advocacy efforts, and access to policymakers (Hojnacki, 1997). Research has particularly emphasized the degree to which collaboration is done to gain or conserve resources, particularly for organizations with limited internal capacity (Galaskiewicz, 1985; Guo and Acar, 2005). Research has also shown that non-advocacy-related collaborations increase the likelihood that human service organizations will be involved in advocacy (Mosley, 2010), so perhaps some organizations simply have a collaborative orientation. Regardless, because collaboration is common among human service nonprofits, is particularly common as an advocacy tactic, and has the potential to allow organizations to participate in advocacy with a minimum outlay of resources, we need additional understanding about the ways in which collaboration may help human service nonprofits overcome advocacy barriers (see Sandfort, chap. 9, this volume, for more on advocacy collaboration).

Second, the relationship between government funding and advocacy involvement is of special interest in regard to human service nonprofits. Privatization has led to an increased dependence on government funds throughout the humans services sector (Smith and Lipsky, 1993). Some fields, like homeless services, have grown considerably as a result of this trend, but they may have also lost some autonomy. Traditional wisdom long held that nonprofits that are more dependent on government funds would be less likely to participate in advocacy because of fear of alienating their government funders, driving away other possible sources of revenue, or because of the limited flexibility of government funding (Alexander et al., 1999; Nicholson-Crotty, 2009). But most research now suggests that government funding either has no effect or is associated with greater advocacy involvement (Chaves et al., 2004; Child and Grønbjerg, 2007; Mosley, 2010).

This project adds more empirical evidence to this debate. Although it now appears that government funding is positively associated with increased advocacy involvement, it is still not clear why. It could be that greater access to government decision makers facilitates involvement, or it could be an increased incentive to make sure government policy and funding decisions are in alignment with organizational priorities. These may not be mutually exclusive. Alternatively, the direction of the relationship may be reversed—it could be that organizations that advocate more wind up with more government funding. More information is needed to determine the influence of this field-level trend.

Third, just as some leadership characteristics may serve as a barrier for advocacy involvement, other characteristics may actually help facilitate advocacy. Clearly, leadership matters, but what causes some leaders to embrace advocacy more than others and overcome those day-to-day barriers? Professional norms around advocacy may be one reason. Nonprofit leaders come from a variety of backgrounds and have different orientations to their work (Suarez, 2010). Research has shown that nonprofit leaders who are management professionals (as opposed to amateurs or people with only substantive expertise) embrace different management tools (Hwang and Powell, 2009). Leaders with different backgrounds also are known to have a variety of interpretations of the field in which they work and share different norms (Fligstein, 1990). Advocacy may be one of these, as research has shown that having a leader with a masters or professional degree is associated with a higher rate of advocacy involvement (Mosley, 2010). Other leadership characteristics that may help facilitate advocacy include having a leader with greater access to policymakers, a better understanding of legal issues, or the execution of management techniques that integrate advocacy into the organization.

These characteristics may or may not be associated with professional norms, too. Advocacy may also be driven by more individualistic differences, such as personal passion or social justice orientation (Bass et al., 2007).

Finally, policy fields come with distinctive regulatory environments, interactions with government administrators, and connections to private resources (Salamon, 1987; Stone and Sandfort, 2009). Studies have shown that nonprofits from different policy fields also vary widely in whether they are involved in advocacy. Nonprofits in the health and environment fields, for example, have higher rates of involvement in advocacy than human service nonprofits (Child and Grønbjerg, 2007). Their higher rates of participation may be because the fields of health and environment are highly politicized, partially as a result of targeted lobbying efforts by private interests, and have strong government regulatory bodies. Additionally, political opportunity theory has long proposed that the friendliness of the political environment, which varies by policy field over time, can serve as a barrier or incentive to political activism (Meyer and Minkoff, 2004). In a recent study of nonprofit reproductive health and family planning providers, Nicholson-Crotty (2007) found that reproductive health organizations were more likely to advocate when either their ability to deliver core services was threatened or when the political environment appeared favorable. I assess these policy field effects by studying a single, regionally constrained, policy field: homeless services.

## Methods

This research focuses on one regional policy field—homeless services—in order to gain insight into how organizational constraints and managerial beliefs interact when it comes to advocacy involvement. Qualitative research methods were used to maximize understanding of how managers interpret potential barriers and incentives, as well as the context in which they act on their beliefs. The units of analysis were homeless service nonprofits, defined as organizations with 501(c)(3) status with at least one of its three largest programs specifically focused on serving the homeless. These organizations include emergency shelters, transitional housing providers, and providers of basic needs services, among others. Using a variety of databases and membership lists, 86 of these organizations were identified in the city of Chicago in August of 2008. All were primarily direct service providers, not advocacy organizations.

Because of the small population size, it was possible to use representative sampling in conjunction with the qualitative approach. The population was stratified by size (as measured by expenditures reported on the organization's most recently available Form 990 tax return) and service provided (e.g., transitional housing, emergency services). The initial sampling frame consisted of 54 organizations, two of which were later found to be defunct, resulting in a final sampling frame of 52 organizations.

The executive directors of the sampled organizations were contacted initially by letter and then by telephone. Forty-two directors agreed to participate and were subsequently interviewed. These semistructured, in-depth interviews lasted between one and two hours and took place between August 2008 and April 2009. The interviews solicited information about a variety of topics related to advocacy involvement, including motivation, barriers, and tactics, as well as other organizational characteristics such as collaboration and government funding. The response rate was 81%, with data collected from half the population of homeless service organizations in Chicago.

All interviews were digitally recorded and then professionally transcribed. All transcripts were used in the analysis, using a coding scheme containing both inductive and deductive techniques. Codes reflected topics of a priori theoretical interest as well as those that emerged from open coding, reflecting new insights (Patton, 2002). Extensive memoing was also used in the analysis. Case summaries were written immediately after each interview, and additional memos regarding connections to existing theories and emerging themes were written during the analysis phase (Miles and Huberman, 1994). Data from the interviews and memos were complemented with field notes written during participant observation at advocacy coalition meetings and other field-level events where advocacy was discussed.

Because of substantial correlation between variables of interest (e.g., size and government funding), negative case analysis was an important part of the analysis, used to provide additional insight into sources of variation (Patton, 2002). Member checking was also used to enhance validity; this was done through sharing initial findings with respondents, requesting feedback, and discussing the findings at several advocacy coalition meetings.

## Results

Responding organizations varied on several characteristics of theoretical interest. Size varied greatly, with expenditures ranging from $7,000 to $11 million. The mean was $2,447,122 and the median was $1,603,824. Respondents also ranged on the degree to which they were financed by government funding, from 0% to 100% of their budgets. About 83% of the organizations had some government funding, and about half of those organizations (51%) had a budget made up of more than 60% government funds. The professionalization of the executive director was assessed qualitatively; leaders differed considerably on variables such as their years of work in the nonprofit sector, level of education, and connections to others in the field. Less variation was seen regarding collaboration; all the organizations that reported advocacy involvement also reported involvement in collaborative groups, albeit to different degrees.

In regard to advocacy, great variation was found in the degree to which organizations participated in advocacy but, surprisingly, not on whether they participated at all. Managers in this sample reported high rates of engagement in policy advocacy. Only three organizations out of the 42 interviewed were not involved in policy advocacy in any way, meaning that 93% did participate. Although many of these organizations participated only in minor ways, this participation rate is substantially higher than is generally found in surveys of nonprofit advocacy. Although there are contextual issues that incentivize advocacy in this field that will be discussed below—specifically, opportunities for collaboration and reliance on government funding—this finding is likely at least a partial result of a qualitative methodology that allowed managers to define for themselves what advocacy meant. These findings are addressed in the first research question.

## What Activities Do Organizational Leaders Consider Advocacy?

In the interview, managers were not given a definition of advocacy, but rather asked to define the term on their own. Sample questions in the interview include, "Even if you don't participate in them, what kinds of activities do you think of when you think about advocacy?" and "Can you give me an example of something you recently did that you would consider advocacy?" Findings revealed that managers often interpreted certain activities they engaged in as "advocacy" that may not be obviously included in the definitions of advocacy used in most surveys. Notably, managers included most types of community outreach (e.g., newsletters, open houses) as advocacy, as well as attendance at meetings with fellow service providers, regardless of whether policymakers were in attendance or advocacy action was discussed.

Examples of responses to this question included, "Let me see. I mean we do hold things like community forums," or "We usually send someone to meetings at the Alliance [the local U.S. Department of Housing and Urban Development continuum of care network]." In both cases these organizations did not participate in advocacy tactics that were more obviously "public policy" work. But these activities are clearly focused externally on improving conditions in the larger political environment and should probably not be automatically excluded from advocacy definitions. Some managers had definitions that were even further afield, however, and acknowledged that their definition of advocacy may differ from that of the researchers. As one manager said, "How we're trying to do [advocacy] is more through educating our volunteers and our constituency about really treating people with dignity and love and care. So I know that's not where you're going with the whole policy thing." It should be noted that, when asked specifically, almost all managers did make a distinction between advocacy and lobbying, although their definition of lobbying was often vague.

A parallel finding is that, later in the interview, managers were asked about their involvement in a variety of activities that researchers commonly consider to be advocacy. These activities included involvement in advocacy coalitions and meetings with government agency administrators. Many times managers who earlier reported that they did not engage in advocacy did report engagement in these activities, a finding similar to that reported by SNAP researchers (Bass et al., 2007; Berry and Arons, 2003). When asked to reconcile these statements, respondents would say something like, "Well, I see how that might seem political. But to us it is just networking."

*What Are the Most Serious Barriers to Advocacy Participation?*

As mentioned above, three barriers are addressed in this section: concerns about IRS regulations, limited capacity, and lack of supportive and knowledgeable leadership.

## Concern about IRS Regulations

As noted above, proponents of nonprofit advocacy and lobbying have long been concerned that many nonprofit organizations are not well versed in the IRS rules governing lobbying activity for 501(c)(3) organizations and worry that this lack of clarity might produce a chilling effect for advocacy involvement. This research revealed that confusion over the rules was common among homeless service providers in Chicago. These misunderstandings clearly did not prevent organizations from participating in advocacy (as 93% were found to participate), however, and usually did not keep them from participating in lobbying, either.

Data from the interviews revealed that 50% of organizations participated in lobbying at some level, but only 24% responded in the affirmative when asked specifically if they lobbied. In other words, about half of the organizations that participated in lobbying were either unwilling to say so, or else did not understand what activities constituted lobbying (even though what they later described doing met the legal definition of the term).

This discrepancy is primarily a result of two common misunderstandings. First, many managers were unsure about what lobbying actually was and so participated in it without knowing they were doing so. When asked if they lobbied, for example, they would say no, and then later talk about a trip they made to the state capital with a group of other service providers to talk to legislators about the proposed state budget cuts.

Second, many managers noted a specific aversion to the word "lobbying" and preferred not to use it. Instead, they referred to their lobbying involvement as "educational," "advocacy," or "public policy." As one director said, "I like the word advocacy a lot better. It doesn't sound so political. It's really me talking about something that I'm passionate about . . . Lobbying kind of has a negative connotation in today's world." Another was even more descriptive: "lobbying, even the term kind of turns my stomach. I mean, I feel like, if I'm Amoco, and need this done so I can make more money, then I need to be lobbying. What we're doing, we're trying to educate them to make right decisions for their constituents . . . I guess in a sense that's lobbying, but this is really, I mean, it's our money, and it's coming back to us . . . Lobbying to me sort of has a more greasy feel to it."

About 21% of managers specifically, and erroneously, stated that they could not lobby because of their nonprofit status or because they received government funding. The rest knew that some lobbying was acceptable, but the vast majority was unsure about what the spending cutoffs were. They simply felt that that whatever they were doing, it certainly wasn't "too much." Only one executive director knew what the 501(h) election was, for example, but he did not bother selecting it because he felt there was no chance that they would spend enough for it to matter. One director, who freely reported involvement in lobbying, said the following when asked about reporting lobbying expenditures: "Well, we don't really have any, so we don't report any, frankly. I mean there's my time, but that's really more, it's public policy work, as opposed to lobbying. It's really minimal, so it's not really worth reporting. Maybe 5% of my salary." "I ain't making a million dollars," he added, laughing.

In sum, these managers felt there was a qualitative difference between any lobbying that they might do and lobbying that is done on behalf of corporate interests. They viewed their work to be primarily educational, or as giving voice to underrepresented constituents. Essentially, lobbying was seen as self-interested. Because they did not see their lobbying work in that light, they did not consider it lobbying. As one respondent noted when asked about the difference between advocacy and lobbying, "I don't see a difference, but we can't call it lobbying if we do it . . . Lobbyists get paid. We don't. Bottom line."

The other half of respondents, who did not participate in lobbying, tended to be the organizations who were less involved with advocacy overall. Although some noted that they believed lobbying to be illegal, they also generally reported they were not interested in engaging in lobbying or did not have the time to go to the state capital (about four hours by car from Chicago). As one manager put it, "When you have a lot of restricted money, it's difficult . . . especially to the degree that it requires travel, because you don't have money in your budget that covers those kinds of expenses, it makes it difficult to accomplish. So sometimes you have to cover those expenses yourself. And depending on how often you do it, it can be expensive."

Finally, the following quote demonstrates that it is not fear or confusion about violating IRS rules that keeps one manager from lobbying; rather, it is the perceived staff time that monitoring takes: "I don't really find them [the lobbying laws] to be overly burdensome . . . I think that people can always get around prohibitions and lobbying if they need to and they want to. It's just not something that I would care to be involved in, because it would take staff time and resources in order to defend against it."

## Limited Capacity

As was seen in a few of the above quotes, instead of legal worries, the advocacy barrier that managers reported to be most severe is limited capacity in terms of time and resources, which is similar to what has been reported in previous research (Bass et al., 2007). When human service providers participate in advocacy, they must do so while simultaneously providing services to clients, maintaining relationships with their community, and raising funds. Balancing these different demands was seen as difficult. "Frankly, part of the reason we're not more involved [in advocacy] is because we're so involved with doing [service] that there just doesn't seem to be enough time left over to do the other part, and shame on us. But that's the reality." Another pointed out, "I mean, we [service providers] have a dual role. We have to push the envelope in terms of social change, and then we have to make sure that the work that we do gets done . . . And so that means that we have to make sure that we're adequately resourced to do the work, and then also to push the envelope. And it's very hard to do." These managers wanted to increase their advocacy effort but simply could not find the time or resources to do so.

When asked what it would take to expand their advocacy involvement, time was the most frequent answer given by managers. For the executive directors of these organizations, there simply is not enough time to manage the organization and participate in policy advocacy, too. As one manager put it, "[We] could be a lot better at advocacy, but we would say the reason we really haven't been is because we are just busy. That's really the main reason. It seems like every day we're putting out some kind of fire, whether it be funding or staff issues or, you know, being understaffed . . . although we know we need to do it more."

A perceived lack of time is strongly related to resource availability. In the minds of managers, with bigger budgets they could afford to hire someone to help with advocacy. "I would like to have a full-time staff person to work on advocacy, outreach, and public awareness. And I don't have it. I have a part-time person who also has an entirely different function. She's my office manager." Speaking about her desire to be more involved in advocacy, one manager said, "We definitely would love, love, love to do that. But, that takes up resources. That's, like, a person working on it and engaging, and—you know, it's not a case manager, because if they're doing that then they're not doing case management . . . maybe it's a program supervisor, but it's another task that she's got to do."

Several complained that finding funding to do advocacy was difficult. Because of resource constraints—both being underresourced and being reliant on inflexible government funding were mentioned—many managers felt that there was simply not enough money in their budget to be fully engaged in advocacy. Accordingly, many felt that specific funding for advocacy would help them be more involved. As manager noted, "We wanted to keep doing advocacy but we couldn't find money for it. So that's another factor that probably keeps us from doing advocacy is, you know, if somebody would throw some money at it . . . We kind of have to do that on the side. There's really no designated money for it that we have found." Laughing, she added, "So—we need to advocate for advocacy funding!"

## Lack of Supportive and Knowledgeable Leadership

The decision to advocate often lies with executive director. Not only is she the leader of the organization, she is also the person with the greatest access to decision makers and stakeholders. Most executive directors interviewed reported that they themselves conducted the vast majority of the organization's advocacy efforts. As reflected in the quotes above, executive directors often reported that other staff members were either too busy serving clients or did not have the necessary expertise. Except in the largest organizations, resources were not available to hire specific advocacy-related staff. Many executive directors also felt that, as the public face of the agency, they were best situated to head up any advocacy involvement. Unfortunately, because they were often busy with other tasks, relying solely on the executive director to do advocacy meant that many organizations were not as involved as they would like. This situation was discussed above as one of limited capacity but can also be conceptualized as a leadership issue.

Involvement was also limited when the executive director did not see advocacy as central to the organization's functioning. A professional orientation to service over advocacy was articulated by several of these directors. Although they generally saw advocacy as a potentially valuable activity, direct service to clients took precedence for them. As one put it: "not that I don't think advocacy isn't important, but . . . if I had $50,000, I frankly would not spend it on an advocacy person. I'd put it into someone's pocket here, or mouth, or pay rent, or buy [medicine] for them. That's not the way I think we would choose to use money, honestly."

Other managers spoke of this in mission-related terms, although their personal beliefs were clear: "We can't get too involved in [advocacy] or else we're not doing our main mission, which is not advocacy in the public sphere. We advocate for the clients all the time, but we're not an advocacy organization, so we lend a hand. We participate a little bit and stay in touch, but try not to get too off topic." Another manager preferred to "Leave it to the Chicago Alliance; they have a staff person, that's that person's job to do that . . . I don't think I'm very good at it, either. So, I mean, I'm all for leaving things to do for people who are good at it. We do one thing and we do it very, very, well, and that is [provide direct services] . . . that's our mission, and we're going to stick with our mission."

Less often, but still present, were managers who felt that they just were not sure how to get more involved. These managers knew that their knowledge and expertise were holding back the organization, but they did not feel positioned to rectify the situation. One executive director of a small, faith-based emergency shelter who had only a high school diploma and limited interactions with other directors said of increasing their advocacy and lobbying involvement, "From what I hear, all the money that they raised and all that, I would love to do that for [name of organization], but I don't know how to do it."

### What Characteristics or Actions Help Overcome Barriers to Advocacy Involvement?

The high rates of advocacy participation in this field provide a useful angle for determining what organizational actions or characteristics help facilitate advocacy involvement. Two types of organizations in particular were useful analytical cases: (1) organizations that were only marginally involved in advocacy (because of the multiple barriers they faced, these organizations probably would not have participated at all if not for one of the characteristics listed below) and (2) organizations that were highly involved in advocacy (as evidenced through use of multiple tactics, frequent engagement, and high levels of sophistication).

I find that the advocacy of both of these types of organizations was greatly facilitated, albeit in different ways, by (1) efficiency gains achieved through advocacy collaboration, (2) organizational reliance on government funding, and (3) professional norms and beliefs. Table 5.1 provides an overview of the findings demonstrating how these three characteristics help overcome the barriers of limited capacity and lack of knowledgeable and supportive leadership, as well as the mechanisms through which this happens. Concerns about IRS regulations were not found to be a major barrier, so they are not included in table 5.1.

## Collaboration

The interviews revealed that participation in advocacy coalitions and other interorganizational networks was the tool managers felt best helped them overcome the barrier of limited capacity. The importance of these collaborations for the involvement of individual agencies is evidenced by the fact that 46% of the organizations that participated in advocacy participated *only* through collaborative methods. The primary mechanism through which collaborative networks facilitate advocacy is by allowing organizations to be

TABLE 5.1.
Barriers to Advocacy and Mechanisms to Overcome Them

| Barrier | Facilitating Action or Characteristic | Mechanism at Work |
| --- | --- | --- |
| Limited capacity | 1. Collaboration | Allows organizations to be involved with a minimum outlay of time and resources |
| | | Secondarily provides access to knowledge and information |
| | 2. Professional norms | Associated with specific management techniques that build advocacy infrastructure |
| Lack of knowledgeable and supportive leadership | 1. Professional norms | Associated with a change in managerial beliefs regarding the role and importance of advocacy in organizational functioning |
| | 2. Government funding | Provides strong incentives for advocacy that leads managers to become more knowledgeable and supportive |

involved with a minimum outlay of time and resources. Collaboration also helped organizations gain knowledge about current policy debates, but this was also seen as a time- and resource-saving feature.

Not surprisingly, the usefulness of collaboration in counterbalancing limited capacity was particularly salient for relatively small organizations. For example, one manager noted that if his organization had to work alone, it might not be involved in advocacy (because he felt it could not accomplish much), but as part of a network, "they can get a lot more done." Another manager of a small organization pointed specifically to how established coalitions make it easy for organizations like his to be involved: "There's a housing group that sends alerts all the time of when issues are coming before the legislature and I always try to support those, either by the phone call or the letter, that kind of thing . . . They make it pretty simple. Like they'll say, 'Please send this to your legislator.' We all do that because that's really simple, it's like a click of a button." Coalitions also help make more complicated advocacy endeavors, like lobbying trips to the state capital, achievable. "I have gone to Springfield. I typically will do that in conjunction with another organization. So one of our funders is [an intermediary organization], and they usually do a lobbying trip where we go down to Springfield. I have gone with [a different coalition] . . . They'll make arrangements for me to come and speak with lawmakers. And I really enjoy doing that."

The institutional context that supports this kind of collaboration is an important background to these comments. Homeless service organizations in Chicago are able to see the field in this way because there are multiple existing coalitions and other interorganizational networks that do advocacy. Most organizations had the choice of which networks to be active in, and there are strong field-level norms that support involvement with these groups. As Jodi Sandfort reports in chapter 9 in this volume, organizations become involved in these collaborations for different reasons, and the groups can have different levels of effectiveness. Most managers in this field, however, believed that the work of these coalitions and other collaborative advocacy structures boosted effectiveness and helped move their field forward. One manager found a coalition to be:

> very effective, and it's really getting funding for services and supportive housing and advocating for that and getting people motivated and letter writing and calling and all of that stuff. So they've been pretty effective at getting people to be involved, so, via email, being very direct on who to call, what to say, here's an example of a letter. Those are really great for people like myself who are busy, and just coming up with a letter just out of the blue is going to take more time that I don't always have. It's good to have a sample I can use and go from there. So I mean ultimately, I think it's been pretty effective.

As a result, this effort on the part of the coalitions was seen as an appropriate division of labor in the field. Another manager explained that the coalitions "aren't doing direct service, they are paid just for advocacy, and so they solicit feedback about needs from the organizations like ours and also incorporate input from people who are using services in our organizations . . . They do a lot of the legwork, so they help us to be more strategic in our advocacy, and they're able to say, this is legislation that is going to impact your organization, so we need you to write a letter to this senator, or we need you to come to Springfield for a lobby day, or things like that." As this quote indicates, managers often see the coalition leaders as experts in advocacy, but themselves as experts in ground-level concerns. Getting these two types of expertise together was seen as an ideal way to be effective while conserving resources.

Finally, as the above quote alludes to, beyond providing opportunities to get involved in ways that are easy and preserve resources, established advocacy coalitions can also increase capacity for advocacy by providing knowledge. This happens in two ways. First, they provide information about specific actions and keep organizations updated as to important policy developments, which allows organizations to essentially outsource this time-consuming task. For example, a certain coalition "is coordinating it or at least is informing us about it. I kind of always fall back to them because they have really been the most vocal source of information for us around the state budget issues with daily, if not multiple times, a daily update on what's going on and weekly conference calls and helping get information about rallies that are occurring all over the place." Second, coalitions provide low-cost, low-overhead ways to help managers educate their staff on how to be involved in advocacy. One manager said, "there's advocacy trainings that [a coalition] does, which is great. And so we had our intern go to that, which was really good. If we have any staff that has any time to do that, then they can go do that as well."

These findings illustrate that nonprofits that join advocacy coalitions often become more deeply involved in advocacy. Furthermore, these findings suggest that collaborative partners may have a large influence on venue choice, as individual providers often depend on these partners to let them know where the best advocacy opportunities can be found.

## Government Funding

The executive directors interviewed in this study were clear that they believed advocacy to be a crucial tool in helping to secure and maintain vital government funding. Not a single manager reported that they thought policymakers would frown upon advocacy, or that their government funding made them less likely to advocate. Instead, for organizations reliant on government funding, advocacy was seen as an important way to keep government officials connected with the activities of the organization, their successes, and their challenges. Most importantly, though, advocacy was seen as an important way of exerting some control over their finances so as to maintain consistent funding for their services. One manager noted, when asked about the primary motivation for their advocacy, "because we need the funding from the government, and so we need to reach out to those people who are in positions of power, you know, to alter that funding . . . Those are the important conversations that we have with them."

Because over 83% of respondents were at least partially funded by the government, such funding is a major incentive that is recognized by all members of the field, not just those that currently receive it. Interestingly, some of the most revealing quotes came from the directors of organizations that were entirely privately funded. Almost all of these managers reported that if they had government funding, they would probably do more advocacy, but since they do not receive government funds, they find themselves prioritizing other activities. "It's not something that we have focused on so much just because, you know, I think you'll find other providers that have a whole lot more to do with advocacy than we do just because our funding base is a little different," one manager explained. The following quote also captures this sentiment well:

> Because we are privately funded, we are in a unique situation. We do get involved, we stay informed about issues that may affect our colleagues . . . But there is a bit of a struggle internally, how much we should do for issues that do not necessarily affect us. We do think that we should be involved in staying on top of things that affect the other organizations, and in turn, some of our former or current clients. But, also, there is our day-to-day operations, and we have to keep our own doors open, so there isn't a terribly large amount of resources that is involved in policy activism.

Sometimes managers of organizations without government funding seemed to feel that policy just did not affect them in the same way as organizations receiving government funding. As one noted, "We don't take governmental monies and so we don't—I mean we can express our opinion about how we feel that the government should run human services and medical care and health plans. But I don't think we probably get as involved as we would if we were receiving government money."

Organizations primarily reliant on government funds were found to advocate more frequently, and to see advocacy as more essential. When asked why his organization had moved to doing more advocacy, one manager forthrightly replied, "Self-interest . . . We've got to prepare for the future. And in order to grow the agency, which is something that we definitely want to do." Another supported this sentiment, making it clear that their increased advocacy involvement was directly tied to their government contract: "You're going to do more advocacy if you have more government dollars, because if you've got the government dollars they're incredibly important to the service you're providing, or you wouldn't have applied for them. They're too much work in all kinds of respects to not fight to keep those dollars."

Overall, government funding served as a major incentive for advocacy. It played this role for organizations of all sizes by shifting managers' calculus about whether advocacy was something their organization should be involved in. Managers of organizations with more government funding felt they did not have the luxury of deciding whether advocacy was an important part of their organizational mission; rather, they talked about it as an important strategy for organizational survival. It also played a role in their choice of which venue to target. Because their advocacy is often focused on maintaining funding streams and relationship building with administrators, managers choose venues that support those goals, namely, administrative agencies that manage contracts and state legislatures that distribute funding.

## Professional Norms

As noted above in the section on lack of supportive or knowledgeable leadership, a subgroup of respondents in this study felt that advocacy did not always mesh with their direct service mission, which presented a major barrier for the organizations they led. It is worth noting that all of these comments were made by managers who had more experience as service providers than as professional managers. Managers with career paths that were firmly focused on nonprofit administration generally found advocacy to be more central to their organization's mission than managers without that professional education or experience. These "management professionals" articulated a different set of professional norms and beliefs than other managers. Instead of seeing advocacy as a distinct activity, separate from their services work, management professionals saw advocacy as important for promoting the organization and its agenda, and as directly connected to their larger mission. Acting on these professional norms helped their organizations overcome both capacity and leadership issues. Meanwhile, characteristics such as personal passion, increased access to policymakers, and understanding of legal issues, while mentioned, were not nearly as influential as this difference in understanding of the role of advocacy in human service nonprofits.

Examples of advocacy-related statements from management professionals include "We're really an organization that focuses on helping [clients] become independent and sustain independence, and advocacy is an instrument of that machine" and "We just feel that that's a part of our job, not only to represent [the organization], but also to be involved in establishing policy and ensuring that needs of people who were homeless or previously homeless are being met." These quotes focus on how advocacy actually promotes services for clients instead of competing with services.

Interestingly, the few managers with business backgrounds but who entered nonprofit work near retirement age, often as a result of being on a board of directors, did not share these norms. These managers were much more committed to the "service first" norms held by managers who had risen through the ranks or who had limited administrative experience outside their current organization. These "second career" managers made statements that indicated they saw nonprofit work as primarily charitable, and not to be sullied by too much interaction with the government.

Some of the management professionals actually set themselves apart from managers who did not see a connection between quality services and advocacy. They often spoke in business-like terms and focused on how advocacy is an important management tool. One such manager noted that "the other part of your mission is to say you're going to run the best business. You know, you're going to run the best administration . . . And I think not everyone does that—bridging relationships—to the degree that could manifest the success that we've had. And people ask, 'Why have you been so successful? How can you do that?' I point to our leadership and vision, and the relationship building that we've done over time. I think that's made the difference for us." From this perspective it is foolish not to be involved because, as another noted, "everything [policymakers] do, every decision they make, is going to make your job harder or easier."

These managers also tended to build infrastructure and capacity for advocacy within their organizations, which was particularly important for organizations that otherwise faced barriers to advocacy because of small size or limited budget. One manager reported, "Because we're fairly small, obviously we don't have a lot of staff. We're pretty lean actually. So we've been using interns actually to do [advocacy] and to work with our clients and to sort of get them involved. So we've been trying to tie in some of those pieces through our interns and trying to get not only the staff more involved but also board members as well as clients." Leveraging interns (to whom almost all homeless service providers have access through local schools of social work) and board members grows the resources of the organization in ways that have little impact on their ability to provide direct services.

Building infrastructure also means building an advocacy culture within the organization. An advocacy culture leads to increased capacity for advocacy, as it removes the burden from the executive director's shoulders and makes advocacy involvement less dependent on the beliefs of any individual director. Overall, while these executive directors still may do the majority of the advocacy work, they find ways to share the load. The following quote exemplifies this approach: "It's also part of the job description of every single person here, down to the part-time staff people, to be involved in the advocacy effort. Whether it be on a committee of something, or representing the agency out in the community in some way, but it's really something that we weave into everyone's role. Our direct service staff may be more involved in micro, so that's why we add policy advocacy stipulations in all of the job descriptions. We actually have two staff members in advocacy training today."

## Conclusions

This study adds to our understanding of the advocacy involvement of human service nonprofits by refocusing attention on ground-level processes and on managers' understanding of why and how advocacy should be carried out. While we have recently learned much about nonprofit advocacy involvement in a general context, research that investigates how specific barriers and incentives may interact with field-level policy and institutional contexts has been lacking. By studying a single population of organizations—homeless service nonprofits in the city of Chicago—I attempt to shed light on both the internal and external processes behind managers' decisions regarding advocacy involvement.

Three research questions are addressed. First, what activities do organizational leaders consider advocacy? This is important information for researchers, as there appears to be a mismatch between definitions used by researchers and definitions held by practitioners, which threatens construct validity in survey research. Second, what are the most serious barriers to advocacy participation? Although this question has been explored in the past, more information is needed on the primacy of specific barriers and how this may differ among policy fields. The third question receives the majority of the analytical attention: what organizational features best position organizations to overcome those barriers?

First, the findings on street-level definitions of advocacy confirm that managers often have a slightly different definition of advocacy than researchers generally do. Managers in this sample defined advocacy more broadly than most surveys, including activities that were externally focused but not policy related. At the same time, however, they were also likely to think of some advocacy tactics as simply "networking" or "education." These findings imply that researchers need to be careful when asking managers about their advocacy involvement. There may be no single best approach; depending on their research question, some researchers may want continue to use traditional definitions of advocacy, while others may wish to explore advocacy from the perspective of practitioners. The important thing is that definitional assumptions are made clear and decisions are made consciously, with full understanding of the implications for findings.

Three barriers were explored in this research: concerns about IRS regulations, limited capacity, and lack of knowledgeable, supportive leadership. Of the three, limited capacity stood out as the most severe barrier for organizations in this study. Leadership issues also were of concern. In particular, there appeared to be a subset of managers that saw advocacy as detracting from their organizations' service mission, thus making advocacy a low organizational priority. Given resource constraints, organizations with these types of managers generally advocated at low levels.

Interestingly, however, concerns about IRS regulations did not appear to be a major barrier for organizations in this study. Although many were confused about the rules governing nonprofit lobbying, that did not generally stop them. Advocacy rates were high (93%), and so were lobbying rates (50%). The organizations that lobbied were about evenly split between those that knew they were lobbying and simply did not worry about going over the stated IRS limits and those that did not call what they were doing lobbying even though it met the legal definition. None of the groups in this study opted for the 501(c)(h) election. Overall, although managers' confusion does bring up concerns about compliance with IRS regulations, in this study concern about IRS regulations was not found to be a major barrier.

Why is it, though, that some organizations overcame barriers around limited capacity and leadership while others did not? Most organizations participated in advocacy, but many only at low levels. Three organizational features were found to help organizations become more deeply involved in advocacy: participation in collaborative networks, government funding, and professional leadership.

First, between coalitions, stand-alone advocacy organizations with collaborative components and other interorganizational networks that do advocacy, homeless service organizations in Chicago have a choice of partners for their advocacy efforts, and essentially all of them do collaborate on advocacy. These networks allow organizations to "plug in" to existing structures and participate in advocacy in ways that are straightforward and require minimal outlays of time and resources. For small organizations in particular, these collaborative networks were essential for their involvement, and even for larger organizations, collaborating allowed the organization to be involved in more advanced ways. By providing structure, information about current policy, and how to get involved, as well as trainings for staff and information about venue selection, these collaborative groups greatly increased the capacity for advocacy involvement in the field and help set the stage for nonprofit advocacy to be more successful.

Next, human service managers come from a wide variety of backgrounds (Hwang and Powell, 2009; Smith, 2002). While some come from professional backgrounds and see themselves as nonprofit management professionals, many rise through the ranks and have limited administrative experience or training outside of their own organizations (Suarez, 2010). This study found that executive directors who considered themselves to be management professionals and came to their organization with administrative training or experience saw advocacy in a different light than did other managers.

Professionalized managers espoused a shared norm that advocacy is an appropriate tool to improve and grow services and did not believe that advocacy was in competition with those services. Contrary to other managers, professionalized managers saw advocacy as an essential part of their job, not as an additional task to be undertaken only in times of emergency or when time and resources allow. They believed that the political connections built through advocacy participation would create opportunities for growth and provide legitimacy; this was true even for organizations less reliant on government funding. Adoption of these professional norms helped leaders overcome limited capacity, as they simply did not view advocacy as optional. They found the time and resources to do it by employing specific management techniques to help overcome limited capacity. For example, they built strong infrastructure for advocacy throughout their agency and often encouraged a "culture" of advocacy where all staff members were encouraged to consider advocacy as part of their jobs. These strategies helped build the conditions for successful advocacy involvement in their agencies and are similar to the strategies highlighted elsewhere in this volume (see Bass et al., chap. 10, this volume).

The other organizational feature that helps organizations overcome leadership barriers is government funding. Government funding appears to incentivize advocacy in the minds of leaders, increasing the likelihood that the organization will be more deeply involved in advocacy. Managers of government-funded agencies saw advocacy as likely to have a direct payoff for the agencies' services. As a result, even managers with a service orientation regarded advocacy as more important as their government funding increased. All managers care about the bottom line. When advocacy is associated with maintaining it, as it was for agencies reliant on government funding, managers came to see advocacy as a more important part of their job.

There are limitations to this work; most notably, its generalizability is unknown. That said, these findings provide an important benchmark against which studies from other fields and other locations may be compared. Similar dynamics may exist in other fields with analogous conditions, such as high levels of government funding and interorganizational networks. Future research should also take note of the findings here regarding definitions of advocacy, especially when determining wording for surveys.

Overall, this research demonstrates that advocacy is often integrated into organizations more deeply when its professional utility is emphasized through professional norms, government funding, and strong ties to existing networks. These specific features of the organizational and institutional context—which differ among policy fields—incentivize or facilitate advocacy involvement. Interestingly, even in the field of homeless services, where beliefs about the need for social justice and wealth redistribution are common, advocacy is not generally spawned from altruistic motives; rather, it often stems from professional and managerial self-interest. Strengthening advocacy in this field and others may be better accomplished by encouraging organizations to view advocacy as a way to balance mission and resource demands (Frumkin and Andre-Clark, 2000), not as a purely mission-driven activity. Interestingly, each of the organizational features mentioned here—professionalization, reliance on government funding, and increased collaboration—are growing across the nonprofit sector. Perhaps we will see a growth of advocacy in the sector as a result.

### REFERENCES

Alexander, Jennifer, Renee Nank, and Camilla Stivers. 1999. "Implications of Welfare Reform: Do Nonprofit Survival Strategies Threaten Civil Society?" *Nonprofit and Voluntary Sector Quarterly* 28: 452–75.

Allard, Scott W. 2009. *Out of Reach: Place, Poverty, and the New American Welfare State*. New Haven, CT: Yale University Press.

Andrews, Kenneth T., and Bob Edwards. 2004. "Advocacy Organizations in the U.S. Political Process." *Annual Review of Sociology* 30: 479–506.

Bass, Gary D., David F. Arons, K. Guinane, and Matthew F. Carter. 2007. *Seen but Not Heard: Strengthening Nonprofit Advocacy*. Washington, DC: Aspen Institute.

Berry, Jeffrey M., and David F. Arons. 2003. *A Voice for Nonprofits*. Washington, DC: Brookings Institution Press.

Chaves, Mark, Laura Stephens, and Joseph Galaskiewicz. 2004. "Does Government Funding Suppress Nonprofits' Political Activity?" *American Sociological Review* 69: 292–316.

Child, Curtis D., and Kirsten A. Grønbjerg. 2007. "Nonprofit Advocacy Organizations: Their Characteristics and Activities." *Social Science Quarterly* 88: 259–81.

Donaldson, Linda Plitt, and Joseph Shields. 2009. "Development of the Policy Advocacy Behavior Scale: Initial Reliability and Validity." *Research on Social Work Practice* 19: 83–92.

Fligstein, Neil. 1990. *The Transformation of Corporate Control*. Cambridge, MA: Harvard University Press.

Frumkin, Peter, and Alice Andre-Clark. 2000. "When Missions, Markets, and Politics Collide: Values and Strategy in the Nonprofit Human Services." *Nonprofit and Voluntary Sector Quarterly* 29: 141–63.

Galaskiewicz, Joseph. 1985. "Interorganizational Relations." *Annual Review of Sociology* 11: 281–304.

Guo, Chao, and Muhittin Acar. 2005. "Understanding Collaboration among Nonprofit Organizations: Combining Resource Dependency, Institutional, and Network Perspectives." *Nonprofit and Voluntary Sector Quarterly* 34: 340–61.

Hasenfeld, Yeheskel. 1992. "The Nature of Human Service Organizations." In *Human Services as Complex Organizations*, edited by Y. Hasenfeld, 3–23. Newbury Park, CA: Sage.

Hojnacki, Marie. 1997. "Interest Groups' Decisions to Join Alliances or Work Alone." *American Journal of Political Science* 41: 61–87.

Hwang, Hokyu, and Walter W. Powell. 2009. "The Rationalization of Charity: The Influences of Professionalism in the Nonprofit Sector." *Administrative Science Quarterly* 54: 268–98.

Meyer, David S., and Debra C. Minkoff. 2004. "Conceptualizing Political Opportunity." *Social Forces* 82: 1457–92.

Miles, Matthew B., and Michael Huberman. 1994. *Qualitative Data Analysis: An Expanded Sourcebook*. Thousand Oaks, CA: Sage.

Mosley, Jennifer E. 2009. "Institutionalization, Privatization, and Political Opportunity: What Tactical Choices Reveal about the Policy Advocacy of Human Service Nonprofits." *Nonprofit and Voluntary Sector Quarterly* 40: 435–57.

———. 2010. "Organizational Resources and Environmental Incentives: Understanding the Policy Advocacy Involvement of Human Service Nonprofits." *Social Service Review* 84: 57–76.

Nicholson-Crotty, Jill. 2007. "Politics, Policy and the Motivations for Advocacy in Nonprofit Reproductive Health and Family Planning Providers." *Nonprofit and Voluntary Sector Quarterly* 36: 5–21.

———. 2009. "The Stages and Strategies of Advocacy among Nonprofit Reproductive Health Providers." *Nonprofit and Voluntary Sector Quarterly* 38: 1044–53.

Patton, Michael Quinn. 2002. *Qualitative Research and Evaluation Methods*. Thousand Oaks, CA: Sage.

Salamon, Lester M. 1987. "Partners in Public Service: The Scope and Theory of

Government-Nonprofit Relations." in *The Nonprofit Sector: A Research Handbook*, edited by W. W. Powell, 99–117. New Haven, CT: Yale University Press.

Salamon, Lester M., and Stephanie Lessans Geller with Susan C. Lorentz. 2008. "Nonprofit America: A Force for Democracy?" Listening Post Project Communique No. 9, Center for Civil Society Studies, Johns Hopkins University, Baltimore. http://ccss.jhu.edu/wp-content/uploads/downloads/2011/09/LP_Communique9_2008.pdf.

Schmid, Hillel, Michal Bar, and Ronit Nirel. 2008. "Advocacy Activities in Nonprofit Human Service Organizations: Implications for Policy." *Nonprofit and Voluntary Sector Quarterly* 37: 581–602.

Schneider, Robert L., and Lori Lester. 2001. *Social Work Advocacy: A New Framework for Action*. Belmont, CA: Brooks/Cole.

Smith, Steven Rathgeb. 2002. "Social Services." In *The State of Nonprofit America*, edited by L. M. Salamon, 149–86. Washington, DC: Brookings Institution Press.

Smith, Steven Rathgeb, and Michael Lipsky. 1993. *Nonprofits for Hire: The Welfare State in the Age of Contracting*. Cambridge, MA: Harvard University Press.

Stone, Melissa M., and Jodi R. Sandfort. 2009. "Building a Policy Fields Framework to Inform Research on Nonprofit Organizations." *Nonprofit and Voluntary Sector Quarterly* 38: 1054–75.

Suarez, David F. 2010. "Street Credentials and Management Backgrounds: Careers of Nonprofit Executives in an Evolving Sector." *Nonprofit and Voluntary Sector Quarterly* 39: 696–716.

# PART TWO

# ORGANIZATIONAL POLITICS, STRATEGY, AND TACTICS

# CHAPTER SIX

# Advocacy in Hard Times

Nonprofit Organizations and the Representation of Marginalized
Groups in the Wake of Hurricane Katrina and 9/11

DARA Z. STROLOVITCH

What are the effects of national crises on nonprofit advocacy, particularly
when it comes to organizations that represent marginalized and underrepresented groups in national politics? Following the 2001 attacks on the World
Trade Center and the Pentagon, the American political landscape has been
influenced by the convergence of a range of "national crises," including the
wars in Iraq and Afghanistan, continued threats of terrorist violence, the
destruction wrought by Hurricane Katrina, and the mortgage and financial
crises.[1] While the convergence of these phenomena has changed American
politics, this terrain continues to be shaped by perennial challenges, among
them enduring racial, gender, and economic inequalities. This chapter ana-
lyzes the intersections between these persistent inequalities on the one hand
and episodic crises on the other, examining their implications for nonprofit
organizations' advocacy on behalf of marginalized groups. Combining original quantitative and qualitative data, I argue that crises present advocacy
organizations with a combination of constraints and opportunities when
it comes to addressing the enduring issues affecting their constituents. In
particular, comparing the responses of organizations to 9/11 and Hurricane
Katrina reveals that each of these two calamitous events has had different repercussions for liberal and conservative advocacy groups. These differences
can tell us a great deal about the political opportunities and policy windows
for nonprofit advocacy on behalf of groups for whom times are "always hard."

## Nonprofit Advocacy in (Pretty) Good Times

Nonprofit organizations, interest groups, and advocacy organizations are crucial conduits for the articulation and representation of the legal, political, and
policy interests of groups such as women, people of color, and low-income

people, who have traditionally been underserved by the two major political parties and underrepresented within the electoral system (Bass et al., 2007; Berry and Arons, 2003; Boris, 1999; Boris and Krehely, 2002; Boris and Mosher-Williams, 1998; Costain, 2005; Dahl, 1967; Frymer, 1999; Heaney, 2004; Minkoff, 1994, 1995; Weldon, 2002, 2011). Organizations advocating on behalf of marginalized groups were once outnumbered, out-resourced, and out-influenced by organizations such as business and professional associations that spoke for more powerful and all-too-often anti-egalitarian interests (Schattschneider [1960] 1975, 35). By 2000, however, there were more than 700 organizations representing women, people of color, and low-income people in national politics, encompassing more than 40 African American organizations, more than 30 Asian Pacific American organizations, and well over 100 women's organizations (Strolovitch, 2007). These organizations continue to make up only a small portion of the broader interest group universe that counts more than 17,000 national organizations representing much wealthier and more powerful interests. Nonetheless, groups like the National Association for Advancement of Colored People, the National Organization for Women, the Center for Law and Social Policy, the National Council of La Raza, and the National Asian Pacific American Law Center have become a significant and visible presence in Washington politics, and many argue that these organizations are among the most important representatives of and advocates for marginalized groups in the United States.

Although the increase in the number of organizations has helped usher in significant legal and policy gains for these and other marginalized groups, the extent to which their promise to equalize the representational playing field has been fulfilled remains the source of much debate. And while scholars continue to echo the long-standing concerns of scholars such as E. E. Schattschneider, who were concerned with biases within the broader pressure group system that favored wealthy and powerful interests, some also express concerns about the development of biases within organizations claiming to represent marginalized populations (Berry, 1999; Hamilton and Hamilton, 1992; Skocpol, 2003; Strolovitch, 2007). Observers allege, for example, that civil rights organizations focus mainly on "middle-class" issues, that feminism is a movement of and for affluent white women, and that economic justice groups marginalize low-income women and people of color (Hamilton and Hamilton, 1992).

My 2007 book *Affirmative Advocacy* took these debates and allegations as its point of departure. In it, I explored how advocacy organizations decide which battles to prioritize in an era marked by subsiding de jure discrimination but often heightened de facto inequalities, both *between* their marginalized constituencies on the one hand and dominant racial, gender, and income groups on the other, as well as *within* the marginalized populations they claim to represent. Faced with limited resources but encompassing large and internally complex constituencies, how do advocacy organizations decide which groups and subgroups warrant the most attention?

To answer these questions, I explored the issues addressed by organizations that represent marginalized populations in American politics. In particular, I examined to what degree and in what ways organizations claiming to speak for marginalized groups attend to the particular challenges associated with advocating on behalf of disadvantaged subgroups of their own marginalized constituencies—what scholars have come to call "intersectionally disadvantaged" groups (Crenshaw, 1989; see also Collins, 1990; Davis, 1981; hooks, 1981, among others). Intersectional frameworks contend that economic and social injustices are not mutually exclusive and that no particular form of domination or social relation—be it race, class, patriarchy, or heteronomativity—is the primary source of oppression (Kurtz, 2002, 38).[2] As I explained in *Affirmative Advocacy*, while recognizing that important inequalities persist *among* racial, gender, or economic groups, intersectional approaches highlight the ways in which social and political forces manipulate the overlapping and intersecting inequalities *within* marginalized groups. These approaches also emphasize the consequent unevenness in the effects of the political, economic, and social gains made by marginalized groups since, and as a result of, the social movements and policy gains of the 1960s and 1970s (McCall, 2013; Strolovitch 2007, 22–28).

Using this intersectional approach, in the summer of 2000, I fielded the Survey of National Economic and Social Justice Organizations, in which respondents were asked a series of questions about the levels and targets of their advocacy activities on four domestic policy issues. The four issues were assigned to different types of organizations based on a four-part policy typology that I created to operationalize key aspects of intersectional theories about power and marginalization and to test them against competing explanations (fig. 6.1): (1) universal issues that affect, at least in theory, the population as a whole regardless of race, gender, sexual orientation, disability, class, or any other identity; (2) majority issues that affect an organization's members or constituents relatively equally; (3) disadvantaged subgroup issues that affect an intersectionally marginalized subgroup of an organization's constituents

|  | Affects Subgroup | Affects Majority of Group |
|---|---|---|
| Low Power | Disadvantaged Subgroup Issue | Majority Issue |
| High Power | Advantaged Subgroup Issue | |
| | Universal Issue | |

*Figure 6.1.* Policy typology. Source: *Affirmative Advocacy* (Strolovitch, 2007)

(i.e., it is disadvantaged economically, socially, or politically compared to the broader constituency); and (4) advantaged subgroup issues that also affect a subgroup of an organization's constituents, but a relatively advantaged or privileged subgroup compared to the broader constituency (though they are nonetheless disadvantaged compared to the general population).

For example, I asked respondents from women's organizations about their advocacy efforts regarding violence against women (VAW) as a majority issue, as all women are, theoretically, equally likely to be victims of gender-related violence, even if not every women is in fact a victim in her lifetime. I asked them about affirmative action in higher education as an advantaged subgroup issue because this issue primarily affects college-educated women, a relatively privileged subgroup of all women. Finally, I asked these same respondents about welfare reform as a disadvantaged subgroup issue, as it intersects gender and class and affects low-income women, an intersectionally disadvantaged subgroup of women. All organizations in the study were asked about Social Security as a "universal" issue.[3] Based on this typology, respondents from different kinds of organizations were asked a series of questions, including one that asked them to estimate the proportion of their constituency that was affected by each of four designated policy issues, and another that asked how active, on a scale of 1 to 5, their organization had been on each issue between 1990 and 2000.

Table 6.1 shows the percentage of organizations that were active and inactive on each issue type, as well as the mean levels of activity on each one

TABLE 6.1.

Mean Level of Activity and Percent of Organizations Active on Each Issue Category, by Type of Organization

| Organization Type | Majority Issue | | Advantaged Subgroup Issue | | Disadvantaged Subgroup Issue | | Universal Issue | |
|---|---|---|---|---|---|---|---|---|
| | Mean | % | Mean | % | Mean | % | Mean | % |
| Asian Pacific American | 3.7 | 76.9 | 3.0 | 84.6 | 2.4 | 69.2 | 1.6 | 30.8 |
| Black/African American | 4.1 | 85.0 | 4.5 | 90.0 | 3.7 | 90.0 | 2.1 | 45.0 |
| Latino/Hispanic | 4.6 | 100.0 | 4.3 | 100.0 | 2.9 | 62.5 | 2.1 | 50.0 |
| Native American/ American Indian | 4.0 | 100.0 | 3.8 | 69.2 | 2.9 | 69.2 | 1.7 | 15.4 |
| Civil rights (other)[a] | 3.3 | 74.4 | 2.9 | 64.1 | 2.7 | 64.1 | 1.6 | 23.1 |
| Labor[b] | 3.8 | 78.6 | 4.0 | 78.6 | 3.5 | 71.4 | 2.9 | 54.8 |
| Economic justice[c] | 3.4 | 69.7 | 3.4 | 71.2 | 1.2 | 12.1 | 1.9 | 30.3 |
| Public interest[d] | 3.3 | 72.7 | 2.4 | 45.5 | 2.1 | 63.6 | 1.8 | 27.4 |
| Women's rights/ feminist[e] | 3.6 | 84.8 | 3.4 | 77.3 | 2.9 | 65.2 | 2.1 | 39.4 |

Source: Survey of National Economic and Social Justice Organizations; see Strolovitch (2007) for details

Organization officers were asked, "Please tell me, on a scale of 1 to 5, where 1 is not active, and 5 is very active, how active has your organization been on each of the following policy issues in the past ten years?" Note that data reflect the percentage of respondents giving answers between 2 and 5.

[a] Includes broadly based civil rights and civil liberties organizations; lesbian, gay, bisexual, and transgender (LGBT) rights organizations; criminal justice organizations; Arab/Muslim organizations; antiracist organizations; some religious minority groups; and multiculturalism organizations. Also includes immigrants' rights organizations.

[b] Includes unions.

[c] Includes antipoverty, welfare rights, antihomeless, and antihunger organizations.

[d] Includes consumer, environmental, and "good government" organizations that advocate in the areas of racial, gender, or economic justice.

[e] Includes women of color, reproductive rights, and women's health organizations.

(based on the 1–5 scale of activity). The data show that the advocacy organizations in the study were involved in many of the issues about which they were asked, thereby confirming that advocacy groups are a critical source of compensatory representation for marginalized groups. But variations in their patterns of involvement also show that they give short shrift to issues that affect intersectionally disadvantaged subgroups of their constituencies, devoting considerably *less* attention to issues affecting such constituents than to issues affecting more advantaged ones.

In the case of women's groups, for example, approximately 85% of the responding organizations were active on the majority issue, VAW. Slightly fewer, about 77%, were active on affirmative action in higher education, an issue affecting an advantaged subgroup of women. But a significant but far smaller proportion of these organizations—just over 65%—were at all active on welfare reform, an issue affecting a disadvantaged subgroup of women.

Figure 6.2 illustrates the effects of these disparities. Probabilities of activity that simulate the contingent effects of the proportion of affected constituents as they vary by policy type (while holding the values of all variables at their means) show that there is a 23.3% chance that an organization will be very active (4 or 5 on the 1–5 scale of activity) on a majority issue with a low level of impact on an organization's constituents (1 on the 1–5 scale of impact). This probability increases to 78.8% in the case of a majority issue with a high level of impact (5 on the 1–5 scale of impact). In the case of disadvantaged subgroup issues, the chances of a high level of activity increase from 14.6% to 45.6% as we move from low to high levels of impact. The simulation also demonstrates, however, that levels of activity for advantaged subgroup issues are likely to be very high (62.8% chance of a high level of activity), even when impact is at its lowest level. Moreover, the probability of a high level of activity on an advantaged subgroup issue increases much less starkly (to 78%) as we move from low to high levels of impact. In fact, the probability that an organization will be active at a high level is greater in the case of an advantaged subgroup issue with a very low level of impact on its constituents than it is for a disadvantaged subgroup issue that affects "almost all" of its constituents.

Together, the analyses in *Affirmative Advocacy* revealed what I characterize as a double standard on the part of advocacy organizations that represent women, people of color, and low-income people in US politics—a double standard in which issues affecting advantaged subgroups receive more attention than disadvantaged subgroup issues and more attention than even majority issues. Moreover, while activity on both majority and disadvantaged subgroup issues is sensitive to levels of impact, levels of activity on advantaged subgroup issues do *not* increase or decrease as the proportion of constituents affected by an issue increases, suggesting that these issues are almost immune to strategic considerations about breadth of impact. Instead, under some circumstances, the broader the potential impact of an issue, the *less* attention it receives.

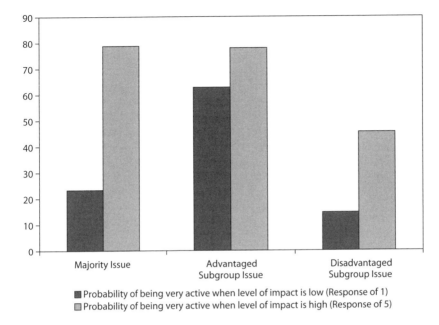

*Figure 6.2.* Predicted probability of activity and inactivity by issue type and level of impact (membership organizations only). Note that organization officers were asked, "Pease tell me, on a scale of 1 to 5, where 1 is not active, and 5 is very active, how active has your organization been on each of the following policy issues in the past ten years?" The black columns reflect the probability of giving a rating of 4 or 5 (holding the other variables in the model constant) when they judge the level of impact on their constituency to be low (1). The shaded columns reflect the probability of giving a rating of 4 or 5 (holding the other variables in the model constant) when they judge the level of impact on their constituency to be high (5). Source: Survey of National Social and Economic Justice Organizations

## Nonprofit Advocacy in Not-So-Good Times

Such evidence of inequalities in representation even among those organizations most concerned with advocating on behalf of marginalized groups is particularly sobering in light of the fact that it is based on data that tracked policy advocacy between 1990–2000, when times were, by many accounts, relatively good. Though the survey and interview questions asked respondents to reflect upon their organizations' activities and priorities going back to 1990—an era that encompassed, among other things, an economic recession and Operation Desert Storm—the period under examination in *Affirmative Advocacy* was one that has come to be considered a decade of relative "peace and prosperity." In addition, while Republicans held the presidency until 1993 and all or some of Congress at various points during the same period, 1992–2000 was dominated by a Democratic administration that is typically portrayed as having been relatively sympathetic to marginalized groups, and the Democrats controlled the House of Representatives and Senate for four years (1990–94). While that era was by no means a utopian one for marginalized groups—characterized as it was by widening wealth and income gaps (Bartels, 2008; Hacker and Pierson, 2010), welfare reform legislation, Don't Ask, Don't Tell military policy, immigration reform, the Defense of Marriage Act, and the Omnibus crime bill—it is normally remembered as having been markedly untumultuous (Robin, 2004).

All that would change as I was analyzing and grappling with the results of this research. I fielded the survey of organizations in the summer and fall of 2000, completing it just a few days after the 2000 election. I then conducted face-to-face interviews during the spring and summer of 2001, completing the last one in mid-August, a month before the events of September 11, 2001. Working on *Affirmative Advocacy* in the wake of 9/11 consequently highlighted important questions about the political effects of catastrophic events, and led me to contemplate the implications of crisis for the questions I was trying to address about representation and intersectional marginalization.

Even during the ostensibly peaceful and prosperous 1990s, respondents had claimed that, as organizations and movements speaking on behalf of weak, minority, and marginalized groups, they first needed to secure their place at the political table before they could be expected to pay attention to "narrow" issues affecting their intersectionally marginalized constituents. Framing such issues as narrow and particularistic "special" interests allowed them to justify both their lack of attention to them as well as their extensive attention to issues affecting advantaged subgroups. Others argued that the concerns of intersectionally marginalized subgroups were not central to their organization's mission, and that other groups were therefore better suited to address them. Still others claimed that the crosscutting issues of race, class, gender, or sexuality would be taken care of by whatever the organization in question considered the more "fundamental" issue. Most centrally, when I probed respondents about their organizations' lack of attention to issues affecting intersectionally disadvantaged subgroups of their constituencies, they often gave answers such as that "the time wasn't right" to address such concerns because resources were scarce, that there were "bigger issues" at stake, or that such issues were divisive in ways that threatened their ability to present a united front to dominant groups (Strolovitch, 2007).

## Crises, Marginalization, and Nonprofit Advocacy

That these responses justifying meager representation for intersectionally marginalized groups were articulated during what are more often than not characterized as relatively good times led me to contemplate what we might expect during the "hard times" that followed 9/11, when the pressure to fight for "the common good" that so often leads to the marginalization of disadvantaged groups intensified almost instantly. While 9/11 undoubtedly and unalterably changed the political terrain, the issues at the core of *Affirmative Advocacy* were not unique to the 1990s. Rather, these issues are related to enduring and deeply embedded structural inequalities and consequently serve to underscore, as Gretchen Ritter writes, the coexistence of order and continuity with "political disorder, disequilibrium, punctuation, and transformation" (Ritter, 2007, 388; see also Jacobs and King, 2009; Strach and Sapiro, 2011). Contemplating organizations' responses from this perspective leads to a second question: How would nonprofit organizations that represent groups for whom times are "always hard" respond to and be affected by the nexus of crises in the midst of the persistent and quotidian inequalities that impact their constituents?[4] To paraphrase an often-invoked expression about people of color in the United States, when America catches a cold, do nonprofits that advocate on behalf of marginalized groups get political pneumonia?

At first blush, the answer to this question would seem to be yes. Although rising tides do not lift all boats, tempests and waning tides do seem to ground smaller ones more violently. Almost by definition, for example, lower-income people are likely to suffer more acutely during economic and financial crises, and because of racial and gender disparities in income and wealth, the effects of economic crises also disproportionately disadvantage blacks, Latinos, and women of all races and ethnicities. At the height of the Great Depression, for example, one quarter of American workers were unemployed, but the rate was double—50%—for blacks (Sundstrom, 1992; see also Strolovitch, 2004, 2013). Analogous disparities were evident in the Great Recession of 2007–9. In 2009, rates of black unemployment in the 15 largest metropolitan areas in the United States were on average seven percentage points higher than rates for whites, with differences as high as 13.8% in Minneapolis-St. Paul (where white unemployment was 6.6% and black unemployment 20.4%) and 10.5%

in Memphis, Tennessee (where white unemployment was 5.1% and black unemployment 15.7%; Austin, 2010).

Crises cut in multiple directions, however, and a great deal of research suggests that, although difficult to disentangle, the political effects of crises may not mirror their material impact. In particular, even if a population group suffers during or as a consequence of a recession, natural disaster, or health pandemic, the organizations that advocate on its behalf might "benefit" through increased visibility, media attention, or donations.[5] A comparison of fundraising by nonprofits in 2009 and 2010 by the Nonprofit Research Collaborative (NRC) found that although 37% reported declines in donations during this recessionary period, a similar proportion (36%) reported increases (NRC, 2010, 32).[6] Similarly, while material conditions might worsen, events such as wars and economic crises might also open what John Kingdon (1995) calls "policy windows" or improve conditions within what social movement scholars label the "political opportunity structure" (Eisinger, 1973; Meyer, 1993a, 1993b). Public sympathy for the poor often increases during recessions, for example (Gilens, 1999; McCall, 2013), and while the Great Depression took a greater toll on already disadvantaged groups, welfare state advocates advanced redistributive policies that they had failed to secure in more prosperous times (Goldfield, 1989; Piven and Cloward, 1977; Skocpol, 1992). Scholars such as Mary Dudziak (2000), Mark Graber (1995), Philip Klinkner and Rogers Smith (1999), and Daniel Kryder (2001) have shown that equality for African Americans has advanced most dramatically during times of war.[7] While women's suffrage faced setbacks during the Civil War and World War I, President Wilson eventually "announced that women's suffrage was urgently needed as a 'war measure,'" and his support for the Nineteenth Amendment was in part a reward to women for their contributions to the war effort (Mayhew, 2005; see also Flexner and Fitzpatrick, 1996; Ritter, 2006).[8] Crises such as wars can also have indirect benefits for nonprofits by stimulating civic engagement (Skocpol, 2002).[9] Suzanne Mettler (2007) and Christopher Parker (2009) have found that wartime military service cultivated a lasting sense of entitlement to full citizenship rights on the political participation on the part of black men.

In contrast to evidence suggesting that crises can have silver linings for nonprofit advocacy, other research finds that they can also bring political constraints, challenges, and setbacks for nonprofits associated with movements seeking expanded civil rights or broad social and political change. Historian Robert Caro told President Barack Obama that the main lesson of the Vietnam War and the Johnson administration is that wars kill movements for domestic reform (Sanger, 2009, 448). During the Civil War and World War I, for example, women's suffrage organizations were attacked as selfish and unpatriotic for not focusing on the war effort (Banaszak, 1996). In the days following 9/11, Northwest Airlines (NWA), facing lost income like almost all airlines at the time but also confronting impending negotiations with its unions, invoked wartime powers to override protections against layoffs and announced that it would cut about 10,000 jobs to make up for financial losses it attributed to the terrorist attacks. The proposed cuts prompted talk of a strike by several NWA unions, which the airline rebuffed, alleging that a strike would be unpatriotic (Kennedy and Phelps, 2001).

## Data and Methods

The foregoing bodies of scholarship have taught us a great deal about the implications of particular crises for particular groups or for specific policy areas, but they also lead to conflicting expectations about the more general implications of crises for nonprofit organizations that advocate on behalf of marginalized groups. Viewed through some lenses, crises would seem to present these organizations with distinct, albeit constrained, opportunities to advance their legal, political, and policy goals. Thinking about crises as policy windows, for example, leads to potentially sanguine assessments of the possibilities that change can take place during "states of exception" (Agamben, 2005). But other work suggests that crises also redirect resources and produce calls for austerity and national unity, closing policy windows, restricting political opportunities, and making some kinds of advocacy more difficult.

To shed light on the conflicting expectations that arise from extant research, I compare the implications of two starkly different crises—9/11 and Hurricane Katrina—for several aspects of the work done by an array of advocacy organizations. To do so, I use data from "Public Interest Organizations in the New Millennium" (PIONM), a survey of 626 advocacy organizations that I conducted in 2007 (table 6.2).[10] The survey follows Robert J. Pekkanen and Steven Rathgeb Smith's definition of nonprofit advocacy as "the attempt to influence public policy, either directly or indirectly," which is articulated in their introduction to this volume. To make sure that all responding organizations engage in advocacy according to this definition, the survey opens with the screening question, "On a scale of 1 to 5, if 1 is 'not important' and 5

TABLE 6.2.
Distribution of Organizations in Public Interest Organizations in the
New Millennium, 2007

| Organization Type | Frequency | % |
| --- | --- | --- |
| AIDS/HIV | 14 | 2.2 |
| Arab/Muslim | 6 | 1 |
| Asian American | 15 | 2.4 |
| Black/African American | 15 | 2.4 |
| Civil liberties | 15 | 2.4 |
| Civil rights (general) | 35 | 5.6 |
| Conservative (general) | 56 | 8.9 |
| Criminal justice/anti–death penalty | 10 | 1.6 |
| Disabled | 16 | 2.6 |
| Environment/ecology/animal rights | 48 | 7.7 |
| Farm/migrant workers | 11 | 1.8 |
| Health care | 4 | 0.6 |
| Immigration | 10 | 1.6 |
| Labor organization or union | 78 | 12.5 |
| Latino/Hispanic | 14 | 2.2 |
| LGBT/Queer | 14 | 2.2 |
| Native American/American Indian | 21 | 3.4 |
| Peace/antimilitarism/antinuclear | 13 | 2.1 |
| Poverty and social justice[a] | 80 | 12.8 |
| Progressive social change (general) | 13 | 2.1 |
| Public interest | 13 | 2.1 |
| Right to life/anti-abortion | 14 | 2.2 |
| Senior citizens | 7 | 1.1 |
| Women of color | 10 | 1.6 |
| Women's health/reproductive rights | 28 | 4.5 |
| Women's rights/feminist (general) | 66 | 10.5 |
| Total | 626 | 100.1 |

[a]Includes welfare rights and homelessness organizations.

is 'very important,' how important is influencing national public policy as a part of your organization's mandate and activities?" PIONM targeted liberal and conservative organizations, and contained general questions about organizations' constituencies, governance, and funding, as well as more specific questions that asked respondents about changes in their organizations' advocacy targets and policy agendas over time and about the effects of the attacks of 9/11 and Hurricane Katrina on several dimensions of their organizations' work.[11] To explore these issues in more depth, and to begin to examine the effects of the Great Recession, I also conducted face-to-face interviews with officials at 45 organizations in 2006, 2007, and 2010.

In what follows I use the information from these two studies to investigate the political effects of crises on political opportunity and policy windows for nonprofit organizations, particularly for organizations that advocate on behalf of marginalized groups. To ascertain whether 9/11 and Hurricane Katrina had differing implications for different kinds of organizations, the responses of liberal organizations are compared with those of conservative groups (based on their self-placement on a 1–10 scale of ideology, where 1 is very conservative and 10 is very liberal). By almost every measure, there are significant differences between the perceived effects of each crisis on liberal groups compared to their conservative counterparts. Taken together, these differences begin to make sense of the conflicting expectations suggested by extant research about the implications of crises for nonprofit advocacy.

## Policy Windows and Political Opportunity after 9/11 and Hurricane Katrina

In his classic book about agenda setting and public policy, John Kingdon (1995) defines policy windows as "opportunities for action on given initiatives" (166). Although crises do not *guarantee* policy change, they are, in many ways, prototypical focusing events that precipitate the opening of policy windows (Solecki and Michael, 1994; see also Baumgartner and Jones, 1993). David Mayhew (2005) has argued that one kind of crisis—war—is "the ultimate 'policy window,' during which favorable political environment comes together with a perceived public "problem" to make policy change possible" (47). More generally, crises might structure political opportunity by encouraging or discouraging mobilization or membership, rendering the public more or less sympathetic to a group's issues and policy goals, and increasing or decreasing access to elected officials (Meyer and Minkoff, 2004). But one organization's policy window opening can be another organization's policy window closing. In this light, the extent to which crises shift political opportunities is likely to vary dramatically among types of organizations.

Extant research also suggests that the resulting variation in policy windows will have significant consequences for policy outcomes. Recessions might open doors for antipoverty advocates, for example, but might also lead to deprioritizing "quality-of-life" issues such as civil rights (Berry, 1999; Inglehart, 1971). Although women's and civil rights organizations fought for and supported the New Deal, for instance, many of its redistributive policies discriminated against black men and women as well as against women of all races. Similarly, a crisis might expand political opportunities in some venues while simultaneously narrowing them in others. Although opportunities may expand in terms of favorable public opinion, they may nonetheless contract when it comes to government attention.

To explore whether, to what extent, and in what ways 9/11 and Hurricane Katrina altered the political terrain for different kinds of nonprofit advocates, respondents were asked about the impact of each crisis on four elements of the political opportunity structure. The first question draws on the insights of a growing body of research about "threat as a motivator," which shows that membership in advocacy organizations often rises in the context of political climates perceived as adverse by their constituents (Huddy et al., 2007; Miller and Krosnick, 2004). Increases or decreases in membership and donations can have significant implications for organizations' capacities to engage in advocacy activities and to make claims as representatives. To assess what this might mean for nonprofit advocacy on behalf of disadvantaged groups after 9/11 and Hurricane Katrina, respondents were asked whether each of these two events led to increases in their membership or donors.

Rises or declines in membership in the wake of a crisis are related to increases and decreases in media sympathy for and public attention to the issues addressed by an organization. I examine these two dimensions of political opportunity using respondents' answers to questions about changes in their perceptions regarding media coverage of and public attention to and support for their issues. I then analyze their answers to questions about the changing level of government attention to their issues. To examine the cumulative effects of these factors on the policy windows available to advocacy groups, respondents were asked whether their policy goals became easier or harder to pursue between 2000 and 2006.

## Donors and Members

Responses to the foregoing questions are presented in table 6.3, and together they begin to sketch the contours of the differential effects of each crisis, as these vary along ideological lines. First, the data show that conservative groups are more likely than liberal ones to report that 9/11 led to increased donations and membership growth, while they report that Hurricane Katrina had much less of an effect on this front. Liberal groups reported that the two events had similar effects on their donations and membership, with 12.5% of these organizations saying that 9/11 led to increased members and 14% reporting that Hurricane Katrina did. Although this is an admittedly

TABLE 6.3.
Indicators of Changes in Political Opportunity

| | 9/11 | | Hurricane Katrina | |
| --- | --- | --- | --- | --- |
| | Conservative (%) | Liberal (%) | Conservative (%) | Liberal (%) |
| Increased members or donors | 18.0 | 12.5 | 4.9 | 14.0 |
| Decreased public attention | 17 | 28.5 | 21.3 | 10.9 |
| Increased public attention | 48.9 | 36.7 | 29.8 | 54.4 |
| Decreased public support | 15.2 | 28.5 | 13.1 | 12.4 |
| Increased public support | 32.6 | 28.4 | 19.6 | 45.1 |
| Decreased government attention | 17 | 30.7 | 17 | 17 |
| Increased government attention | 34 | 26.8 | 14.9 | 32.8 |
| Led organization to change mandate/ shift issues | 13.1 | 20.1 | 4.9 | 21.2 |

Source: Public Interest Organizations in the New Millennium, 2007

incomplete measure of resources, increased membership and donations are key indicators of support for and resources available to an organization, as well as indirect indicators of the salience of the issues with which they are associated among members of the public. As such, the patterns of increases in members and donors are quite telling, suggesting that the two crises raised the salience of different issues that resonated in particular ways with different constituencies. More specifically, that 9/11 led to a much larger uptick in support for conservative groups than for liberal groups suggests that the attacks raised the salience of policy issues such as national security and law and order that are more likely to be on the agendas of conservative groups, while the policy issues associated with Hurricane Katrina failed to resonate to the same degree among the conservative groups. The executive director of a conservative organization told me that 9/11 "kind of gave us an issue that's always been percolating below the surface, but 9/11 really brought it out." Before 9/11, he said, "Americans thought of terrorism as something distant. That's what happens in London, Madrid, Spain." More importantly, these concerns have perhaps, in his opinion, "spilled over into the immigration debate, securing our borders. Because it's not just securing our borders for people who are getting here legally and who want to work, but people getting into here legally who want to hurt us . . . So I think that goes over well with our donor base."[12]

While 9/11 and Hurricane Katrina each resonated in different ways among conservative groups, respondents from liberal organizations reported that the two catastrophic events had similar effects on membership in and donations to their organizations. Although neither crisis led to as large of an increase for liberal groups as 9/11 did for conservative ones, 9/11 seems to have raised the salience of civil liberties issues among liberals. Hurricane Katrina, on the other hand, raised issues of racialized poverty and government neglect in particularly salient ways for the constituents of liberal organizations. As such, it is understandable that 9/11 was associated with increased members and donors for both liberal and conservative groups while Hurricane Katrina stimulated increases primarily among liberal organizations.

Evidence from the face-to-face interviews I conducted with advocacy group officers suggests that because of the complicated politics associated with civil liberties during times of war, the opportunities presented by 9/11 for growth among liberal organizations were fraught. Even after 9/11, a majority of Americans remained unwilling to give the federal government a blank check when it came to limiting civil liberties to fight terrorism. However, a greater-than-usual proportion of the population was willing to tolerate certain restrictions that had been controversial before the attacks (Berinsky, 2009; Merolla and Zechmeister, 2009). Many liberal advocacy organizations found themselves trying to navigate demands from their long-standing members that they take firm stands against any and all threats to civil liberties, while at the same time trying to appeal to potential members who might be newly concerned about possible subversions of freedom, but who also felt threatened by the possibility of further attacks. As one interviewee from a civil liberties group put it, "bring the Patriot Act back in line with the Constitution" is a message that "sells with Middle America." The challenge, however, was that this position was not "strong enough" for the group's "most hard-core supporters," who, he argued, wanted the organization "to say 'repeal, repeal, repeal.'" But taking this position, he said, "gets us nobody. The people already believe us and love it, and we don't grow by a person."[13]

To illustrate his point, the respondent recounted what happened when he was on a panel soon after the USA PATRIOT (Uniting and Strengthening America by Providing Appropriate Tools Required to Intercept and Obstruct Terrorism) Act was passed. After concluding his remarks, a panelist representing another civil liberties organization said, "I like a lot of what [he] said." The respondent told me that as his co-panelist was saying this, he was thinking, "Here comes the 'but,'" and that he cringed as his co-panelist went on to say, "But I don't know why they're not talking about creeping fascism." "I'm sorry?," said my interlocutor, "Not only did we just lose middle America, we just lost Stockton. We can't even get out of the Bay Area." I explore in further detail below the implications of this and related tightropes that organizations often find themselves walking.

## Media Sympathy and Public Attention and Support

Increasing membership is one indicator of changing political fortunes; two other important dimensions of political opportunity concern how attentive and sympathetic the media and the public are to the issues advocacy organizations address. The differences between liberal and conservative organizations' answers to questions about these issues are telling. For example, respondents from liberal organizations were more likely than those from conservative groups to indicate that the media had become more sympathetic to the issues addressed by their organizations. When asked whether the media was more sympathetic to their cause after 9/11, 30.2% of conservative organizations agreed (versus 69.6% that disagreed), and 47.6% of liberal organizations agreed (versus 52.4% that disagreed).

The trend is somewhat different when it comes to the effects of 9/11 and Hurricane Katrina on support for and attention to their organization's issues among members of the public, however (note that the PIONM questions about media sympathy do not ask about its relationship to 9/11 and Hurricane Katrina). In that case, almost half of the respondents from conservative organizations (49%) reported that 9/11 led to increased public attention and support for their issues, while only 30% of these respondents said the same was the case for Hurricane Katrina. Conversely, a far smaller proportion of respondents from liberal groups (36.7%) said that 9/11 had increased attention among members of the general public to the issues addressed by their organizations, while a far greater proportion of these respondents (54%) believed the same was true of Hurricane Katrina (see table 6.3).

Similar patterns are evident in the perceived effects of the two calamitous events on public support for the issues addressed by organizations, with just under a third of conservative groups saying that 9/11 led to increased public support for their issues and only a fifth reporting the same was true of Hurricane Katrina. While 28% of respondents from liberal groups said that 9/11 led to increased public support for their organizations' issues, 45% gave this response when asked about Hurricane Katrina. The proportions of respondents in organizations of each type who said that each event led to decreases in public support for their issues are just as significant as these perceived increases in support. For example, 15% of conservative groups, but almost 29% of liberal groups, said that 9/11 had led to declines in support. The proportions of liberal and conservative groups giving this answer regarding Hurricane Katrina was roughly even, however, with approximately 12% saying that it led to decreased public support for their issues.

## Government Attention and Policy Windows

Membership, media attention, and support from members of the general public are all important factors when it comes to structuring political opportunities for advocacy, but this advocacy requires attention from policymakers if it is to contribute to policy changes. To understand perceptions among advocates about whether and how Hurricane Katrina and 9/11 influenced this attention, respondents were asked to assess whether each event had greatly decreased, somewhat decreased, somewhat increased, greatly increased, or had no effect on government attention to the issues addressed by their organizations.

The patterns in the responses to these questions in table 6.3 are similar to some of those for the measures that I have described thus far, but they also reveal some significant departures that are suggestive about the ways in which political opportunities vary, with some kinds of groups finding openings where others find less receptivity. Although more than half of respondents from liberal groups reported that Hurricane Katrina had increased public attention to their issues, for example, and almost as many said that it had led to increased public support as well, only a third (32.8%) reported that it had led to increased government attention. This finding is nonetheless approximately twice the proportion of respondents from conservative groups (14.9%) who thought that Hurricane Katrina had led to expanded opportunities for their issues. And whereas these latter respondents had reported that 9/11 led to vastly expanded public attention to the their issues, only about a third of respondents from these conservative groups (34%) reported that it had led to increased government attention. Although respondents from liberal groups were only somewhat less likely than their conservative counterparts to report increased government attention as a consequence of 9/11 (34%

for conservative groups, 26.8% for liberal groups), however, they were almost twice as likely to say that it had led to decreased attention from policymakers.

To assess the extent to which these factors come together to open windows of opportunity for advocacy, respondents were asked how each event affected the ability of their organizations to achieve their policy goals during the years 2000 through 2006. Table 6.4 presents the mean responses to these questions disaggregated by organization type. A few results stand out. First, among almost all types of organizations associated with progressive causes, 9/11 is viewed as, on average, having made it harder to achieve their policy goals. But the pattern is less consistent when it comes to the effects of Hurricane Katrina, and respondents from liberal organizations do not necessarily view it as having opened policy windows.

TABLE 6.4.
Perceived Effects of 9/11 and Hurricane Katrina on Ability to Achieve
General Policy Goals

|  | 9/11 | Hurricane Katrina |
|---|---|---|
| AIDS/HIV | −1.00 | −0.33 |
| Arab/Muslim | −1.50 | 0.00 |
| Asian American | −0.45 | −0.36 |
| Black/African American | −0.89 | 0.11 |
| Civil liberties | −0.89 | 0.11 |
| Civil rights (general) | −0.97 | −0.14 |
| Conservative | 0.11 | −0.03 |
| Criminal justice/anti–death penalty | −1.00 | −0.17 |
| Disability | −0.33 | 0.07 |
| Environmental | −0.66 | 0.32 |
| Farm/migrant workers | −1.29 | −0.14 |
| Health care | 0.00 | 0.75 |
| Immigration | −1.78 | −0.56 |
| Labor organization or union | −0.61 | 0.08 |
| Latino/Hispanic | −0.33 | 0.11 |
| LGBT/Queer | −0.40 | 0.00 |
| Native American/American Indian | −1.23 | −1.00 |
| Peace/antimilitarism/antinuclear | −1.11 | 0.12 |
| Poverty and social justice | −0.80 | 0.41 |
| Progressive social change (general) | −1.18 | −0.45 |
| Public interest | −0.75 | −0.08 |
| Right to life/anti-abortion | 0.00 | −0.14 |
| Senior citizens | 0.17 | 0.17 |
| Women of color | −0.80 | −0.40 |
| Women's health/reproductive rights | −0.88 | −0.59 |
| Women's rights/feminist (general) | −0.55 | −0.31 |

Source: Public Interest Organizations in the New Millennium, 2007

Note that data reflect mean responses on a scale between −2 and +2, in which −2 is "much harder" and +2 is "much easier."

To explore the ways in which such openings and closings of policy windows translate into changes in advocacy, respondents were asked whether 9/11 and Hurricane Katrina had led to changes in their mandate or in the issues addressed by their organizations (see table 6.3). Once again, conservative organizations were more likely to report that 9/11 had such an effect than they were regarding Hurricane Katrina. Even more striking, however, is that approximately equal proportions of respondents from liberal groups—20%—claimed that each event led to changes in their mandates or agendas.

My conversations with officers from a range of advocacy organizations help to make sense of some of the changes in advocacy resulting from 9/11 and Hurricane Katrina, particularly for understanding the expanding and contracting political opportunities they faced between 2000 and 2006. A respondent from a civil liberties group told me, for example, that the magnitude of the sense of crisis brought about by 9/11 was so overwhelming that progressive groups quickly realized that they "couldn't make any real immediate inroads into it. We couldn't stop the Patriot Act, we couldn't stop a lot of stuff that was going on." "We knew," she said, "we were emailing each other the afternoon of 9/11, and our email was not, 'Oh, goody, this is an opportunity to get attention to this stuff,' but 'Oh, my God, there is gonna be such a huge, horrible bill.'" She continued, "We didn't think we were gonna pass anything good. We were just trying to limit the damage. Nobody in their right mind thought they were gonna do anything—that there was any good legislation gonna come out of that."[14] But while her organization was unable to influence the substance of public policy, the nature of these policies raised the salience of many civil liberties issues that have long been central to their mission, and her organization was consequently able to "mobilize a tremendous people on the right and left." Moreover, she continued, the "ACLU made a trillion and a half dollars, I don't know what the number was, but it was a huge amount of money, and got a lot of supporters."

Finding themselves stymied at the national level, organizations like the one above also pursued opportunities in other venues, engaging in the process that Doug McAdam and his collaborators call "scale shift," through which "contention at one level is transposed" to a higher or a lower level of government. In this case, many civil liberties organizations shifted their focus from trying to change federal policies to trying to support such efforts at the state and local levels (McAdam et al., 2001). For example, this respondent explained that while advocates at many national organizations felt "somewhat powerless" when it came to trying to challenge national policies such as the

Patriot Act, they nonetheless wanted to register their concerns and decided that it was best to do so locally. "So," she said, "you had . . . 500 and some ordinances" passed by states and municipalities saying, "'We want to repeal the Patriot Act, we don't want our city or county or state to enforce what we consider to be overreaching, unconstitutional violations of civil rights,' and whatever else."[15]

While some organizations were able to retool in these ways, others found that 9/11 had mainly a chilling effect on their work. The director of operations at another liberal civil liberties group explained that among her organization's many projects are databases that aggregate information about environmental toxins. The databases are all compiled from publicly available information, but after 9/11 the organization was told by the government to remove them from its website. The idea "that you could [ask anyone to] take down any data set that was public because terrorists might read it," she explained, became "a kind of mantra for a while . . . All of a sudden they created a new classification that it wasn't a 'classified document,' it was 'sensitive but unclassified,' where they could just take things off from anywhere and just say, 'It's a security risk.' You didn't even know what was in the document, but it wasn't classified, so it couldn't be unclassified later on . . . And our work got really more difficult."

The hurdles to advocacy associated with such measures extend beyond their "chilling effects" on organizations to their substantive effects on the nature and scope of organizations' agendas. That is, rather than focusing on the policy issues that are at the core of their agenda—in this case, cleaning up environmental toxins—the organization's energy became focused on battling government efforts to "hide that data from terrorists."[16]

While the foregoing statements illustrate some of the constraints faced by progressive organizations following 9/11, other interviews are suggestive about the kinds of opportunities that a crisis like Hurricane Katrina can present to liberal organizations, particularly to ones that focus on issues of race and poverty. The policy director of a civil rights group told me, for example, "here's this festering problem, the problem of inequality and race and class-based injustice, something that threatens this democracy and has for a long time." Hurricane Katrina, he said, put these issues "on TV in such a dramatic way that no one could resist it" and, he argued, did so in a way that "made clear the Republicans are both uncaring and incompetent in a fundamental way." He continued, "That's a huge opening for Democrats to say, 'OK, we're taking a baby step next month. We'll pass the minimum wage. We're gonna put it on the table . . . We're gonna make it very hard for [Republicans] to say no on this.'"

## Plus Ça Change . . .

Although the survey and interviews provide evidence that both 9/11 and Hurricane Katrina affected the political opportunities and policy windows available to advocacy groups, equally significant is the evidence suggesting that for many organizations and issues, the more things change, the more they stayed the same. As the executive director of a criminal justice organization put it, 9/11 "doesn't seem to have affected our work on a day-to-day basis. The problems we face, the issues, are not that much different than they were before."[17] The executive director of a lesbian, gay, bisexual, and transgender (LGBT) rights group went even further, saying that "nothing linked to 9/11 caused any changes" for her organization.[18] Indeed, although many respondents from liberal groups reported that Hurricane Katrina opened important policy windows, many others told me that, in their view, it was a fleeting opportunity. The executive director of an antipoverty group argued that "people were disgusted by the scene of it all . . . People were just horrified by the magnitude of the disaster, and they wanted people's lives to be better, if you will. But it only lasted for so long, and people go back to what's occupying them."[19] Another interviewee said that Hurricane Katrina provided "an opening . . . to participate in a debate about poverty," to ask "what are we doing for the underclass, the widening gap, and how we fit into the problems?" However, he continued, "press interest in poverty is waning . . . It's more than it was, but it's . . . certainly not what it was many, many years ago."[20] Another respondent put it this way: "Katrina was huge and shameful and brought the attention of the poor inescapably to America's TV sets, but it's disappeared. But I don't think that . . . it plays a continuing role in helping to raise poverty issues."[21]

## Policy Issues and Political Opportunity

To get additional purchase on the meaning of the continuities and changes in political opportunity structures for nonprofit policy advocacy that I have discussed thus far, I turn now to evidence from a series of questions in which PIONM respondents were asked to list up to five policy issues that had been most important to their organization in 2000. They were then asked to answer a series of questions about each one, including a question that asked whether their organizations had experienced changes in the difficulty of pursuing their goals on the issues they mentioned; that is, had these goals become harder, easier, or had there been no change since 2000?

The data in table 6.5 disaggregate the answers to this question by the ideological self-placement of the organizations, and then more finely by organization type. Comparing the responses of liberal organizations to those of conservative groups shows that although respondents may have experienced openings in policy windows or political opportunity at a general level, a plurality of respondents nonetheless felt that it had become more difficult to pursue their goals on most of the issues that were important to their organizations. While this was true of 40% of respondents from conservative groups, however, it was far more common among respondents from liberal groups, a strong majority of which (54.6%) reported that their goals had become more difficult to achieve. Among those from conservative groups, responses were more evenly distributed, with over 60% saying that their goals had become easier or that they had experienced no change.

These differences between liberal and conservative groups generally persist when the responses are disaggregated by organization type. For example, immigration, civil liberties, American Indian, women of color, and HIV/AIDS groups were particularly likely to say that it had become harder to achieve their policy goals, while this response was uncommon among conservative movement organizations and anti-abortion groups. The disaggregated responses also reveal provocative deviations from this pattern, however. In particular, among organizations associated with progressive issues, immigration and LGBT organizations both stand out—immigration organizations because they were most likely to report that their policy goals had become more difficult (71.1%), and LGBT groups because, at 64.5%, they were more likely than any other organization type in the survey to report that their goals on the issues they named had become easier.

Looking at the particular issues mentioned by respondents from these organizations reveals that in most of the cases in which respondents from LGBT groups reported that an issue had become easier, it was an issue related to lifting the Don't Ask, Don't Tell (DADT) prohibition on gays and lesbians serving openly in the military. Efforts to repeal DADT gained traction as the wars in Iraq and Afghanistan progressed, particularly after the release of a 2006 report from the General Accounting Office, which found that over 300 language experts, including over 50 who speak Arabic, had been discharged under DADT. In 2007, the US Department of Defense issued a statement

TABLE 6.5.
Perceived Change in Difficulty of Achieving Specific Policy Goals Listed by Respondent
by Organization Type, 2000–2006

| | Easier (%) | No Change (%) | Harder (%) |
|---|---|---|---|
| Conservative (1–5 on scale) | 29.4 | 31 | 39.5 |
| Liberal (6–10 on scale) | 22.8 | 22.7 | 54.6 |
| AIDS/HIV | 22.2 | 16.7 | 61.1 |
| Arab/Muslim | 25.0 | 25.0 | 50.0 |
| Asian American | 25.8 | 22.6 | 51.6 |
| Black/African American | 31.4 | 20.0 | 48.6 |
| Civil liberties | 16.1 | 12.9 | 71.0 |
| Civil rights (general) | 29.2 | 19.8 | 51.0 |
| Conservative (general) | 28.0 | 36.0 | 36.0 |
| Criminal justice/anti–death penalty | 31.6 | 31.6 | 36.8 |
| Disability rights | 19.0 | 25.9 | 55.2 |
| Environment/ecology/animal rights | 17.3 | 25.3 | 57.4 |
| Farm/migrant workers | 27.8 | 22.2 | 50.0 |
| Health care | 33.3 | 6.7 | 60.0 |
| Immigration | 7.9 | 21.1 | 71.1 |
| Labor organization or union | 17.3 | 25.3 | 57.4 |
| Latino/Hispanic | 36.4 | 25.0 | 38.6 |
| LGBT/Queer | 64.5 | 9.7 | 25.8 |
| Native American/American Indian | 14.3 | 20.4 | 65.3 |
| Peace/antimilitarism/antinuclear | 25.7 | 14.3 | 60.0 |
| Poverty and social justice | 22.3 | 27.2 | 50.5 |
| Progressive social change (general) | 25.0 | 37.5 | 37.5 |
| Public interest | 8.7 | 30.4 | 60.9 |
| Right to life/anti-abortion | 33.3 | 45.5 | 21.2 |
| Senior citizens | 13.3 | 26.7 | 60.0 |
| Women of color | 29.2 | 12.5 | 58.3 |
| Women's health/reproductive rights | 21.8 | 29.1 | 49.1 |
| Women's rights/feminist (general) | 22.3 | 27.7 | 50.0 |

Source: Public Interest Organizations in the New Millennium, 2007

making the unprecedented suggestion "that lesbian and gay service personnel should continue to use their skills in support of national security efforts, even after facing dismissal under the law" (PRNewswire, 2007). In late 2010, Congress passed and President Obama signed the Don't Ask, Don't Tell Repeal Act of 2010 and the new policy went into effect in 2011.

That efforts to repeal DADT gained traction and were eventually realized in the context of the wars in Iraq and Afghanistan illustrates some of the ways in which crises can interact with enduring inequalities to produce variations in the political opportunities and policy windows encountered by advocates for marginalized groups. In particular, it suggests that organizations might be best able to exploit the instabilities of crises by framing their claims as extending rights to a "worthy" group—in this case lesbian and gay military personnel—who need fuller citizenship in order to serve national interests (Schneider and Ingram, 1997). Conversely, the experiences of immigrants' rights groups are suggestive about the ways in which crises can intensify the constraints faced by advocates. In particular, the issue that leads to the strongly negative mean for immigration organizations is the increased difficulty associated with the pursuit of issues related to undocumented immigrants. That is, it is partly related to the increased complexity of trying to frame undocumented immigrants as a morally worthy group and of regularizing their status as being in the national interest.

Although the case of undocumented immigrants is a telling example of the constraints faced by advocates for marginalized groups during a time of crisis, considering military and immigration issues together also illustrates the kinds of struggles over the *constructions* of marginalized groups that can take place in such a context, particularly during a time of war. Specifically, while political opportunities to address issues related to undocumented immigrants seemed to contract after 9/11, in July 2002, President George W. Bush announced that "the thousands of non-citizens serving in the US armed forces would immediately be eligible for naturalization." Proclaiming military service "the highest form of citizenship" (Krebs, 2006), President Bush essentially said that these immigrants were "worthy," and that they should be rewarded with citizenship rights for serving the national interest (see also Novkov, 2010).

In fact, as has been the case before, the wars that followed 9/11 seemed to allow many veterans' issues to gain traction (Dudziak, 2000; Graber, 1995; Klinkner and Smith, 1999; Kryder, 2001; Mettler, 2007; Parker, 2009; Ritter, 2006). Table 6.6 makes clear that, across all types of organizations in the study, respondents typically reported that issues related to rights and resources for members of the military—including the repeal of DADT as well as issues such as women in combat and benefits for wounded veterans—became easier. As the data in table 6.6 demonstrate, however, organizations of all types reported immigration issues typically became more difficult. These two clusters of issues are essentially mirror images, with 75% of those mentioning military-related issues reporting that they had become easier while 76.5% of those mentioning immigration-related issues reporting that it had become more difficult to achieve their goals. As the legislative director for a veterans' organization told me during an interview, the wars in Iraq and Afghanistan "put a lot of focus on us and our issues. It's terrible to say, but in a way, it's helped us get our issues enacted into law. There's just that type of

TABLE 6.6.
Perceived Change in Difficulty of Achieving Policy Goals for Selected Issues,
2000–2006

|  | Easier (%) | No Change (%) | Harder (%) |
|---|---|---|---|
| Immigration-related issues | 11.8 | 11.8 | 76.5 |
| Military-related issues (e.g., wounded veterans, women in combat, DADT repeal) | 75.0 | 4.0 | 20.1 |

Source: Public Interest Organizations in the New Millennium, 2007

sentiment right now, following 9/11." For over a decade and a half, he said, his organization was "fighting for reform of the VA healthcare budget process. Last year, we finally got it enacted into law."[22]

It may not be surprising that, as has been the case before, the need for bodies to fight wars can present political opportunities to members of marginalized groups who can be framed as worthy and constructed as patriots (Schneider and Ingram, 1997). But while rights and policy gains such as the repeal of DADT, benefits for disabled veterans, or the conferral of citizenship to immigrants who serve in the military might be things that, as Gayatri Spivak argues, "we cannot not want," they also replicate and reinforce narrow and normative racial, gender, class, and nationalist ideals and claims to citizenship (Spivak, 1993, 45–46). Policy changes are often tied to these constructions, of course, but such connections are tightened by links among "worthiness," "citizenship," and the "national interest" that are so often heightened during wars, depressions, pandemics, and disasters.

## Conclusions

Organizations that advocate on behalf of marginalized groups often represent unpopular or underresourced constituencies, and the issues that they address are frequently divisive and controversial. As a consequence, such organizations typically face significant constraints and often give short shrift to issues affecting intersectionally disadvantaged subgroups of their constituencies, even during relatively untumultuous times. Given the difficulties they face when times are good, it is important to examine how they fare during hard times, such as the period that followed 9/11 or post Hurricane Katrina.

The evidence that I have presented suggests that the crises brought about by events such as 9/11 and Hurricane Katrina do not necessarily mirror their material impact on members of marginalized groups. Rather, they present advocacy organizations with a combination of constraints and opportunities when it comes to addressing the ongoing social, economic, and political issues that affect their marginalized constituents. Comparing the responses of organizations to 9/11 on the one hand and to Hurricane Katrina on the other also reveals that each crisis has had different implications for liberal and conservative advocacy groups. Moreover, while these crises affected the political opportunities and policy windows faced by advocacy groups, my research also suggests that for many organizations, particularly ones that advocate on behalf groups for whom times are "always hard," the more things change, the more they stay the same. Taken together, the evidence holds several implications for our understandings of advocacy strategies, about the types of issues in which nonprofit groups engage, and about the effects of crises on the political opportunities they present to nonprofit organizations vis-à-vis their members, the policy process, and their roles as advocates for marginalized groups.

First, this study confirms that a sense of urgency can be helpful to an advocacy group, particularly in terms of resource development, member recruitment, and public attention. In particular, since crises can increase the sense of urgency around some kinds of issues, they can present organizations with important opportunities for fundraising, public education, and media outreach. They can also present organizations with opportunities to reinvigorate their relationships with their constituents, as well as to recruit new members. While nonprofit advocacy organizations should certainly be attentive to the potential opportunities presented by crises, they should also be aware of their potential tradeoffs. If outreach or appeals to new members or donors entails watering down agendas, for example, advocacy efforts stimulated by crises can risk alienating long-standing ones.

Second, crises not only open up opportunities to increase membership and resources, they can also lead to shifts in the locations of political opportunity. As the example of the Patriot Act suggests, crises can open policy windows at the state and local levels even as they close them at the national or international levels. Conversely, Hurricane Katrina allowed advocates to leverage a crisis that affected a few states as a way to draw national attention to issues of race and poverty, if only briefly. Organizations should prepare for and be attentive to the possibilities of such scale shifts by maintaining strong ties to state, local, and perhaps even international and transnational organizations along the lines of those that I advocated in my 2007 book.

Third, and perhaps most importantly, organizations that advocate on behalf of disadvantaged groups must not lose sight of or neglect the longer-term, quotidian, and structural problems that affect their constituents, even as they may exploit the political opportunities associated with episodic crisis. This "moving picture" approach is important for several reasons (Pierson, 2004). First, it is helpful and important for developing a sustainable business model and strategic plan. Taking a long-term view can also help to mitigate the likely "media cycles" that accompany attention-getting crises by reminding advocates that they need to continue to work on issues even—and perhaps especially—after the media or Congress loses interest in them. In addition, maintaining a long-term view can help organizations to combat the chilling effects that can accompany crises associated with wars or security crises. Finally, such an approach can help them to maintain proactive agendas and what I have called "utopian visions," and to do what they can to make sure that the most vulnerable and intersectionally marginalized members of their communities do not bear a disproportionate share of the retrenchments of rights and resources that so often accompany national crises (Strolovitch, 2007).

NOTES

1. That events such as wars, terrorist attacks, depressions, health pandemics, and natural disasters are "national crises" often seems self-evident, but I acknowledge that their status as crises is also the product of political contestation, interventions, and the exercise of power. In other work, I explore the processes through which a subset of problems become figured as "urgent crises" that demand urgent policy responses.

2. Examples of intersectionally marginalized groups include women of color, whose disadvantage is constituted by the intersection of racial and gender-based marginalization.

3. Though not everyone is affected in exactly the same way by Social Security, it is relatively "equal opportunity" in its potential impact, both among constituencies of the organizations in the study and among general public.

4. I borrow this formulation from Brown-Dean (2010).

5. Any distinction between material and political effects is, to some degree, plastic and further complicated by the difficulty of disentangling the political effects of crises from the effects of regularized political events such as elections. Can we separate the effects of an exogenous crisis like 9/11, for example, from those of the 2000 election and the political agenda of President George W. Bush? In spite of these and related complexities, extant research suggests that it is worth trying to tease out the ways in which crises might open political opportunities or close policy windows, even in cases in which they do not lead to immediate gains or losses.

6. Disaggregating these data uncovered significant variations by type of organization (NRC, 2010).

7. While several scholars argue that war can open up possibilities for mobilization, others suggest that such openings are quite contingent. For Klinkner and Smith (1999), inclusive wartime rhetoric and an established protest vehicle are necessary as well.

8. David Mayhew (2005) writes that "no doubt this reform, effected by the Nineteenth Amendment, would have succeeded sooner or later, but energetic contributions by women to wartime mobilization seem to have brought the proximate winning argument. Suffrage extension was 'necessary to the successful prosecution of the war,' President Wilson argued; 'We have made partners of the women in this war.' . . . Women won the vote in many other countries during World War I or its near aftermath, evidently through a logic of wartime contribution or various other democratizing impulses associated with war. The instances include Britain (for women over thirty), Canada, Germany, Austria, Poland, Czechoslovakia, Sweden, Belgium, and the Netherlands. Women in France, Italy, Hungary, and Japan had to wait until the close of World War II, when a comparable logic seems to have obtained" (478).

9. Skocpol (2002) argues that the extent to which this is true depends upon whether the government calls for or otherwise encourages citizen involvement and whether voluntary associations are available and structured in ways that allow people to "volunteer together" and "to link face-to-face activities in local communities to state and national projects" (539). For example, the government relied heavily on voluntary associations during the Civil War, World War I, and even during World War II, even though it did not need them to the same degree. She argues, however, with the rise of professionally managed associations, the focus after 9/11 was on "managerial coordination and professional expertise" rather than on mobilization and engagement (538).

10. The University of Chicago Survey Lab administered the PIONM. The sample is composed of 626 respondents out of an original list of 1,249 organizations, for a response rate of 50.1%. Respondents could complete the survey by phone, on the Internet, or on paper. The sample of organizations was generated by assembling a database of national progressive and conservative advocacy organizations using information from published directories of organizations, websites, and movement publications.

11. In order to distinguish between these events and changing political conditions, respondents were also asked about the effects of the 2000 presidential election and the 2006 midterm elections, with the expectation that the 2000 election would provide a baseline and that 9/11 and Hurricane Katrina would show variations. Although these expectations are borne out, the results are beyond the scope of this chapter, and I focus my discussion here on the effects of 9/11 and Hurricane Katrina.

12. Interview with organization officer, July 2007.

13. Interview with organization officer, May 2010.

14. Interview with organization officer, June 2010.

15. Ibid.

16. Ibid.

17. Interview with organization officer, December 2006.

18. Ibid.

19. Ibid.
20. Ibid.
21. Ibid.
22. Interview with organization officer, May 2010.

## REFERENCES

Agamben, Giorgio. 2005. *State of Exception*. Chicago: University of Chicago Press.

Austin, Algernon. 2010. *Uneven Pain*. Washington, DC: Economic Policy Institute.

Banaszak, Lee Ann. 1996. *Why Movements Succeed or Fail: Opportunity, Culture and the Struggle for Woman Suffrage*. Princeton, NJ: Princeton University Press.

Bartels, Larry. 2008. *Unequal Democracy*. Princeton, NJ: Princeton University Press.

Bass, Gary D., David R. Arons, Kay Guinane, and Matthew Carter. 2007. *Seen but Not Heard: Strengthening Nonprofit Advocacy*. Washington, DC: Aspen Institute.

Baumgartner, Frank R., and Bryan D. Jones. 1993. *Agendas and Instability in American Politics*. Chicago: University of Chicago Press.

Berinsky, Adam. 2009. *In a Time of War*. Chicago: University of Chicago Press.

Berry, Jeffrey M. 1999. *The New Liberalism*. Washington, DC: Brookings Institution Press.

Berry, Jeffrey M., and David F. Arons. 2003. *A Voice for Nonprofits*. Washington, DC: Brookings Institution Press.

Boris, Elizabeth T. 1999. "Nonprofit Organizations in a Democracy: Varied Roles and Responsibilities." In *Nonprofits and Government: Collaboration and Conflict*, edited by Elizabeth T. Boris and C. Eugene Steuerle, 1–36. Washington, DC: Urban Institute Press.

Boris, Elizabeth T., and Jeff Krehely. 2002. "Civic Participation and Advocacy." In *The State of Nonprofit America*, edited by Lester M. Salamon, 299–330. Washington, DC: Brookings Institution Press.

Boris, Elizabeth T., and Rachel Mosher-Williams. 1998. "Nonprofit Advocacy Organizations: Assessing the Definitions, Classifications, and Data." *Nonprofit and Voluntary Sector Quarterly* 27, no. 4: 488–506.

Brown-Dean, Khalila. 2010. "From Exclusion to Inclusion: Promoting Civic Engagement when Times Are Always Hard." Paper presented at the American Political Science Association Annual Meeting, Washington, DC.

Collins, Patricia Hill. 1990. *Black Feminist Thought*. Boston: Unwin Hyman.

Costain, Anne N. 1992. *Inviting Women's Rebellion*. Baltimore: Johns Hopkins University Press.

Crenshaw, Kimberlé. 1989. "Demarginalizing the Intersection of Race and Sex." *University of Chicago Legal Forum* 39: 139–67.

Dahl, Robert A. 1967. *Pluralist Democracy in the United States*. Chicago: Rand McNally.

Davis, Angela Y. 1981. *Women, Race, and Class*. New York: Random House.

Dudziak, Mary. 2000. *Cold War Civil Rights*. Princeton, NJ: Princeton University Press.

Eisinger, Peter. 1973. "The Conditions of Protest Behavior in American Cities." *American Political Science Review* 81: 11–28.

Flexner, Eleanor, and Ellen Fitzpatrick. 1996. *Century of Struggle: The Woman's Rights Movement in the United States*. Cambridge, MA: Belknap Press of Harvard University Press.

Frymer, Paul. 1999. *Uneasy Alliances: Race and Party Competition in America*. Princeton, NJ: Princeton University Press.

Gilens, Martin. 1999. *Why Americans Hate Welfare*. Chicago: University of Chicago Press.

Goldfield, Michael. 1989. "Worker Insurgency, Radical Organization, and New Deal Labor Legislation." *American Political Science Review* 83: 1257–82.

Graber, Mark. 1995. "Counterstories: Protecting and Expanding Civil Liberties in Times of War." In *The Constitution in Wartime: Beyond Alarmism and Complacency*, edited by Mark Tushnet, 95–123. Durham, NC: Duke University Press.

Hacker, Jacob, and Paul Pierson. 2010. *Winner-Take-All Politics*. New York: Simon and Schuster.

Hamilton, Donna Cooper, and Charles V. Hamilton. 1992. "The Dual Agenda of African American Organizations since the New Deal: Social Welfare Policies and Civil Rights." *Political Science Quarterly* 107, no. 3: 435–53.

Heaney, Michael. 2004. "Issue Networks, Information, and Interest Group Alliances: The Case of Wisconsin Welfare Politics, 1993–1999." *State Politics and Policy Quarterly* 4: 237–70.

hooks, bell. 1981. *Ain't I a Woman?* Boston: South End Press.

Huddy, Leonie, Stanley Feldman, and Christopher Weber. 2007. "The Political Consequences of Perceived Threat and Felt Insecurity." *Annals of the American Academy of Political and Social Science* 614: 131–53.

Inglehart, Ronald. 1971. "The Silent Revolution in Europe: Intergenerational Change in Post-Industrial Societies." *American Political Science Review* 65: 991–1017.

Jacobs, Lawrence, and Desmond King. 2009. "America's Political Crisis: The Unsustainable State in a Time of Unraveling." *PS: Political Science and Politics* 42, no. 2: 277–85.

Kennedy, Tony, and David Phelps. 2001. "NWA Will Lay Off 10,000; $15 Billion Airline Aid OK'd; 4,500 Workers Will Be Cut in Minnesota." *Star Tribune*, September 22, 21A.

Kingdon, John W. 1995. *Agendas, Alternatives, and Public Policies*. New York: HarperCollins.

Klinkner, Philip A., and Rogers M. Smith. 1999. *The Unsteady March*. Chicago: University of Chicago Press.

Krebs, Ron. 2006. "The Father of All Things? Hypotheses on the Effects of War on Democracy." Paper presented at the International Studies Association Annual Convention, San Diego, CA.

Kryder, Daniel. 2001. *Divided Arsenal: Race and the American State during World War II*. New York: Cambridge University Press.

Kurtz, Sharon. 2002. *Workplace Justice: Organizing Multi-Identity Movements*. Minneapolis: University of Minnesota Press.

Mayhew, David R. 2005. "Wars and American Politics." *Perspectives on Politics* 3: 473–93.

McAdam, Doug, Sidney Tarrow, and Charles Tilly. 2001. *Dynamics of Contention.* New York: Cambridge University Press.

McCall, Leslie. 2013. *The Undeserving Rich: American Beliefs about Inequality, Opportunity, and Redistribution.* New York: Cambridge University Press.

Merolla, Jennifer L., and Elizabeth Zechmeister. 2009. *Democracy at Risk: How Terrorist Threats Affect the Public.* Chicago: University of Chicago Press.

Mettler, Suzanne. 2007. *Soldiers to Citizens: The G.I. Bill and the Making of the Greatest Generation.* New York: Oxford University Press.

Meyer, David S. 1993a. "Peace Protest and Policy: Explaining the Rise and Decline of Antinuclear Movements in Postwar America." *Policy Studies Journal* 21: 35–51.

———. 1993b. "Protest Cycles and Political Process: American Peace Movements in the Nuclear Age." *Political Research Quarterly* 46: 451–79.

Meyer, David S., and Debra Minkoff. 2004. "Conceptualizing Political Opportunity." *Social Forces* 82, no. 4: 1457–92.

Miller, Joanne, and Jon A. Krosnick. 2004. "Threat as a Motivator of Political Activism: A Field Experiment." *Political Psychology* 25: 507–24.

Minkoff, Debra C. 1994. "The Institutional Structuring of Organized Social Action, 1955–1985." *Research in Social Movements, Conflict, and Change* 17: 135–71.

———. 1995. *Organizing for Equality: The Evolution of Women's and Racial-Ethnic Organizations in America, 1955–1985.* New Brunswick, NJ: Rutgers University Press.

Novkov, Julie. 2010. "Sacrifice and Civic Membership: The War on Terror" (paper presented at the Annual Meeting of the American Political Science Association, Washington, DC).

NRC. Nonprofit Research Collaborative. 2010. "November 2010 Fundraising Survey." Arlington, VA: NRC. http://foundationcenter.org/gainknowledge/research/pdf/nrc_survey2010.pdf.

Parker, Christopher S. 2009. *Fighting for Democracy: Black Veterans and the Struggle against White Supremacy in the Postwar South.* Princeton, NJ: Princeton University Press.

Pierson, Paul. 2004. *Politics in Time.* Princeton, NJ: Princeton University Press.

Piven, Frances Fox, and Richard Cloward. 1977. *Poor People's Movements: Why They Succeed, How They Fail.* New York: Pantheon.

PRNewswire. 2007. "Department of Defense Issues Revised Statement about 'Don't Ask, Don't Tell.'" *PRNewswire,* June 26.

Ritter, Gretchen. 2006. *The Constitution as Social Design: Gender and Civic Membership in the American Constitutional Order.* Palo Alto, CA: Stanford University Press.

———. 2007. "Gender and Politics over Time." *Politics and Gender* 3, no. 3: 386–97.

Robin, Corey. 2004 *Fear: The History of a Political Idea.* New York: Oxford University Press.

Sanger, David E. 2009. *The Inheritance: The World Obama Confronts and the Challenges to American Power.* New York: Harmony Books.

Schattschneider, E. E. [1960] 1975. *The Semisovereign People.* New York: Harcourt Brace Jovanovich.

Schneider, Anne Larason, and Helen Ingram. 1997. *Policy Design for Democracy*. Lawrence: University Press of Kansas.

Skocpol, Theda. 1992. *Protecting Mothers and Soldiers: The Political Origins of Social Policy in the United States*. Cambridge, MA: Harvard University Press.

———. 2002. "Will 9/11 and the War on Terror Revitalize American Civic Democracy?" *PS: Political Science and Politics* 35, no. 3: 537–40.

———. 2003. *Diminished Democracy: From Membership to Management in American Civic Life*. Norman: University of Oklahoma Press.

Solecki, William, and Sarah Michael. 1994. "Looking through the Postdisaster Policy Window." *Environmental Management* 18: 587–95.

Spivak, Gayatri. 1993. *Outside in the Teaching Machine*. New York: Routledge.

Strach, Patricia, and Virginia Sapiro. 2011. "Campaigning for Congress in the '9/11' Era: Considerations of Gender and Party in Response to an Exogenous Shock." *American Politics Research* 39: 264–90

Strolovitch, Dara Z. 2004. "Politics and Federal Policy." In *The Encyclopedia of Poverty and Social Welfare*, edited by Gwendolyn Mink and Alice O'Connor, 548–52. Santa Barbara, CA: ABC-CLIO.

———. 2007. *Affirmative Advocacy: Race, Class, and Gender in Interest Group Politics*. Chicago: University of Chicago Press.

———. 2013. "Of Mancessions and Hecoveries: Race, Gender, and the Political Construction of Economic Crisis and Recovery." *Perspectives on Politics* 11: 167–76.

Sundstrom, William 1992. "Last Hired, First Fired?" *Journal of Economic History* 52: 415–29.

Weldon, S. Laurel. 2002. *Protest, Policy and the Problem of Violence against Women*. Pittsburgh: University of Pittsburgh Press.

———. 2011. *When Protest Makes Policy: How Social Movements Represent Disadvantaged Groups*. Ann Arbor: University of Michigan Press.

# CHAPTER SEVEN

# Gender Identity and the Shifting Basis of Advocacy by US Women's Groups, 1920–2000

KRISTIN GOSS

American democracy is increasingly responsive to political elites and moneyed interests (Bartels, 2008; Gilens, 2012; Hacker and Pierson, 2010; Skocpol, 2003). These factions are not representative of the American public (Bartels, 2008; Fiorina and Abrams, 2009; Gilens, 2012). While the elite bias in American democracy is nothing new (Schattschneider, 1960), political Washington has been transformed in ways that have exacerbated that bias. Public interest groups and political parties, which once effectively spoke for marginalized people and diffuse publics, are overpowered by groups attentive to narrow, advantaged constituencies (Hacker and Pierson, 2010). At the same time, the types of organizations that often serve as the default "representative" of diffuse and disadvantaged citizens—public charities—face severe legal and organizational barriers to political action (Berry and Arons, 2003). Even interest groups purporting to represent marginalized citizens are disproportionately attentive to their most privileged members (Strolovitch, 2007).

In light of these trends, this chapter takes a step back and examines how one diffuse and historically marginalized group—American women—made themselves heard before Congress. Long before they had the right to vote, American women organized in membership organizations to influence policy making from the outside. In the process, they spoke not only for their own particular needs and desires, but also for those of other groups such as the poor, children, racial minorities, and even humanity at large. Using two original data sets of women's organizations' public engagement, I examine how women's organizations constructed their moral authority to advocate before Congress on the important issues of the day. Rather than taking women's political marginalization as a given, I examine how all-female groups persuaded elected officials that women's voices should count.

Despite their marginalization, women historically have constituted one of the most vibrant sectors of the US interest group universe. As historians have noted, women helped to create what we now term "interest group politics" (Cott, 1987). Long before the explosion of public interest groups in the 1960s and 1970s (Berry, 1997), women's groups spearheaded a dizzying array of concerns: abolition, temperance, charity reform, suffrage, kindergartens, clean food and drug laws, maternal and child health, free trade, peace, multilateral engagement, juvenile justice, environmental protection, black civil rights, women's rights, universal health care—the list goes on. Women's organizations often paid attention to issues that male politicians and male-dominated associations did not. Women played an important agenda-setting role by bringing to elites' attention issues that affected everyone, but that women encountered first in their domestic roles (Jeffreys-Jones, 1995). Indeed, women received more elite attention than might have been expected based on their political clout, as was also true of children (see Imig, chap. 8, this volume).

Although "women's impact has, in many senses, been greatest when they worked through women's organizations" (Sapiro, 1984, 135), their collective advocacy evolved in significant and often counterintuitive ways throughout the late nineteenth and twentieth centuries. These changes included the types of groups representing women's collective concerns, the authority claims offered on women's behalf, and the substantive issues and issue dimensions that women's groups embraced. I suggest that changes in these various dimensions of women's collective advocacy are related to shifting understandings of women's collective identity.

This study uses women's organizations' congressional testimony to examine how women's groups established their bona fides before political elites and how those strategies evolved over time. Testifying before Congress is one important form of nonprofit advocacy, which this book defines as "the attempt to influence public policy, either directly or indirectly" (see Robert J. Pekkanen and Steven Rathgeb Smith's introduction to this volume). Because it is typically done in person before congressional committee members, testimony constitutes direct advocacy of the "insider" variety (see Pekkanen and Smith, introduction, this volume). But testimony also can work indirectly, as when organizations use it to educate the broader public, to communicate with members, and to reinforce their status as power players in Washington. As Jeffrey M. Berry (1997, 164) notes: "The most visible part of an interest group's effort to influence pending legislation takes place at congressional hearings . . . Interest group leaders like to testify because it bestows status on them and their organizations, because it shows members that their group is playing an important part in the legislative process, and because it helps to legitimize further participation."

A careful analysis of hearing testimony illuminates the three major themes of this book: *venue choice*, factors associated with *success* in the legislative realm, and *limitations* on advocacy by nonprofit organizations. First, Congress is the most prominent target of advocacy by nonprofit organizations in Washington, and congressional testimony is a particularly common—and coveted—opportunity for nonprofit organizations to try to influence public policy directly (Berry, 1997; Grossmann, 2012). Second, organizations use hearings to develop messages that will reinforce their stature with, and sway, wavering policymakers. As this study shows, those advocacy messages have changed significantly over time, illuminating shifting strategies to influence lawmakers. Finally, congressional hearings illustrate the ebbs and flows in different groups' prominence on Capitol Hill and remind us that organizations that were important in one era may be severely limited in another.

Appearances by women's organizations before Congress are captured in two original data sets. The first contains every appearance by a women's organization before a congressional committee or subcommittee hearing between 1878 (the first such appearance) and 2000. There are more than 10,400 appearances and more than 2,100 groups in the data set. The second data set consists of 368 systematically selected sets of testimony by women's organizations in two broad policy domains: international affairs and national health-care provisions. Congressional testimony provides a unique, systematic measure of two constructs: (1) those policies on the government agenda that women collectively decided to try to influence, and (2) those policies on which members of Congress considered women's input to be authoritative.

As a vehicle for analyzing policy authority, I invoke the concept of *civic place*, which I define as the intersection of a group's civic identity, its organizational advocates, and their policy agenda. A civic identity is a political construction that signifies collective beliefs about citizens' claims against and duties toward the state. Identities with strong civic connotations might include laborer, pauper, veteran, and mother. Each is rooted in some facet of individual experience that helps to establish one's role in the political order. Organizations representing different identity groups (in this case, women) construct rationales to link civic identities to policy demands. In so doing, organizations seek to establish a civic place for their constituents. The notion of civic place is akin to the notion of "place" more generally—a metaphorical location that anchors a claim to rightful inclusion.[1] Groups reveal their civic place through the symbols and narratives that they use as a basis for establishing their authority to "count" in public policy discussions.

To structure the historical analysis, I elaborate on the familiar, if questionable, dichotomy upon which much feminist theory and analysis are based: the "sameness versus difference" dichotomy. In the next section, I briefly review theories of how women are the same as, or different from, men and describe the creative ways in which women's groups have combined or reconciled these supposedly dichotomous understandings. Next, I introduce the data and methods of analysis. I then trace the evolution of women's groups' authority claims through the three civic identities that emerged from the testimony: a maternal identity, a "good citizen" identity, and an equal claimant identity. Generally speaking, the maternal identity maps onto the difference understanding; the equal claimant identity maps onto the sameness understanding; and, as I describe below, the good citizen identity constitutes a clever combination of the two. I show how these identities shifted over time as the foundation of women's groups' policy advocacy. I conclude with a set of hypotheses about how these patterns may relate to broader questions about women's voice and influence in national policy debates.

## Women's Sameness, Women's Difference

Understandings of women's civic identity have revolved around a core question: whether women are at root the same as or different from men. Sameness arguments characterize women as *independent* political actors "endowed by their Creator" with the same citizen rights enjoyed by men. The sameness paradigm was present in the 1848 first-wave women's movement's "Declaration of Sentiments," which adapted the Declaration of Independence to state that "all men *and women* are created equal" (italics mine). The sameness paradigm also guided the rhetoric of the early suffrage movement (Kraditor, 1971). Likewise, sameness was the underpinning of the brand of liberal, or equality, feminism that came to dominate the so-called second-wave women's movement, which emerged in the 1960s and peaked in the 1970s. The doctrine infused the founding statement of purpose of the second wave's flagship organization, the National Organization for Women (NOW). NOW's mission statement stressed that women were "human beings, who, like all other people in our society, must have a chance to develop their fullest human potential" (Carabillo et al., 1993, 159). And it was the lodestar of the uncompromising feminist strategy that characterized the Equal Rights Amendment struggles of the 1970s and early 1980s (Mansbridge, 1986).

The notion that women were the same as men informed women's activists' understanding of their relationship with the state. In this understanding, the state has a duty to protect the rights claims of women, including equal political rights and the right to equal treatment under the law. When the state fails to treat women equally, women have the prerogative to voice their grievances and claims for redress through the political process. Sameness understandings, then, stress what the state owes to the citizen, namely equal political rights and equal treatment under law. This relationship puts the natural rights conception of citizenship front and center. Women join men as carriers of the classical liberal tradition in American political culture.

But "difference" arguments conceptualize women as distinctive, *relational* actors. This perspective holds that, whether by nature or nurture or some combination thereof, women demonstrate an "ethic of care" toward others (Lister, 2003). This ethic of care in turn undergirds women's proper role in strengthening democracy. The post-Revolutionary period gave rise to the notion of "republican motherhood," for example, in which women's public contribution was to train their sons to be good citizens (Kerber, 1976). It also informed Progressive Era frameworks for collective action, such as social reformer Jane Addams's suggestion that communities were just extensions of families and that women consequently could bring their domestic caretaking skills to improving government performance—what has been termed "social feminism" (O'Neill, 1971) and "municipal housekeeping" (Skocpol, 1992). The difference paradigm also informed early twentieth-century suffragists' arguments that the franchise would allow women to use their experiences in charitable and reform organizations to improve the performance of government (Kraditor, 1971). And it informed women's peace movements from the early to mid-twentieth century (Alonso, 1993; Goss, 2009; Jeffreys-Jones, 1995).

Like the equality framework, the difference framework serves as a basis for women's relationship with the state. In the difference framework, women assume the role of engaged members of the polity, bringing their special experiences and caring sensibilities—especially as mothers and dependents—to their civic work. Women's role in public life is to use what economists would call their comparative advantage. This understanding of women's role stresses what citizens owe or can contribute to the polity—and to the state, as the democratic embodiment thereof—as opposed to what the state owes to the citizen. The difference framework, as developed by nineteenth- and early twentieth-century women, harks back to the founders' civic republican tradition, a subordinate yet important strain in American political culture emphasizing engagement, community, consensus, and civic virtue.[2]

The second-wave women's movement had a complex and sometimes fraught relationship with the difference argument as articulated in the Progressive Era. Some offshoots of the feminist movement, such as ecofeminism and portions of the women's peace and antinuclear movements, were comfortable using a language of maternal care as a source of legitimacy and authority (Alonso, 1993; Somma and Tolleson-Rinehart, 1997). However, the core cadres of the feminist movement, first consciousness-raising groups and later rights-based advocacy groups, viewed difference feminism as a threat to women's liberation and equality. They feared that difference reinforced "damaging sex stereotypes" (Davis, 1999) that could be "co-opted by those hostile to women's emancipation to fuel arguments for their continued subordination" (Offen, 1988, 154). As Nancy Fraser (1997, 99) writes, "Equality feminists saw gender difference as an instrument and artifact of male dominance . . . To stress gender difference is to harm women. It is to reinforce our confinement to an inferior domestic role." With this understanding, "the political task was thus clear: the goal of feminism was to throw off the shackles of 'difference' and establish equality, bringing women and men under a common measure" (Fraser, 1997, 100).

One line of attack was on the female tradition of volunteer work, which fueled the philanthropic and social reform efforts that had distinguished women's organizations in the Progressive Era. The flagship movement group NOW in 1971 "issued a resolution telling women they should only volunteer to effect social change, not to deliver social services . . . The new woman of the 1970s could be an activist; she could work for free to change an inequitable system but could not be a volunteer" (Kaminer, 1984, 4). Women's peace advocates took this resolution to be a "denigration of volunteerism as female exploitation" (Swerdlow, 1993, 158). Difference arguments made a bit of a comeback in the 1980s, when "cultural feminism" arose to reclaim femininity (Fraser, 1997, 100) and theorists such as Jean Bethke Elshtain (1981), Carol Gilligan (1982), and Sarah Ruddick (1989) argued that maternal experiences and relational orientation contribute to a more moral, peaceful, and just society.

These scholarly efforts to re-embrace difference notwithstanding, the wariness of difference arguments persisted throughout the 1980s and 1990s. Many equality feminists perceived care rhetoric as a threat to women's advancement, particularly in the professional realm. To many women who did not or could not aspire to motherhood—and even to many mothers—difference arguments reduced women to one-dimensional, easily oppressed beings. By the early 1990s, Theda Skocpol (1992, 538) concluded that "in the United States today no such unproblematic connections of womanhood and motherhood, or of private and public mothering, are remotely possible—not even in flights of moralism and rhetorical fancy."

The sameness and difference constructs have thus "run like two currents through the stream of feminist theory and politics since the late eighteenth century" (Lister, 2003, 96). Issue entrepreneurs have used accepted understandings about women's essence to frame women's collective action, to assemble issue agendas, and to legitimize women's authority to advance them. Understandings of sameness and difference have also been subject to debate and tension within women's movements, from suffrage through the second wave and beyond.

Even as these understandings have been in tension, however, they have also provided a diverse repertoire of symbols, metaphors, and narratives from which women's advocates could draw as the political and social context warranted. Scholars have documented the many instances in which women throughout American history have moved between, conflated, combined, or sampled from these two supposedly dichotomous understandings to advance their political and policy goals. Such strategies have allowed women's leaders to fit innovative, hybrid narratives to changing times (Goss and Heaney, 2010).

Such hybrid perspectives have been used to advance both explicitly feminist goals, such as women's rights and status, as well as more universalistic concerns. With respect to feminist goals, Eileen McDonagh (2009) argues that suffragists blended equality and difference rationales to win the vote.[3] Likewise, Wendy Sarvasy (1992) observes that Progressive Era women's advocates pushed mothers' pensions as a means of caring for women as a group with particular needs (difference) *and* advancing women's equality (sameness). Echoing that synthesis, second-wave feminists of the 1980s advocated policies to protect classes of women who were uniquely vulnerable or underrepresented—pregnant workers, battered women—with an end of providing them with equal freedoms and opportunities (Costain, 1988). In other cases, women's groups have synthesized sameness and difference understandings to mobilize women around causes that are not explicitly about women's rights or status. Such campaigns have included promoting environmental protection (Somma and Tolleson-Rinehart, 1997), advancing gun control (Goss and Heaney, 2010), and opposing war (Goss and Heaney, 2010).

Hybridizing is possible because, as Joan Scott (1988, 38) has argued, "equality is not the elimination of difference, and difference does not preclude equality." Both constructs acknowledge women's distinctiveness in the political realm: difference theorists because they find meaning in women's sensibilities, and equality theorists because they have supported separatist strategies of feminist organizing and in some cases supported policies (such as those dealing with pregnancy) that must acknowledge women's difference to achieve their equality. Karen Offen (1988, 156) has suggested that it is time for women to claim a hybrid "relational feminism" that would "reclaim the power of difference . . . and . . . reweave it once again with the appeal to the principle of human freedom that underlies the individualist tradition." Likewise, Scott (1988, 43) suggests that it is to women's advantage to include both sameness and difference constructs in their discursive repertoire, for difference has been women's "most creative tool," while equality speaks to "the principles and values of our political system."

Sameness, difference, and hybrid rationales have served as the foundation of women's collective work in the public sphere. They have informed frameworks of collective action, providing purposive and solidary incentives for women to join in social movements and other voluntary associations. As I demonstrate, they have also formed the basis for women's claims to speak authoritatively before elected officials at the highest level. This analysis is not a simple tour through women's discursive repertoires. Rather, it provides a bird's-eye view of what turns out to be a significant evolution in women's civic place in the United States, one with implications for their presence and voice in American democracy.

## Data and Methods

The question of "who matters" in Washington has long preoccupied scholars and led them to examine the laws, congressional routines, and organizational norms that structure access to political decision makers (Berry and Arons, 2003; Grossmann, 2012; Kasniunas, 2009; Leyden, 1995; Strolovitch, 2007). This study uses the testimony of women's organizations before congressional committees and subcommittees to illuminate and theorize about the dimensions of women's participatory citizenship. Besides constituting a common and highly visible form of direct and indirect advocacy, congressional testimony represents a valuable, underutilized source of data for studying the public discourse of politically relevant organizations. For one, testimony is systematically archived, allowing researchers to construct scientific samples of organizational rhetoric, as opposed to samples of convenience. Testimony also represents groups' unfiltered arguments, eliminating any concerns about media bias in selecting which ideas to report (Bennett, 2004). And testimony is consistent in its format, allowing for comparative analysis across issues and over time.

This study employs two sets of data: (1) an original data set of every appearance before a congressional committee or subcommittee by a women's organization from the first such appearance, in 1878, through 2000; and (2) transcripts of women's organizations' testimony in two key policy realms—foreign policy and health care—from the 1920s through the 1990s. Like Doug Imig (chap. 8, this volume), I approach nonprofit advocacy by starting with an agenda-setting institution, in this case Congress. Also like Imig, I utilize systematic, longitudinal data to capture the ebb and flow of issue agendas. The women's groups in my sample cut across Imig's categories of governmental representatives, religious groups, advocacy organizations, nongovernmental service providers, professional groups, and business groups. The data sets are described in turn.

## Quantitative Data

The quantitative data set ($n = 10,464$) was culled from the Congressional Information Service's *CIS Index*, a series of massive volumes that list every person who has ever testified before Congress and the organization represented. A total of 2,130 women's groups testified, with national organizations and their chapters counted separately. These hand-assembled data were then crosschecked through a variety of methods against the online records in the LexisNexis congressional database. For any individual organization, the listing in both the paper and electronic sources includes a brief, general description of the hearing and the year or Congress in which the hearing took place.[4] These data were coded according to a number of variables, three of which are important to this study. First, each appearance was assigned a subject matter policy code as defined by the Policy Agendas Project.[5] There were 228 possible subject matter codes, such as "U.S. foreign aid" (code 1901) and "comprehensive health care reform" (code 301), spanning 21 major policy categories. Second, each appearance was coded according to whether a significant part of the testimony centered on women's rights, status, advancement, or well-being. In some cases, the content was apparent from the organization and hearing topic (e.g., NOW testifying at a women's rights hearing). But in most cases, the testimony was reviewed and coded accordingly. Finally, appearances were coded as to whether the group represented women's occupational interests. The quantitative data set documents trends in the types of organizations that testified and the issues they advocated.

### Qualitative Data

The second source of data, derived from the first, consists of a carefully constructed sample of hearing transcripts from women's organizations' appearances before Congress on two policy questions: foreign policy and government provision of health care. These issues were selected because they are different enough to increase confidence in the findings and because they are issues that drew concerted attention from women's groups throughout the twentieth century. I coded 368 pieces of witness testimony. These policy case studies allow for a fine-grained, qualitative analysis of women's organizations' authority claims.

Each piece of testimony was examined to uncover the rhetorical strategies that women's groups used over the course of the twentieth century to connect their civic identities to their policy advocacy and thereby to establish their civic place. For each piece of testimony, I asked "How does this organization establish its bona fides to speak on the issue at hand?" Emerging organically from the testimony, the answers included narratives about women's individual and collective experiences, normative ideas about women's proper role in the private and public spheres, and accounts of the procedures and philosophies of organizations that purported to speak for female constituents. Synthesizing these key themes, I identified three civic identities that served as springboards for collective policy advocacy in the twentieth century: (1) a "maternal" identity rooted in women's roles as family caretakers; (2) a "good citizen" identity rooted in women's roles as stewards of the public interest; and (3) a "professional" identity rooted in women's work-related expertise. Let us now turn to an analysis of each of these three identities.

### The Maternal Roots of Women's Civic Place

In the first four decades of the twentieth century, in both the international and domestic realms, women's groups derived their authority from the special knowledge, skills, and civic responsibilities that women claimed by virtue of their roles as caretakers of the family and its traditions. In my sample of foreign policy and health-care hearings, women were especially engaged in two policy debates: (1) US participation in the World Court (1920s) and its nationality convention (1930s) and (2) the Maternity and Infancy Protection Act of 1921 (also known as the Sheppard-Towner Act), which provided federal aid to states in an effort to lower maternal and child mortality rates. Although these legislative proposals occupied different policy realms and appeared differently amenable to a maternal frame, women's groups in both cases capitalized on their authority as guardians of the family. Women's family authority took various forms rooted in biological motherhood, social motherhood, and family heritage.

## Biological Motherhood

Passage of the Sheppard-Towner Act constituted one of the top priorities for women's associations, which organized the Women's Joint Congressional Committee to advocate for the program. It is perhaps axiomatic that women's groups' authority over maternal and child health policy would derive from members' status as mothers. Women's groups such as the League of Women Voters and the National Consumers' League rooted their advocacy in their "special experience and knowledge" of the health needs of women and children.[6] A representative of the National Congress of Mothers and Parent-Teacher Associations noted that her organization was "rather unique because we have rich and poor, wise and ignorant, and all of them working together for the good of the children." She suggested that the bill would give women "knowledge and proper care" to have "many healthy children," an aim reinforced by the Great War's "tragic wiping out of so many precious lives."[7] As scholars have argued, women's groups' "appeal to male politicians' reverence for motherhood was a powerful and shrewd political tactic" that gave women an opening wedge into a broader critique of the domestic social problems of the industrial era (Ashby, 1984; Wilson, 2007, 45, 29).

Maternal authority also proved a powerful lever for women in foreign policy debates from the 1920s through the 1950s. Women's groups lobbied for greater engagement in international institutions, such as the World Court and later the United Nations, as well as for European reconstruction aid. These debates unfolded against the backdrop of World Wars I and II; as the mothers of soldiers, women staked a collective claim on foreign policy questions. Women's patriotic organizations and military auxiliaries were more likely to employ maternal rhetoric than were multipurpose civic groups, but these groups also drew authority from mothers' sacrifices.

Interestingly, women's groups used maternal authority both to justify and to oppose international engagements. In the 1920s, women's groups used motherhood arguments to lobby for US entry to the World Court. Mothers had given up their sons for war, draining women's physical, economic, moral, and spiritual resources, argued an American Association of University Women representative.[8] However, mothers' groups in the 1940s often opposed US engagement in the United Nations. These groups claimed to speak for the voiceless "loyal fighting men who are paying in what Mr. Churchill calls blood, sweat, and tears for this conflict"[9] and for the "millions of mothers and fathers of boys and girls now serving in the United States armed forces."[10] By the 1950s, mothers' groups were firmly on the side of international engagement, as evidenced by this representative quotation from a witness for the World Organization of Mothers of All Nations, or WOMAN: "I am a mother of four sons, two of whom are war veterans. I know I am expressing the fears and bewilderment of millions of mothers, confronted with the obvious fact that although we stand today in the very shadow of onrushing atomic catastrophe, virtually nothing is being done by our Government and the government of our Allied Nations to stop this catastrophe."[11] The group's chairman used a family metaphor to describe the Cold War, saying "WOMAN does not maintain that communism and democracy cannot live in the same world. As women we are conscious of the infinite variety between members of the same family—in our own children."[12]

### Social Motherhood

In the period from 1920 through 1950, women's groups located their authority not just in biological motherhood, but also in the social caretaking that women performed as an extension thereof. For purposes of establishing policy authority, women were social mothers as well as biological ones. With respect to health care, the social conception of motherhood meant enlisting the government to supplement women's voluntary work in what Paula Baker terms "the domestication of politics" (Baker, 1984, 642). Stating flatly, "the Government has a responsibility for things like the care of mothers and babies," Mary Stewart of the Women's National Republican Executive Committee argued that "the new times bringing women into politics have brought new ideas of Governmental responsibility," including federal support for maternal and child health care.[13] But conservative women's groups opposed to the Sheppard-Towner Act argued that, far from assisting women in family caregiving, the federal government threatened to undermine the family by taking over its functions. These women saw their political role as protecting their sphere of authority—the family—from what they branded as the paternalistic and socialistic designs of progressive reformers. Said Mrs. Albert T. Leatherbee of the Massachusetts Antisuffrage Association: "The chief object of attack in the battle of socialism against our established Christian civilization is the family. Socialists know that so long as the legitimate legalized family remains the unit of society, they can never control the State. It is the first necessity to break up the family that amid the resulting chaos may endeavor to build a society based upon individualism in which children become wards of the State."[14]

Besides threatening family cohesion, the bill would undermine families by invading the privacy of the home and by promoting birth control, according to opponents. Decrying the interference "with the domestic relations of private life" and the looming policy decision by "the National Government to supervise the pregnancy of the country," Mrs. Leatherbee and other conservative witnesses connected family protection to the protection of core American values. In their view, women had a duty to use their moral authority as mothers to stave off threats to the family and hence to the nation. Progressive reformers used maternal rationales to counter such claims: "That a bill whose only purpose is the saving of life should be attacked as 'destructive of the family' seems fantastic. Nothing so certainly destroys the family as death."[15]

### Family Heritage

A third way in which women's groups used family roles as their source of policy authority was by casting women as guardians of their ancestors' patriotic legacy. Women's patriotic groups confine membership to women who can trace their heritage to soldiers who fought in eighteenth- and nineteenth-century wars to establish or preserve the union. To these groups, female citizens must honor their ancestors' sacrifices by defending American values and institutions, particularly the Constitution (which a representative of the Kentucky chapter of Daughters of the American Revolution, or DAR, called "the greatest document that was ever written, and we love it"[16]). Women's groups' authority to defend the Constitution was derivative, the product of family lineage. A witness for the Minnesota DAR acknowledged that her freedoms are "precious legacies I inherited from the young soldier from Virginia" and vowed that young soldiers would not have died in vain if modern-day women, "in whose hands the priceless gift of liberty has been placed . . . are true to that trust and preserve and strengthen our freedom."[17]

## Maternal Rationales over Time

Figure 7.1 documents the presence of maternal rationales in women's groups' testimony over time. As figure 7.1 shows, women's groups drew on women's family roles frequently in the 1920s through the 1950s, but they clearly had other rhetorical strategies at their disposal. Although scholars have suggested that suffrage rendered maternalism obsolete (Baker, 1984; Cott, 1987), the evidence indicates that women commonly used their family roles as a source of political authority at least through the 1950s.[18]

The maternal understanding of women's civic place was rooted in gender difference. With the emergence of second-wave feminism, we see a dramatic drop in women's groups' use of maternalism such that it was virtually obsolete by the 1970s. Why did maternal rationales rooted in women's role as

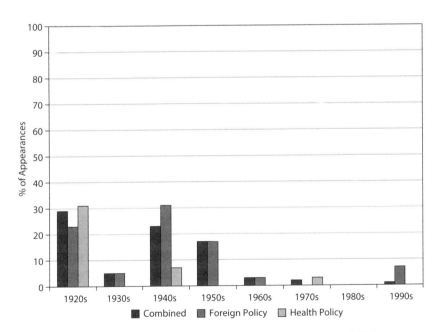

*Figure 7.1.* Women's policy authority rooted in maternal sensibilities.

family and community caretakers decline so dramatically in the feminist era? There are two possibilities: long-established groups shifted away from maternal rationales over time, or the types of groups using maternal rationales faded from the scene. A closer inspection of the data reveals that the latter explanation is driving most of the change. The types of groups that relied on maternal rationales—chiefly women's patriotic organizations and women's clubs—had all but disappeared from congressional hearing rooms by the 1970s. Groups such as the League of Women Voters and the American Association of University Women used maternalist rhetoric in the early decades and then shifted away—but their adaptation was not the major reason for the observed pattern. At the same time, by the 1970s and 1980s, as discussed below, the types of groups that were dominating health and foreign policy testimony were drawing on different female identities to make their case.

## Women's Civic Place as Good Citizens

Beginning in the 1920s and continuing through the 1970s, voluntary associations afforded women a different basis for female policy authority: the good citizen identity. In the wake of suffrage, women's leaders were eager to educate the newly enfranchised in the norms and habits of democratic citizenship. What is more, women's leaders were keen to prove that women were worthy of their inclusion in the polity, that they would be conscientious citizens and bring improvements to democratic governance. Like the maternal identity, the good citizen identity was other oriented. It thereby provided a flexible platform from which to engage in a broad array of public issues. But the good citizen identity offered an even broader platform than the maternal identity, for the civic-minded woman could speak to issues not traditionally associated with, or easily linked to, maternal experiences. Women's groups used the good citizen identity to weigh in on everything from civil liberties to water resources policy. The good citizen rationale had three interrelated components. It dodged the sameness-difference question, stressed the effort required of thoughtful citizenship, and invoked the public and national interest.

### Dodging the Question of Sameness versus Difference

The good citizen rationale sought to avoid a head-on reckoning with the age-old, divisive question of women's essential nature; that is, the question of whether women were fundamentally different from or the same as men.

The avoidance strategy meant that major women's organizations in the mid-twentieth century rarely constructed their narratives around gender identity. Absent were sentimental appeals to women's particular virtues as caretakers. Also absent were pleas based on assumptions of women's inequitable treatment. As Anne Costain points out, women leaders "worked to erase the perception of distinctiveness" in the hopes of being "accepted as equals of other voters" (Costain, 1988, 150). There were no female citizens and male citizens—just American citizens.

At the same time, women's groups' testimony carried the implicit message that women were distinct from men. Women were supercitizens: more conscientious and public-interest oriented than their male counterparts, as well as less reflexively partisan and self-interested. Women's groups' difference rhetoric operated like a "dog whistle," to use a now-popular term, audible only to those who were attuned. Women's groups emphasized their nonpartisanship, implicitly distinguishing themselves from male-dominated political parties (Sharer, 2004). And women's groups drew on their expertise derived from voluntary work in the nonprofit sphere. By withholding explicit appeals to female virtue while elaborating on the practices associated with care for others, women's groups cleverly elided the sameness-difference distinction and created a hybrid civic identity that captured the best of both.

### *Elaborating on Civic Effort*

The second component of the good citizen rationale was the frequent invocation of the laborious processes that women's groups undertook to develop their positions on policy issues. Women's groups discussed processes of careful, objective study that was implicitly nonpartisan. They portrayed themselves as promoters of good policy, untainted by crass political considerations. A particularly rich, but by no means unrepresentative, example of such discussion came from Mrs. Harry G. Long of the United Church Women of Ohio in testimony before a Senate subcommittee in 1954:

> Since the inception of the United Nations and long before that, I organized study groups, led discussions, moderated panels, and have spoken with scores of church and club groups locally and over the State, on various phases of world affairs, with emphasis on world organization, and accent on the work of the United Nations. And as a member of the Christian world relations committee of United Church Women, I have visited the United Nations a number

of times. This summer I was a member of a European seminar made up of writers, speakers, ministers, and teachers, who spent the summer on a study tour of social, political, and economic conditions of Europe. I visited FAO in Rome, UNESCO in Paris, and the European headquarters of the U.N. in Geneva . . . I know something of the great humanitarian achievements and the social good accomplished by the specialized agencies of the United Nations.[19]

Many times throughout hearings, particularly at midcentury, congressional committee members took care to compliment the female witnesses on the thoughtfulness of their positions. For example, Representative Pete Jarman (a Democrat from Alabama) said of the Women's Trade Union League and the League of Women Voters, which testified on postwar aid for Europe: "To me it is outstanding that the women of this country, or at least those represented by the two ladies who have addressed us, and I imagine they represent a cross section, are far ahead in their thinking, I believe, either of the people in general, or of the Congress."[20]

### Invoking the Public and National Interest

The third component of the good citizen rationale was its reliance on appeals to the public interest generally and the national interest specifically. Against the backdrop of World War II and the Cold War, women sought a civic place alongside men as defenders of the American way of life. In foreign policy, women's groups maintained their traditional interest in questions of war, peace, and international cooperation, but the maternalist rhetoric that had dominated in the earlier decades was confined to small, conservative, isolationist mothers' groups. The larger women's groups, whether internationalist or isolationist in orientation, adopted gender-neutral language. In debates over the United Nations charter, for example, the conservative Ladies of the Grand Army of the Republic warned of "a very stealthy scheme for a One World Government, which if put into effect would abolish the United States of America,"[21] while the internationalist National Council of Jewish Women stated that the United States had a "position of leadership" in the world that necessitated full participation in the United Nations.[22]

### The Good Citizen Rationale over Time

Figure 7.2 charts the fraction of women's groups' health, foreign policy, and combined testimony in which the witness couched her presentation in terms

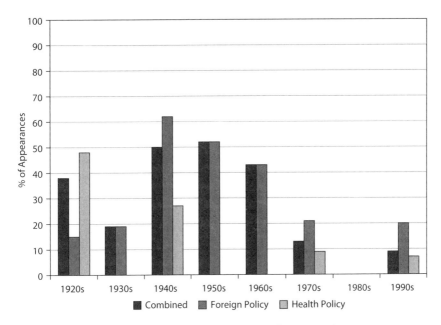

*Figure 7.2.* Women's policy authority rooted in national interest.

of defending the national economic or political interest. As the darkest bars show, such appeals became a declining share of all appeals as the twentieth century wore on. As was the case with the maternal rhetoric described above, the evolution was driven mostly by changes in the types of groups testifying over time, as opposed to changes in rhetorical claims within the same groups.

Women's groups thus reconciled the sameness-difference tension by continuing to organize as women, in deference to their common experiences as mothers, wives, and politically marginalized citizens, while making nongendered claims on behalf of the public good. Women organized as women but did not call attention to gender as the basis for collective action. Their approach to policy advocacy was based on principles of rational study and analysis. Women's contributions as citizens would be informed by female experience but pursued on male terms.

## Embodying the Good Citizen: The League of Women Voters

The League of Women Voters was the most prominent organization to ground its advocacy in the good citizen framework. The League and its affiliates testified more than any other women's group in American history. Its mission from the outset was to "develop the woman citizen into an intelligent and self-directing voter and to turn her vote toward constructive social ends" (Young, 1989, 49). Because of the League's importance to women's advocacy, and because the good citizen rationale has not been well studied, I use the League to illustrate how this novel civic identity functioned in practice.

As noted, the first component of the good citizen identity is ambiguity surrounding the question of sameness and difference. In the League's case, the ambiguity showed up as ambivalence about whether it was even a women's organization. Although "women" was part of its name at its founding in 1920, within a year president Carrie Chapman Catt advocated changing the name to the "League of Voters" and admitting men. A 1946 report on the League's history noted that members did "not think of their organization as a 'woman's organization,' but rather, as a citizen organization whose work is carried on by women simply because they happen to be able to organize their time and energies in a convenient working pattern" (Stone, 1946, 16). This same report remarked that the "League has never been feminist in its thinking or approach."

And yet, much as it hesitated to identify as a women's group, the League clearly was and in all practical respects continues to be one. Its founding mission was "to finish the fight" of suffrage; to incorporate women so as to provide "the *fresh challenge* needed to revitalize democracy"; and to represent the ongoing interest in the equal rights of women (Stone, 1946, 5–6, 15; League of Women Voters, 1994, 4–5; italics mine). Since its founding, the League has been an organization whose membership and leadership are overwhelmingly female. Men were not admitted as members until 1974; the first and only male member of the national board was not elected until 2008; and active members at the local, state, and national levels are almost all women. What is more, ninety years after Carrie Chapman Catt suggested dropping it from the organization's name, the word "women" remains.

In sum, the League's conflicted reactions to the gender question exemplified the first component of the good citizen rationale: a simultaneous denial and embrace of women's difference. The League, like other organizations utilizing the good citizen rationale, found a way to allow members simultaneously to be undifferentiated from men, when equality was politically expedient, and civically superior to men in political conditions when traditional notions of gender were more likely to resonate.

The League also embodied the second component of the good citizen identity: the emphasis on intensive deliberation and participation. The League deploys elaborate internal rituals of study, consensus, and parliamentary procedure to formulate its policy positions. In the words of Marguerite M. Wells, the League's president from 1934 to 1944, "To consider well before undertaking action and to prepare well before beginning to act—this may be called a religion with the League of Women Voters" (Wells, [1938] 1962, 11). The League's dedication to consensus-based deliberation and democratic processes dominated its external activities, as well. For example, those values guided the League's "Wartime Service" campaign during World War II (in which "every member would educate the public about the importance of American democracy"), its postwar "Take It to the People" campaign to generate support for the United Nations, and its 1950s "Freedom Agenda" to combat McCarthyism (League of Women Voters, 1994, 11, 22, 24). As League president Percy Maxim Lee told the national convention in 1952, "The League within itself must be a vital force demonstrating democracy at its best . . . To support democracy, we must *be* democracy" (Stuhler, 2003, 251). The League's internal practices gave weight to its implicit claims to civic virtue.

Finally, through its broad policy agenda, the League self-consciously sought to speak for the public interest. In its early years, the League inherited a policy agenda of traditional women's concerns, such as child welfare and gender discrimination; within the first three years, state League chapters had successfully championed some 420 "women's bills" (Young, 1989, 75). In subsequent years, the League's energies were directed at issues such as international relations, citizens' rights, the well-being of disadvantaged people, and the conservation of natural resources (Young, 1989, 162). In the decades after suffrage, the League went from having a "difference" orientation focused on maternalist concerns and women's rights to a "hybrid" orientation that implicitly drew on notions of women's civic virtue to advance nongendered causes. In so doing, the League "succeeded in establishing itself in many quarters as the spokesman for the general interest" (Bauer et al., 1963, 393).

In advocating for progressive domestic legislation and internationalist policy, League representatives couched their arguments in the language of the nation's interests and responsibilities. In interpreting such interests and responsibilities for Congress, the League sought to speak for the general public interest. Interestingly, the League's conception of the US role in the world closely paralleled the League's conception of its own role in the civic sphere. In both cases, the proper path was intensive engagement, which would simultaneously serve as a means to achieve political leadership on an equal footing and to fulfill the responsibilities of good citizenship. The good citizen rationale allowed women to perform caregiving on a national scale, without requiring them to resort to sentimental appeals based on maternal nurturing. In this account, women were looking out for others but were not grounding such concern in explicit claims of gender difference. Rather, the League exemplified the promise of a fulsome citizenship rooted in the public interest.

## The Equal Claimant Identity and Women's Civic Place

The third identity is one I have termed "the equal claimant." This identity is rooted in women's experience of disadvantage and the expectation of recourse to bring about equal conditions and treatment. Roughly speaking, this identity maps onto the sameness construct, the notion that women are inherently equal to men and thus have claims on the state to redress inequities. The equal claimant identity was present in women's advocacy on certain key policy domains, such as (logically) women's rights. Testimony shows, however, that over time equality narratives came to dominate women's testimony in policy domains *other than* women's rights. The equal claimant identity had two variants: one that promoted women's equality through the identification of women's different needs and one that promoted women's equality through the lens of women's sameness.

### Claims for Equality through Different Needs

Witnesses using difference-based equality claims grounded their testimony in discussions of the ways in which women, by virtue of their physiology or social roles, had particular vulnerabilities or disadvantages. Such traits gave rise to what Nancy Fraser (1989) has termed "needs claims." In the interest of women's equality, policymakers had a duty to address women's needs born of women's difference. Such rationales become increasingly important beginning in the 1970s in both health and foreign policy.

During the 1970s and 1990s, when national health insurance was on the congressional agenda, feminist groups called attention to women's unique health needs and disparate treatment under the existing system. In 1975 testimony, for example, a representative of the Women's Lobby stated, "No health care legislation should be considered by this Congress which does not address itself to the specific needs of more than one-half of our population: women." She cited various ways in which women's needs were distinctive. Women make more doctor and hospital visits. Women stay home with sick children. Women take more prescription drugs, often with understudied or serious side effects. Women constitute more health-care workers but fewer health-care policymakers. Women face discrimination in insurance rates. Women face particular diseases that could be prevented with better care.[23] In 1994, Representative Patricia Schroeder (D-CO), representing the Congressional Caucus for Women's Issues, echoed these concerns, noting that women's health differences affect "every system from cardiovascular, to urological, to psychological," as well as reproductive, and "that means research, treatment and insurance must respond appropriately."[24] At the same time, Schroeder made clear that, while rooted in difference, her claim was unabashedly in the egalitarian tradition: "We are here because we are terrified that the health care train is going to leave the station and women are not going to be on it in equal seats . . . we are full citizens and we want to be treated the same as any other citizen."[25]

In the foreign policy realm, the equality-through-difference claims show up in earnest in the 1990s, by which time women's groups' dominant foreign policy concern had shifted from international organizations to human rights, particularly violations against women. A representative of the Women's Commission for Refugee Women and Children, for example, returned from a trip to the Balkans and declared that "women are the targets of this war." She cited the use of rape as a weapon of war and urged the United States to open its doors to these "traumatized women and children."[26] Echoing those sentiments, a representative of the Women's Rights Project of Human Rights Watch cited an epidemic of violence against women perpetrated for political objectives and urged that, for this reason, women's rights must be made a more integral part of US foreign policy.[27]

## Claims for Equality through Sameness

While difference-based equality arguments recognized women as a special class requiring targeted policies to effect equity, sameness-based claims saw gender distinctions as artifacts of patriarchal systems. Here the role of public policy was to make a public statement that downplayed differences and to create legal mechanisms to advance women's equal treatment.

In the health-care domain, nurses' associations voiced equality claims. Roughly 110 nursing groups cumulatively testified more than 800 times from 1910 to 2000, constituting more than 7% of all appearances by women's groups. For the most part, this testimony staked a claim that nurses' perspectives and experiences with patients made them just as worthy as doctors, and arguably more so, to speak to shortcomings in the health-care system and to suggest reforms. Nursing organizations thus drew on their members' professional experiences to stake a claim for equal status in health-care debates. At the same time, nurses' organizations testified that government programs unjustly treated nursing services as inferior to services provided by doctors for purposes of reimbursement formulas. Anyone reading nursing organizations' testimony would hear a clear message, emerging in 70–80% of the testimony: (female) nurses were just as qualified as (male) doctors to speak authoritatively about health-care policy, and the government must treat nursing services as equally worthy.

Within foreign policy, the equality-as-sameness rationale emerged in the debate over ratification of the United Nations Convention on the Elimination of All Forms of Discrimination Against Women (CEDAW). The debate over CEDAW, which in my sample unfolded on Capitol Hill in 1990 and 1994, pivoted on the same question that had bogged down the Equal Rights Amendment in the 1970s. Liberal feminist groups insisted that CEDAW was necessary to ensure equal treatment; conservative women's groups insisted that equal treatment would harm women by ignoring real gender differences; and moderate groups sought to thread the needle by arguing that equality could be gained without trampling on difference. A representative of Women's Rights Action Watch articulated the equality-as-sameness view: CEDAW would provide "full citizenship to women."[28] Interestingly, harking back to the good citizen rationale, she invoked US national interest and leadership on women's rights as reasons to support ratification.[29]

But a representative of the conservative Concerned Women for America argued that, while the group supported equality under law for women, CEDAW would eliminate "commonsense distinctions between men and women."[30] Even in embracing an equality-as-difference rationale in this particular case, Concerned Women for America accepted the premise that public policy should, within reason, promote gender equality.

## The Emergence of the Equal Claimant Identity

These narratives reflect the confluence of three developments: the expansion of the state as a locus for constituency claims making; the movement of women into professional roles; and the development of a second-wave feminist consciousness in the 1960s and 1970s, together with a backlash in the

1980s and 1990s. The movement of women into the paid labor force helped to fuel the creation of women's occupational and policy advocacy organizations and encouraged the spread of women's emerging feminist consciousness. These groups brought that consciousness to their critique of federal programs. As the state expanded into areas such as foreign development aid and health-care provision, feminist and women's occupational groups staked women's claims to government resources. The conservative backlash created women's groups that were uncomfortable with what they saw as overly expansive interpretations of women's sameness with men. In sum, women's occupational and professional advocacy groups identified grievances and brought claims for redress to Congress.

## The Equal Claimant Rationale over Time

As was the case above, the shift toward the equal claimant identity was driven not so much by changes in rhetorical strategies on the part of the same groups over time, but rather by changes in the types of groups that came to testify. Although women's occupational groups—such as those representing nurses, tradeswomen, and lawyers—had testified on foreign policy and health-care issues throughout the twentieth century, the second-wave women's movement brought about a flowering of occupational and feminist advocacy organizations. These groups generally disregarded claims rooted in a female ethic of care or good citizenship. Figure 7.3 charts the shifting types of groups involved in my sample of foreign policy and health testimony over time.

The trends observed in the foreign policy and health fields generalize to women's testimony across issue domains. More than 600 new second-wave feminist groups appeared before Congress from 1966 through 2000 (Goss, 2013). The fraction of women's group testimony given by just the seven most prominent second-wave groups rose from none before the 91st Congress (1969–70) to 20% in the 94th Congress (1975–76). The story is similar for women's occupational groups. They constituted at most 10–15% of testimony in the decades before the 1960s, but by the 1990s, that percentage was close to 55% (Goss, 2013). Through these two pathways—the professional feminist and the occupational lobby—women developed new sources of authority.

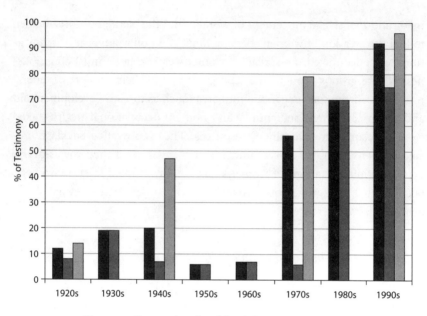

*Figure 7.3.* Occupational and feminist group testimony.

## Does Civic Identity Have Broader Implications for Women's Voice?

Throughout the twentieth century, women's groups drew on female identities rooted in family responsibilities, good citizenship, and equality claims. Yet, over time, the balance of these civic identities evolved, as did the types of policies that women's groups advocated. Women's identity as biological and social mothers, as well as stewards of family legacies, dominated the early decades after suffrage and continued to be important through midcentury. Such relational identities allowed women to forge a civic place in which they were considered expert on everything from children's health to peace to national sovereignty.

In the decades around midcentury, women's groups elaborated an identity of women as good citizens who were both equal to and implicitly superior to men. America at midcentury faced threats to its national interests, founding values, and global leadership, and women were eager to take their place alongside men in articulating a defense of all three. After all, women at midcentury were still on a path to fulfilling the promises they had made in exchange for the vote: that they would use their political inclusion as the basis for a deeply engaged, conscientious citizenship advocating for government that would serve all people. The good citizen identity formed the basis for women's civic place as guardians of the public interest.

The postwar progression of women into the paid labor force (particularly educated women, wives, and mothers), together with the feminist movement's attentiveness to gender inequalities, laid the groundwork for a third civic identity: the equal claimant. Groups drawing on this identity used it to critique systematic gender inequities in society and policy and to make the case that the state had a duty to redress them. The women's groups that staked these claims tended to be associations of female professionals and second-wave feminist advocacy groups. These groups articulated a vision of women as inherently equal to men. These groups' handling of gender difference was distinct from that of their foremothers. In the traditional formulation, difference was a strength—it gave women a distinctive perspective and source of policy authority. In the modern formulation, difference was a social artifact or even a necessary evil of biology. Rather than serving as a rhetorical springboard, difference served as the basis for claims of redress. Women were different, but they aspired to be equal; the state's role was to enact policies that kept difference from impeding equality. Women had become, in a sense, a "special interest" or, rather, an amalgamation of interests with claims against the state for recognition of their equal rights and contributions in the professional sphere.

## Conclusions

This chapter has explored women's civic place—or "places"—as developed by women's organizations and articulated on Capitol Hill to advance policy goals. Throughout the nineteenth and twentieth centuries, women's organizations interpreted the social and political environment to identify and articulate civic identities for women as a basis for collective participation in national policy debates. Women's groups linked female identities to public issues—mothers to children's health programs, good citizens to internationalist foreign policy, professionals to equal treatment in government programs. In so doing, they carved out a civic place for themselves.

These notions of civic place evolved with women's lives and political opportunities. Women's place was rooted in family, in nation, and in the workplace, and each place implied different rhetorical claims and policy agendas. Each identity and corresponding civic place was present throughout the twentieth century, for their philosophical foundations of women's sameness and difference remained alternately vibrant and unresolved. Yet a clear pattern emerged. Claims to women's civic place as family caregivers were more prominent in the early twentieth century than in the late twentieth century, "civic place as good citizenship" peaked in the middle decades, and "place as equal claimant" came to dominate as second-wave feminism birthed occupational and advocacy groups focused on gender discrimination.

Civic identities provide a basis for group claims to authority over policy issues. One might infer that the availability of civic identities has implications for groups' capacity to insert themselves in policy debates. The more civic identities upon which women's groups can draw, we might hypothesize, the greater women's role in national policy debates will be. According to this hypothesis, women's groups should be most prominent on Capitol Hill—and testifying on the broadest range of issues—when they can credibly and compellingly activate maternal, good citizen, *and* equal claimant identities. In other words, women's groups should be most prominent when they are free to call upon the full range of women's identities, whether rooted in difference, sameness, or some hybrid of the two, as the political context warrants. In a related work (Goss, 2013), I document that women's groups in the twentieth century were most active on Capitol Hill when they could credibly invoke the broadest possible array of identity narratives.

This chapter has offered an account of how a politically marginalized population can effectively navigate around the sources of its disadvantage to be heard in the halls of power. Congress, the principal venue for issue advocacy groups at the national level, proved more receptive than might be expected to the voices of women, regardless of their political status. It was and remains an important locus for women's collective advocacy. While nonprofits' testimony does not necessarily change laws, just being invited to appear is a measure of organizational credibility, "insider-ness," and influence among elite decision makers. At the same time, as this study makes clear, organizations' access to power evolves over time, even as they strive to maintain political relevance. Insider advocacy strategies such as congressional testimony pose clear limitations, as organizations that once enjoyed access find themselves losing ground to others with stronger claims to politically relevant resources, policy expertise, and moral language.

NOTES

1. In adopting the term "place," I am cognizant of its historically pejorative usage signifying the oppression of less advantaged groups, as in "keeping women in their place." Here I wish to reclaim the term as one signifying group empowerment through political engagement.

2. Historians have rightly observed that civic republican theory at times romanticizes unequal relations among people. I employ the term because it continues to resonate as the conventional signifier of America's communitarian tradition, as opposed to its individualistic one. I thank Nancy MacLean for pointing me to the critique of the term. In a fascinating history, Leonard and Tronto (2007) argue that the gendered division between the liberal (male) and civic republican (female) citizen was in a sense "invented" not long after the nation's founding. The division arose when masculinity was redefined to center on self-interest and private economic gain; that is, individualism. Such a conception was anathema to the traditional view of manly citizenship as being oriented around civic responsibility. Under the gendered partitioning of citizenship roles, women were to be the standard bearers for the participatory, community-oriented, other-regarding citizenship that civic republicans celebrate, while men were freed to represent the individualistic, rights-centered conception of classical liberals.

3. McDonagh (2009) challenges Kraditor's (1971) argument that difference ("expediency") rationales largely replaced equality rationales in the lead-up to ratification.

4. The LexisNexis congressional online service contains all published hearings and unpublished hearings through 1976 for the House and through 1984 for the Senate. Unpublished hearings tend to focus on District of Columbia affairs, minor legislative action, or sensitive issues (such as national security or matters involving private individuals). Historically, women's groups' appearances at unpublished hearings were rare, bordering on nonexistent.

5. The codebook is available at http://www.policyagendas.org/page/topic-codebook. Each hearing in my data set has been given the same topic code that the Policy Agendas Project coders assigned in their data set of all congressional hearings (which at the time of this research covered 1946–2004). For earlier hearings, I extrapolated from the coding rules used by the Policy Agendas Project coders.

6. Senate Committee on Education and Labor, *Protection of Maternity*, 67th Cong., 1st Sess. 15 (April 25, 28, May 5, 1921) (testimony of Maud Wood Park, League of Women Voters). See also the testimony of Florence Kelley, National Consumers League, esp. 136–37.

7. House Committee on Interstate and Foreign Commerce, *Public Protection of Maternity and Infancy*, 66th Cong., 3rd Sess. 55 (December 20–23, 28, 29, 1920) (testimony of Mrs. Milton P. Higgins, president, National Congress of Mothers and Parent-Teacher Associations).

8. Senate Subcommittee on Permanent Court of International Justice, Senate Foreign Relations Committee, *Permanent Court of International Justice*, 68th Cong., 1st Sess. 147 (April 30, May 1, 1924) (testimony of Mrs. Martin Hutchins, American Association of University Women).

9. Senate Committee on Foreign Relations, *Charter of the United Nations*, 79th Cong., 1st Sess. 570 (July 9–13, 1945) (testimony of Mrs. L. Benge, Mothers of Sons Forum).

10. Senate Committee on Foreign Relations, *Charter of the United Nations*, 79th Cong., 1st sess. 351 (July 9–13, 1945) (testimony of Agnes Waters, National Blue Star Mothers).

11. Senate Committee on Foreign Relations, *Revision of the United Nations Charter*, 81st Cong., 2nd Sess. 561 (February 2, 3, 6, 8, 9, 13, 15, 17, 20, 1950) (testimony of Jane L. Hayford, World Organization of Mothers of All Nations).

12. Senate Committee on Foreign Relations, *Revision of the United Nations Charter*, 81st Cong., 2nd Sess. 561 (February 2, 3, 6, 8, 9, 13, 15, 17, 20, 1950) (Dorothy Thompson, "The Progress of a Journal Editorial," *Ladies Home Journal* February 1950, reprinted in hearing record).

13. Senate Committee on Public Health and National Quarantine, *Protection of Maternity and Infancy*, 66th Cong., 2nd Sess. 42 (May 12, 1920) (testimony of Mary Stewart, Women's National Republican Executive Committee).

14. House Committee on Interstate and Foreign Commerce, *Public Protection of Maternity and Infancy*, 67th Cong., 1st Sess. 68 (July 12–16, 18–23, 1921) (testimony of Mrs. Albert Leatherbee, Massachusetts Antisuffrage Association).

15. Senate Committee on Education and Labor, *Protection of Maternity*, 67th Cong., 1st Sess. 147 (April 25, 28, May 5, 1921) (testimony of Mrs. Larue Brown, National League of Women Voters).

16. Senate Committee on Foreign Relations, *Review of the United Nations Charter, Part 5*, 83rd Cong., 2nd Sess. 516 (June 17, 1954) (testimony of Mrs. Clark Bailey, Kentucky Society, Daughters of the American Revolution).

17. Senate Committee on Foreign Relations, *Review of the United Nations Charter, Part 7*, 83rd Cong., 2nd Sess. 62 (July 10, 1954) (testimony of Mrs. Howard M. Smith, Minnesota Daughters of the American Revolution).

18. In her study of women's groups' rhetoric, Wendy Sharer (2004, 18) likewise noted that "claims about gender difference and women's moral nature would be used by various women's groups to justify their entry in to domains of political control in the post-suffrage era."

19. Senate Committee on Foreign Relations, *Review of the United Nations Charter, Part 2*, 83rd Cong., 2nd Sess. 116 (February 12, 1954) (testimony of Mrs. Harry C. Long, United Church Women of Ohio).

20. Senate Committee on Foreign Relations, *European Recovery Program, Part 2*, 80th Cong., 2nd Sess. 1058 (January 16, 19–24, 26–28, 1948) (statement of Rep. Pete Jarman, D-AL).

21. Senate Committee on Foreign Relations, *Revision of the United Nations Charter*, 81st Cong., 2nd Sess. 716 (February 2, 3, 6, 8, 9, 13, 15, 17, 20, 1950) (statement of Mrs. Margaret Hopkins Worrell).

22. Senate Committee on Foreign Relations, *Review of the United Nations Charter*, 84th Cong, 1st Sess. 935 (March 17, 1955) (statement of Mrs. Niels Jacobson).

23. House Committee on Ways and Means, *National Health Insurance, Vol. 7*, 93rd Cong., 2nd Sess. 3066 (June 28, 1974) (testimony of Carol Burris, president, Women's Lobby).

24. House Committee on Energy and Commerce, *Health Care Reform, Part 8*, 103rd Cong., 2nd Sess. 16 (January 26, 1994) (testimony of Patricia Schroeder, co-chair, Congressional Caucus for Women's Issues).

25. Ibid.

26. Commission on Security and Cooperation in Europe (Joint Congressional Commission), *Implementation of the Helsinki Accords: War Crimes and the Humanitarian Crisis in the Former Yugoslavia*, 103rd Cong., 1st Sess. 10–14 (January 25, 1993) (testimony of Catherine O'Neill, chairwoman, Women's Commission for Refugee Women and Children).

27. House Committee on Foreign Affairs, *Human Rights Abuses against Women*, 103rd Cong., 1st Sess. 17–22 (September 28, 29, October 20, 1993; March 22, 1994) (testimony of Dorothy Q. Thomas, director, Women's Rights Project, Human Rights Watch).

28. House Committee on Foreign Affairs, *International Human Rights Abuses against Women*, 101st Cong., 2nd Sess. 12 (March 21, July 26, 1990) (testimony of Arvonne S. Fraser, International Women's Rights Action Watch).

29. Senate Committee on Foreign Relations, *Convention on the Elimination of All Forms of Discrimination against Women*, 101st Cong., 2nd Sess. 71–79 (August 2, 1990) (testimony of Arvonne S. Fraser, International Women's Rights Action Watch).

30. Senate Committee on Foreign Relations, *Convention on the Elimination of All Forms of Discrimination against Women*, 101st Cong., 2nd Sess. 82 (August 2, 1990) (testimony of Ellen Smith, field legislative counsel, Concerned Women for America).

### REFERENCES

Alonso, Harriet Hyman. 1993. *Peace as a Women's Issue: A History of the U.S. Movement for World Peace and Women's Rights*. Syracuse, NY: Syracuse University Press.

Ashby, LeRoy. 1984. *Saving the Waifs: Reformers and Dependent Children, 1890–1917.* Philadelphia: Temple University Press.

Baker, Paula. 1984. "The Domestication of Politics: Women and American Political Society, 1780–1920." *American Historical Review* 89, no. 3: 620–47.

Bartels, Larry M. 2008. *Unequal Democracy: The Political Economy of the New Gilded Age*. New York: Russell Sage.

Bauer, Raymond A., Ithiel de Sola Pool, and Lewis Anthony Dexter. 1963. *American Business and Public Policy: The Politics of Foreign Trade*. New York: Atherton Press.

Bennett, W. Lance. 2004. *News: The Politics of Illusion*. 6th ed. New York: Pearson, Longman.

Berry, Jeffrey M. 1997. *The Interest Group Society*. 3rd ed. New York: Longman.

Berry, Jeffrey M., and David F. Arons. 2003. *A Voice for Nonprofits*. Washington, DC: Brookings Institution Press.

Carabillo, Toni, Judith Meuli, and June Bundy Csida. 1993. *Feminist Chronicles*. Los Angeles: Women's Graphics.

Costain, Anne N. 1988. "Women's Claims as a Special Interest." In *The Politics of the Gender Gap*, edited by Carol M. Mueller, 150–72. Newbury Park, CA: Sage.

Cott, Nancy F. 1987. *The Grounding of Modern Feminism*. New Haven, CT: Yale University Press.

Davis, Flora. 1999. *Moving the Mountain: The Women's Movement in America Since 1960*. Urbana: University of Illinois Press.

Elshtain, Jean Bethke. 1981. *Public Man, Private Woman*. Oxford: Martin Robertson.

Fiorina, Morris P., and Samuel J. Abrams. 2009. *Disconnect*. Norman: University of Oklahoma Press.

Fraser, Nancy. 1989. "Talking about Needs: Interpretive Contests as Political Conflicts in Welfare-State Societies." *Ethics* 99, no. 2: 291–313.

———. 1997. "Equality, Difference and Democracy: Recent Feminist Debates in the United States." In *Feminism and the New Democracy*, edited by Jodi Dean, 98–109. London: Sage.

Gilens, Martin. 2012. *Affluence and Influence: Economic Inequality and Political Power in America*. New York: Russell Sage.

Gilligan, Carol. 1982. *In a Different Voice*. Cambridge, MA: Harvard University Press.

Goss, Kristin A. 2009. "Never Surrender? How Women's Groups Abandoned Their Policy Niche in U.S. Foreign Policy Debates, 1916–2000." *Politics and Gender* 5, no. 4: 1–37.

———. 2013. *The Paradox of Gender Equality: How American Women's Groups Gained and Lost Their Public Voice*. Ann Arbor: University of Michigan Press.

Goss, Kristin A., and Michael T. Heaney. 2010. "Organizing Women as Women: Hybridity and Grassroots Collective Action in the 21st Century." *Perspectives on Politics* 8, no. 1: 27–52.

Grossmann, Matt. 2012. *The Not-So-Special Interests: Interest Groups, Public Representation, and American Governance*. Palo Alto, CA: Stanford University Press.

Hacker, Jacob S., and Paul Pierson. 2010. *Winner-Take-All Politics*. New York: Simon and Schuster.

Jeffreys-Jones, Rhodri. 1995. *Changing Differences: Women and the Shaping of American Foreign Policy, 1917–1994*. New Brunswick, NJ: Rutgers University Press.

Kaminer, Wendy. 1984. *Women Volunteering: The Pleasure, Pain, and Politics of Unpaid Work From 1830 to the Present*. Garden City, NY: Anchor Press.

Kasniunas, Nina Therese. 2009. "Impact of Interest Group Testimony on Lawmaking in Congress." PhD diss., Loyola University, Chicago.

Kerber, Linda K. 1976. "The Republican Mother: Women and the Enlightenment— An American Perspective." *American Quarterly* 28, no. 2: 187–205.

Kraditor, Aileen. 1971. *The Ideas of the Woman Suffrage Movement: 1890–1920*. Garden City, NY: Doubleday.

League of Women Voters. 1994. *The League of Women Voters in Perspective*. Washington, DC: League of Women Voters.

Leonard, Stephen T., and Joan C. Tronto. 2007. "The Genders of Citizenship." *American Political Science Review* 101, no. 1: 33–46.

Leyden, Kevin M. 1995. "Interest Group Resources and Testimony at Congressional Hearings." *Legislative Studies Quarterly* 20, no. 3: 431–39.

Lister, Ruth. 2003. *Citizenship: Feminist Perspectives*. 2nd ed. New York: New York University Press.

Mansbridge, Jane J. 1986. *Why We Lost the ERA*. Chicago: University of Chicago Press.

McDonagh, Eileen. 2009. *The Motherless State: Women's Political Leadership and American Democracy*. Chicago: University of Chicago Press.

Offen, Karen. 1988. "Defining Feminism: A Comparative Historical Approach." *Signs* 14, no. 1: 119–57.

O'Neill, William L. 1971. *Everyone Was Brave: A History of Feminism in America*. New York: Quadrangle/New York Times.

Ruddick, Sara. 1989. *Maternal Thinking: Towards a Politics of Peace*. London: Women's Press.

Sapiro, Virginia. 1984. *The Political Integration of Women: Roles, Socialization, and Politics*. Urbana: University of Illinois Press.

Sarvasy, Wendy. 1992. "Beyond the Difference versus Equality Policy Debate: Postsuffrage Feminism, Citizenship and the Quest for a Feminist Welfare State." *Signs* 17, no. 2: 329–62.

Schattschneider, E. E. 1960. *The Semi-Sovereign People*. New York: Holt, Rinehart and Winston.

Scott, Joan W. 1988. Deconstructing Equality-versus-Difference: Or, the Uses of Poststructuralist Theory for Feminism. *Feminist Studies* 14, no. 1: 32–50.

Sharer, Wendy B. 2004. *Vote and Voice: Women's Organizations and Political Literacy, 1915–1930*. Carbondale: Southern Illinois University Press.

Skocpol, Theda. 1992. *Protecting Soldiers and Mothers*. Cambridge, MA: Belknap Press of Harvard University.

———. 2003. *Diminished Democracy: From Membership to Management in American Civic Life*. Norman: University of Oklahoma Press.

Somma, Mark, and Sue Tolleson-Rinehart. 1997. "Tracking the Elusive Green Women: Sex, Environmentalism, and Feminism in the United States and Europe." *Political Research Quarterly* 50, no. 1: 153–69.

Stone, Kathryn. 1946. *25 Years of a Great Idea*. Washington, DC: National League of Women Voters.

Strolovitch, Dara Z. 2007. *Affirmative Advocacy: Race, Class, and Gender in Interest Group Politics*. Chicago: University of Chicago Press.

Stuhler, Barbara. 2003. *For the Public Record: A Documentary History of the League of Women Voters*. Washington, DC: League of Women Voters.

Swerdlow, Amy. 1993. *Women Strike for Peace*. Chicago: University of Chicago Press.

Wells, Marguerite M. [1938] 1962. *A Portrait of the League of Women Voters*. Washington, DC: League of Women Voters.

Young, Louise M. 1989. *In the Public Interest: The League of Women Voters, 1920–1970*. New York: Greenwood Press.

# CHAPTER EIGHT

# The Political Voice of American Children

## Nonprofit Advocacy and a Century of Representation for Child Well-Being

DOUG IMIG

Public interest groups, citizens' groups, nonprofits, and social movement organizations play a critical representative role in American democracy (Berry, 1977; Schlozman and Tierney, 1986; Truman, 1951). In the words of a recent Aspen Institute study, "active participation in the policy process is a fundamental function of the nonprofit sector in a democratic society" (Salamon and Geller, 2008). In fact, nonprofits may be the "primary vehicles by which people . . . pressure government to respond to disadvantaged groups . . . and attend to unresolved problems" (Child and Grønbjerg, 2007, 260). The capacity of nonprofits to offer political representation to marginalized and silent constituencies has gained urgency as recent studies suggest that levels of social capital and civic engagement are widely in decline (Andrews and Edwards, 2004; Putnam, 2000; Skocpol, 2003).

In spite of the importance of their representative capacity, our understanding of the extent to which nonprofits actually engage in advocacy is limited. In part, this is a function of the sources of empirical information available on nonprofit advocacy. Our principal insights into nonprofits come from two types of information.

First, organizational directories like the *Encyclopedia of Associations* and national databases maintained on tax-exempt organizations provide a range of insights into nonprofits, including information on their size, range of reported activities, and membership status. These data sources also allow us to comment on dimensions of the nonprofit sector more generally, including key periods of organizational formation (Lowery and Gray, 2004; Meyer and Imig, 1993). From organizational directories and tax data, for example, we can chart the major surge in public interest organizing that began in the 1960s (Berry, 1977). We also are able to sketch the lapses and redundancies of representation that continue to characterize the American pressure system, leaving the "heavenly chorus" of interest representation to sing with a decidedly "upper-crust accent" (Edwards and McCarthy, 2004; Schattschneider, 1960; Schlozman, 1984).

But organizational directories prove to be less helpful when it comes to documenting other critical facets of the nonprofit sector, particularly when we seek to understand advocacy and lobbying activities. To learn more about nonprofit activity including advocacy, we generally turn to survey data (cf. Child and Grønbjerg, 2007). Survey data offer powerful insights into the tactical and strategic venue choices made by nonprofits. But even when they are taken together, organizational directories, charitable databases, and surveys of nonprofits offer uneven insights into what nonprofits actually do. This is certainly true when it comes to advocacy. In part, this uncertainty is likely to reflect nonprofits' own ambivalence toward advocacy (cf. Berry and Arons, 2003; Child and Grønbjerg, 2007). Consider these examples:

- Boris and Krehely (2002) find that fewer than 2% of 501(c)(3) organizations reported lobbying expenses across a recent ten-year period.
- Meanwhile, a survey of more than 2,200 nonprofits active at the state level indicates that roughly a quarter of nonprofits are engaged in advocacy, broadly defined (Child and Grønbjerg, 2007, 266).
- Still a third story emerges from surveys conducted with leaders of 872 nonprofit organizations in four key fields (Salamon and Geller, 2008). A total of 73% of these leaders reported that their groups engage in some form of policy advocacy or lobbying (Salamon and Geller, 2008, i).
- A key insight into the political efficacy of nonprofits is offered by Carol J. DeVita and her collaborators (chap. 4, this volume), who find that 64% of nonprofits believe that they have no or little political influence in the geographic area that they serve.

What accounts for this broad range of findings? There is no doubt that some of the differences uncovered by these studies follow from the range of definitions of advocacy employed. In order to clear some of this definitional underbrush, Robert J. Pekkanen and Steven Rathgeb Smith in their introduction to this volume clarify advocacy as the "attempt to influence public policy, either directly or indirectly." But even under this broad net, there are vast differences between nonprofits oriented toward *direct* and *indirect* advocacy (see Boris and Maronick, chap. 3, and Mosley, chap. 5, this volume), and these difference both follow from and bear direct implications on the venues advocates choose and the constraints on their efforts. Direct strategic action is "intended to change policy or regulation by working directly with policy makers and other institutional elites" (Mosley, 2011, 439). Related tactics may include "participating in government commissions and committees, providing testimony on public policy issues, and participating in the development or revision of public policy."

Indirect advocacy, meanwhile, includes tactics that are "generally intended to raise concern about the problem among the general public and to help shape solutions that are considered desirable" (Mosley, 2011, 440). Often associated with the repertoire of social movements, tactics in this category include "providing public education, writing letters to the editor, . . . joining coalitions, issuing policy reports, . . . demonstrations and boycotts" (Mosley, 2011, 440; see also Tarrow, 2011).

There are other limitations on our empirical understanding of advocacy by nonprofits. First, we know a great deal more about certain types of organizations, including public charities, Washington-based national organizations, and groups within particular *fields of activity*, or movement sectors (Foley and Edwards, 2002). But we know much less about nonprofits at the state and local level; about faith-based groups; or about organizations too new, amorphous, or small to appear in national databases and directories (Child and Grønbjerg, 2007, 265).

A number of these lapses are addressed directly by the essays in this volume. Jeffrey M. Berry and Kent E. Portney in chapter 1, for example, offer compelling evidence that local, municipal policy systems are much more porous to nonprofit advocacy efforts than state or national policy systems. When their engagement with local government endures, nonprofits are more likely to be successful as they come to be recognized as substantial and trusted partners in decision making and service provision. Advocacy efforts—particularly when they are conducted in multiple venues and locales—are costly in terms of time, personnel, and related resources, and nonprofits need to concentrate their efforts in those venues where they are able to maximize their return on investment. In this sense, a lack of strategic focus imposes a limitation on advocacy effectiveness. In terms of political efficacy, Carol J. DeVita, Milena Nikolova, and Katie L. Roeger (chap. 4, this volume) find that larger organizations oriented toward action at the national level are much more likely than smaller and locally focused nonprofits to believe that their efforts make a difference.

These findings certainly leave room for further research concerning the degree to which nonprofits offer political representation to marginalized and silent constituencies, the tactics they use, and the issues they champion.

## Outcomes—and Successes—of Nonprofit Advocacy

The greatest lacuna in the study of nonprofit advocacy concerns organizations' level of influence. Once we discover that an organization is committed to policy representation and political advocacy, how do we identify the effectiveness of that strategic effort? What measures of influence would persuade us that *this* voice rather than *that* voice was influential in shaping the direction of public policy? As DeVita and her colleagues indicate (chap. 4, this volume), larger nonprofits, 501(c)(4) organizations, and groups that employ a lobbyist are significantly more likely than their smaller or resource-constrained colleagues to feel that they wield political influence. But this leaves open the conditions under which such groups are actually able to effect change.

At the national level, some studies have sought to gauge levels of policy efficacy in terms of the range of voices invited to deliver testimony before congressional committees (Hansen, 1991; see also, Goss, chap. 7, this volume). Meanwhile, at the local level, other studies have sought to chart the rich networks of interaction that constitute the foundations of city politics (Dahl, 1961; Stone, 1989; see also Berry and Portney, chap. 1, this volume).

Still a third promising avenue for discussing advocacy influence is suggested by studies of the policy process (e.g., Baumgartner and Jones, 1993; Nelson, 1982) and studies of the interaction between *political processes* and social movements (e.g., Costain, 1992; Imig and Tarrow, 2001; McAdam, 1982). Taking advantage of the record left by the daily press, these studies attempt to identify the range of voices engaged in the policy process *who also managed to gain media coverage for their actions* (often no small feat in itself). In a sense, these studies are designed to help us understand the macrolevel conditions under which advocacy is likely to emerge and to be successful, the venue choices of advocates, and their tactical and strategic choices.

Media-generated event data offer several other advantages that suggest it might provide useful insights into nonprofit advocacy as well.

1. Archives of media data (particularly newspaper archives) are available for most regional and national (and even international) markets.
2. These archives often cover long historical periods, allowing for comparisons across time (adjusting for differences in reporting style and language use over many decades). The historical article archives of the *New York Times*, for example, are available at the daily level from

1851 forward. This capacity allows us to build an understanding of how public policy issues gain and lose media salience, and can also provide insights into the ways that issue representation has evolved over time.

3. Working from media archives allows us to avoid the limitations of defining a field of activity a priori from organizational directories or nonprofit databases. Theoretically, the media record allows us to glimpse the full range of voices that have gained media attention for their activity in a relevant policy arena. Working from that picture, we can then try to identify the voice of nonprofits within that historical conversation.

4. Media-generated event data allow us to identify not only active organizations, but also their tactics, targets, and issues.

5. Media data offer insights into both the historical ebb and flow of a macro policy area (or field of activity), as well as insights into shifting patterns of representation and framing within that general arc. (For example, we can comment on the shifting proportion of advocacy events within a policy sector initiated by churches, charities, professional associations, and academic and research groups across time.)

6. Organizations named in the media record can then be tracked across other measures of policy engagement such as congressional hearings.

These advantages lead us to wonder: what if we were to stand a number of traditional questions concerning nonprofit advocacy on their head? What insights might be gained into the nature of nonprofit advocacy if, rather than begin with the nonprofit as the unit of analysis, we instead looked at the range of voices and activity within a particular policy arena identified by the media?

## The Political Representation of Children across the Last Century

One policy arena that we can examine in this respect is political advocacy for children. Across the last century, reformers have both railed against the many threats to American children and championed public policies to improve their well-being (Imig and Wright, 2010; Michel, 1999; Mintz, 2004). As Julia Lathrop, the first head of the Children's Bureau, argued in the early twentieth century: "the mere business of being a baby in the United States must be classified as an extra-hazardous occupation, and those children who weathered the storms of the first year grew up in a battered, weakened, and crippled condition" (quoted in Lindenmeyer, 2004, 111). Yet in spite of nearly constant advocacy efforts, the United States has embraced a much less coherent or generous system of support for children and families than other developed nations (Adamson, 2010). In fact, the share of federal funding devoted to children has dropped over the last half century, and it is projected to continue on a downward trajectory (Ingelhart, 2007; Lesley, 2011).

Some observers have suggested that children draw the short straw when it comes to public policy because they do not have a vote. But at the same time, their welfare is the focus of thousands of nonprofits, constituting one of the largest cohorts within the nonprofit sector (cf. Salamon and Geller, 2008, i). In fact, the most recent edition of the *National Directory of Nonprofit Organizations* lists over 10,000 American nonprofits that include children's issues within their mission (Gale, 2010). Children may be politically silent but, based on the number of organizations speaking for them, they are extremely well represented. This paradox makes them a strong case for examining the nature of the representation of weak, silent, and marginalized groups within American society.

Often called the national newspaper of record, the *New York Times* offers a robust source of media data with which to follow advocacy for public policies across time. What insights does the historical archive of the *Times* suggest when it comes to advocacy for children in this country over the last century, and the role of nonprofit organizations in that conversation?

Some preliminary answers to these questions can be found in a data set containing more than 7,100 *New York Times* news articles on child advocacy filed between 1901 and 2009. Articles in the data set touch on four broad categories of American children's policy:

- Child care and early education policy (including day nurseries, crèches, preschool, nursery school, kindergarten, universal pre-kindergarten, center-based care, and Head Start).
- Child health and nutrition policy (including infant mortality, breast-feeding, nutritional support, WIC, immunizations, and prenatal and well-child care).
- Child labor policy (principally including regulation of the industrial and agricultural employment of children under age 16 in the United States).
- Child abuse, cruelty, neglect, and abandonment (including a broad range of policy discussions concerning the physical, mental, and sexual abuse of children; the protection of children from such abuse; and shifting policies concerning abuse reporting regulations).

Articles were pulled from the *New York Times* article archives using keyword searches and were then cleaned and coded to arrive at a final data set of 7,127 media reports of events over the last century that concerned one of these four aspects of children's policy. News reports of advocacy efforts were included in the data set. Other types of articles (such as reports of natural disasters or birth, marriage, and death announcements) were excluded. Coding decisions, protocols, and coding schemes are based on the Integrated Data for Events Analysis (IDEA) project, directed by Doug Bond. For more information, visit http://vranet.com/IDEA.aspx.

The resulting data set offers a historical overview of advocacy for children, as that history has been recorded by the daily press and is contained in the media archive. These data shed light onto the full range of tactics associated with child advocacy, their venues of choice, as well as the full range of voices participating in the historical conversation over children's policy as catalogued in the *New York Times*.

A broad range of events are uncovered by this method. Many of these events were press releases or policy statements. Others centered on the release of research reports, announcements of workshops, and findings reported at conferences. Another share of the press reports discussed efforts to contact officials, announcements of support for legislation, and the launch of advocacy campaigns. There are also a small number of more contentious events, including marches, demonstrations, sit-ins, and other types of protest actions. A final cluster of events concerns advocacy organization dynamics, including reports of new groups being formed, holding fundraising events, merging or splitting from other groups, and disbanding over time.

## Historical Patterns of Children's Issue Salience

What does the historical media record tell us about the general ebb and flow of children's advocacy over the last century? Figure 8.1 offers a picture of advocacy over time, as documented in the *New York Times* database. It offers a graphic representation of the public salience of child advocacy in this country over the last century based on the record compiled a day at a time by the reporting staff of the *New York Times*. (The break in the trend line acknowledges a difference between the two sections of the *Times* article archives that existed at the time these data were collected.) Figure 8.1 shows us year-by-year counts of the number of children's advocacy events reported by the media. As it suggests, attention to children's issues crested in two identifiable waves over the last century. Children's issues first peaked in public salience in the 1930s, consistent with the broad sweep of progressive politics, before fading from public consciousness. Aligning with the emergence of the "interest group society," we find a second wave of rising salience of children's advocacy since the 1960s (Berry, 1977). As with the earlier wave of salience, the second period of expanded attention to children also appears to have declined from its 2002 peak.

The issue-attention cycles identified in these data suggest that there have been historical moments in which dimensions of political opportunity have been more favorable to children's advocacy (Downs, 1972). These waves of rise and decline raise interesting questions about the efficacy and limitations on advocacy across different historical moments, and confirm that policy attention and political opportunity have been distributed unevenly over time in the United States (Meyer and Imig, 1993).

The cyclic pattern of rise and decline found in these trends also supports the literature on children's policy (cf. Grubb and Lazerson, 1988; Hayes, 1982; Michel, 1999; Steiner, 1976) as well as more general observations of American public policy, interest group activity, and social movement mobilization (Baumgartner and Jones, 1993; Berry, 1977; Salisbury, 1969; Tarrow, 1989).

Within the broad contours of children's advocacy, can we identify individual aspects of the children's cause that have generated the largest share of advocacy activity at different points in time? By identifying the specific issue motivating each of the advocacy events reported in the *Times*, we are able to comment on the evolving focus of the national concern with children. That picture is presented in figure 8.2, which suggests that media data offer an important extension to the argument that there are issue-attention cycles in American politics. Under the broad category of children's policy, we identify a historical *sequencing* of attention to dimensions of child well-being. To paraphrase Anthony Downs (1972), when it comes to children, our issue attention span proves short, and even during periods of rising issue salience, our focus tends to wander. These findings also suggest that the framing of child well-being may be as significant a choice for advocates as their choice of venue.

## What Voices Have Dominated Child Advocacy?

Turning from the general ebb and flow of children's salience, figure 8.3 reports on the range of actors identified by the media data as initiating advocacy events for children over the last century. We identify nine principal

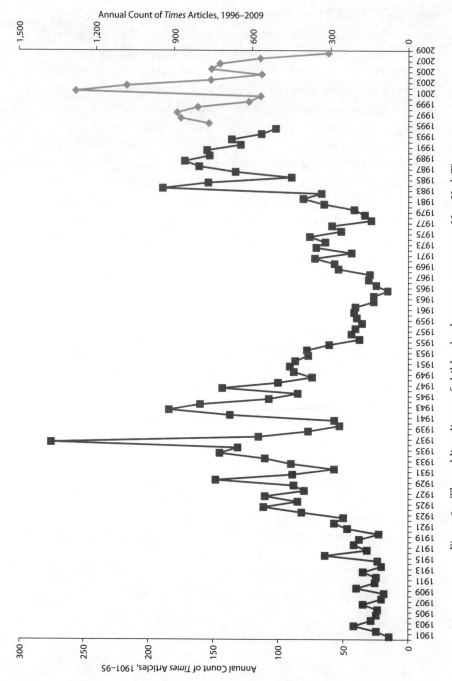

*Figure 8.1.* The public salience of children's advocacy, 1901–2009. *New York Times*

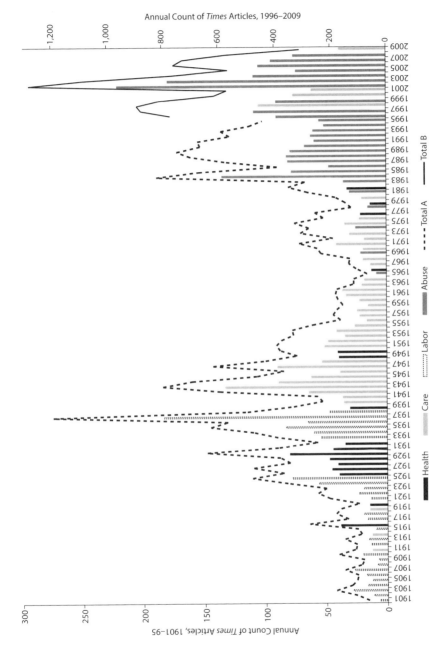

Annual Count of *Times* Articles, 1996–2009

Health    Care    Labor    Abuse    Total A    Total B

Annual Count of *Times* Articles, 1901–95

*Figure 8.2.* Principal issues in media coverage of child policy, 1901–2009.

sets of actors active in this policy arena. These include government, business groups, and nonprofit organizations:

- Governmental entities and agencies (including municipal, state, and federal government representatives) account for 58% of the total set of advocacy events.
- Advocacy organizations (including antipoverty groups, children's advocates, citizen's advocacy groups, women's groups, parent and family groups, civil rights groups, and labor union organizations) were responsible for another 21% of these instances of advocacy.
- Nongovernmental service providers were identified as the source of 5% of events.
- Professional groups (including physicians' organizations such as the American Medical Association and American Academy of Pediatrics; this category also includes nurses, social workers, and other organizations identified by their professional status, such as lawyers) initiated 4% of the total.
- Religious groups authored 3% of the total.
- Business groups headed 4% of events.
- Education and research groups (including both stand-alone research organizations and university-affiliated research centers) initiated another 3%.
- Charities (including organizations identified as philanthropies and foundations) were responsible for 1% of the total.
- Political parties initiated the final 1% of the sample.

Figure 8.3 displays the share of events over each decade of the twentieth century that were initiated by each group of actors.

As figure 8.3 indicates, the media data set tells us a great deal about who has championed children's issues in each decade across the twentieth century. One striking feature of this picture is the continuing and central involvement of governmental actors in this field of activity. Government-initiated events account for the largest share of the total sample (58%). Governmental actors included city and county governments, state governors, and federal agencies. As the data set affirms, across the century, appointed and elected government officials have been a strong force in the process of articulating children's needs and in linking these issues to specific policy responses.

The importance of governmental leadership in establishing the children's agenda is exemplified by federal legislative action during the Second World War, as Congress and the White House took bold action on child-care policy.

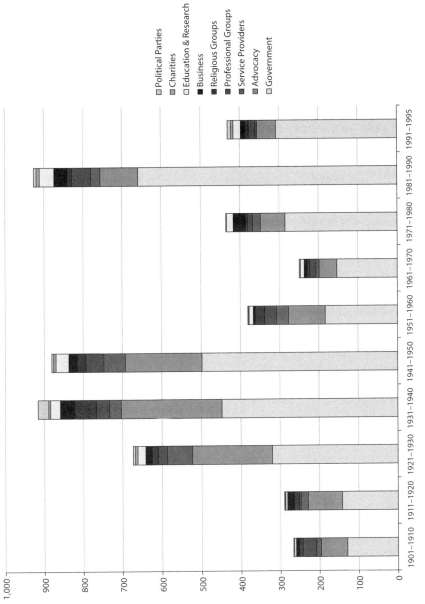

*Figure 8.3.* Organizations initiating children's advocacy events, 1901–95.

This activity led to passage of the Lanham Act and eased the entry of mothers into defense industry jobs by subsidizing child-care centers. All told, before the end of the war, some $50 million in federal funds was directed toward child care, and more than a million and a half children were cared for in federally subsidized centers. In this case, the national crisis of World War II represented a moment in which early childhood policy was reframed as an emergency war measure that was needed in order to expand the size of the domestic labor pool. More generally, external shocks to established policy systems provide moments of expanded political opportunity for new or more marginalized policy claimants.

Scanning trends over the century, we see that the share of children's events initiated by government entities has risen over this period. In recent decades, governmental actors initiated 61% of events in the 1960s, 65% of events in the 1970s, and 71% of events recorded during the 1980s and 1990s.

## Nonprofit Advocacy for Children

But there is also much in this story that points to the active role played by the nonprofit sector in the political representation of American children. As figure 8.4 indicates, a broad range of nonprofits has appeared in the media data, too. The largest share of nonprofit advocacy events was initiated by organizations that self-identify as advocates. At different historical moments, this broad category of actors contained such recognizable children's advocates as the National Child Labor Committee, the Child Welfare League of America, and the Children's Defense Fund. But we also identify a broad sweep of other advocacy groups who took action on behalf of children's concerns. At different moments, these have included parents' groups and parent-teacher organizations, women's clubs, youth groups, civil rights organizations, and trade unions.

These findings underscore the significant role that a broad range of social movements have played in representing children's issues (cf. Steiner, 1976). In successive decades, children's interests have been hosted, given voice, and framed by progressive, trade union, women's, and civil rights movements. This was evident early in the twentieth century, as labor activists Mother Mary Jones and John L. Lewis demanded child labor reform. Significantly, this advocacy emerged in the context—and reflected the needs—of the labor movement more broadly. In consequence, the actions of both Jones and Lewis to reform child labor were consistently framed in terms of the larger

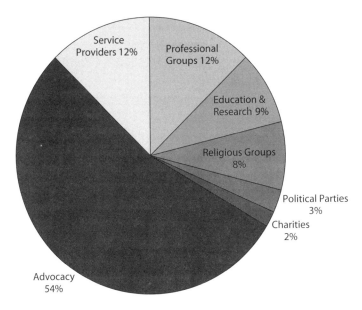

*Figure 8.4.* Nonprofits advocating for children, 1901–95.

objectives of the labor movement. In general, the reliance by child advocates on their association with other social movements represents both a condition of potential success and a limitation on advocacy. "Host" movements offer much-needed resources including funding, members, and organizational and communications infrastructure. At the same time, as the example of child labor suggests, such advocates also articulate children's issues in terms of the host movement.

From the beginning of the twentieth century, the tactical repertoire of advocacy organizations found in our sample included press releases, issue briefings, and announcements of policy positions. By the 1920s, activists increasingly were reported to be engaging in a range of activities designed to more immediately influence the policy process. These included legislative action campaigns. Into the 1920s, the combined efforts of progressive reformers, the Settlement House Movement, the Consumer Movement, the City Beautiful Movement, and the General Federation of Women's Clubs pushed the issues of child labor, child health, and child care onto the policy agenda. During these early decades, children's concerns were part of the social justice agendas of churches, charities, and women's clubs. As a 1916 *Times* headline suggests, the club women were hot on the trail of meaningful child labor reform: "Women Club Members to Bombard Senators with Telegrams for Child Labor Legislation."

From the mid-1920s and into the 1930s, the largest share of children's policy events reported in the *Times* focused on children's health, nutrition, and labor. During this period, two organizations dominated the public representation of children's issues: the US Children's Bureau and the American Child Health Association. From its formation in 1912, the Children's Bureau worked to implement a nationwide system of birth certificates as part of its campaign to gain an empirical understanding of the scope of infant mortality. Aligning state birth certificates made it possible to grasp the magnitude of the problem of infant mortality in America.

By the 1940s, the media database indicates that the tactical repertoire of advocates had expanded still further, with advocates launching broad legislative campaigns, letter-writing campaigns and holding marches, demonstrations, and rallies. In the postwar years, the media data suggest that the repertoire of advocacy organizations had become much more subdued. Almost all advocacy activity reported during the 1980s, for example, concerned the release of research findings, while *none* of the events from this historical period in our sample involved contentious political action. In part, this tactical shift away from more contentious methods may be a reflection of increased scrutiny of advocacy by tax-exempt organizations during this period.

During these same decades, nonprofits accounted for a shrinking share of advocacy events. Figure 8.5 reports on the decade-by-decade changes in the share of advocacy events in our sample that were initiated by nonprofit organizations. As it suggests, the share of events initiated by nonprofits has diminished by nearly 23% since the 1950s.

One possible interpretation of this shrinking role is that advocacy agendas have been embraced by governmental agencies. This interpretation would be supported if we could point to expanding policy support for children's programs. But the picture is much less clear. In fact, public spending on children has declined during the same period in which children's advocacy has diminished. It also appears that nonprofits have chosen a less contentious repertoire during this same period. While nonprofits continue to undertake educational and research activities, there are far fewer instances of direct action or concerted legislative campaigns in recent decades. In general, an antipathy to advocacy by nonprofits has likely tempered their activism in recent years.

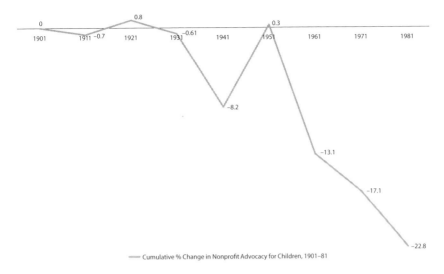

*Figure 8.5.* Change in share of advocacy events for children initiated by nonprofits, 1901–81.

## Conclusions

This chapter considers the ways that nonprofits advocate for children in America. An analysis of the historical media record offers insights into the pattern of nonprofit engagement in children's policy over the last century. The findings from that analysis paint a picture of the ebb and flow of child advocacy over time and allow us to identify two periods in which waves of child advocacy have surged before retreating. The media database also offers evidence suggesting that the issue focus of children's advocacy has shifted over time. In other words, it explains what we mean when we say the well-being of children has evolved across the century.

Returning to our central question: what are the dimensions of nonprofit advocacy for children? This examination has identified a broad range of actors engaged in advocacy for children over the last century. These actors include both governmental and nongovernmental entities that have played instrumental roles in shaping the public salience as well as the political representation of children across time. More than half of all advocacy events contained in the data set were initiated by governmental entities, and the share of events initiated by governmental actors has only increased in recent years. By comparison, through the first half of the twentieth century, nonprofits represented the largest cohort of voices advocating for children.

Within the nonprofit sector, the data set identifies a broad range of organizations that have been active on behalf of children. These organizations include not only the likely suspects—social movement organizations, children's advocates, and service providers—but also a wide range of professional associations, educational and research groups, religious organizations, political parties, churches, charities, and foundations. Across the century, nonprofits initiated 38% of all events contained in the database. (The narrowly defined category of advocacy organizations alone was responsible for 21% of all events in the sample.)

When it comes to the capacity of nonprofits to provide effective political voice to weak, marginalized, and silent constituencies, this study reveals several troubling trends. The data suggest that nonprofits have initiated a shrinking share of advocacy events discussed in the press over the last 50 years (down 23% from the 1960s). The data also suggest that the tactical repertoire of nonprofit advocacy has become more subdued over this same period of time. While nonprofits in the sample continue to engage in a full range of educational activities (including producing and publishing issue briefs, holding workshops and conferences, and issuing policy statements and research reports), in recent years they have been much less inclined to engage in direct action campaigns to influence legislation or to mobilize the public. A growing reliance on mainstream activity potentially reflects the increasing institutionalization and normalization of nonprofits in the policy process (see also Mosley, chap. 5, this volume). Conversely, this silence may have significant implications for related aspects of political participation, such as forming collective identity, translating collective identity into collective action, and mobilizing the mass public in support of policy agendas. The absence of this dimension of the tactical repertoire of advocates is troubling given the historical centrality of direct action and mobilization efforts to the historical successes of activist campaigns (Fantasia and Hirsch, 1995).

But before giving too much weight to these findings, more study is needed. While the media record certainly offers a glimpse of the broad range of organizations that gave voice to children's concerns at different points in our history, these data alone provide little insight into the tax status of these groups. One way to respond to this limitation would be to collect more information on the organizational and tax status of the (more than 2,200) named organizations identified in the media data set.

Another limitation concerns the assumed link between issue salience and political action. While *New York Times* data are likely to be a robust measure of public issue salience, a corresponding measure of policy engagement would be helpful in order to verify that the advocates gaining press attention also gain a seat at the policy-making table. Ideally, we would work to connect the data on issue salience to other measures of policy involvement—such as participation in congressional hearings—in order to expand our understanding of the policy outcomes that followed from the advocacy efforts identified in this investigation.

But even with these cautions, this investigation confirms that nonprofits have played a vigorous role in representing children in this country. Early in the last century, nonprofits accounted for the largest share of advocacy activity on behalf of children. More troubling, however, is our second key finding. Echoing patterns of representation of American women (Goss, chap. 7, this volume), nonprofit organizations representing children have proliferated over time, and yet their advocacy presence appears to have diminished in both frequency and intensity in recent years.

## NOTE

I thank Doug Bond for kindly sharing the IDEA system.

## REFERENCES

Adamson, P. 2010. "The Children Left Behind: A League Table of Inequality in Child Well-Being in the World's Rich Countries." Innocenti Report Card 9, UNICEF Innocenti Research Center, Florence. http://www.unicef-irc.org/publications/pdf/rc9_eng.pdf.

Andrews, Kenneth T., and Bob Edwards. 2004. "Advocacy Organizations in the U.S. Political Process." *Annual Review of Sociology* 30: 479–506.

Baumgartner, Frank, and Bryan Jones. 1993. *Agendas and Instability in American Politics.* Chicago: University of Chicago.

Berry, J. 1977. *The Interest Group Society.* 3rd ed. New York: Longman.

Berry, Jeffrey M., with David F. Arons. 2003. *A Voice for Nonprofits.* Washington, DC: Brookings Institution Press.

Boris, Elizabeth T., and Jeff Krehely. 2002. "Civic Participation and Advocacy." In *The State of Nonprofit America*, edited by Lester M. Salamon, 299–330. Washington, DC: Brookings Institution Press.

Child, Curtis D., and Kirsten A. Grønbjerg. 2007. "Nonprofit Advocacy Organizations: Their Characteristics and Activities." *Social Science Quarterly* 88, no. 1: 259–81.

Costain, A. 1992. *Inviting Women's Rebellion: A Political Process Interpretation of the Women's Movement.* Baltimore, MD: Johns Hopkins University Press.

Dahl, Robert A. 1961. *Who Governs?* New Haven, CT: Yale University Press.

Downs, A. 1972. "Up and Down with Ecology: The Issue-Attention Cycle." *Public Interest* 28: 38–50.

Edwards, B., and J. McCarthy. 2004. "Resources and Social Movement Mobilization." In *The Blackwell Companion to Social Movements*, edited by David A. Snow, Sarah A. Soule, and Hanspeter Kriesi, 116–52. Malden, MA: Blackwell.

Fantasia, Rick, and Eric L. Hirsch. 1995. "Culture in Rebellion: The Appropriation and Transformation of the Veil in the Algerian Revolution." In *Social Movements and Culture*, edited by Hank Johnston and Bert Klandermans, chap. 8, 144–60. Minneapolis: University of Minnesota.

Foley, Michael W., and Bob Edwards. 2002. "How Do Members Count? Membership, Governance, and Advocacy in the Nonprofit World." In *Strategies and Finances, Exploring Organizations and Advocacy 2*, edited by Elizabeth J. Reid and Maria D. Montilla, 19–32. Washington, DC: Urban Institute. http://www.urban.org/url.cfm?ID=410532.

Gale. 2010. *National Directory of Nonprofit Organizations*. New York: Gale.

Grubb, W. N., and M. Lazerson. 1988. *Broken Promises: How Americans Fail Their Children*. Chicago: University of Chicago Press.

Hansen, J. 1991. *Gaining Access: Congress and the Farm Lobby, 1919–1981*. Chicago: University of Chicago Press.

Hayes, C. D. 1982. *Making Policies for Children: A Study of the Federal Process*. Washington, DC: National Academy Press.

Imig, D., and S. Tarrow, eds. 2001. *Contentious Europeans: Protest and Politics in an Emerging Polity*. Lanham, MD: Rowman and Littlefield.

Imig, D., and F. Wright. 2010. "Health and Science." In *A Cultural History of Childhood and Family in the Modern Age*, edited by J. Hawes and N. Hiner, 179–94. Oxford: Berg Publishers.

Inglehart, John K. 2007. "Insuring All Children—The New Political Imperative." *New England Journal of Medicine* 357: 70–76.

Lesley, B. 2011. "Getting Back to Basics for Our Nation's Children." *Huffington Post*, July 27, http://www.huffingtonpost.com/bruce-lesley/children-budget-cuts_b_905113.html.

Lindenmeyer, K. 2004. "The Federal Government and Child Health." In *Children in Sickness and in Health: A Historical Handbook and Guide,* edited by Janet Golden, Richard Meckel, and Heather Munroe Prescott, 107–25. Westport, CT: Greenwood Press.

Lowery, D., and V. Gray. 2004. "Bias in the Heavenly Chorus." *Journal of Theoretical Politics*. 16, no. 1: 5–29.

McAdam, D. 1982. *Political Process and the Development of Black Insurgency*. Chicago: University of Chicago Press.

Meyer, D., and D. Imig. 1993. "Political Opportunity and the Rise and Decline of Interest Group Sectors." *Social Science Journal* 30, no. 3: 253–71.

Michel, S. 1999. *Children's Interests/Mother's Rights*. New Haven, CT: Yale University Press.

Mintz, S. 2004. *Huck's Raft*. Cambridge, MA: Belknap Press of Harvard University.

Mosley, J. 2011. "Institutionalization, Privatization, and Political Opportunity: What

Tactical Choices Reveal about the Policy Advocacy of Human Service Nonprofits." *Nonprofit and Voluntary Sector Quarterly* 40, no. 3: 435–57.

Nelson, B. J. 1982. *Making an Issue of Child Abuse: Political Agenda Setting for Social Problems*. Chicago: University of Chicago Press.

Putnam, R. 2000. *Bowling Alone: The Collapse and Revival of American Community*. New York: Simon and Schuster.

Salamon, Lester M., and Stephanie Lessans Geller with Susan C. Lorentz. 2008. "Nonprofit America: A Force for Democracy?" Listening Post Project Communique No. 9, Center for Civil Society Studies, Johns Hopkins University, Baltimore. http://ccss.jhu.edu/wp-content/uploads/downloads/2011/09/LP_Communique9_2008.pdf.

Salisbury, R. H. 1969. "An Exchange Theory of Interest Groups." *Midwest Journal of Political Science* 13, no. 1: 1–32.

Schattschneider, E. 1960. *The Semi-Sovereign People: A Realist's View of Democracy in America*. New York: Holt, Rinehart and Winston.

Schlozman, K. 1984. "What Accent the Heavenly Chorus? Political Equality and the American Pressure System." *Journal of Politics* 46, no. 4: 1006–32.

Schlozman, K., and J. Tierney. 1986. *Organized Interests and American Democracy*. New York: Harper and Row.

Skocpol, T. 2003. *Diminished Democracy: From Membership to Management in American Civic Culture*. Norman: University of Oklahoma Press.

Steiner, G. 1976. *The Children's Cause*. Washington, DC: Brookings Institution Press.

Stone, Clarence N. 1989. *Regime Politics*. Lawrence: University Press of Kansas.

Tarrow, S. 1989. *Struggle, Politics and Reform: Collective Action, Social Movements and Cycles of Protest*. Western Societies Occasional Paper 21. Ithaca, NY: Cornell University Press.

———. 2011. *Power in Movement*. New York: Cambridge University Press.

Truman, D. B. 1951. *The Governmental Process: Political Interests and Public Opinion*. New York: Alfred A. Knopf.

# CHAPTER NINE

# Analyzing the Practice of Nonprofit Advocacy

## Comparing Two Human Service Networks

JODI SANDFORT

Engaging in public policy is an important and well-established role for non-profit organizations. Yet, as other contributors to this volume explain, initial research about nonprofit advocacy assessed public policy in relation to abstract frames from social science, considering nonprofit agencies as merely another form of interest groups, vehicles for social movement organizing, or civil society associations enabling democratic participation (Andrews and Edwards, 2004; Boris and Krehely, 2002; Mosley, 2010a; Warren, 2004). This volume and other more recent scholarship try to understand advocacy itself to center stage, or to consider, as Robert J. Pekkanen and Steven Rathgeb Smith articulate in their introduction, "How do nonprofits advocate?"

Significant numbers of nonprofit agencies engage in civic engagement, policy advocacy, and lobbying. Many large and formalized nonprofit organizations deploy a range of tactics to share their knowledge and expertise in the public policy arena. Much of this research grows out of larger consideration of how public funding might influence nonprofit board governance, professionalization, formalization, and organizational effectiveness (Grønbjerg, 1993; Sandfort et al., 2008; Schmid et al., 2008; Smith and Lipksy, 1993; Stone, 1996). While scholars initially worried that nonprofits' resource dependency on government created disincentives for policy advocacy, empirical research has found little support for this concern. In fact, there is growing evidence that organizations receiving government funding are more likely to engage in public policy engagement (Berry and Arons, 2003; Chaves et al., 2004; Child and Grønbjerg, 2007; Mosley, 2010b; Salamon and Geller, 2008).

Beyond this question, scholars have not explored many other essential questions about capacity and result. National policy engagement is certainly differentiated from activities at the state and local levels (Berry and Arons, 2003; Child and Grønbjerg, 2007). National nonprofits engaged in policy advocacy are often sizable, able to mobilize their memberships, and pursue sophisticated tactics informed by political practices (Berry, 1999; DeVita and Mosher-Williams, 2001; Strolovitch, 2007). In contrast, nonprofits at the state and local levels engage in much more modest activities; researchers document that confusion about basic legal rules and regulations and lack of familiarity with simple tactics decreases policy advocacy engagement among the whole population of nonprofits (Bass et al., 2007; Berry and Arons, 2003; Reid, 2006).

But more recent descriptive accounts of nonprofits public policy activity by Johns Hopkins Center for Civil Society Studies point to new topics for research. Their 2007 survey and subsequent roundtables of nonprofit leaders highlight the significant role of coalitions and networks for many organizations (Belzer, 2011; Geller and Salamon, 2009; Newhouse, 2010). While Jennifer E. Mosley (chap. 5, this volume) also highlights that collaboration with other organization is a common phenomenon, the mechanism of influence and capacity among networks is not well understood. In fact, this issue inspired the analysis I undertook for this chapter. Through investigating nonprofit advocacy in a unique study of nonprofit service delivery organizations in one state, I highlight what is not yet visible in most research about nonprofit advocacy—the way network participation influences how organizations develop, reinforce, and sustain advocacy practices.

In this exploration, I examine the workings of two networks of human service organizations, both of whose members provide a safety net and social service programs to low-income individuals and families. The statewide Community Action Partnership (CAP) was formalized in 1971 and strengthened in the early 1980s after federal retrenchment and funding consolidation. As such, it emerged in response to government-initiated, top-down policy change. The other network, the Alliance for Connected Communities (hereafter the Alliance), was founded in 1999 by agencies in the state's metro area with deep community roots as historic settlement houses and community centers. As such, it emerged from a bottom-up movement of agency directors who wanted to build power in light of growing environmental uncertainty. Each network is held together by a unique history and a similar struggle for stable and flexible revenue to support daily operations within service-based organizations. Important to our purposes here, while agencies in both networks focus on service provision, they also engage in local and state community building and policy advocacy like many other community-based human service organizations (Marwell, 2004; Mosley, 2011).

In this chapter, I draw upon multiple sources of data to better understand how advocacy capacity is built in such direct service organizations. Like other past research (Berry and Arons, 2003; Mosley et al., 2003; Salamon and Geller, 2008), I capture a point-in-time report by surveying organizational leadership about their policy advocacy tactics. While individual organizations in this sample report used a comparable number of advocacy tactics, and the descriptive analysis points to results consistent with previous research, analysis of qualitative data gathered over time suggests that critical capacity resides at the network level. While surveys offer one picture, a deeper exploration of how advocacy is practiced highlights other dynamics.

While the practices used, capacity they reveal, and results generated differ significantly across the two networks, my interpretation draws upon practice theory to showcase a comparable underlying dynamic. Practice theory starts from the presumption that what people do and how they do it have substantive impact. My application here unpacks how shared experiences and understandings activate or impede the development of critical resources. This lens departs from the conventional understanding of resource as financing provided through a foundation grant or government contract. It also is distinct from other scholarship in this area that sees advocacy as a tool to reduce resource dependency on the sources of finances and legitimacy (Child and Grønbjerg, 2007; Mosley, 2010a; Pfeffer and Salancik, 1978). Rather, it stresses that critical resources also may be human talent, collective strategy, or organizing tools. They can be activated, squandered, or depleted. This interpretative lens emerged from longitudinal, qualitative data and privileges the way each network actually attempts to execute its various advocacy tactics. As we describe what is actually done and how the tactic unfolds and is understood in the network, we can better see the significance of the resourcing process in what subsequently occurs. This close analysis responds to other scholars' entreaties (Berry and Arons, 2003), which we further explore to understand what is involved in developing nonprofit advocacy capacity so that organizations and networks can effectively deploy a range of tactics.

## Research Design and Methodology

This chapter uses data from an in-depth study of two human service networks I conducted from 2007 to 2010. Unlike some case studies, I did not seek to identify cases with strong reputations for effectiveness, either as networks or organizations, when designing this study; instead, I identified two networks with similar characteristics to allow for systematic comparison. Both the Alliance and community action agencies (CAAs) exist in one state, allowing us to hold constant the policy environment in the comparison. Both are organized by the same overall structure, a formal network with an incorporated nonprofit at the hub. At the time of this study, the Alliance had two full-time staff and a budget of $450,000 and the CAP had four full-time staff and a budget of $1 million, both supported largely by membership dues and contracts. All local member agencies committed their executive directors to each network's governing board. Table 9.1 summarizes the organizational members on some key dimensions. As shown, while the Alliance member organizations are smaller than the community action agencies, with average employment half as large, less revenue, and fewer overall programs, organizations in both networks are large, formalized, and professional human service agencies. All receive significant levels of funding from public sources and are thus easily recognized as significant in the day-to-day operations of the American social welfare state.

One source of data comes from an organizational survey of all network members conducted during the spring of 2008. This survey garnered a 75% response rate among the Alliance agencies and 86% among the CAP organizations. The survey captured descriptive information about all agencies regarding programming, size, finances, governance, management capacity, and policy engagement. A comparable survey also was fielded in a statewide random sample of Minnesota's nonprofit sector to allow for comparison between that population and organizations in these two networks (Sandfort and Rogers-Martin, 2008).[1] Measures about policy engagement activities were adapted from a survey of human service organizations in Los Angeles (Mosley et al., 2003).

I also conducted 45 semistructured formal interviews with leaders during 2007–8, distributed equally across each network, about the network's history, accomplishments, and major activities. A portion of these interviews uses a modal narrative approach (Clark et al., 2007) in which hypothetical situations about three major trends in government and nonprofit relationships are posed systematically. This data collection technique helps capitalize on the richness of semistructured interviews and yet enables more systematic comparison about how perception and action are related.

Additionally, I consulted network documents and conducted regular participant observation throughout the four-year period. The field notes (Emerson et al., 1995) captured observations and informal interactions from

TABLE 9.1.
Comparison of Two Human Service Networks, 2008

|  | Alliance of Connected Communities | Community Action Partnership |
|---|---|---|
| Legal status | 501(c)(3) established in 1999 | 501(c)(3) and 501(c)(4) established in 1971 |
| Members | 24 nonprofit organizations: half founded in early twentieth century, half in the 1970s | 27 nonprofit organizations: all founded in the mid-1960s to early 1970s as a result of a federal initiative |
| Geographic reach | seven-county metro area | statewide |
| Board | full representation of all members | full representation of all members |
| Member clients | low-income individuals and families | low-income individuals and families |
| Network services/ resources | executive and staff development, program development access to administrative services | executive and staff development, legislative advocacy, federal and state funding |
| Average total employment of member organizations | 45 | 83 |
| Median revenue | $2,281,767 | $6,558,509 |
| Source of revenue (percent of members receiving) | 76% federal 89% state 89% local | 100% federal 100% state 81% local |
| Programs | average = 19, range 5 to 90 | average = 23, range 5 to 100 |
| Four most common programs of member organizations | youth services family stabilization services senior services juvenile supervision | Head Start weatherization and energy assistance family financial services senior services |

training programs, board meetings and public events, phone conversations, and other professional interactions. They recorded both notable events and participants' interpretations of events. This source was an important supplement to the more formal interviews and added an ethnographic dimension to the research, probing the ways network participation shaped perceptions and actions among their membership.

Survey results were analyzed with SPSS, and descriptive comparisons were made between both networks and our statewide sample of human service organizations. The indices of different types of advocacy tactics were developed using data from the full statewide survey. I also compare results from network organizations with the 239 human service organizations in the statewide sample in this chapter.[2] All qualitative data were transcribed or audio recorded and introduced into NVivo for systematic analysis, using both inductive and deductive coding. Analytical memos were used to capture emerging themes that inform the development of the grounded theory presented here. Because data collection occurred over a number of years, there was systematic refinement of coding scheme and understanding over the course of the study.

This comprehensive data collection and analysis of both qualitative and quantitative information about these two cases enables triangulation and improves the validity of the conclusions drawn. Specifically, the analysis provides rich description that allows me to illuminate important dynamics largely obscured in most research based upon specifying constructs presumed in existing theory to predict policy advocacy.

## Research Context

The organizations in these two networks focus on providing human services for low-income citizens. They are multiservice organizations offering a range of programming such as emergency food and shelter, early childhood and family services, senior services, and support to vulnerable families and youth. They are not in any sense advocacy organizations (Berry and Arons, 2003; Child and Grønbjerg, 2007; Mosley, 2010a). While these two cases are comparable in many ways, there are some distinctions to note. Organizations across each network share similar struggles for stable and flexible funding and espouse values of social justice as central motivations, but each is held together by a unique history. Their stories illustrate how developing an orientation to advocacy is often an incremental process within nonprofit service organizations (Berry and Arons, 2003, 164).

The organizations in the Alliance are traditional social service agencies or community-based organizations (Smith and Lipsky, 1993). Started in the early twentieth century, these settlement houses and mutual aid associations provided language instruction, childhood enrichment, and other family services for those in need. They were originally funded through private donations and community chests but began receiving increasing amounts of public funding during the 1970s and 1980s (Fabricant and Fisher, 2002; Smith and Lipsky, 1993). Much of these organizations' public funding comes from county and city governments and school districts, but table 9.1 also shows that the large majority of organizations receive at least some funding from federal, state, and local sources. Private philanthropy—from foundations, corporations, and individuals—and the United Way were significant funding streams for these organizations throughout much of their existence. Starting in the 1970s, many Alliance agencies began experimenting with community organizing. As social welfare agencies, they saw the importance of community mobilizing and sought private funding to support it and the accompanying advocacy to promote policy change. Yet this type of private funding was always in short supply (Salamon and Geller, 2008).

The formal Alliance network grew from informal meetings among agency directors starting in the mid-1990s. While many had known each other for years, they began to come together more regularly to trade information about funders and emerging opportunities for influence and service innovation. By 1999, they incorporated as a stand-alone nonprofit. As one of the directors of a large nonprofit explained, "I had tried for ten years to get something together; I realized that, as non-profits, we had to get bigger to command respect. Otherwise, we were going to get nicked to death." The Alliance affiliated with the national United Neighborhood Centers of America and more members began attending the national meeting, which put local service experience in a larger, systemic context.

Unlike the CAAs, which have distinct geographic service areas and designated funds, the Alliance members initially were as much competitors as they were collaborators. But they worked diligently to build trust and collaborative capacity (Huxham, 2003). At first they focused on joint buying of products, but they slowly began to talk about sharing management services, program development, and policy engagement. By 2001, they hired staff and, a few years later, a full-time executive director. By 2007, when this formal study began, they had developed and were executing a shared public policy strategy. Although agencies varied in size, all executive directors on the network board initially agreed that building a policy advocacy strategy was a valuable collective good.

While the CAAs operate within the same state and provide similar programs and services to low-income citizens, they have a different history and funding legacy as government-established nonprofits (Smith and Lipsky, 1993). In fact, twenty-five local CAAs were founded in 1965 across the state to lead local efforts on the war on poverty, as was done throughout the country.[3] Today, twenty-seven nonprofits span the state and receive the federal Community Services Block Grant and designated state funding, both valuable and unusual public funds because they support general operating costs. Many implement the federal Low Income Home Energy Assistance Program (targeted to low-income families to help defray high energy costs during winter), Weatherization Assistance Program (which helps improve low-income homes), and Head Start (a family support and early childhood education program). Virtually all agencies also receive state and local public funding, and some garner support from local United Way chapters.

At the core of the statewide network is the statewide Community Action Partnership. Formally established as a nonprofit in 1971, soon after local CAAs were founded, its activities initially focused on sharing program knowledge, promoting development of local resources, and coordinating resources across the full network.[4] In the early years, it was not easy for members to work effectively together, and agency programs and operations varied in quality. But many saw themselves as the frontlines of the federal war on poverty focused on organizing low-income Americans. To formalize their network, they hired an executive director for a new nonprofit and soon thereafter secured the state-level appropriation to support the general operations of the state's CAAs.[5] When the Reagan administration's 1981 Omnibus Budget Reconciliation Act significantly cut federal programs, the network again activated. Working together, the nonprofits encouraged state legislators to pass the first state law designating certain nonprofits as CAAs, just when the federal special designation was rescinded.[6] They also affiliated with the national Community Action Partnership, a membership organization of direct service and state agencies across the country. Legislative successes and subsequent participation in governor-appointed task forces built experiences of policy engagement into the foundations of the network.

My study of these organizations and networks occurred over a number of years during which funding for social welfare service was contracting. The Great Recession affected individual donations, philanthropic endowments, grant making, and government sources at all levels (see Boris and Maronick, chap. 3, this volume). While the state's foundation association reported consistent funding for human services during this period, there were significant changes in large funders who had been important supporters of these agencies. Leaders in both networks agreed with the sentiment expressed by one Alliance member: "It used to be we would talk about the perfect storm [with each funding source fluctuating]. But things aren't really that any more. Now we are thinking more like an earthquake . . . as this hits the county, state, and feds, United Way, foundations and individuals."

One additional relevant element of the research context is the state's nonprofit sector. Both networks exist in a state with a vibrant and growing nonprofit sector.[7] Significant to our purposes here, the state association of nonprofits (one of the largest in the country) is deeply involved in building the sector's capacity for effective public policy engagement. The association regularly offers training on legal responsibilities and regulations, publishes newsletter stories about legislative initiatives, and communicates about instances in which nonprofits act as a resource to government officials. It disseminates tool kits to enable direct service organizations to easily host get-out-the-vote activities and forums for candidates. During the period of this study, in fact, "Working with Government" was the theme of one association's annual conferences, which attracted over 3,000 participants. As such, the state association is widely perceived as one of the more general intermediary organizations recognized as building individual organizational capacity for policy advocacy (Belzer, 2011; Newhouse, 2010). This resource should positively influence the deployment of advocacy tactics for all agencies across the two study networks and comparison sample.

## One View of Advocacy Tactics

Within existing research, a common method of documenting nonprofits' policy advocacy tactics is the use of cross-sectional organizational surveys (Berry and Arons, 2003; Child and Grønbjerg, 2007; Mosley et al., 2003; Schmid et al., 2008), and I draw upon that source of data here. My survey results illustrate that few human service organizations in the statewide sample (7%) and even fewer in both of the case study networks (less than 5%) report hiring lobbying consultants or filing a 501(h) election with the Internal Revenue Service to report lobbying expenses. But like other scholars' work (Bass et al., 2007; Berry and Arons, 2003; Mosley, 2010a), my survey also explores other advocacy activities beyond formal lobbying. I conceptualize public policy engagement in three additional dimensions, ranging on a continuum from insider to indirect tactics (Mosley, 2011). The first, *acting as a resource to public officials*, documents insider activities in which staff or board members formally bring their expertise to those with authority: participating in the development or revision of regulations; having meetings with policy officials; serving on a commission or task force; providing formal testimony at a public hearing; or signing a letter to express their opinion to public officials. Table 9.2 provides details about the index developed from these measures in our survey and illustrates that both Alliance and CAP agencies acted as such a resource more than typical human service agencies (statistically significant). On the five-point scale, Alliance members reported an average of 2.88 such activities over the previous two years and CAP members reported 3.27 incidences, compared to 1.83 in the general population of human service agencies in Minnesota. Mosley (2011) suggests that while these insider tactics require more expertise and are more resource intensive, they offer potentially more benefit because nonprofits develop closer ties to decision makers through using them.

The second dimension of public policy engagement focuses on general activities to *educate the general public about policy-relevant issues.* These activities include writing editorials or letters to the editor; issuing reports related to public policy issues; purchasing advertising to influence public policy; or hosting nonpartisan candidate forums. They are less direct than being a resource to a public official but still require substantive expertise. Again, the organizations in both the Alliance and CAP networks were statistically more likely to be involved in these types of activities than other organizations. On the four-point scale, Alliance members reported an average of 2.30 incidences and the CAP organizations 2.75, compared to 1.0 in the other human service agencies in the state. Comparatively, these organizations use the direct means (resource to public officials) in similar amounts to this more general approach.

The final dimension of public policy engagement focuses on activities related to *organizing constituencies about systems-level issues.* Among these indices, this dimension is the least direct and includes participating in nonpartisan voter registration efforts and other get-out-the-vote activities; working to pass or defeat ballot measures; and organizing citizens to influence policy making. While these tactics might influence the general civic environment, they are less focused on particular organizational or client objectives. Once again, organizations in both the Alliance and CAP networks were statistically more likely to demonstrate these activities than the statewide sample of other human service agencies. On the four-point scale, Alliance members reported an average of 1.5 activities and CAP members reported 1.67 activities, compared to 0.65 in the larger human service agency comparison group. Comparatively, however, the survey suggests less use of these indirect methods than the other two approaches.

TABLE 9.2.
Survey of Advocacy Activities: Comparison between Two Service Networks with
Human Service Organizations from a Statewide Nonprofit Survey

| | Average Response | | |
|---|---|---|---|
| | Alliance | CAP | Other Human Service Agencies |
| Resource to Public Officials[a] | 2.88 | 3.27 | 1.83[b] |
| • Participated in development or revision of public regulation | (.96)[c] | (1.16) | (1.51) |
| • Met in person with a public official | | | |
| • Served on government commission, committee, or task force | | | |
| • Provided testimony to elected officials at a public hearing | | | |
| • Signed on to a letter expressing an opinion to public officials | | | |
| Public Education about Policy Issues[d] | 2.30 | 2.75 | 1.0[e] |
| • Issued a report on a public policy issue | (1.06) | (1.19) | (1.27) |
| • Wrote an editorial or letter to the editor of a newspaper or magazine | | | |
| • Purchased advertising to influence public policy | | | |
| • Hosted or cohosted a nonpartisan candidate forum | | | |
| Organizing Constituencies about Systems-Level Issues[f] | 1.50 | 1.67 | .65[e] |
| • Participated in nonpartisan voter registration efforts | (.96) | (.91) | (.90) |
| • Participated in nonpartisan get-out-the-vote efforts | | | |
| • Participated in an effort to pass or defeat a ballot measure within the past two years | | | |
| • Organized members of the community to influence public policy | | | |
| | $n = 18$ | $n = 22$ | $n = 239$ |

Index measures are calculated from the full random sample of the state's nonprofit organizations.
[a]Index mean = 1.75 (2.78), Cronbach alpha = 0.784.
[b]Where $p < 0.05$.
[c]Parenthetical values indicate standard deviation.
[d]Index mean = 0.70 (1.04), Cronbach alpha = 0.683.
[e]Where $p < 0.01$.
[f]Index mean = 0.51 (.844), Cronbach alpha = 0.689.

The survey also asks about levels of government the agencies sought to influence with these tactics. As table 9.3 reflects, the descriptive results suggest that organizations direct advocacy tactics toward levels of government most relevant to their own agency survival. Alliance organizations are more heavily dependent upon state and local resources to support their range of service programs. They respond to state- and county-issued requests for proposals to secure funding for their food pantries, early childhood programs, and employment services. The CAP organizations secure financial resources from the state government for energy assistance, food programs, and employment, and they enjoy a designative fund that supports general operations. Yet they also receive significant federal resources as the main implementers of some federal programs. As a result of their particular financial dependencies, the leaders in these organizations report focusing their policy advocacy activities on the relevant levels of government. The organizations in both of these networks report statistically more attention to these levels of government than human service organizations in the statewide survey.

To this point, these results paint a picture consistent with previous research. In this sample, few organizations report direct lobbying, but many are involved in a range of advocacy activities, from resource-intensive insider tactics to more indirect tactics such as public education about issues or organizing constituents. The organizations involved in both the Alliance and CAP networks are more engaged in public policy advocacy efforts than other human service agencies. We would expect so because they are larger, more formalized organizations (Bass et al., 2007; Child and Grønbjerg, 2007; Mosley, 2010a, 2011; Salamon and Geller, 2008; Schmid et al., 2008). They also operate at the state and local level, where it is easier to use such tactics to gain access to public officials (Berry and Arons, 2003). The survey results are also consistent with a resource dependency theory (Pfeffer and Salancik,

TABLE 9.3.
Areas of Focus for Organizations' Public Policy Advocacy Activities

|  | Federal (%) | State (%) | Local (%) |
|---|---|---|---|
| Alliance organizations | 39[a] | 89 | 72 |
| CAP organizations | 73 | 96 | 50[a] |
| Other human service organizations | 18[a] | 43[a] | 32[a] |

Data are from responses to the question "what level(s) of government has your organization sought to influence through these activities?"
[a]Statistically different at $p < 0.001$.

1978) account in which advocacy targets and tactics are chosen to maximize influence on the environment. Managers act strategically to minimize environmental uncertainty, targeting entities that allocate financial and other resources, and engaging citizens to increase perceived influence. As we will see, however, this explanation is incomplete when we delve more deeply into the qualitative data collected in this comparative case study. The similarity between these organizations and networks—their size, formalization, dependence on public revenue—would predict similar advocacy tactics and results. Yet significant differences exist in how these organizations and networks actually carry out their advocacy practice.

## Another, More Complete View of Advocacy Tactics

Over a number of years, my research team and I gathered qualitative data that align with the constructs in the quantitative analysis: lobbying, serving as resources to public officials, supporting public education about policy issues, and organizing citizens around policy issues. We also observed and documented events that unfolded as both networks vied to participate in the implementation of federal stimulus funding. What emerges from this careful attention is a deeper understanding of the actual practice of policy advocacy within service organizations and networks.

### *Lobbying*

As would be expected by low reports in the survey, organizational leaders are not strong supporters of formal lobbying. One way they isolate risk for their individual agency is to focus formal lobbying activity in the central agency at the center of each network. Yet the social dynamics among network members shape their understanding of the tactic and how it is implemented.

At board meetings, Alliance members talk more abstractly about lobbying, speaking frequently about the need to engage in "systems change" or to build new "power bases." Often when this value is expressed, other agency directors challenge the presumption, evoking various experiences or rumors that lend an air of uncertainty about the legitimacy of lobbying activities. When I followed up with one vocal critic, he explained that his organization "does not have the capacity to do [lobbying]. And it is not who I am. I was hired to run the organization the best way I can, provide the best services I can to the community. My board is not that type of board." He and others consulted subsequently estimate that 40–50% of Alliance members have deep ambivalence about lobbying. This belief goes unchallenged by experience because few Alliance organizations are familiar with lobbying practice. One notable exception is an agency that for years used philanthropic grants to support community organizing and lobbying. This expertise was one of the resources the executive director eagerly offered to the network when her organization joined. As she explained, "We are we are really known for our public policy, even though we only have two people on staff [doing it]. I believed we needed to come together with the others to help build the power." The Alliance executive committee initially embraced this idea and contracted with her registered lobbyist for 20 hours a month to lobby on behalf of the network. But this effort was short lived. The deep ambivalence felt by large numbers of Alliance members caused them to back away from this tactic when private philanthropic funding became uncertain. While they could have used board meetings to assemble funding or plan alternative lobbying activities, Alliance members merely resumed their ongoing discussion about the lack of policymaker interests in low-income people and despair that the situation would ever change. This shared belief—plus the individual director's ambivalence about the value—created little impetus to sustain lobbying capacity within the network.

In contrast, the CAP annually develops a public policy statement, articulating particular legislative objectives. At the network level, they contract with a part-time lobbyist, and the executive director and up to two additional staff also register as lobbyists. But like the Alliance, there is not uniform support for lobbying within the CAP network. Thinking about the board table, one director reflected, "half the table doesn't care about the lobbying . . . [They] get money and do good things and don't care where it comes from. Part of it is geographic, related to the sophistication of agencies and philosophy. But it also depends on the background of the executive director." Lobbying is recognized as legitimate activity for advancing the shared objectives of the network, however. Membership dues support the associated expenses, and updates are a regular segment in board meetings. The ambivalence of individual leaders manifests in unequal engagement in the network's legislative committee rather than a decision for the network not to engage at all.

In fact, the CAP network regularly engages in heated debates about particular legislative issues and tactics. As Mosley (2010a) points out, both lobbying and advocacy tactics can be directed toward either organizational or client concerns. Chuck Atwood, the network's director, characterizes it as oriented toward "business" or "mission" and recounts many experiences in the network history where one or the other focused network lobbying efforts. For the network, *business* lobbying focuses on ensuring that the state and federal funding streams important to the network are protected from attacks. For some, network lobbying effectiveness is assessed on this dimension. As one leader reflected, "Our lobbying receives a B+ or A– because we've weathered some pretty rough storms. When the times come we need to do something, we do it. The minus comes because we are not as good at shaping policy as we should be." *Mission* lobbying in these cases focuses on policy issues related to the well-being of low-income citizens—minimum wage legislation, access to health care, changes to food stamp eligibility, establishing a legislative commission to end poverty. Assessing network effectiveness along these lines, another network member came to less favorable conclusions: "We aren't on the foreground of changing social justice issues. I would give us a C. We're passing, but not doing great. We aren't rabble rousing like [other low-income policy advocates] but we offer services to those in need." Yet differing perspectives are live within the network, shaping heated debates around the board table about the relative costs and benefits of business- and mission-oriented lobbying strategies.

Because of their general similarities, a resource dependency lens does not explain the variation across these two networks. It would lead one to assume that lobbying is most strategic when focused on "business" issues, overlooking the nuanced ways that individuals debate, compromise, and ultimately integrate their perspectives to enable actual practice. While executive directors' attitudes about lobbying are significant, these attitudes were deterministic for individual organizations and, ultimately, the whole network. In the Alliance case, there were not enough experiences to overpower the predominant belief that policymakers have little commitment to low-income people. In the CAP network, individual directors' attitudes were merely mediating forces in determining the scope and direction of the overall advocacy strategy.

### Resource to Public Officials

As the survey results suggest, the organizations in both networks engage in a range of advocacy tactics beyond lobbying. The most common advocacy activities focus on proactively engaging in both legislative and administrative advocacy and developing relationships with public officials (Berry and Arons, 2003; Mosley, 2010a). Again, while organizations in both networks carry out these tactics statistically more often than other human service agencies, how this ambition is carried out varies in important ways.

In early 2007, the Alliance board decided it would develop a full strategy to improve its standing with state and local officials and formed a policy working group. This group deliberated and decided to invite legislators to a meeting at the state capital. A few elected officials showed up, and the agency directors talked about their programming. But, as network members reflected on it later, it seemed difficult for the officials to fully comprehend the core mission of the network or the constituencies they represented. As a result, the network decided to catalogue its own assets; mimicking the success of a health membership organization, it hired a firm to develop a staff survey across its members to document latent talents and skills. While such information helped increase internal information and was shared with member agencies, it was not effectively leveraged like the health membership agency's experience of working with state officials. Instead of exploring the cause of the mismatch, members resorted to stories of other missed opportunities in building credibility with legislative officials: state representatives who showed up at their organization on Thanksgiving or for flu shots but not asking them to testify at the legislature, or conversations where their knowledge of community issues was not appreciated.

More progress occurred at the local level. Through another survey of their members, the director, Juanita Larson, discovered one metro county contracted with the network for a total of $8 million in various services, requiring 40 different staff members to manage all the contracts. She used this information to access the county's administrator, who was interested in increasing administrative efficiencies. They met over a number of months, and as a result a county staff member was asked to join the network's monthly meetings. The county began to regularly consult with network members about community concerns. While this positive development allowed county officials to better appreciate the breadth and scope of the Alliance's work, a relationship with one county did not translate into relationships with others. In interviews, leaders repeatedly referenced the myriad state, county, city, and school districts that influenced their work. Assessing the overall progress, one network member said, "There are just so many municipalities. We can't establish this type of relationship with all of them." The task of positioning the network as a true resource to public officials, to invest the time in building the trusting relationships, felt overwhelming because of its scope.

In contrast, the CAP network carries out proactive development of relationships with public officials. Unlike the contested value of lobbying, network members uniformly believe it is important to offer policy leaders their expertise. "We must be able to show working poor people who are in danger of becoming undefined families on the political radar. We need to always remind decision-makers that working poverty is important—and not to be replaced by the homeless or methadone addicts—especially in rural areas." When the Legislative Commission to End Poverty was constituted, members opened local offices for visits and hosted community meetings. This type of investment yielded results. Many members recount being called by state legislators for opinions about policy issues or antipoverty program details. These relationships made them comfortable asking administrators for technical modifications in state legislation or county process when modest tweaks could improve service options. In recounting one such story, one director explained, "If I didn't have a trusting relationship with a legislator he wouldn't have done this for me at all. Also, knowing the funding agency folks, developing a trusting relationship with them, that's also important. When you . . . do what you say you're going to do, then they trust you."

Like the Alliance, the CAAs enjoy trusting relationships with administrative officials at the state and county levels, but they have a broader scope. Although local agencies receive significant resources from various state departments, the state's Office of Economic Opportunity (OEO), so named because of its War on Poverty–era origins, has a unique relationship with the entire network. They invest federal funds in the network that assist with general operations, research, and data analysis; regularly communicate the network staff and agency directors; and conduct monitoring visits in ways emphasizing mutual partnership. When creating a training program for the networks' emerging leaders, program designers all assumed that the office's director, Linda Miller, would be a featured speaker. In that session, she told a story of implementing total quality management within state government and her realization that low-income people were not technically her office's customers. Nonprofits were. As she explained, "We are the voice for the poor in state government. [But] someone needs to make sure that you get the resources you need. If we take care of you, you are able to care of the poor people." In this way, Miller conveyed the shared mission between her office and the network, subtly communicating the special relationship existing between them.

Agencies in the network also enjoy a unique relationship with local public officials. By federal law, CAA boards reflect a "tripartite board structure";

one third of the members are local elected officials, one third are community members, and one third are low-income citizens. While this structure takes different forms in each locality, it helps ensure that these nonprofits have unique access to county officials. Conservative board members appreciate how these agencies leverage local volunteers and help ensure that federal funding reaches rural areas. Policy briefs from the state CAP network also provide timely information about state policy changes to local officials. One consequence of this unique board arrangement—and its difference from the Alliance whose board members are more typical nonprofit volunteers—was documented in our survey; 85% of CAP agencies report that their boards are somewhat or very active in influencing public policy, compared to only 45% of Alliance agencies.[8]

Applying resource dependency theory suggests that nonprofit leaders interested in acting as a resource for public officials should go through a rational, strategic planning process to identify and target their activities to minimize main dependencies. Yet examination of these comparable networks shows that relationships often evolve in ways more haphazard and opportunistic. All of these organizations have complex revenue portfolios, making it difficult to identify or act upon all dependencies. For the Alliance, that reality immobilized further action. For the CAP, the historical relationships with the state's OEO took precedence over other, more significant state-level financial dependencies. Relationships are shaped through experiences of success and failure, from repeated contact over time or stories of past embarrassments. External mandates, such as the metro county's sudden interest in the Alliance or the law dictating community action board composition, create opportunities that can be capitalized upon with sufficient attention.

## Public Education about Policy Issues

Educating others is a less direct and less common approach to advocacy in these organizations. For the Alliance, mobilizing the resources to do public education about policy issues is challenging. Members operate different programs—youth development, child care, preschool, mental health groups, food shelves, and employment programs—each with distinct funding sources. The network does not have much research capacity to document the scope of these programs or their collective impact. The active working group on youth development draws staff from all agencies, but its activities focus on sharing program information and establishing common program outcomes. When asked about the potential of working through the network to educate citizens about the policy issues driving their work, staff and leaders found it difficult to imagine. In service-oriented organizations, resources to proactively engage in this way are scarce.

As part of the Alliance's intentional public policy strategy developed in 2007, however, a number of organizations hosted candidate forums. They developed a subcommittee of member organizations and worked through logistics. While there was good turnout at some agencies, it was not uniform. As a result, fewer organizations hosted the following year. After a few years, this tactic faded from collective discussion. While individual agencies might occasionally write letters to the editor of neighborhood papers or use food shelf statistics when trying to raise funds from individuals, leaders never discuss proactively engaging the media around the networks' board tables. When asked about this lack of public outreach, many were surprised by the question. It never occurred to them that public education would be a viable tactic if they collectively pursued it. They also never considered that this constrained viewpoint likely contributed to public officials' lack of understanding of their value to communities.

In contrast, the CAP network has many tactics focused on educating the public about policy issues related to both their work and their clients' needs. The network publishes a comprehensive, 80-page report every two years documenting current policy or program issue and profiling individual organizational successes. It lists each network member, contact information, and key program areas and results. It presents comparable data about clients served and longer-term results assessed through a self-reliance scale implemented throughout the network. Lobbyists use this report and data when working with legislators and county officials; leaders share copies with important stakeholders from state agencies, universities, private foundations, and local business leaders.

Other tactics are used to carry out public education. As a network of service-based organizations, the statewide Community Action Partnership is an important venue that state-level advocacy groups use to disseminate research, solicit volunteers for pilot programs or research, or implement outreach efforts to low-income citizens. Niche advocacy organizations focused on employment, public assistance benefits, and free tax preparation and regularly attended network meetings to discuss policy challenges and potential solutions, asking the network to get the word out. These direct service organizations are essential in other nonprofits' strategies to educate others about policy issues. Moreover, the network proactively cultivates media attention in areas like asset development or home weatherization, where its member organizations have particular expertise. Even when time and resources are limited, the CAP can showcase local organizations' expertise, and it has developed many different tactics for educating the public about policy issues.

### Organizing Constituencies about Systems-Level Issues

This dimension of advocacy is less common among all human services organizations, and in Alliance and CAP members and human service agencies in general. Yet examining these practices illuminates a few additional factors important in better understanding advocacy capacity.

One commitment uniting the Alliance organizations is a formal goal: "to create assets and tools to amplify community voice." Members claim it is a distinguishing characteristic of the network, differentiating members from other human service agencies. Some shared petitions about local economic or social justice issues. Others hosted brown-bag presentations about new programs, listened to citizen concerns, and responded with staff support for community leadership. But their iconic illustration of this ambition was a get-out-the-vote tool kit developed and branded as Community Power Vote. With promotional materials, voter guides, and contact tracking for staff and volunteers, it was uniformly recognized among members as a significant experiment consistent with their values embracing community organizing. In 2007, they contacted training across the agencies and registered 1,000 voters using the tool kit. Juanita Larson then tried to take their model to the state's nonprofit association and was shocked to discover they had developed their own voter initiative. Rather than partnering with the association, she decided to distribute the kits nationally in their national association of settlement houses and community centers. But the next year, the network registered far fewer voters and discovered few were using the Community Power Vote materials. In fact, rather than building more capacity within their own network for this activity by 2009, the Alliance decided to join a larger coalition—ironically spearheaded by the state's nonprofit association—to participate in get-out-the-vote activities.

The CAP network also evokes the tradition of community mobilization as part of the War on Poverty legacy when they discuss their work. Like the Alliance, however, it is difficult to sustain this tradition in the current environment. One federal funding source, the Community Services Block Grant, mandates "community needs assessments" on a regular basis, and agencies comply. Some organizations use the results of these assessments to inform planning, but none use it to inform a policy agenda. When agencies' programs are threatened, the network has the ability to mobilize staff and clients through email that creates constituent pressure or legislative testimony. The network also aligns with the state's nonprofit association and many other organizations in get-out-the-vote efforts.

In fact, the network's previous executive director hired a consulting firm to develop a statewide grassroots organizing plan for particular legislative districts. During that period, the network employed a full-time organizer who tried to build a deeper base of constituent support for antipoverty policy. But the following network director did not sustain this approach. Members were ambivalent. In discussing it later, network leaders recounted that campaign-style organizing just felt too risky. They remembered the fights during the early years of the national network, when local agencies received significant scrutiny if they pushed too hard to mobilize the poor around electoral change. Targeting particular districts felt quite different than the network's conventional responsive activity when threats were made to a specific program.

### Assessing Network Advocacy Capacity

Members' own assessments of policy advocacy effectiveness align with the picture painted in this analysis. Conventional wisdom encourages nonprofits to be modest in their aspirations of effectiveness, to be prudent in their activities, and to educate funders and board members that long time horizons are often necessary. Such sentiments are heard often within the Alliance. While many members speak frequently about the need to engage in "systems change" work and board meetings focus on desires to share expertise and influence public officials, little progress is made. Survey results confirmed that members did not value the advocacy activities attempted by the Alliance. Among a list of nine different network activities, they rated policy advocacy activities near the bottom. Although the Alliance pursued many different tactics during this study period—hiring a part-time lobbyist, convening a policy work group, hosting annual briefing meetings at the capital, commissioning research to gather data, developing a get-out-the-vote initiative—members could point to no real achievements.

In contrast, CAP's advocacy tactics create significant benefits in the minds of members. Their advocacy successfully curtailed challenges to their state appropriation—a significant accomplishment given growing state budget deficits—and secured federal funds to expand programs and develop a network-wide performance management system and leadership development initiative. Beyond these narrow "business" interests, their efforts also helped to pass an increase in the minimum wage, stabilize a state-funded asset development program, and increase general awareness through the a legislative commission. In our survey, when asked about a comparable list to Alliance members of nine network activities, community action agency leaders rated business and mission policy advocacy as the first and third most important, respectively. In open-ended responses, members drew particular attention to the consequence that access to the legislature, rapid response, and general understanding of lobbying had on building their capacity during critical times.

Although these data about member assessments of network capacity were gathered through our 2008 survey, an unprecedented opportunity emerged during the Great Recession to demonstrate the advocacy capacity of both networks. By early 2009, the community circumstances seemed dire. As layoffs grew, low-income working families were losing their homes to foreclosure, struggling to make ends meet and to pay for food and energy bills. While all nonprofits serving low-income working people could have benefited from the passage of the American Recovery and Reinvestment Act (ARRA), the implementation took a different turn. As a moment experienced by both human service networks in this study, the events provide an opportunity to better understand how advocacy capacity functioned in both networks.

With the new Democratic leadership in the White House and stimulus funding flowing, Alliance members tried to garner the attention of public officials. For the third year in a row, they held a board meeting at the state capital and invited their own legislators to join them. Few showed up. They then asked one member's lobbyist to try and insert the whole network into an employment bill, an emergency assistance bill, or any legislation that might be able to tap federal stimulus funding. All attempts to engage as a full network went nowhere. While they could read the legislative summaries showing increases in funding for the very services they provided for needy families, child care, and unemployed workers, there was no way for them to leverage their collective expertise.

So Alliance leaders tried another strategy focused on the local level. Juanita Larson met multiple times with the same county executive with whom she had previously developed a relationship and asked him to convene a meeting with historic foundation partners. At that meeting, the Alliance described the needs of communities, the potential of a significant public–private partnership, and their unique ability to respond as a network. Yet nothing resulted. While the county continued to imagine there would be a way to contract with the network as a whole and save administrative dollars, the internal barriers to making this change impeded progress. Foundations merely acknowledged that financial resources were short all around.

The network changed course yet again. The Alliance policy work group recommended, and members voted for, joining a statewide coalition, HIRE, of over 70 nonprofit members initially focused on "advocating for the fair allocation of federal stimulus dollars." They believed this coalition would create more contact points with the legislators than Alliance-only efforts. They mobilized staff and board members to attend a rally at the state capital, where the coalition argued that public investments should lift people out poverty. Reflecting immediately afterward, Larson felt it was one of their most successful efforts to engage in public policy process because it was visible, tangible, out in the open. Yet, in reality, like many indirect advocacy tactics, it did little to change the allocation of stimulus funding.

At this unique moment when public funds were available to meet clients' needs, the Alliance's inability to influence the policy process was glaringly apparent, and it caused dissention among them. Many board meetings during the spring and summer focused on diagnosing the challenge and possible solutions. After the dust settled, one organization secured a new group of AmeriCorps volunteers and shared them with other network agencies. But this rather modest benefit also carried costs (a required agency financial match and supervision). It was a small consolation. As one member said, "We were on the outside looking in; all the while we knew that others were benefiting disproportionately."

The CAP experience was strikingly different. From the beginning, the network focused on the ARRA funding. In fact, lobbying of the National Community Action Foundation helped assure specific expansions in CAP program staples—Community Services Block Grant, Weatherization Program, Head Start—and enabled specific information about other programs, such as energy-efficiency tax credits, increased food and shelter assistance, and expanded federal housing programs, to be shared early within the network. From the local and state vantage point, it was relatively easy to activate the network's advocacy practices. Staff and paid lobbyists tracked relevant committees at the state legislature and communicated about federal legislative development to members. In testimony before the state's House Finance and Policy Committee, one network member stressed the network's unique ability to provide a nimble and effective infrastructure for state implementation. He emphasized, "The stimulus package for someone in my line of work is like a kid in the candy store. There are so many things, so many programs funded it in." Local agency staff mobilized for supportive phone calls or emails at critical moments. As the HIRE coalition (which the Alliance joined) mobilized, the network's director, Chuck Atwood, decided to lay low even though proposed cuts to their state funding was on the table; he wanted to proceed with caution, lest the network's own advocacy capacity become a liability.

As the potential for significant federal investment in the Weatherization Program began to crystallize, the network hired an additional lobbyist. The state's OEO also stepped in. While the office technically had oversight of funding sources with relatively modest increases, Linda Miller believed they should share information with the network. She convened a special session of the network's board and, after that initial information sharing, helped ensure that future network meetings focused on sharing implementation plans, management experiences, and problem-solving strategies. From Miller's perspective, doing so was mutually beneficial. Her participation allowed state officials to learn more quickly the implementation challenges and document modifications that could prove helpful to the congressional delegation. In the end, the 28 CAAs accessed over $118 million of federal ARRA funds from various funding streams over a 15-month period.

There certainly are many potential causal factors behind each network's experiences during implementation of ARRA. The institutional embeddedness of the CAP was a significant factor, but its significance was not inevitable. Chuck Atwood's care around the HIRE coalition reflects his awareness that even though advocacy capacity might exist, it is not always prudent to deploy it. The Alliance's own repeated attempts to influence unfolding events reveal their own understanding of the possibility of being strategic agents. These actions, and many others described with our qualitative data, are unpredictable and perplexing through a lens of resource dependency theory. To understand them, and to place them in a more accurate interpretative lens, we must consider other options. This analytical turn has both theoretical and practical importance. The management directive stemming from resource dependency theory—to target advocacy activities to reduce dependency—may overlook other practices important to understanding the development and deployment of policy advocacy capacity among service organizations.

## Interpreting Variation in Policy Advocacy Capacity

This study provides a unique window into the more nuanced process used by nonprofit organizations who engage in policy advocacy. In these comparative cases, service organizations depend on a collective to help build their own advocacy capacity. From a management perspective, this strategic choice makes sense. The knowledge and skills necessary for effective advocacy are distinct from what people managing a service organization, supervising staff, or delivering programs possess. Within the collective, more potential resources existed; they could hire staff with knowledge of legislative processes, utilize and cultivate relationships with other policy advocates and officials, and use effective planning and prioritizing processes. They could also build concrete tools such as LISTSERVs, reports with program facts, and organizing tool kits. Actors within both cases attempted all of these tactics. Yet, as the comparison reveals, such collective resources are not always directed effectively and are not always further developed or sustained. Not all network activity yields resources for use in advocacy, in spite of clear intent.

Interpreting this evidence requires that we turn to a body of theory concerned with the consequentiality of every day action. This theory, called practice theory, enables us to better understand the core logic of how practices are produced, reinforced, and changed, as well as the results of that activity (Feldman, 2004; Feldman and Orlikowski, 2011; Orlikowski, 2002; Nicolini et al., 2003). In the contexts within which they find themselves, people both develop understandings and use artifacts such as research reports, formal data, and marketing materials to inspire certain actions. Practices thus both come out of a particular context and help to constitute that context going forward. As Feldman and Orlikowski (2011, 1240) explain, there is an empirical approach to practices that focuses on how people act in organizational or network contexts, a theoretical focus probing the relationship between actions and social structures, and a philosophical focus exploring the way practices constitute and produce organizational reality. The first approach is relevant as a means for understanding the different views of advocacy practice gleaned from the survey and qualitative data in these cases.

The cross-sectional survey accounts, and resulting attention to variables easy to measure such as size and receipt of government funding (Bass et al., 2007; Child and Grønbjerg, 2007; Mosley 2010a, 2011; Salamon and Geller, 2008), overlook the significance of shared, historical experiences in creating and reinforcing share values and underlying assumptions about advocacy.

But my detailed examination of these two cases highlights its significance. While the Alliance members shared a tradition of responding to community needs through services, their experiences with public policy lobbying and other tactics, such as community organizing, reinforced ineffective timing and unstable financial support. Similarly, when their major federal funding was slashed in the 1980s, CAA leaders learned graphically the consequences of being unprepared to engage in policy advocacy. Yet that period also yielded important successes, creating a state funding appropriation and governor-appointed task forces. These successes convinced them, in ways that eluded many leaders of Alliance organizations, that advocacy tactics could yield significant changes. This mind-set is communicated through stories and rituals. The socialization transmits underlying assumptions about the practical importance of policy advocacy (Schein, 2004). The shared understandings of historical experiences create a background within which the legitimacy of policy-level work is rarely questioned, even though these direct service agencies face many competing demands.

This practice-oriented account is consistent with other research stressing that resources are important in advocacy. But unlike resource dependency theory, which assumes externally situated and constrained resources, this theory posits that resources are not static, not constituted by the objective presence of a budget line item, hired lobbyist, or get-out-the-vote campaign. The data analysis of these cases highlights that resources have to be activated. It is consistent with a stream of practice theory by Martha Feldman (Feldman, 2004; Feldman and Quick, 2009) highlighting a *process of resourcing*, rather than attending to static definitions of resources.

The Alliance kept busy executing a number of advocacy tactics, but their activities depleted, rather than built, the network's resources. The policy work group developed a proactive strategy. A lobbyist worked part time. Yet board meetings focused on topics understood to be important—management and program collaborations, financial uncertainty, changes at historic funding partners—rather than discussing advocacy efforts. Their network acted together on these other topics but did not focus much attention on how they could sustain their lobbying work. From the beginning, network leadership assumed that the only way to do so was to raise external dollars from foundation grants. But this is a difficult path because of changeable philanthropic priorities (Belzer, 2011; Newhouse, 2010). Because of their ambivalence and belief in an external locus of control, the network thought through alternative revenue strategies. They also did not activate other potential resources:

the policy committee had unstable membership; the annual process of establishing a network-level policy agenda happened only sporadically; and staff professional development trainings did not discuss policy advocacy or dispel myths about government relations. While a few members received national legislative updates or funding from national advocacy organizations, they only rarely shared it within the network. There seemed to be many more important things on the Alliance's collective agenda. This reality quelled the potential resources of time, strategic thinking, and program insight from being unleashed for policy-level change.

The CAP network similarly used a number of tactics for public policy advocacy. Yet, as discussed above, they were deployed in different ways. For this network, public policy engagement was a means for using and enhancing resources, building the network's overall strength. Built upon historical experience, network practices focused on sharing information about federal, state, and local policy successes and failures, enhancing the overall knowledge base. They developed common performance measures to share with decision makers and regularly invited other nonprofit advocacy groups to board meetings. Interpreted through a practice theory lens, all such actions help activate multiple types of resources within the network, including funding, time, strategic thinking, and program expertise.

Finally, while these different practices emerge from historical context and shared understanding, the process also helps define what is possible in the future. When tactics such as working with legislators are successful, then training programs with emerging network leaders include daylong modules focused on legislative processes. When lobbyists use network reports about performance and results, a just-in-time performance system is deemed to be important to the network in the future. Once email lists are built or cross-agency working groups assembled, they can be tapped again in the future because operational details are worked out. With this capacity, advocacy practices can focus on execution rather than trying to build competency. The practices reinforce a feeling of agency rather than disillusionment, sustainable even when success is not immediate.

Practice theory helps us to differentiate between potential resources and resources in use. In assessing the ways networks may build the capacity of organizations to effectively carry out policy advocacy practices, the theory emphasizes the recursive way that shared understanding and resources operate. Resources do not exist only because of philanthropic gifts or a brilliant leader. Rather, they are activated and can be further developed when a network is willing to work through ambiguity and roadblocks. Resources can also be squandered and depleted when found in a network unwilling to overcome past challenges.

## Conclusions

With this unique comparative case study, I have tried to move the emerging research focused on nonprofit advocacy beyond categorizing or predicting particular advocacy tactics. Doing so has yielded some interesting insights.

First, this approach highlights the potential significance of the contexts within which nonprofit organizations operate. If we merely see advocacy tactics as bounded by organization, we will miss many elements important in how advocacy is practiced. As Salamon and Geller (2008, 16) conclude, "Squeezed by an increasing need to interact with the policy process but limited resources with which to do so, organizations have turned to intermediary organizations and advocacy coalitions to help, gaining in the process expertise and focused attention that they cannot easily provide internally." Networks provide significant platforms for creating pools of potential resources to support advocacy, some which can be mobilized quickly. They help reduce the confusion surrounding advocacy for many nonprofit managers (Bass et al., chap. 10, this volume) and allow a collection of activities to be understood as the way advocacy is done.

Second, policy advocacy capacity is not merely focused on proactively developing and winning legislative agendas. As these cases illuminate, it can be evoked to assist in policy implementation or deployed reactively to stave off legislative assaults. It can be an essential competency of effective service organizations (Crutchfield and Grant, 2007; see also Bass et al., chap. 10, this volume), but because there are so many potential sites of advocacy activity, capacity involves being able to frame collective understanding of the issue at hand and use resources to enable effective action. While using various advocacy tactics, the Alliance did not actually build capacity. Instead, they reacted haphazardly to events, never quite gaining traction on systems-level change. While carrying out a similar number of tactics, the Community Action Partnership deployed them in ways that built collective will, knowledge, and insider relationships.

Third, this chapter highlights that research merely reporting frequency of advocacy tactics might reveal little about the capacity involved or the effectiveness of those efforts. The notion of capacity suggested here is inherently dynamic; it is not attained but rather created and demonstrated through its execution. It requires activity, insight, reflection, and adjustments, and capacity is enacted to respond to events. The Alliance's collective ambivalence surrounding policy advocacy was visible in what they did and did not do. It also quelled the potential resources of time, strategic thinking, and program insight from being unleashed. The positive collective experience in CAP enabled their practices to form a whole repertoire, activated when unexpected events like stimulus funding occurred. These comparative cases suggest how networks can build and sustain advocacy capacity through their practices. Both small and large events and experiences contain potential for change because people choose how to interpret events, and create, use, or enhance the resources collectively available. Fundamentally, understanding advocacy capacity as practice shifts our analytical attention to how capacity is experienced (Mosley, chap. 5, this volume).

These results have implications for how management support organizations or private funders conceptualize capacity-building efforts in the field. My informants and those interviewed by Jennifer E. Mosley (chap. 5, this volume) certainly experience real funding constraints for advocacy activities. Engaging in policy advocacy is resource intensive for nonprofits; it requires time to develop strategies; knowledge about policy systems, programs, communications; and relationships, which are often in short supply in service organizations like those examined here. One answer would be to support networks. But this analysis suggests that networks may or may not effectively resource policy advocacy. While financial support is necessary, it is not sufficient. This analysis showcases that advocacy capacity is more iterative. Organizations gain capacity through a process of engaging ideas and using tools. While financial resources are always in short supply, some nonprofit leaders act to build shared experiences and collective understanding, which can actually generate or deplete available resources. Using this insight, we hope to move closer to appreciating what it takes to build the capacity of nonprofits to engage more fully in policy processes on behalf of the citizens for whom too few institutions speak.

## NOTES

1. To create an accurate sampling frame that defines the entire population of nonprofit organizations in the state, we defined four strata according to the following revenues (during 2005 or 2006): under $100,000; $100,000 to $1 million; over

$1 million; and no financial data. In total, the stratified random sample included 3,113 organizations across these strata. The distribution by field reflected that of the population. A total of 622 organizations completed the survey for a 20% response rate, which is similar to other mailed surveys of nonprofit organizations (Durst and Newell, 2001; Zimmermann and Stevens, 2006). Analysis comparing survey respondents with the complete random sample showed no statistical differences on either total revenue (criteria of sampling) or the National Taxonomy of Exempt Entities (NTEE; denoting substantive field expertise), suggesting no response bias.

2. In the statewide survey, we used the conventional way of classifying NTEE codes to define human service agencies: Education NEC (B99); Crime and Legal related (I); Employment (J); Food, Agriculture, and Nutrition (K); Housing and Shelter (L); Public Safety; Disaster and Relief (M); Youth Development (O); Human Services (P); and Community and Neighborhood Development (s20).

3. By 1968, there were more than 1,000 in the national network, covering more than 65% of the nation's counties (Clark, 2000).

4. Material in this section was drawn from an unpublished document, "History of Community Action," written circa 1999 for the Office of Economic Opportunity by Sirius Communications.

5. This approach is also maintained in other states. As of 2007, eight other states made state-level appropriations totaling more than $13 million to supplement the federal Community Services Block Grant.

6. This state law became the model for eleven other states, including New Jersey, Florida, Virginia, and Missouri, that developed similar designation in state law.

7. From 1995 to 2005, the state's nonprofit sector grew 67% to 7,339 organizations in IRS data.

8. In the statewide survey of human service organizations, only 21% of agency report boards are active at this level.

## REFERENCES

Andrews, Kenneth T., and Bob Edwards. 2004. "Advocacy Organizations in the U.S. Political Process." *Annual Review of Sociology* 30, no. 1: 479–506.

Bass, Gary D., David R. Arons, Kay Guinane, and Matthew Carter. 2007. *Seen but Not Heard: Strengthening Nonprofit Advocacy.* Washington, DC: Aspen Institute.

Belzer, Hillary. 2011. "Building Advocacy from Within: Report on the West Coast Listening Post Project Roundtable on Nonprofit Advocacy and Lobbying." Center for Civil Society Studies, Johns Hopkins University, Baltimore.

Berry, Jeffrey M. 1999. *The New Liberalism: The Rising Power of Interest Groups.* Washington, DC: Brookings Institution Press.

Berry, Jeffrey M., and David F. Arons. 2003. *A Voice for Nonprofits.* Washington, DC: Brookings Institution Press.

Boris, Elizabeth, and J. Krehely. 2002. "Civic Participation and Advocacy." In *The State of Nonprofit America*, edited by L. Salamon, 299–330. Washington, DC: Brookings Institution Press.

Chaves, Mark, Laura Stephens, and Joseph Galaskiewicz. 2004. "Does Government Funding Suppress Nonprofits' Political Advocacy?" *American Sociological Review* 69: 292–316.

Child, Curtis D., and Kirsten A. Grønbjerg. 2007. "Nonprofit Advocacy Organizations: Their Characteristics and Activities." *Social Science Quarterly* 88, no. 1: 259–81.

Clark, Peter, Charles Booth, Michael Rowlinson, Stephen Procter, and Agnes Delahaye. 2007. "Project Hindsight: Exploring Necessity and Possibility in Cycles of Structuration and Co-Evolution." *Technology Analysis and Strategic Management* 19: 83–97.

Clark, Robert F. 2000. *Maximum Feasible Success: A History of the Community Action Program*. Washington, DC: National Association of Community Action Agencies.

Crutchfield, Leslie, and Heather McLeod Grant. 2007. *Forces for Good: The Six Practices of High-Impact Nonprofits*. Jossey-Bass: New York.

DeVita, Carol J., and Rachel Mosher-Williams, eds. 2001. *Who Speaks for America's Children? The Role of Child Advocates in Public Policy*. Washington, DC: Urban Institute Press.

Durst, Samantha L., and Charldean Newell. 2001. "The Who, Why, and How of Reinvention in Nonprofit Organizations." *Nonprofit Management and Leadership* 11, no. 4: 443–69.

Emerson, Robert, Robert Fretz, and L. Shaw. 1995. *Writing Ethnographic Field Notes*. Chicago: University of Chicago Press.

Fabricant, Michael, and Robert Fisher. 2002. *Settlement Houses under Siege: The Struggle to Sustain Communication Organizations*. New York: Columbia University Press.

Feldman, Martha S. 2004. "Resources in Emerging Structures and Processes of Change." *Organization Science* 15, no. 3: 295–309.

Feldman, Martha S., and Wanda Orlikowski. 2011. "Theorizing Practice and Practicing Theory." *Organization Science* 22, no. 5: 1240–53.

Feldman, Martha S., and Kathryn S. Quick. 2009. "Generating Resources and Energizing Frameworks through Inclusive Public Management." *International Public Management Journal* 12, no. 2: 137–71.

Geller, Stephanie L., and Lester Salamon. 2009. "Listening Post Project Roundtable on Nonprofit Advocacy and Lobbying: Washington, DC." Listening Post Project Communique No. 13. Center for Civil Society Studies, Johns Hopkins University, Baltimore.

Grønbjerg, Kirsten. 1993. *Understanding Nonprofit Funding: Managing Revenue in Social Service and Community Development Organizations*. San Francisco: Jossey Bass.

Huxham, Chris. 2003. "Theorizing Collaboration Practice." *Public Management Review* 5, no. 3: 401–23.

Marwell, Nicole P. 2004. "Privatizing the Welfare State: Nonprofit Community-Based Organizations as Political Actors." *American Sociological Review* 69, no. 2: 265–91.

Mosley, Jennifer. 2010a. "The Policy Advocacy Role of Human Service Nonprofits: Incentives, Involvement, and Impact." In *Human Services as Complex Organizations*, edited by Y. Hasenfeld, 505–31. Los Angeles: Sage.

———. 2010b. "Organizational Resources and Environmental Incentives: Understanding the Policy Advocacy Involvement of Human Service Nonprofits." *Social Service Review* 84, no. 1: 57–76.

———. 2011. "Institutionalization, Privatization, and Political Opportunity: What

Tactical Choices Reveal about the Policy Advocacy of Human Service Nonprofits." *Nonprofit and Voluntary Sector Quarterly* 40, no. 3: 435–57.

Mosley, Jennifer, H. Katz, Yeheskel Hasenfeld, and Helmut Anheier. 2003. "The Challenge of Meeting Social Needs in Los Angeles: Nonprofit Human Service Organizations in a Diverse Community." University of California School of Public Policy and Social Research, Los Angeles.

Newhouse, Chelsea. 2010. "Report on the Listening Post Project Roundtable on Nonprofit Advocacy and Lobbying." Center for Civil Society Studies, Johns Hopkins University, Baltimore.

Nicolini, Davide, Silvia Gherardi, and Dvora Yanow, eds. 2003. *Knowing in Organizations: A Practice-Based Approach.* Armonk, NY: M. E. Sharpe.

Orlikowski, Wanda J. 2002. "Knowing in Practice: Enacting a Collective Capacity in Distributed Organizing." *Organization Science* 13: 249–73.

Pfeffer, Jeff, and G. Salancik. 1978. *The External Control of Organizations: A Resource Dependence Perspective.* New York: Harper and Row.

Reid, Elizabeth. 2006. "Advocacy and the Challenges It Presents for Nonprofits." In *Nonprofits & Government: Collaboration and Conflict*, edited by E. Boris and C. E. Steuerle, 343–72. Washington, DC: Urban Institute Press.

Salamon, Lester, and Stephanie L. Geller. 2008. "Nonprofit America: A Force for Democracy?" Listening Post Project Communique No. 9. Center for Civil Society Studies, Johns Hopkins University, Baltimore.

Sandfort, Jodi, and Nicole Roger-Martins. 2008. "Exploring the Nature and Consequences of Nonprofit Management Capacity." Paper presented at the Association for Research on Nonprofit and Voluntary Associations, Pittsburgh.

Sandfort, Jodi, Sally C. Selden, and Jessica Sowa. 2008. "Do the Tools Used by Government Influence Organizational Performance? An Examination of Early Childhood Education Policy Implementation." *American Review of Public Administration* 38, no. 4: 412–38.

Schein, Edgar. 2004. *Organizational Culture and Leadership.* 3rd ed. New York: Jossey-Bass.

Schmid, H., M. Bar, and R. Nirel, 2008. "Advocacy Activities in Nonprofit Human Service Organizations: Implications for Policy." *Nonprofit and Voluntary Sector Quarterly* 37, no. 4: 581–602.

Smith, Steven R., and Michael Lipsky. 1993. *Non-Profits for Hire: The Welfare State in the Age of Contracting.* Cambridge, MA: Harvard University Press.

Stone, Melissa. M. 1996. "Competing Context: The Evolution of a Nonprofit Organization's Governance System in Multiple Environments." *Administration and Society* 28, no. 1: 61–89.

Strolovitch, Dara. 2007. *Affirmative Advocacy: Race, Class and Gender in Interest Group Politics.* Chicago: University of Chicago Press.

Warren, M. 2004. "What Is the Political Role of Nonprofits in a Democracy?" In *In Search of the Nonprofit Sector*, edited by P. Frumkin and J. Imber, 37–50. New Brunswick, NJ: Transaction.

Zimmerman, Jo An, and Bonnie Stevens. 2006. "The Use of Performance Measurement in South Carolina Nonprofits." *Nonprofit Management and Leadership* 16, no. 3: 315–27.

# CHAPTER TEN

# Effective Advocacy

## Lessons for Nonprofit Leaders from Research and Practice

GARY D. BASS, ALAN J. ABRAMSON, AND EMILY DEWEY

Most of the chapters in this volume report on original research studies that have as their main goal the scholarly objective of deepening understanding of nonprofit advocacy. In contrast, this chapter has a more applied purpose: to draw on scholarship—from this volume and beyond—and the experience of leading nonprofit practitioners to provide guidance to nonprofit managers about their advocacy work. In particular, in the pages that follow we consider what systematic research and lessons drawn from practice have to say about these critical questions: Should nonprofits become engaged in advocacy? If so, how can their engagement be facilitated? And if nonprofits become engaged, how can they maximize the impact of their advocacy?

## What Is Advocacy?

Before addressing these questions, we pause to note that providing guidance to nonprofit leaders about advocacy is complicated by the fact that there is no universally agreed upon meaning of the term "advocacy" in the nonprofit sector. In their introduction to this volume, Robert J. Pekkanen and Steven Rathgeb Smith note that the lack of a common definition means advocacy "resists scholarly analysis."

Pekkanen and Smith make the point that not only is there a lack of a common definition of "advocacy," but also of "nonprofit." If researchers have no common definitions of what they are researching, it makes it hard to apply lessons from scholarly research, placing a higher premium on experience. Yet Pekkanen and Smith do attempt to bring common ground by defining advocacy as "the attempt to influence public policy, either directly or indirectly."

While research in this volume generally follows the Pekkanen and Smith definition, the authors of this chapter have some preference for a broader definition of advocacy given by Ohio State University sociologist Craig Jenkins. Jenkins has defined advocacy as "any attempt to influence the decisions of any institutional elite on behalf of a collective interest."[1] Note that under Jenkins's definition, activity undertaken by nonprofits to affect decisions by both governmental and nongovernmental elites (e.g., corporate leaders) is considered advocacy. For example, the nonprofit that tries to shape a particular corporation's behavior (e.g., change workplace conditions, limit release of pollution, bring CEO pay in line with other pay) is engaged in advocacy under Jenkins's definition but not under Pekkanen and Smith's because the nonprofit was not attempting to influence public policy.

While Pekkanen and Smith's definition of advocacy may be helpful for the purposes of this book, we have a more expansive definition and believe that advocacy is fundamentally about speaking out and making a case for something important. The target of the advocate's voice is most often a person, group, or institution that holds some power over what the advocate wants.

For a variety of reasons, advocacy can be a challenging concept. The word "advocacy" is often used interchangeably with related words such as "lobbying" and "public education." Some groups use it to describe what others would call lobbying; other groups say they do advocacy work, but to an outsider it is not clear that they are engaged in public policy or any other type of advocacy (Bass et al., 2007, 157–61).

Too often, lobbying and advocacy are perceived as synonymous. In fact, the Internal Revenue Service (IRS) narrowly defines lobbying as an attempt to influence *legislation* at the local, state, or federal level. Thus discussions of broad policies or efforts to influence executive branch actions are not lobbying communications. Lobbying always involves advocacy, but advocacy does not always involve lobbying.

It may be more useful to define advocacy by the activities in which a nonprofit engages when trying to "influence the decisions of any institutional elite," as described by Jenkins. (Although we have a broader definition of advocacy than Pekkanen and Smith in this volume, we concur that studying the different types of advocacy behavior will "advance our overall understanding" of the field.) There are countless ways for nonprofits to engage in advocacy; some common methods include educating, public speaking, commissioning polls, mobilizing, petitioning, holding or attending public meetings, performing media outreach, protesting, or filing lawsuits (Bass and Mason, 2010; Donaldson, 2008; Reid, 2000; see also DeVita et al., chap. 4, and Mosley, chap. 5, this volume. Even commenting on proposed regulations or policies is a form of advocacy. In other words, advocacy is much broader than lobbying.

*There is no legal restriction on any advocacy activities that charitable tax-exempt organizations may undertake—with the exception of electioneering and lobbying.* Charities are prohibited from electioneering and are limited in the amount of lobbying they can undertake.[2] Even with lobbying restrictions, however, few nonprofits are likely to exceed the permissible limits. Moreover, only lobbying activities need to be monitored and reported to the IRS on annual tax returns.

Let us describe some examples of permissible advocacy activities for charitable nonprofits.[3] We have used the "advocacy cycle" developed by Bass (2009), as shown in figure 10.1, to characterize different types of advocacy activities. Although figure 10.1 is drawn as a circle, advocacy is not a cycle in which one activity leads automatically to another. Rather, it is amoeba-like, moving from one type of activity to another, back and forth, with nonprofit leaders employing strategies in ways that make sense for their particular issues and circumstances. No single nonprofit is likely to tackle all types of advocacy activities; instead, nonprofit leaders tend to be more skilled at specific types of advocacy. But an effective leader also recognizes the importance of all types of advocacy activities, thinks strategically about the application of each, and knows on whom to rely for such actions.

There is no starting point for entering the advocacy cycle. Some nonprofits may be better skilled at one activity (e.g., research or organizing demonstrations) and will jump in with those types of action when they make the most sense. The successful advocate is strategic about the timing of advocacy activity. The nonprofit advocate that is skilled at policy analysis, for example, may have little to do if the primary focus at a particular moment in time is litigation. What follows is a short description of each of the items in the advocacy cycle.

Research—empirical, public opinion, and policy analysis—provides the foundation for policy positions. Even though research findings are essential to developing or reforming policy options, many nonprofit executives do not think of their research as a form of advocacy. Applying and utilizing research is an essential advocacy tool, however, because it helps to identify or explain policy problems that need to be addressed.

Doing research and developing policy options are not the only examples of advocacy. Advocacy also includes educating the public or subsets of the public about the need for change. When nonprofit leaders talk about social

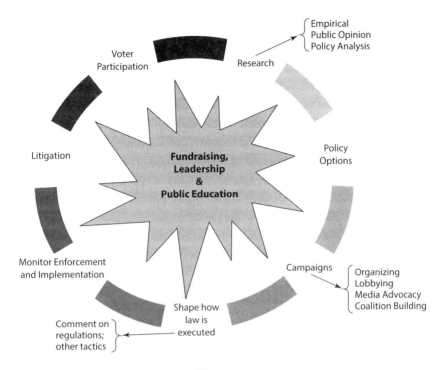

*Figure 10.1.*

issues or major societal problems, they are engaging in a form of advocacy. People tend to think of advocacy as a type of campaign, such as letter writing, protesting, petitioning, awakening power, coalition building, or lobbying. But note in the advocacy cycle in figure 10.1 that campaigns are only one category of advocacy activities.

Although we have listed organizing as a type of advocacy activity, many organizers would object to that classification. The heart of organizing is empowering others to speak for themselves. The organizer thus helps people identify issues and concerns that are important but never attempts to speak for them. According to Dave Beckwith of the Needmor Fund, "Community organizing is the process of building power through involving a constituency in identifying problems they share and the solutions to those problems that they desire; identifying the people and structures that can make those solutions possible; enlisting those targets in the effort through negotiation and using confrontation and pressure when needed; and building an institution that is democratically controlled by that constituency that can develop the capacity to take on further problems and that embodies the will and the power of that constituency."[4]

Advocacy, however, is perceived as nonprofit organizations speaking on behalf of others or launching an action agenda that tries to cajole others to join their cause. Beckwith distinguishes advocacy from organizing by noting that advocacy is "characterized by doing FOR people." While we concur that there is a world of difference in purpose and style between organizing and advocacy, both seek to create social change and attempt to "influence the decisions . . . on behalf of a collective interest," as Jenkins notes. Thus we consider both in our list of advocacy activities.

Nonprofit advocacy also includes efforts to ensure that policy is executed in the manner that was intended. When legislation is enacted, for instance, nonprofit groups often monitor the implementation and enforcement of that policy, moving into administrative advocacy: commenting on rule makings, tracking enforcement, and participating in governmental advisory committees and other meetings of decision makers.

If working through legislatures and executive branches does not accomplish the desired results, litigation is another option. Advocacy includes suing the government or powerful companies. It also includes filing friend-of-the-court, or amicus, briefs to highlight important concerns. At times, nonprofits create campaigns of amicus briefs with sign-ons and media advocacy.

Charities are also permitted to engage in nonpartisan political activities, but not electioneering. Nonprofits can conduct voter registration drives and candidate forums and can craft and distribute voter guides and more if done in a manner that does not support or oppose a particular candidate or political party. This is one area in which the IRS rules could be improved, because the determination of what is and is not allowed is based on the "facts and circumstances" of each case. Accordingly, it may be advisable for charities to get legal advice from experts when engaging in nonpartisan political activity.

Integral to the entire cycle is fundraising and leadership, which are at the center of the circle. Too often fundraising staff members within nonprofits are not engaged in the advocacy work, making it harder to raise resources. Advocacy is a hands-on team effort, calling on the skills of all staff, including the development team and information technology experts. Involving all staff is but one example of leadership that is an essential element of all advocacy efforts.

Because the definition of advocacy is so broad, many nonprofit leaders do not even realize when they are engaging in advocacy. Hence they do not say they are involved in advocacy when asked. Conversely, doing one item from the advocacy cycle such as research, for example, does not necessarily mean the organization is engaged in advocacy unless the intention is to influence the decisions of institutional elites. This ambiguity over what counts as advocacy adds to the enormous problem researchers have in quantifying or describing nonprofit advocacy.

One final comment on definitions: nonprofit advocacy is distinct from similar activities undertaken by the for-profit sector. Nonprofit policy participation is in the public interest, regardless of whether it is in pursuit of conservative, liberal, or nonideological objectives. In contrast, for-profit sector lobbying usually has a private pecuniary gain as its motive. While policy participation by all parties—nonprofit and for profit—is an essential ingredient of democracy, there is something special about nonprofit participation that should be strongly encouraged and supported by our national leaders.

## Should a Nonprofit Organization Engage in Advocacy?

The underlying goal of this chapter is to provide useful advice to nonprofit leaders about whether and how to engage in advocacy. In deciding whether to become involved in advocacy, nonprofit leaders will want to weigh the pros and cons of advocacy work, and to consider how engaged their peers—especially those nonprofits considered "best in class"—are in advocacy.

## Arguments for and against Engaging in Advocacy

There is a story about a nonprofit executive whose Midwest organization published a variety of analyses to influence state policy on services to children and families.[5] When asked whether his organization did advocacy, he said no. Figuratively tying himself into a pretzel to avoid the word "advocacy," he added, "We do impact analysis." Then there is the story of the head of the human services nonprofit organization in the South who described repeated meetings with staff in the state legislature to argue for more money for her organization and others like it. When asked whether she lobbied, she said no. We could go on, but you get the picture: nonprofit leaders are hesitant to engage in advocacy, and even when they do, they are nervous about calling it such.

In interview after interview, nonprofit grant makers and grant seekers talk about the importance of advocacy in fulfilling their organizational mission.

Yet foundations are apprehensive about making grants for advocacy, and charities are equally squeamish about undertaking advocacy, often putting other organizational priorities such as service delivery, fundraising, board development, strategic planning, and personnel issues ahead of advocacy. Nonprofit leaders cite limited resources, federal tax law and regulatory restrictions, and lack of skills as their top barriers to participating in advocacy. They also talk about the antipathy that board members, donors, and the public show toward advocacy as an additional obstacle to advocacy engagement.

These are significant barriers that are not new and are not likely to be overcome easily or quickly. Brazilian Archbishop Dom Helder Camara may have captured the challenge nonprofits face when thinking about advocacy: "When I give food to the poor, they call me a saint," he famously said. "When I ask why the poor have no food, they call me a communist."[6] In other words, according to the point of view held by many, the appropriate role for nonprofits is to provide or engage in palliative services; trying to promote systems change or address underlying problems may lead to negative repercussions. Even within the nonprofit sector, many believe that the sector's nonpartisan nature means that it should not be involved in policy or political work. As Catholic University of America professor Linda Plitt Donaldson writes, "The common image of nonprofit human service agencies as providers of shelter, food, clothing, and other forms of treatment for the symptoms of intractable social problems overshadows their important history as social change agents."[7]

It seems that over the years nonprofits have become increasingly specialized: for example, it is not just an organization that works on children's issues, it targets children age two to five. This type of specialization has occurred in every area of the nonprofit sector and creates silos where nonprofits become increasingly alienated from their colleagues in related areas. As nonprofits become more specialized and more professionalized in their service delivery, they become more focused on service delivery.[8] Whereas nonprofit organizations historically engaged in advocacy *and* service delivery, today's nonprofits tend to engage in advocacy *or* service delivery. There may be many reasons for this split, including less diversified funding sources, less flexibility in how funds can be used, or more narrowly focused staff. Whatever the reason for the split between advocacy and service, it has fostered more antipathy toward advocacy, and where advocacy does occur it is less grounded in information about the needs of people.

Whether because of competing priorities, limited staff time, lack of skills, confusing tax rules, negative attitudes of donors and board members about advocacy, a focus on service delivery, or other reasons, the costs associated with advocacy may simply be too high for many nonprofit executives.[9]

Yet there are many reasons why nonprofit organizations should be involved in advocacy. As far back as 1831, Alexis de Tocqueville noted during his trip to the United States the role nonprofits play in addressing national problems. "Americans of all ages, all conditions, and all disposition constantly form associations . . . Whenever at the head of some new undertaking you see the government in France, or a man of rank in England, in the United States you will be sure to find an association," he wrote.

We have a long history of nonprofit advocacy in this country. In fact, nonprofits have had a hand in most major laws and policies that exist today. In some ways, engaging in advocacy is part of the nonprofit ecology, part of our cultural heritage. As early as "1793, popular associations sprang up in the new republic to debate public questions, criticize government, and influence public policy."[10] As Schudson (1998) notes, these associations eventually "developed strong political agendas. It began in the churches. Out of the churches emerged groups to . . . end drinking, to abolish slavery, to work for peace."[11] Others have described this rich history, which led to the Emancipation Proclamation and subsequent civil rights laws, Townsend Clubs that advocated for policies that led to Social Security, the women's suffrage movement, modern-day environmental protections, food safety laws, worker protections, support for low-income programs, government support for arts and culture, and much more.[12]

This active and engaging history of nonprofit advocacy is supported in tax law and regulation. The IRS is clear that engaging in advocacy is consistent with being a charity. According to IRS regulations: "The fact that an organization, in carrying out its primary purpose, advocates social or civic changes or presents opinion on controversial issues with the intention of molding public opinion or creating public sentiment to an acceptance of its views does not preclude such organization from qualifying under section 501(c)(3)."[13]

This historical and legal context alone should provide motivation for nonprofit leaders to be advocates. But there are more selfish reasons: in today's tough economic times, advocacy on behalf of an organization's mission is essential. In their study, Elizabeth T. Boris and Matthew Maronick (chap. 3, this volume) note that because more human services are being provided by nonprofits rather than government, nonprofits must organize themselves to be ready to advocate both for more funding to provide services to a larger pool and also for policies that will have a direct impact on their missions.

Boris and Maronick (chap. 3, this volume) echo a sentiment found in focus groups conducted as part of the Strengthening Nonprofit Advocacy Project, or SNAP (Bass et al., 2007). As a leader of a Pennsylvania disability association said in one focus group, "We carry out a core function of government; therefore we insist on a partnership with government. But that sometimes means we have to pressure government for a place at the table and to act upon our recommendations." An executive director of a small human services organization in Nebraska added, "I try to sit on as many committees and commissions as possible so I can try to influence public policy."

This type of advocacy can help a nonprofit organization gain visibility for its mission, secure funding for a cause, change public policy on issues central to the purpose of the charity, or some combination of the above. In fact, the nonpartisan nature of charities can be a tool that strengthens its voice when advocating. Since charities are prohibited from supporting or opposing candidates for elective office, they can present themselves to the public as above the fray, focused not on profit-making, pecuniary self-interest but rather the public interest. Of course, the fact that charities are nonpartisan can also be a reason why nonprofit executives and board members argue that they should not be involved in advocacy; it is perceived as beyond the purpose of the organization. These arguments are illustrated in table 10.1.

TABLE 10.1.
Arguments for and against Engaging in Advocacy

| Arguments for Engaging in Advocacy | Arguments for Not Engaging in Advocacy |
|---|---|
| *Historical:* It is part of the nonprofit culture. | *Purpose of organization:* It is not the primary purpose of the nonprofit. |
| *Constitutional:* First Amendment's "right of the people peaceably to assemble, and to petition the Government for a redress of grievances." | *Stakeholders:* It may alienate some board members, donors, government funders, or other important stakeholders. |
| *Moral:* It is consistent with the values of charity. | *Resources:* There is not enough time or resources to do advocacy. |
| *Legal:* Tax law and IRS regulations permit advocacy but put limits on the amount of lobbying. | *Skills:* Staff does not know how to do advocacy. |
| *Mission driven:* Helps elevate visibility, secure funding, and pursue needed policy changes. | *Nonpartisan:* The organization is nonpartisan or nonpolitical. |

## Common Practice: Limited Engagement in Advocacy and Lobbying by Many Nonprofits

So, how do real-life nonprofits weigh the costs and benefits of advocacy? While there is limited, comprehensive data about the extent of nonprofit advocacy and lobbying, the best information available (which is sometimes contradictory) suggests that many nonprofits engage in at least some advocacy activity. The engagement is often limited in scope, however, and only modest organizational resources are spent on advocacy and especially lobbying. In its national survey of nonprofits in 2000, SNAP found that roughly three quarters of nonprofits say they have engaged at least once in key types of public policy activity, such as direct or grassroots lobbying or testifying at a legislative or administrative hearing (Bass et al., 2007, 17). A more recent 2007 survey by the Johns Hopkins University Listening Post Project found that 73% of respondents reported engaging in some type of policy advocacy or lobbying during the year leading up to the survey (Salamon and Geller, 2008).

But while policy activity may be widespread among nonprofits, it is generally limited and not very well resourced. The Johns Hopkins University Listening Post Project reported that the vast majority (85%) of survey respondents devoted less than 2% of their budget to either lobbying or advocacy (Salamon and Geller, 2008). According to IRS Form 990 data from the Urban Institute's National Center for Charitable Statistics, the percentage of charities reporting lobbying expenditures has increased in recent years but remains quite low—about 2% of nonprofits—and the ratio of lobbying expenditures to total organizational expenses remained nearly constant at .08% from 1996 to 2006 (Boris and Maronick, 2012). According to data collected under the Lobbying Disclosure Act and provided by the Center for Responsive Politics, nonprofits have never contributed more than 2% of the overall money spent on lobbying in the nation's capital. Similarly low percentages apply to the number of lobbyists that represent nonprofits, as shown in figure 10.2.

## Best Practice: High-Performing Nonprofits Engage in Advocacy

While many nonprofits engage only in limited amounts of advocacy activity, those nonprofits considered "best in class" are more active advocates. Based on interviews with 250 leading thinkers on philanthropy and 250 executive

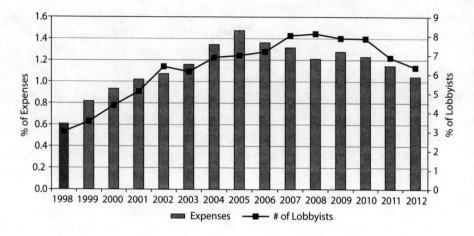

*Figure 10.2.* Share of lobbying done by nonprofits federal lobbying disclosure act data. Source: Center for Responsive Politics; derived from data on Open Secrets, http://www.opensecrets.org/lobby/indusclient.php?id=W02&year=2010, accessed February 2013

directors of some of the nation's most effective nonprofits, Paul Light concludes that there is no one best way to achieve higher performance. But he finds that a commitment to advocacy remains a critical element to higher performance (Light, 2002). Eight years later, building on that initial work, he provides in-depth information on the importance of social change for non-profit organizations (Light and Reynolds, 2010).

Complementing Light's work is a study by Leslie Crutchfield and Heather McLeod Grant of 12 high-impact nonprofits that identified six practices that these nonprofits use to achieve extraordinary results (Crutchfield and Grant, 2007). The first important practice they identified was advocacy. According to these authors in a preview to their book, "High-impact organizations . . . eventually realize that they cannot achieve large-scale social change through service delivery alone . . . Ultimately, all [the high-impact organizations we studied] bridge the divide between service and advocacy."[14]

The authors of this chapter share the views of Light, Crutchfield, and Grant that advocacy ought to be a core activity of many more nonprofits. US charities play a critical role in advocating for change. Whether it is about a local school board issue, a state policy regarding home health care, or national immigration reform, two things are certain. First, nonprofit organizations will be involved in the debate on the issues, and second, society will be just that much better off because of the charitable sector's engagement.

If civic participation is vital for the success of democracy, then nonprofit advocacy is a driving force that frames a vibrant democracy. Since the founding of this country, nonprofits have played an active role in promoting social change and challenging unfair practices and policies. For virtually every major national policy, nonprofits have been part of the inner circle in generating research, providing ideas, and lobbying that shapes that policy. At its core, the nonprofit sector is devoted to making improvements for the common good, and advocacy has been among its most potent weapons.

Given the central role nonprofit advocacy plays in improving our quality of life and enhancing our civil society, it is important to find ways to encourage it and strengthen its effectiveness.[15] The authors of this chapter are committed to drawing on research in this volume and elsewhere and the experience of high-performing nonprofits to strengthen the capacity of nonprofits to engage in advocacy.

## Getting Engaged: How Nonprofit Organizations Become More Involved in Advocacy

What factors facilitate a nonprofit organization's involvement in advocacy? Some factors that promote advocacy are part of a nonprofit's "nature" and cannot be easily controlled by a nonprofit's leadership, at least in the short run; other factors are more controllable.

### *Core, Hard-to-Control, Organizational Features*

In the first category of factors that are part of an organization's nature, organizations whose missions include educating the public, are larger or older, have an involved membership, and who receive substantial government funding are all more likely to have a public policy presence (see Rathgeb and Smith, introduction, Boris and Maronick, chap. 3, DeVita et al., chap. 4, and Mosley, chap. 5, this volume). Nonprofits tasked with educating the public tend to have advocacy as a central component of their work in the community. Older organizations have built up knowledge in their issue area and credibility in the community and with policymakers, giving them an advantage in reaching out to politicians and government institutions to help set the policy agenda and bring their issues to the fore. Larger organizations are less prone to the resource limitations that prevent smaller organizations from getting involved in advocacy work. Organizations with a strong constituency or active membership find it easier to get involved in advocacy because they have built-in support to help them achieve their policy goals.

## What Nonprofit Leaders Can Do

While the organizational features above are items that nonprofit executives cannot easily control, we have also identified other factors that are more controllable, which studies show are highly correlated with either helping to get nonprofits engaged in advocacy or increasing the frequency of advocacy activity.

1. *Create a supportive environment for advocacy.* It all starts with the organization's leadership. Saidel and Harlan (1998) found that leadership was a key factor influencing advocacy activities, and DeVita et al. (2004) also found leadership to be a key link between an organization's capacity and its advocacy work. In other words, top leadership, including the board, executive director, and senior staff, needs to be openly supportive of advocacy in order for it to thrive. Bass et al. (2007) found that when it comes to advocacy, the executive director is the most influential figure in the organization, followed by the board chair and the board itself or a board committee.

There are numerous mechanisms for creating a friendly advocacy climate within an organization. Some include establishing a governmental affairs or policy committee at the board level to discuss advocacy issues. Another is to ensure that advocacy issues are discussed during board and staff meetings. Other approaches include adding language about the importance of advocacy to the mission, vision statement, or goals of the organization. In sum, advocacy must be a part of the organization's ecology, and that can only happen with a supportive environment.

2. *Assign staff and board responsibilities.* Donaldson (2008) highlights the importance of leveraging staff skills. She writes, "it is incumbent on the advocacy staff to ensure that their advocacy is being done in support of and in coordination with the service programs by communicating regularly with service staff through meetings or e-mail to share information and to engage them in advocacy activities" (31). This statement suggests that the advocacy staff should involve all departments within an organization. Too often key staff, such as those in development, are left out of advocacy conversations. They should be involved so that they can help raise resources and explain the importance of advocacy to potential donors. All staff skills are necessary for meaningful engagement in advocacy.

Bass et al. (2007) noted the importance of assigning advocacy work to specific staff. But they found that when the executive director had the lead, day-to-day responsibility, the organization was less likely to be engaged in advocacy than other organizations that assigned the responsibilities to nearly anyone else in the organization. This finding makes some sense, as the executive director has a broad range of day-to-day responsibilities and can unintentionally give less priority to advocacy work even when supportive of it.

A key suggestion is to assign day-to-day advocacy responsibilities to lobbyists, other staff, board members or a board committee, or volunteers before assigning them to the executive director. Doing so does not reduce the importance of the executive director setting the overall direction on public policy matters (Mosley, chap. 5, this volume). Furthermore, designating a staff member as a lobbyist is correlated with a higher likelihood of advocacy (DeVita et al., chap. 4, this volume). An organization structured with staff dedicated to advocacy can be more effective in the field because other staff provide useful information or knowledge to support the staff member tasked with engaging policymakers and the community (Donaldson, 2008).

3. *Make rules on policy decision making clear and simple.* Advocacy often requires fast decisions and quick action. Bass et al. (2007) emphasize the importance of having guidelines within the organization for such decision making. The organization should have clear rules on who makes the decisions on specific policies—a board committee, the full board, or the chair of the board? Or is it the executive director or senior staff? Do separate people or entities make decisions for different types of policy issues? It is important that all staff, especially any who may be involved in advocacy, know these guidelines.

But clarity is not always enough. One nonprofit executive explained that there was a clear procedure within his organization for tackling advocacy issues. The staff needed to obtain board approval for all policy positions big and small. Yet the board met only four times a year, even though policy decisions needed to be made on a faster time line. They found over time that their advocacy activities withered until they stopped altogether. The lesson is that the internal procedures must be clear *and* logical. The procedures must fit the situational needs of conducting advocacy activities.

4. *Preserve time for advocacy.* Donaldson (2008) discusses the importance of having full-time, dedicated advocacy staff. But not all organizations can afford that. Whatever staff structure is created, it is essential to give the staff time to do advocacy. Remember, advocacy is often about nurturing relation-

ships and can take time. In an organization where staff time is highly valued, there may be a tendency to pull back on the time reserved for advocacy if there are few advocacy successes in the short term.

5. *Build lobbying and advocacy skills.* Nancy Amidei (2010) says advocacy skills are like exercise: if you do not do it regularly, you get out of shape. The same is true with advocacy: if you do not advocate regularly, you get out of practice. Donaldson (2008) and Bass et al. (2007) describe the importance of providing training to build advocacy and lobbying skills.

According to research on the subject, an executive director who is committed to advocacy is the most important step toward an organization participating in advocacy. An advocacy-friendly board also increases the likelihood of an organization engaging in advocacy (Bass et al., 2007; Donaldson, 2008). Executive directors with high levels of education or who have professional managerial backgrounds, as opposed to those with more experience as service providers, are more likely to value advocacy (Mosley, chap. 5, this volume). Executive directors who have good relationships with policymakers are also more likely to engage in advocacy (Mosley, chap. 5, this volume).

Providing training for executive directors who are not dedicated to advocacy may help them overcome their concerns and become more engaged in the policy process. Emphasizing the potential of advocacy as "an appropriate tool to improve and grow services," rather than a distraction from a direct service mission, could help them reorient their perception of advocacy (Mosley, chap. 5, this volume), which also applies to training for board members.

Other training topics might include: the importance of engaging in the public policy process, how to build organizational capacity to support advocacy goals, effective advocacy techniques, and lessons on the public policy process (Bass et al., 2007). The last topic is important; while many organizations might realize that lobbying for the passage of a bill is critical, there are numerous ways to effect policy change through regulations, and by protecting the law from attacks after its passage. There is no end to the policy process, and action must always be taken to support a friendly agenda. So nonprofits must learn how to maintain their advocacy momentum. A final idea for training could be effective mobilization of constituents. Because nonprofits work on the front lines of the community, they have a built-in base of potential advocates for an issue. Learning to effectively mobilize their communities could allow nonprofits to advocate without needing to hire additional staff by creating interest and ownership in the community.

## Joining Coalitions and Associations

One way to overcome many of the hurdles for getting started in advocacy—or to strengthen an organization's advocacy presence—is to join a coalition or association. According to Steven Smith (2010, 623), "funding cutbacks often promote nonprofit organizations to join together to influence public policy, sometimes through formal coalitions and associations representing nonprofit interests." Boris and Maronick (chap. 3, this volume) emphasize that "coalitions provide opportunities to pool resources, forge partnerships, and share innovative programming ideas with other nonprofits."[16]

In one survey of nonprofit managers, those interviewed reported that advocacy through coalitions was the best way to overcome the barriers they faced to engaging in advocacy on their own (Mosley, chap. 5, this volume). In a study of nonprofit organizations in the Washington, DC, area, Carol J. DeVita, Milena Nikolova, and Katie L. Roeger (chap. 4, this volume) found that "advocacy work in the nation's capital is conducted primarily through coalitions. Only 8% of nonprofits that engaged in advocacy did so exclusively on their own. Nearly half (48%) conducted their advocacy both in coalitions and sometimes alone, and about two in five nonprofits (44%) worked only in coalitions." A related but surprising finding in the same study was that larger organizations were much more likely to participate in advocacy only through coalitions.

By combining their knowledge of issues and strategy in their implementation of an advocacy agenda, nonprofit coalitions can leverage credibility and gain the trust of policymakers. Research also shows that smaller organizations are less likely to engage in advocacy than larger organizations, but that coalitions may serve as a means to help smaller organizations engage in advocacy.

In addition to joining coalitions, Bass et al. (2007) found joining state and national associations significantly increased the likelihood of becoming involved in advocacy. This might be counterintuitive because many nonprofits join associations to be represented on policy matters. Nonetheless, the data show that groups become more involved in advocacy particularly when they join national associations.

## Ways for Smaller Organizations to Participate

In DeVita et al.'s study of Washington, DC, area nonprofits (chap. 4, this volume), researchers also found that 80% of large nonprofits (with annual budgets of $1 million or more) participate in advocacy activities, compared to only 56% of small nonprofits (with annual budgets below $1 million); other studies have found similar results (Boris and Maronick, chap. 3, this volume). Similarly, a much higher proportion of national nonprofits are active in advocacy than local nonprofits (Mosley, chap. 5, this volume), potentially because larger national organizations have more resources and staff to dedicate to advocacy (Boris and Maronick, chap. 3, this volume). Nevertheless, small and local nonprofit organizations can achieve significant impacts if they engage in advocacy, without needing to have vast resources at their disposal.

Gaining access to policymakers can be much simpler at the local level than at the national level, so it is not necessary to expend as much time and effort to achieve similar progress (see Jeffrey M. Berry and Kent E. Portney's chap. 1 in this volume). In Berry and Portney's research, based on a survey of local officials and advocates in 50 large US cities, 92% of all advocacy group respondents said that they are able to reach local officials most of the time, which is close to the level of access that for-profit entities have and considerably greater access than reaching officials in Washington, DC.[17] Berry and Portney caution that one-time access may not mean much. So they looked at how often local officials reached out to nonprofit groups: a little over 30% of nonprofit leaders reported their organization being contacted by city officials twice a month or more, and 13% reported contact four or more times a month. While the frequency of contact for nonprofit groups was less than for business groups, "the bottom line on access, whether seen from the perspective of city officials or group leaders, whether involving contacts initiated by groups or by city officials, is that groups appear to have a significant opportunity to affect local policy," according to Berry and Portney (chap. 1, this volume).

The lesson is that small nonprofits can more easily engage in local than state or federal policy making because they can gain more access to local policymakers, making it easier to break into advocacy. Additionally, as discussed above, smaller groups can join coalitions, which may also enhance participation.

## Government Funding

Research has been somewhat ambiguous about the impact government funding has on nonprofit advocacy. Some researchers and commentators have found that government funding constrains advocacy (Alexander et al., 1999;

O'Connell, 1994; Reinelt, 1994; Wolch, 1990). Smith and Lipsky (1993) noted that nonprofits dependent on government funds were less likely to engage in advocacy for fear of alienating government funders, driving away possible sources of new funding or reducing the flexibility of funding. Other authors in the 1990s, such as Brian O'Connell, noted repercussions of the possible loss of federal funds when nonprofits engage in advocacy. Fear of such repercussions was voiced in focus groups conducted in SNAP (Bass et al., 2007). In the 1990s, some also worried that federal proposals to prohibit or limit federal nonprofit grantees from engaging in advocacy was a strong message to avoid policy engagement if getting government funds.[18]

But most current research finds that as government funding increases so, too, does the amount of advocacy by nonprofits (Bass et al., 2007; Chaves et al., 2004; Child and Grønbjerg, 2007; Donaldson, 2004; Grønbjerg, 1993; Kramer, 1994; Mosley, 2010; Salamon, 1987, 1995). Pekkanen and Smith's more recent research (chap. 2, this volume) found that as government funding increased for nonprofits in King County, Washington, so did nonprofit advocacy. "For every one percentage point increase in government funding, the likelihood that an organization engages in advocacy increases by a factor of 0.014." Pekkanen and Smith (chap. 2, this volume) and DeVita et al. (chap. 4, this volume) found the same relationship between government funding and advocacy with nonprofits in the Washington, DC, area. Boris and Maronick (chap. 3, this volume) also found a similar pattern: nonprofits with five or more government contracts or grants were far more likely to be advocates (63%) than those groups that had only one (42%).

These findings are consistent with those from the Bass et al. (2007) study, which included a nationwide survey of charities. They found that diversifying funding sources was strongly tied to nonprofit policy engagement. They also found that as government funding increases, nonprofit executives report increased barriers to advocacy participation. Ironically, however, as government funding goes up, the nonprofit organization is significantly more likely to become involved in advocacy and on a more frequent basis (Bass et al., 2007, 205–10). The Bass et al. (2007) study had the same findings with revenue from foundations: nonprofits complained about barriers to advocacy when receiving foundation funding, but engaged more often as foundation funding increased.

The lesson is that nonprofit executives need not think of government funding as an inhibiting factor to engaging in advocacy. In fact, such funding is likely to increase advocacy engagement.

## Coping with IRS Regulations

There is widespread agreement in the research literature that nonprofit leaders find the IRS regulations on lobbying confusing, if not intimidating. In survey after survey, nonprofit executives say they are fearful of engaging in advocacy because of these regulations. To address this problem, there are two things nonprofit executives can do.

First, they can elect to fall under the "expenditure test" for lobbying. The expenditure test provides a sliding scale on how much money can be spent on direct and grassroots lobbying depending on the budget size of the organization. For organizations with exempt purpose expenditures below $500,000, the charity can spend up to 20% on direct lobbying and one quarter of that (5%) on grassroots lobbying. Larger organizations, over $17 million, are capped at $1 million for lobbying and one quarter of that ($250,000) for grassroots lobbying. It is easy to register for (or elect) the expenditure test. Obtain a copy of IRS Form 5768 at http://www.irs.gov/pub/irs-pdf/f5768.pdf; it requires an organization's name, address, employer identification number, start date, and signature from an officer or trustee.

If a nonprofit does not elect the expenditure test, the default is that the organization operates under the "substantial part test." Table 10.2 provides a comparison of the substantial part test and the expenditure test.

The selection of the expenditure test or the substantial part test applies only to disclosure and limits on lobbying communications, not to other forms of advocacy. A charity does not need to disclose its other advocacy activities, and there are no legal limits other than the need to be performing charitable actions. This reduces a top concern often cited by nonprofit executives for not participating in advocacy—fear of running afoul of IRS regulations on lobbying for charitable organizations (Bass et al., 2007).

Some argue that the use of the expenditure test increases the likelihood that nonprofits will be more involved in advocacy. The data provide less certainty that this is true. SNAP research showed a strong correlation between the expenditure test and engaging in advocacy (Bass et al., 2007, 191–94). But the same research demonstrated that the expenditure test was *not* a predictor of advocacy. For those nonprofits already motivated to be advocates, the choice of the expenditure test is an enabler.

Second, nonprofit leaders should make time to learn the IRS rules, for which there are many useful publications and training materials. For example, a number of state nonprofit associations provide basic training on IRS

TABLE 10.2.
Comparison of the Substantial Part Test and the Expenditure Test for Lobbying

| Substantial Part Test | Expenditure Test |
|---|---|
| • No clear definitions of lobbying<br>• No clarity on how much money or time can be spent on lobbying<br>• One-year violation may result in the loss of tax-exempt status | • Clear definitions of lobbying that only include communications that cost the organization money<br>• Clearly defined amounts of money that can be spent on lobbying<br>• Clear definitions of exceptions to what constitutes lobbying<br>• No jeopardy to tax-exempt status for one-year violation |

regulations. Organizations such as the Alliance for Justice also provide publications and training sessions.

## Motivation

Pekkanen and Smith (chap. 2, this volume) provide a helpful regression analysis using data from a survey of nonprofits in King County, Washington, and Washington, DC, to identify factors explaining why nonprofits engage in advocacy. All of the elements—budget size, age of the organization, sources of funding, staff issues, whether the organization's mission is to educate the public—are vitally important factors to consider in assessing what will encourage nonprofits to engage in advocacy. The bottom line remains, however, that if the senior leadership of an organization is not motivated or does not see how advocacy will benefit the agency, the organization will not become engaged in advocacy.

In focus groups conducted as part of SNAP (Bass et al., 2007), it was not uncommon to find board members and senior staff who talked about the dangers of advocacy. In one focus group in Texas, a board member of a local nonprofit repeatedly emphasized that he did not want the organization involved in advocacy. He felt he had a "fiduciary responsibility" and that advocacy would inevitably anger a local politician or official, which in turn would affect the organization's funding. That line of thinking was not uncommon.

Emmett Carson notes that the same reticence about advocacy exists in foundations:

The proposition that foundations should engage in public policy because it is essential to the development and interchange of ideas integral to maintaining a democratic society, while true, does not motivate many foundations to engage in public policy. The recognition (in the abstract) that public policy work is worthwhile to society rarely sparks a foundation to take on the work—especially if the foundation perceives that there are risks in doing so. Economists call this phenomenon the "free-rider" problem, where individuals acknowledge that a specific activity is beneficial for all (for example, national defense) but no single individual is likely to take the responsibility to provide it because they think that someone else will.

Similarly, it is not enough to say that foundations should engage in public policy because the effort will leverage their grant funds. True, foundation engagement in public policy can mean that relatively small grants can hold the prospect of making significant impact. Unfortunately, this explanation doesn't generate the necessary passion for foundations to engage in public policy.[19]

The above statement could have been written about any nonprofit—grantor or grantee. The solution, according to Carson, is to focus on the mission or vision of the organization. These mission and vision statements remind board and staff why the organization exists; often it is to change communities, the nation, and the world, to improve quality of life in our society. Exploring those objectives rekindles the passion and energy, and draws a recognition that advocacy is a key way to move closer to that vision.

Bass et al. (2007) emphasize that simply reducing barriers does not mean that nonprofits will suddenly get more involved in advocacy. If nonprofits had more resources, would they use them for advocacy? If they thoroughly understood the tax law and knew that advocacy was permissible, would it mean they would do it? Data from SNAP (Bass et al., 2007) show that the key to getting nonprofits engaged in advocacy is first and foremost to provide strong motivation. Of those nonprofits that either lobby, encourage others to lobby, or testify, 86% said that promoting government policies that support the organization's mission was a significant inducement for becoming an advocate. Similarly, three quarters of respondents said that raising public awareness about important issues or protecting government programs that serve the organization's constituents or community were also highly motivating factors for engaging in public policy.

Nonprofit leaders look to these mission-driven reasons for engaging in public policy. Strikingly, in the SNAP survey, nonprofit leaders said that opportunities for obtaining government funding provided the least incentive for advocacy of the list presented to them, because nonprofit leaders consistently put their constituency, issues, and mission above their own organizational needs, such as fundraising. The challenge, then, is finding ways to link policy advocacy to advancing an organization's mission.

By way of conclusion, the Seen but Not Heard research by Bass et al. (2007) identified ten characteristics of nonprofits that are more likely to be advocates: [20]

1. They are environmental, health, and social action groups. (The least engaged tend to be involved in the arts, recreation, religion, and philanthropy.)
2. They have larger budgets and multiple funding sources.
3. They receive government and/or foundation funding.
4. They are membership based, particularly with organizational members.
5. Regardless of staff size, they have senior staff beyond the executive director or a board committee specifically assigned to government relations.
6. They are members of associations or coalitions.
7. They receive frequent calls to action from associations or coalitions.
8. They receive requests for information from public officials.
9. They have elected to follow federal lobbying rules that specify an expenditure limit, authorized under Internal Revenue Code §501(h) and §4911.[21]
10. They tend to be more Internet savvy than those not engaged in advocacy.

## Effective Advocacy: How Nonprofit Organizations Maximize the Impact of Their Advocacy Activities

There are numerous books, articles, and helpful hints from organizations on becoming an effective advocate. Many focus on lobbying techniques, such as what to do in a lobbying meeting with an elected official or how to write a letter to an elected official. One particularly helpful guide for instructing nonprofits in how to engage in advocacy is Marcia Avner's (2004) handbook.[22] It describes how to establish a lobbying plan, including strategies and tactics, and methods for implementing the plan. There are numerous helpful techniques on lobbying, testifying, coalition building, and more. Notwithstanding these helpful publications, there are no magical guideposts to ensure effective advocacy; there is no recipe for advocacy that assures a successful outcome.

One reason advocacy is not like following a recipe is that every situation is different. Though there are common threads that run through all advocacy efforts, there are also nuances, context, and personalities that make each case unique, which is why case studies can be useful learning tools: one can capture common elements while also identifying unique applications. For example, Jodi Sandfort (chap. 9, this volume) looks at two human services networks, the Community Action Partnership and the Alliance for Connected Communities, to understand how advocacy capacity is built. She concludes that successful engagement on policy matters is not simply about the leadership of specific agencies, but also about the context and culture of the community or network that the organization is part of: "service organizations depend on a collective to help build their own advocacy capacity . . . Within the collective, more potential resources existed; they could hire staff with knowledge of legislative processes, utilize and cultivate relationships with other policy advocates and officials, and use effective planning and prioritizing processes . . . [Yet] not all network activity yields resources for use in advocacy, in spite of clear intent." Moreover, the strategies and tactics on similar issues can differ vastly from one network to another. Some of this is the result of cross-fertilization from those within a network. "The shared understandings of historical experiences create a background within which the legitimacy of policy-level work is rarely questioned, even though these direct service agencies face many competing demands."

## Coalitions

Much of the research in this book places a heavy emphasis on the role of coalitions in making groups more effective in their advocacy. (Above we indicated that research showed that participating in coalitions likely results in more advocacy activity, but we did not comment on effectiveness.) As noted by Pekkanen and Smith in their introduction to this volume, "it has been a truism of the field that organized interests will be advantaged over unorganized interests in the policy arena." Coalitions offer a straightforward way for organizations to organize and partner with each other.

In one survey of nonprofit managers, those interviewed reported that advocacy through coalitions was the best way to overcome the barriers they faced to engaging in advocacy on their own (Mosley, chap. 5, this volume). They help nonprofits leverage scant resources, allowing them to have a much larger impact as part of a group than they could have achieved alone.

Advocating through a coalition is often a much more cost-effective way to get involved in the policy process (Boris and Maronick, chap. 3, and Mosley, chap. 5, this volume), which is especially crucial in a time of decreased funding and economic uncertainty.

Aside from these benefits, coalitions also bring together different types of expertise. Combining one organization's advocacy ability with another group's issue knowledge can create a much more effective partnership. Similarly, by bringing together the different perspectives of a variety of nonprofits, a coalition can bring a more nuanced, realistic view of their issue of interest to the attention of policymakers.

There are many examples of how coalitions have strengthened advocacy effectiveness. A national coalition, Let America Speak, was formed in the 1990s to stop legislative proposals that would limit nonprofit advocacy. The leaders of that coalition, Alliance for Justice, Independent Sector, and OMB Watch (now known as the Center for Effective Government), acknowledged the importance of involving local, state, and national nonprofits in fighting against these proposals.

A team from the Urban Institute's Center on Nonprofits and Philanthropy recently wrote about the effectiveness of coalition building among nonprofits in the metropolitan Washington, DC, area dealing with immigrant integration issues (de Leon et al., 2009). Their study highlights the importance of advocacy in immigrant integration but notes that many nonprofits do not have the capacity, resources, or opportunity to engage. These nonprofits were more empowered and more effective by working through coalitions, according to the study.

Coalitions are beneficial in helping organizations, especially smaller nonprofits, gain legitimacy through association with other reputable organizations. With a larger group available to advocate for an issue, lawmakers may become more receptive to their message (Boris and Maronick, chap. 3, and Mosley, chap. 5, this volume). At the same time, coalitions can be counterproductive, depending on the situation. They can sap considerable time, there can be infighting on a host of issues, personality differences can be distracting, and in some cases the coalitions can be costly to some of the key players.

Moreover, creating a coalition may not be the best strategy or tactic for every policy fight. Sandfort (chap. 9, this volume) states that her "analysis suggests that networks may or may not effectively resource policy advocacy . . . advocacy capacity is more iterative. Organizations gain capacity through a process of engaging ideas and using tools."

## Social Media and Information Technologies

In recent years there has been growing discussion about the value of social media and information technologies for nonprofits (McNutt, 2000; Shirky, 2011; Suárez, 2009). Because the rise of the Internet as an important communication tool took place only in the last decade or so, little empirical evidence is available on the efficacy of technology for advocacy engagement. The debate is ongoing about whether technology in general and social media specifically are effective tools for nonprofit advocacy (Miller, 2011; Suárez, 2009). In this context, we have gathered commentary from each side, and we explore some examples of how nonprofit organizations have successfully used technology and social media to accomplish their advocacy goals.

A 2009 study by David Suárez of charities that file IRS Form 990 in the San Francisco area found that 19% of these organizations used their websites to convey information about social change and to passively inform readers about policy issues. In addition, 28% of survey respondents used their websites for promoting civic engagement, defined as "volunteer enrollment, petition signing or letter writing, chat rooms or blogs for citizen discussion, advocacy LISTSERVs, and downloadable materials for social change activities" (Suárez, 2009, 276). He found that organizations already highly involved in advocacy were statistically more likely to engage in online advocacy, although organizations in any issue area or of any size can easily make use of Internet technology if they so desire.

Entrance costs to engaging in online advocacy are relatively low; it is not necessary to have a high-tech website to effectively communicate an organization's policy positions, so long as information is well organized and easy to navigate (Miller, 2011). In addition, the Internet and social media tools make it possible for smaller organizations to have equal presence as large, national organizations. In one study of people who use social media, for example, half of the respondents said they monitored a nonprofit organization at the local level as opposed to a national organization (Miller, 2011), suggesting that smaller or local organizations can compete with larger or national groups.

McNutt and Barlow (2012) looked at use of Internet technologies by child advocacy nonprofits from 2000 to 2008 and found that while the technology has not changed much, how the technology is deployed has. For example, many child advocacy nonprofits used email at about the same rate in 2008 as in 2000. But the use of email sent to decision makers jumped dramatically over that same period.[23] The increase could be a result of the 9/11 terrorist attacks and barriers imposed on sending US mail, the increased ubiquity of email, or both. Given that the use of email to reach people outside the organization for advocacy purposes also increased, however, it would suggest that ubiquity of email has played a key role.[24] McNutt's (2008) data also show a rapid rise in Web 2.0 tools, which are often referred to as social media. At the same time, McNutt found that the greatest barrier to use of new information technologies in 2000 was the same as in 2008: expertise. The tools still remain confusing to many of the leaders in the child advocacy nonprofits that were surveyed.

Even though Internet technologies may be confusing and many nonprofits do not have the expertise to fully use them, effective nonprofits must bring themselves into the cyberactivism age. A powerful YouTube video by Erik Qualman, author of *Socialnomics*, highlights how social media is changing the way we communicate. According to the video, it took 38 years for radio and 14 years for television to reach 50 million people. Facebook added over 200 million users in less than a year, and iPod application downloads hit one billion in nine months.[25] Adding that 96% of millennials have joined a social network, Qualman is quoted as saying, "We don't have a choice on whether we do social media, the question is how well we do it." In other words, nonprofits that choose to ignore social media will be increasingly irrelevant in today's society and in reaching new audiences.

Nonprofits today use the Internet and social media in many different ways for advocacy purposes. Some observers have tried to characterize the various methods used. In his 2003 study on the World Bank, for example, Sandor Vegh (2003) provided three dimensions of online activism: awareness/advocacy, organization/mobilization, and action/reaction. Others, such as McNutt and Menon (2008), provided three spheres of cyberactivism: adjuncts to traditional advocacy and activism, such as for political rallies, demonstrations, or letter-writing campaigns; transnational advocacy; and activism in virtual communities. Some talk about "NetActivism" in terms of Web development: Web 1.0, Web 2.0, and Web 3.0. Under Web 1.0, websites are mainly read only; the focus is on developing content owned by the nonprofit and presenting it to the public in attractive ways. Under Web 2.0, websites are both read and written; it is a mix of content provided by the nonprofit and user-generated information. Web 2.0 is characterized by blogs, common formats (e.g., extensible markup language, or XML), web applications, and social networks. Under Web 3.0, websites are portable and personal; content is in the cloud (meaning the Internet), and data can be shared or mashed up from disparate databases.

Regardless of the elements used, it is clear that effective nonprofit advocacy utilizes the Internet and social media. Those with social media expertise have differing strategies when it comes to advocacy. Some argue that bigger is better; the metrics become how many visits a web page garners, how many friends you have on Facebook, or how many people are following your tweets. Others argue that it is not the size that matters but who is getting the information. It may not matter that 100,000 people are following your comments on Twitter if the objective is to target those in the news media or key elected officials. Instead, the objective is to build an elite following that can reach the targeted audience. Whatever the metric, social media has become a lightning rod when it comes to advocacy.

Internet pundit Clay Shirky has been a huge fan of social media. In his 2008 book *Here Comes Everybody: The Power of Organizing without Organizations*, Shirky makes the argument that social media is empowering new types of advocacy and organizing that makes traditional organizations, including nonprofits, passé. In 2009, when protests broke out in Iran, Shirky was adamant "that this is it. The big one" that will demonstrate the power of social networks and Twitter in particular. According to Shirky: "This is the first revolution that has been catapulted onto a global stage and transformed by social media. I've been thinking a lot about the Chicago demonstrations of 1968 where they chanted 'the whole world is watching.' Really, that wasn't true then. But this time it's true . . . and people throughout the world are not only listening but responding."[26] Shirky was touting the capabilities of services such as Twitter to allow dissidents to communicate not only to the international audience and news services, but also among themselves in order to protest and organize effectively. The ability to communicate immediately with a huge audience is an enormous boon for advocates, who can have a much wider impact than they would otherwise have through traditional organizing strategies (Shirky, 2011; Suárez, 2009).

Some have dubbed the Arab Spring uprising in 2011 in the Middle East the Twitter Revolution because of the role social media played in helping to mobilize people. "Facebook is the soapbox they stand on, and Twitter is the Megaphone through which they speak," was the blog post on *Before It's News*.[27] Yet critics do not completely agree: Libyan author Hisham Matar called that claim an "exaggeration."[28] And Saudi blogger Ahmed Al Omran, who participated in a conference of Arab bloggers, pointed out that "most people on the panel seemed to agree that, while Twitter was important to have people to organize and also to get the word out, in the end it's just a tool.

We cannot call this a Twitter revolution, or a Facebook revolution; it's a revolution of the people. And the people in that revolution would use whatever tools that are available to them."[29]

Moving beyond the Arab Spring, some commentators are not as positive as Shirky about organizing via social media. Critics argue that online advocacy and organizing do not hold a candle to in-person advocacy activities undertaken in previous generations, such as the sit-ins in Greensboro, North Carolina, during the civil rights movement, because online connections create weaker ties than direct personal connections, and it is therefore harder to motivate online connections to act on behalf of a policy goal (Gladwell, 2010).

Notwithstanding the various critiques of social media, there is enormous potential for nonprofit organizations to harness the power of Internet technology and to replicate the successes of the international organizing campaigns that Shirky and others have highlighted. Organizations can use the Internet to engage in traditional advocacy practices, whether through email campaigns, online petitions, or email alerts on policy issues (Miller, 2011; Suárez, 2009). They can also take advantage of Web 2.0 technology, such as blogs or social networks, to engage their members or the community at large. Studies have shown that 21% of the voting-age population uses social networks to communicate with their peers about policy issues; the largest age group using social networking technology includes those between the ages of 18 and 25 (but this group is growing daily, especially among older women); most users have at least some college education and are on the left of the political spectrum.[30] Social media can be an effective tool to communicate with this traditionally hard-to-reach demographic.

Social media and Internet technology have also been successfully employed domestically. Barack Obama's 2008 campaign for the presidency relied heavily on social media to turn out voters of all demographics (Helfenbein, 2010). Local campaigns can also use social media effectively. A key to success is to have a real-world "ask," or to use social media as a tool to coordinate real-world action (Shirky, 2011; West, 2011). The nonprofit organization Invisible Children used several Internet tools—Facebook, Twitter, YouTube—to coordinate its campaign to pass legislation that aims to reduce the number of child soldiers. The nonprofit organized students across the country through social media to stage rallies that succeeded in getting national media attention for its issue (West, 2011).

A recent study by the University of Massachusetts Dartmouth Center for Marketing Research found that up to 97% of nonprofits are using social media for various purposes and to varying degrees of effectiveness (West, 2011). But less is known about why they are using social media; most seem to be using it for fundraising purposes as opposed to advocacy. There is still much to learn about the use of social media for advocacy.

Even so, there are several steps nonprofits can take to compete successfully in this new virtual arena. First, they should strike a good balance for updating their followers. Leaving a social media site without updates for long periods of time could cause followers to lose interest, but bombarding followers with useless information just for the sake of keeping in touch may also turn them off (Miller, 2011; West, 2011). Instead, nonprofits should try to communicate as much critical information as possible in an easily understandable format with each email blast, Facebook post, or tweet. Also, organizations should make sure their materials are appropriate for the demographic they are targeting. Requests for large donations should not be sent to young people who cannot afford to contribute, and references to popular culture should not be included in updates for older members (West, 2011). Another strategy is for nonprofits to build a narrative around an issue before they get to the "ask." When followers feel more engaged in a campaign, they are more likely to take action on the organization's behalf; building relationships, even virtual ones, is crucial for effective organization (West, 2011). Lastly, organizations must take care not to pigeonhole themselves; just because an organization can successfully organize a network on Facebook or amass a large cohort of followers on Twitter does not mean they should neglect other Internet tools. By diversifying their online presence, organizations can reach a much larger audience (West, 2011).

## Best Practices for Effective Advocacy

All in all, it appears that effective advocacy is situational and that it is difficult to generalize about effective strategies and tactics. While some tools work well in one situation, they might not in another. A host of conditions can influence strategies for effective advocacy: personalities of the people involved, the political externalities, historical context, resources available, amount of time, and many other factors.

Craig Jenkins's (2006) authoritative review of existing research on nonprofit policy advocacy identifies effective advocacy strategies that can be used at three critical stages: getting an issue on the policy agenda, enacting favorable legislative and other decisions, and ensuring that these decisions are implemented appropriately. With respect to framing, as Jenkins sees it, "the major function of advocacy leaders is framing issues so that they have broad appeal and gain media coverage" (321). The most effective frames invoke moral principles, like equity and fairness, which have broad appeal. Protesting and influencing party agendas are other avenues for nonprofit groups to gain access to policy agendas.

As far as securing favorable legislation, Jenkins (2006) concludes that the literature on congressional lobbying finds that "the most effective approach is informational lobbying that emphasizes research and insider information, avoids 'burning bridges,' and creates information dependency" (322). Overall, combining insider strategies with protest may be the most effective strategy to secure favorable policy decisions (323).

"Double-barreled," inside, and outside strategies are similarly effective at the implementation stage, according to Jenkins (2006, 324). Actual and even threatened litigation can also influence implementation. Overall, the organizational strength of nonprofit advocates and their use of multiple strategies against relevant targets are critical (324).

A recent exhaustive study of lobbying by Frank Baumgartner et al. (2009) emphasizes the importance of nonprofits and other groups having allies in middle- and high-level elected government positions in order to secure favorable policy outcomes. Moreover, the researchers found that while an individual group's financial and other resources have some impact in the policy process, what is much more important is whether there is a big difference in resources between the two sides of a policy debate. The researchers also found that much of an organization's lobbying involves playing defense and guarding against threats to favorable aspects of the status quo. For defenders of the status quo, vigilance, listening, talking, and monitoring are among the most important lobbying activities. For challengers, their work is much more difficult and often requires a long-term effort to secure the desired change in policy.

In addition to reviewing the existing research on high-impact advocacy, we organized our own informal effort to identify best practices in effective nonprofit advocacy. One of the authors of this chapter, Gary Bass, teaches a certificate program for nonprofit executives that includes a session on advocacy.[31] At two sessions over two years (2011 and 2012), Bass invited David Cohen, a venerated nonprofit advocacy leader, to identify best practices in advocacy.[32] The nonprofit executives then reflected on Cohen's speech and identified what they considered best practices. Bass, also a nationally recognized advocate for more than three decades, summarized the outcome in writing after the event and sent the summary to all participants for input. What follows is the outcome of that process.

1. *The difference between nonprofit and for-profit advocacy should be celebrated.* For-profit advocacy mostly deals with issues that have financial motive for the company, industry, or shareholder: it is advocacy primarily to promote self-interest. Nonprofit advocacy is about causes, organizations that have no profits, or broad social problems. It is advocacy primarily to promote a common good that extends beyond the narrow economic or sectarian goals of nonprofits' members or supporters. This distinction is something nonprofits should be proud of and publicly acknowledge.

2. *Culture within a nonprofit organization.* It is essential to create the right environment within a nonprofit to allow advocacy to flourish. This process can involve structures within the organization as well as attitudes of leadership. Successful advocates understand they will be involved for the long haul, and their organization should plan as such.

3. *Advocacy is about relationships.* Advocacy is about building relationships between and among people, which applies to nurturing relationships with elected leaders and their staff and working collaboratively with colleagues in the nonprofit sector. Too often nonprofit leaders work in silos, or areas of specialization. As a result, they lose opportunities to strengthen their advocacy voice by joining forces with others. Additionally, advocacy success often involves working with unlikely allies, which requires reaching outside of one's own silo.

4. *Advocacy is about changing power dynamics.* Advocacy is often about those with less power trying to shift the balance so they have more. Successful advocates understand this power dynamic. One key step is analyzing the type of power a nonprofit leader has (and the limits of such power). This power may include expertise, authority as an institution, experience, energy, or other items. Often this power must be used to countervail the role of money in politics. Another key step in changing power dynamics is to know the enemies: effectiveness often hinges on understanding the messages and objectives of the opposition, and knowing who the targets are.

5. *Establish credibility.* Once nonprofit leaders have defined their power, they need to establish their bona fides. Others must see them as

credible and reliable for certain things. Effective advocates are not necessarily always the experts, but they always have access to experts. There are many skills beyond substantive expertise that help to establish credibility, but none may be as important as passion. Passion is a strength that is endemic to the nonprofit advocate.

6. *Organize, organize, organize.* Successful advocates are always eager to organize. The top five organizing steps are to (1) get other people engaged; (2) have people speak for themselves, which will empower them; (3) establish the right frames, messages, and language; (4) be ready for next steps whether internal or external to the organization; and (5) be an attentive and active listener—an advocate needs to understand the concerns and issues others may have. Listening is essential to successful coalition building and finding solutions to problems.

7. *Engage in the full policy cycle.* As advocates, nonprofit leaders too often think that once they have won a legislative battle, they are done. After a winning campaign to pass state legislation, for example, do not let the coalition or organization stop working on the issue. Engaging in regulations and implementation of regulations is equally as important for the successful advocate as passing the law was.

8. *Keep the big picture in mind.* Too often advocates are so engaged in one piece of the fight they miss the bigger picture. The successful advocate needs to be able to work on a narrow, even technical, issue while also having a holistic perspective. The successful advocate may also use data to support key points, but must also be skilled in storytelling. Effective use of data can further help to tell a story.

9. *It is never over.* Just as engaging in the full policy cycle is important, it is also vital to take the long view. A loss can turn into a win at a later point; a win can also turn into a loss. So be in the fight for the long haul.

10. *Create space for reflection and celebration.* Reflect on what has worked and not worked personally, as an organization, and as a collective (e.g., a coalition). Take time to debrief and identify positives and negatives with a focus on turning the negatives into positives. Along the way, it is also important to celebrate successes. Enjoy these moments; they help to recharge the batteries for the longer term.

A recent study by Independent Sector (2012) came up with an alternate list of successful advocacy practices, but incorporating many of the points raised by the studies referenced in this chapter:

- Sustain a laser-like focus on long-term goals.
- Prioritize building the elements for successful campaigns.
- Consider the motivations of public officials.
- Galvanize coalitions to achieve short-term goals.
- Ensure strong, high-integrity leadership.

Similar to the list and the qualities of high-impact advocacy laid out earlier in this chapter, coalitions and leadership rise to the top as crucial elements of successful advocacy. The first two criteria from Independent Sector (2012) have to do with the culture of a nonprofit and in some ways are related to quality leadership, as well. In order for organizations to be conscientious about maintaining their commitment to long-term goals and prioritizing building a foundation for campaigns, there must be strong leadership at the top with a clear vision for the organization.[33]

## Conclusions

As indicated at the start, three questions motivated this analysis: Should nonprofits be engaged in advocacy? If yes, how can their involvement be facilitated? If nonprofits become engaged, how can they maximize the impact of their advocacy? Advocacy ought to be a more significant activity for many more nonprofits than it is now. Why? Advocacy is an important way for many nonprofits to advance their missions. Nonprofits can advocate and lobby to secure increased government funding so they can help more clients, for example. But nonprofit advocacy is important not only for advancing the missions of individual nonprofits, but also because it serves important societal functions. Nonprofit advocates often provide useful information to policymakers about new community needs that should be addressed and about existing government programs that are not working and need to be changed. They can also challenge corporate power or inequities in society. Nonprofit advocacy strengthens our democracy by engaging more voices in the policy process and by checking institutional elites. It is especially the vehicle through which otherwise voiceless interests can make their views known and can bring accountability to unchecked power.

Many organizational characteristics facilitate nonprofit advocacy—large size, government support, a supportive internal culture, a staff that is knowledgeable about advocacy, and others. One relatively easy and low-risk but potentially rewarding way for nonprofits to get involved in advocacy is by joining coalitions. Coalitions can be an effective way to advocate because they increase the resources and expertise brought to bear on an advocacy effort. Finding allies in government is often a critical ingredient of successful lobbying. Even so, advocacy is typically a long-term effort, especially if the goal is to change rather than defend the status quo.

Nonprofit staff have much to learn about advocacy from researchers and reflective practitioners. But our hope is that scholars and experienced practitioners will have even more useful advice for nonprofit managers about advocacy in the years to come. In order to provide this guidance, thoughtful practitioners will need more time and space to reflect on what works and what does not in advocacy. And scholars will need to conduct more of the systematic, large-scale studies of the type undertaken by Baumgartner et al. (2009). Especially needed is more research on factors that promote high-impact advocacy.

Additional forums for scholars and practitioners to meet and share their expanding knowledge about nonprofit advocacy are also needed, as both scholars and practitioners have much to gain through these exchanges. Nonprofit managers on the ground can learn from scholars about evidence-based advocacy practices that have proven effectiveness. For their part, scholars can glean useful insights about advocacy from practitioners and learn about cutting-edge practices that they should be studying. Through increased dialogue between scholars and practitioners, we can learn and put into practice many more useful lessons about nonprofit advocacy.

ACKNOWLEDGMENTS

Portions of this chapter appeared in an earlier version as Gary D. Bass and Lee Mason, "Strengthening Nonprofit Advocacy," in *Perspectives On: Social Action in California*, Scan Foundation, June 2010, 26, http://thescanfoundation .org/perspectives-social-action-california; used with permission. The authors also wish to thank Dana Kaasik, a graduate research assistant at George Mason University, for assistance with this chapter.

NOTES

1. Jenkins (2006).
2. Charities may not lobby more than a substantial amount. Since the definition

of "substantial" is not clear, Congress passed another option in 1976, called the "expenditure test," under which a charity must elect to fall and which has clear rules about how much a charity can spend on lobbying. Lobbying is divided into direct lobbying expenditures and indirect (or grassroots) lobbying expenditures. For information on the expenditure test, see the IRS guidelines on lobbying expenditures at http://www.irs.gov/publications/p557/ch03.html.

3. See, e.g., Reid (2000).

4. Beckwith and Lopez (2010).

5. These stories come from focus groups conducted under the Strengthening Nonprofit Advocacy Project described in Bass et al. (2007).

6. As quoted in John Dear, *Peace behind Bars: A Peacemaking Priest's Journal from Jail* (New York: Rowman and Littlefield, 1995), 65; it is a translation of "Quando dou comida aos pobres chamam-me de santo. Quando pergunto por que eles são pobres chamam-me de comunista."

7. Donaldson (2008, 25).

8. As Jennifer E. Mosley points out in chapter 5 in this volume, a professional orientation to service delivery in a nonprofit's leadership may correlate with lower levels of advocacy, while a professional orientation to nonprofit management may be associated with more advocacy activity.

9. Donaldson's (2008) literature review identifies a perception by nonprofits that advocacy is not worth the time or resources required to get involved. Nonprofit leaders generally do not understand the return on investment from engaging in advocacy, or that advocacy activities do not require the dedication of substantial time or money.

10. Schudson (1998, 55).

11. Ibid., 102.

12. See, e.g., Bass et al. (2007, 56–121); Joyce Johnson, "Nonprofit Advocacy," *Learning to Give*, accessed August 5, 2013, http://learningtogive.org/papers/paper40 .html; or "The Nonprofit Sector's Proud Tradition of Serving America," National Council of Nonprofits, accessed August 5, 2013, http://www.councilofnonprofits.org /nonprofit-advocacy/power-nonprofits.

13. IRS Regulations, Section 1.501(c)(3)–1(d)(2).

14. To be sure, because of the limits of their methodology, Grant and Crutchfield's (2007) findings should be taken as suggestive rather than as definitive. Because the authors did not examine a set of low-impact nonprofits, for example, we do not know whether it is just high-impact nonprofits that engage in both service and advocacy or whether low-impact organizations may do both activities, too. It would be harder to hold up advocacy as a best practice for nonprofits if advocacy was a common practice of both less successful and more successful nonprofits.

15. A cross-sector leadership group convened by the Aspen Institute in 2000 similarly agreed that "active participation in the policy process is a fundamental function of the nonprofit sector in a democratic society and one that must be encouraged in the future" (Aspen Institute Nonprofit Sector Strategy Group, 2000, 5).

16. See Boris and Maronick's chapter 3 in this volume.

17. The survey of "interest group" advocates was not a random sample. The authors found it challenging to find a directory of "city-level" advocacy organizations,

so they searched newspapers and websites and talked to various people to develop a list of roughly 25 advocacy groups in each city.

18. In January 1983, the Reagan administration proposed a modification to OMB Circular A-122, Cost Principles for Nonprofit Organizations, that would make unallowable for federal reimbursement all costs of "political advocacy," which was broadly defined as "attempting to influence a government decision" of any type (e.g., legislative, administrative, judicial) at any level of government. That proposal was stopped by a national coalition of nonprofits. In August 1995, the new Republican leadership in the House of Representatives passed a rider to an appropriations bill sponsored by Representatives Ernest Istook (R-OK), David McIntosh (D-IN), and Robert Ehrlich (R-MD) that repeated many of the advocacy restrictions in the 1983 proposals related to OMB Circular A-122 but went even further. Not only would the Istook Amendment, as it was called, prohibit using federal funds for "political advocacy" (also broadly defined), but it also prohibited nonprofits from receiving a federal grant if they spent 5% or more of their private funds for "political advocacy" or if they associated with any entity spending 15% or more on "political advocacy." There were a series of similar amendments and bills introduced in subsequent months and years, nearly all of which were ultimately defeated. But these proposals left a chilling legacy.

19. Carson (2007, 13).

20. This list is based on a bivariate analysis of the data set collected by Bass et al. (2007). Many of these points have been confirmed by Salamon and Geller (2008) and contributors to this volume (Pekkanen and Smith, chap. 2, Boris and Maronick, chap. 3, and Mosley, chap. 5, this volume). On the last point in the list, McNutt and Barlow (2012) reach the same conclusion and note that "electronic advocacy provides a competitive advantage for advocacy groups that make use of it."

21. As described above, charities have the option of having lobbying activities be regulated under a substantial part test (basically meaning that lobbying cannot consume more than a "substantial" portion of an organization's resources) or an expenditure test (which allows charities to lobby up to a specified dollar amount). The expenditure test has clear definitions of lobbying, whereas the substantial part test does not.

22. Avner (2004).

23. According to the Congressional Management Foundation, constituent communications to the U.S. Congress have jumped between 200% and 1,000% in different offices over the past decade. Their October 2011 report states that the "bulk" of these communications come through advocacy campaigns. The report also estimates that 5,000 to 10,000 nonprofits and businesses have sections of their websites with services to send email directly to Congress. "Communicating with Congress: How Citizen Advocacy Is Changing Mail Operations on Capitol Hill" (Congressional Management Foundation, Washington, DC, 2011), http://congressfoundation.org/storage/documents/CMF_Pubs/cwc-mail-operations.pdf.

24. The Congressional Management Foundation report additionally described that there was a "dramatic increase" in email in 2009, which they suggest was because of major legislative initiatives such as economic stimulus, health-care reform, and cap and trade. This seems to suggest that the ubiquity of email has made it much easier to communicate with Congress.

25. Erik Qualman, "Social Media Revolution 2 (Refresh) by Socialnomics," You-Tube video, 4:26, posted by Monique O'Reilly, June 9, 2011, http://www.youtube.com/watch?v=tGzAHbBmcnk.

26. Anderson (2009).

27. "Arab Spring—The Ultimate Social Media Guide," *Before It's News*, March 24, 2011, http://beforeitsnews.com/global-unrest/2011/03/arab-spring-the-ultimate-social-media-guide-508003.html.

28. Anita Singh, "Role of Twitter and Facebook in Arab Spring Uprising 'Overstated,' Says Hisham Matar," *Telegraph*, July 11, 2011, http://www.telegraph.co.uk/culture/books/ways-with-words/8629294/Ways-With-Words-role-of-Twitter-and-Facebook-in-Arab-Spring-uprising-overstated-says-Hisham-Matar.html.

29. "Arab Bloggers Gather in Tunisia After Arab Spring," NPR's *Morning Edition*, October 6, 2011, http://www.npr.org/2011/10/06/141103837/arab-bloggers-gather-in-tunisia-after-arab-spring.

30. Email communications with Kathy Bonk and Jason Shevrin of Communications Consortium Media Center (CCMC), September 21, 2011. The findings are part of regular polling by CCMC and are consistent with the Pew Research Center's Internet and American Life Project; see, e.g., Lee Rainie, "The Social Media Landscape" (presentation, Pew Research Center, Washington, DC), http://pewinternet.org/Presentations/2011/Sept/Social-Media-Landscape.aspx, and Keith Hampton, Lauren Sessions Goulet, Lee Rainie, *and* Kristen Purcell, "Social Networking Sites and Our Lives" (report, Pew Research Center, Washington, DC), http://pewinternet.org/Reports/2011/Technology-and-social-networks.asp.

31. The Nonprofit Management Executive Certificate program is run by the Center for Public and Nonprofit Leadership at Georgetown University's Public Policy Institute. See http://cpnl.georgetown.edu/ for a description of the program. One part of the curriculum is devoted to advocacy.

32. David Cohen has been an advocate and strategist on many of the major social justice and political reform issues in the United States since the early 1960s. These issues include civil rights, antipoverty, and reforming US political processes by eliminating abuses of power and the corrupting influence of money on American politics. He played a leading role in the fight for Congress to end its support for the Vietnam War. From 1984 to 1992 David led the Professionals' Coalition for Nuclear Arms Control—composed of physicians, scientists, lawyers, and social workers—to stop the US nuclear arms buildup by supporting arms control agreements and reducing the military budget. He served as president of Common Cause, the largest voluntary membership organization in the United States working on government accountability issues from 1975 to 1981. David's contributions are recognized in biographies and histories of the period. He cofounded the Advocacy Institute and has been a senior statesman in the nonprofit sector.

33. The Independent Sector (2012) report includes a helpful literature review of scholarly research on nonprofit advocacy that supports many of the points made in this summary (15–23). Following the literature review is a series of case studies that provide insight on well-funded advocacy campaigns organized at the federal level, mainly by 501(c)(4) organizations (25–107).

REFERENCES

Alexander, Jennifer, Renee Nank, and Camilla Stivers. 1999. "Implications of Welfare Reform: Do Nonprofit Survival Strategies Threaten Civil Society?" *Nonprofit and Voluntary Sector Quarterly* 28: 452–75.

Amidei, Nancy. 2010. *So You Want to Make Difference: Advocacy Is the Key*, Washington, DC: OMB Watch. http://www.ombwatch.org/makeadifference.

Anderson, Chris. 2009. "Q&A with Clay Shirky on Twitter and Iran." *TED Blog*, June 16, http://blog.ted.com/2009/06/qa_with_clay_sh.php.

Aspen Institute Nonprofit Sector Strategy Group. 2000. "The Nonprofit Contribution to Civic Participation and Advocacy." Draft Statement for Public Discussion. Washington, DC: Aspen Institute.

Avner, Marcia. 2004. *The Lobbying and Advocacy Handbook for Nonprofit Organizations: Shaping Public Policy at the State and Local Level*. St. Paul, MN: Amherst H. Wilder Foundation.

Bass, Gary D. 2009. "Advocacy in the Public Interest." In *Essays on Excellence*. Washington, DC: Georgetown University Center for Public and Nonprofit Leadership. http://cpnl.georgetown.edu/document/1242781108519/Advocacy+in+the+Public +Interest.pdf.

Bass, Gary D., David F. Arons, Kay Guinane, and Matthew F. Carter. 2007. *Seen but Not Heard: Strengthen Nonprofit Advocacy*. Washington, DC: Aspen Institute.

Bass, Gary D., and Lee Mason. 2010. "Strengthening Nonprofit Advocacy." In *Perspectives on: Social Action in California*, 26–35. Long Beach, CA: SCAN Foundation.

Baumgartner, Frank R., Jeffrey M. Berry, Marie Hojnacki, David C. Kimball, and Beth Leech. 2009. *Lobbying and Policy Change: Who Wins, Who Loses, and Why*. Chicago: University of Chicago Press.

Beckwith, Dave, and Cristina Lopez. 2010. *Community Organizing: People Power from the Grassroots*. Washington, DC: Center for Community Change. http:// comm-org.wisc.edu/papers97/beckwith.htm.

Boris, Elizabeth T., and Matthew Maronick. 2012. "Civic Participation and Advocacy." In *The State of Nonprofit America*. 2nd ed., edited by Lester M. Salamon, 394–422. Washington, DC: Brookings Institution Press.

Carson, Emmett D. 2007. "On Foundations and Public Policy: Why the Words Don't Match the Behavior." In *Power in Policy: A Funder's Guide to Advocacy and Civic Participation*, edited by David F. Arons, 11–22. Saint Paul, MN: Fieldstone Alliance.

Chaves, Mark, Laura Stephens, and Joseph Galaskiewicz. 2004. "Does Government Funding Suppress Nonprofits' Political Activity?" *American Sociological Review* 69: 292–316.

Child, Curtis D., and Kirsten A. Grønbjerg. 2007. "Nonprofit Advocacy Organizations: Their Characteristics and Activities." *Social Science Quarterly* 88: 259–81.

Crutchfield, Leslie R., and Heather McLeod Grant. 2007. *Forces for Good: The Six Practices of High-Impact Nonprofits*. New York: Jossey-Bass.

de Leon, Erwin, Matthew Maronick, Carol J. DeVita, and Elizabeth T. Boris. 2009. *Community-Based Organizations and Immigrant Integration in the Washington,*

*D.C., Metropolitan Area*. Washington, DC: Urban Institute. http://www.urban .org/UploadedPDF/411986_community_based_organizations.pdf.

DeVita, Carol J., Maria D. Montilla, Betsy Reid, and Omolara Fatiregun. 2004. *Organizational Factors Influencing Advocacy for Children*. Washington, DC: Urban Institute Press.

Donaldson, Linda Plitt. 2004. "Toward Validating Therapeutic Benefits of Empowerment-Oriented Social Action Groups." *Social Work with Groups* 27, no. 2/3: 159–75.

———. 2008. "Developing a Progressive Advocacy Program within a Human Services Agency." *Administration in Social Work* 32, no. 2: 25.

Gladwell, Malcolm. 2010. "Small Change: Why the Revolution Will Not Be Tweeted." *New Yorker*, October 4.

Grant, Heather McLeod, and Leslie R. Crutchfield. 2007. "Creating High-Impact Nonprofits." *Stanford Social Innovation Review* Fall 2007: http://www.ssireview .org/articles/entry/creating_high_impact_nonprofits/.

Grønbjerg, Kirsten A. 1993. *Understanding Nonprofit Funding: Managing Revenues in Social Services and Community Development Organizations*. San Francisco, CA: Jossey-Bass.

Helfenbein, David. 2010. "How Malcolm Gladwell Misses the Mark in His Recent *New Yorker* Piece on Social Revolution." *Huffington Post*, October 2, http://www .huffingtonpost.com/david-helfenbein/how-malcolm-gladwell-misses-the-mark -_b_739345.html.

Independent Sector. 2012. *Beyond the Cause: The Art and Science of Advocacy*. Washington, DC: Independent Sector. http://www.independentsector.org/beyond_the _cause.

Jenkins, J. Craig. 2006. "Nonprofit Organizations and Political Advocacy." In *The Nonprofit Sector: A Research Handbook*. 2nd ed., edited by Walter W. Powell and Richard Steinberg, 307–32. New Haven, CT: Yale University Press.

Kramer, Ralph M. 1994. "Voluntary Agencies and the Contract Culture: Dream or Nightmare?" *Social Service Review* 68, no. 1: 33–60.

Light, Paul C. 2002. *Pathways to Nonprofit Excellence*. Washington, DC: Brookings Institution Press.

Light, Paul C., and Catherine B. Reynolds. 2010. *Driving Social Change: How to Solve the World's Toughest Problems*. New York: Wiley.

McNutt, John G. 2000. "Coming Perspectives in the Development of Electronic Advocacy for Social Policy Practice." *Critical Social Work* 1, no 1: http://www .uwindsor.ca/criticalsocialwork/coming-perspectives-in-the-development-of -electronic-advocacy-for-social-policy-practice-0.

———. 2008. "Advocacy Organizations and the Organizational Digital Divide." *Currents* 7, no. 2: 1–16.

McNutt, John G., and Janet Barlow. 2012. "A Longitudinal Study of Political Technology Use by Nonprofit Child Advocacy Organizations." In *E-Governance and Civic Engagement: Factors and Determinants of E-Democracy*, edited by A. Manoharan and M. Holtzer, 405–21. Harrisburg, PA: IGI Books.

McNutt, John G., and Goutham M. Menon. 2008. "The Rise of Cyberactivism: Implications for the Future of Advocacy in the Human Services." *Families in Society: The Journal of Contemporary Social Services* 89, no. 1: 33–38.

Miller, David. 2011. "Nonprofit Organizations and the Emerging Potential of Social Media and Internet Resources." *SPNHA Review* 6, no. 1: article 4.

Mosley, Jennifer E. 2010. "Organizational Resources and Environmental Incentives: Understanding the Policy Advocacy Involvement of Human Service Nonprofits." *Social Service Review* 84: 57–76.

O'Connell, Brian. 1994. *People Power: Service, Advocacy, Empowerment*. Washington, DC: Foundation Center.

Reid, Elizabeth J. 2000. "Understanding the Word 'Advocacy': Context and Use." In *Advocacy and the Policy Process: Structuring the Inquiry into Advocacy*, edited by Elizabeth J. Reid, 1-8. Washington, DC: Urban Institute Press.

Reinelt, Claire. 1994. "Fostering Empowerment, Building Community: The Challenge for State-Funded Feminist Organizations." *Human Relations* 47, no. 6: 685–704.

Saidel, Judith R., and Sharon L. Harlan. 1998. "Contracting and Patterns of Nonprofit Governance." *Nonprofit Management and Leadership* 8, no. 3: 243–59.

Salamon, Lester M. 1987. "Partners in Public Service: The Scope and Theory of Government-Nonprofit Relations." In *The Nonprofit Sector: A Research Handbook*, edited by W. W. Powell, 99–117. New Haven, CT: Yale University Press.

———. 1995. "Exploring Nonprofit Advocacy." Paper presented at the Independent Sector Spring Research Forum, Alexandria, VA.

Salamon, Lester M., and Stephanie Lessans Geller with Susan C. Lorentz. 2008. "Nonprofit America: A Force for Democracy?" Listening Post Project Communique No. 9, Center for Civil Society Studies, Johns Hopkins University, Baltimore. http://ccss.jhu.edu/wp-content/uploads/downloads/2011/09/LP_Communique9 _2008.pdf.

Schudson, Michael. 1998. *The Good Citizen: A History of American Civic Life*. New York: Free Press.

Shirky, Clay. 2008. *Here Comes Everybody: The Power of Organizing without Organizations*. New York: Penguin.

———. 2011. "The Political Power of Social Media." *Foreign Affairs Journal* 90, no. 1: 28–41.

Smith, Steven Rathgeb. 2010. "Nonprofit Organizations and Government: Implications for Policy and Practice." *Journal of Policy Analysis and Management* 29, no. 3: 621–25.

Smith, Steven Rathgeb, and Michael Lipsky. 1993. *Nonprofits for Hire: The Welfare State in the Age of Contracting*. Cambridge, MA: Harvard University Press.

Suárez, David F. 2009. "Nonprofit Advocacy and Civic Engagement on the Internet." *Administration and Society* 41, no. 3: 267–89.

Vegh, Sandor. 2003. "Classifying Forms of Online Activism: The Case of Cyberprotests against the World Bank." In *Cyberactivism*, edited by Martha McCaughey and Michael D. Ayers, 71–96. New York: Routledge.

West, Maureen. 2011. "How Nonprofits Can Use Social Media to Spark Change." *Chronicle of Philanthropy*, February 20, http://philanthropy.com/article/How -Nonprofits-Can-Use-Social/126402/.

Wolch, Jennifer. 1990. *The Shadow State: Government and Voluntary Sector in Transition*. Washington, DC: Foundation Center.

ALAN J. ABRAMSON is a professor in the Department of Public and International Affairs at George Mason University and founding director of Mason's Center for Nonprofit Management, Philanthropy, and Policy. He is also a senior fellow at the Aspen Institute and an affiliated scholar at the Urban Institute.

GARY D. BASS is executive director of the Bauman Foundation and an affiliated professor at Georgetown University's McCourt School of Public Policy.

JEFFREY M. BERRY is the John Richard Skuse Professor of Political Science at Tufts University.

ELIZABETH T. BORIS, PhD, is director of the Center on Nonprofits and Philanthropy at the Urban Institute. The center conducts research on the nonprofit sector and develops and provides data to the public through its National Center for Charitable Statistics. Author of many research publications, Boris also serves on numerous nonprofit boards and advisory committees.

CAROL J. DEVITA is a former senior fellow at the Center on Nonprofits and Philanthropy at the Urban Institute.

EMILY DEWEY is the Colorado Health Coverage Guide for the Small Business Majority.

KRISTIN GOSS is an associate professor of public policy and political science at Duke University and is the director of the Duke in D.C. Program.

DOUG IMIG is a professor of political science at the University of Memphis and resident fellow at the Urban Child Institute. His work concerns efforts to build an effective political voice for children over the last century.

MATTHEW MARONICK is a PhD candidate and adjunct professor at the School of Social Service Administration at the University of Chicago.

JENNIFER E. MOSLEY is an associate professor at the School of Social Service Administration at the University of Chicago.

MILENA NIKOLOVA is a PhD candidate in international development at the University of Maryland, College Park, and nonresident researcher at the Brookings Institution.

ROBERT J. PEKKANEN is a professor at the Henry M. Jackson School of International Studies and an adjunct professor in the Department of Political Science at the University of Washington.

KENT E. PORTNEY is a professor of political science at Tufts University. He is author of *Taking Sustainable Cities Seriously: Economic Development, Quality of Life, and the Environment in American Cities*, 2nd edition. He is also coauthor of *The Rebirth of Urban Democracy* and numerous other books.

KATIE L. ROEGER is the former assistant program director of the National Center for Charitable Statistics, a program of the Center on Nonprofits and Philanthropy at the Urban Institute.

JODI SANDFORT is an associate professor at the Humphrey School of Public Affairs at the University of Minnesota, as well as chair of the school's leadership and management concentration.

STEVEN RATHGEB SMITH is the executive director of the American Political Science Association. He was most previously the Louis A. Bantle Chair in Public Administration at the Maxwell School at Syracuse University. He was also the Nancy Bell Evans Professor at the Evans School of Public Affairs at the University of Washington, editor of *Nonprofit and Voluntary Sector Quarterly*, and president of the Association for Research on Nonprofit Organizations and Voluntary Action.

DARA Z. STROLOVITCH is an associate professor at Princeton University, where she teaches in the Program in Gender and Sexuality Studies and the Department of Politics.

YUTAKA TSUJINAKA is a professor of humanities and social sciences and vice president for international affairs at the University of Tsukuba, Japan.